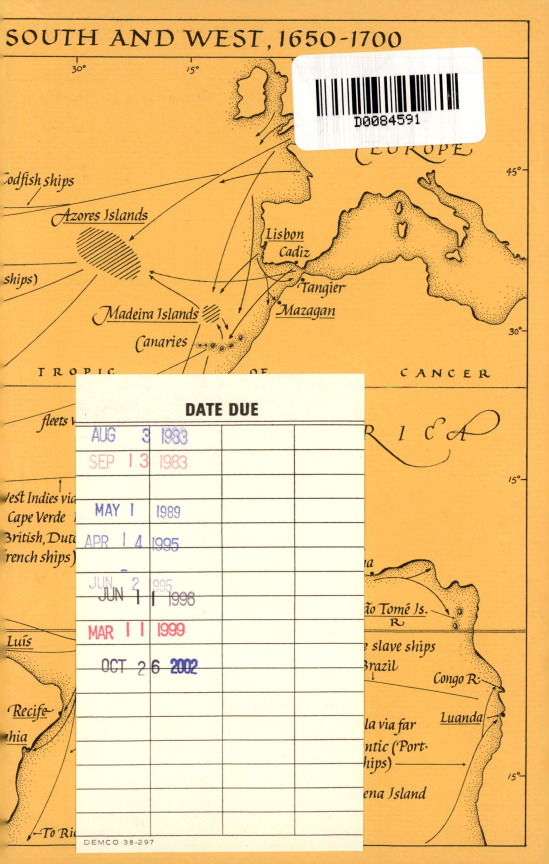

ATLANTIC ISLANDS

ATLANTIC ISLANDS

Madeira, the Azores and the Cape Verdes in Seventeenth-Century Commerce and Navigation

T. Bentley Duncan

THE UNIVERSITY OF CHICAGO PRESS
CHICAGO AND LONDON

The University of Chicago Press, Chicago 60637
The University of Chicago Press, Ltd., London

©1972 by The University of Chicago
All rights reserved. Published 1972
Printed in the United States of America

International Standard Book Number: 0-226-17001-2
Library of Congress Catalog Card Number: 72-80157

To Eva

Contents

vii

Maps

Tables

xi

Preface

An awareness of the Portuguese islands has lain buried somewhere in my mind for many years. In the course of numerous sea voyages between Brazil (the land of my birth) and Britain (the land of my parents), I became aware of the islands at an early age. I remember the dim shapes of the Cape Verdes, or, more vividly, the clever boys of Madeira diving for coins in the waters of the Bay of Funchal and never missing a single one — coins tossed into the sea by passengers from the deck of a ship while she lay at anchor, well offshore, in the days before there was a dock at Funchal.

These early experiences, however, meant very little in any intellectual sense, and many years were to pass before I thought seriously about the history and character of the Portuguese Atlantic islands. This book, in a certain way, is something of a surprise, even to its author. No formal academic course of study evoked it, no professor suggested it, and the published literature about Portugal and islands (with one exception) hardly anticipates it. The book was, in short, very much my own idea, and emerged gradually as the unexpected by-product of a study I did on Anglo-Portuguese relations in the seventeenth century.

First, in going through documents in Portuguese and English archives, I was struck by the number of references to the islands, particularly to the commerce of the islands and to foreign merchants there resident. Second, the wider functions of the islands, in support of general Atlantic shipping, became apparent to me. Third, when I read Frédéric Mauro's *Portugal et l'Atlantique au XVIIe siècle,* I was impressed by his account of the rich archives in Madeira and the Azores; I desired very much to visit them and was soon able to do so.

Yet, once well launched on a study of the islands, it was only when I arrived at Terceira, in the Azores, in 1969, that I finally read something that anticipated, in part, my conclusions about the maritime functions of the Portuguese islands in past ages. The work to which I allude was an unpublished licentiate thesis for the University of Lisbon entitled "Os Açores na Economia Atlântica" (The Azores in the Atlantic Economy), written by Dr. Helder de Sousa Lima, who kindly allowed me to read it. To Dr. Sousa Lima, an able student of Azorean history, I am most grateful.

In the course of visits to Portugal (in 1963, 1966, 1969, and 1971) and to the islands (in 1969 and 1971) I have accumulated numerous obligations to many persons, particularly to staff members in several libraries and archives. I wish to thank, by name, Dr. Luís Silveira, inspector general of Portuguese libraries; Professor António da Silva Rego, the director of many enterprises connected with the scholarly research of the Portuguese overseas world; Dr. Alberto Iria, director of the Arquivo Histórico Ultramarino; and Alfredo Machado Gonçalves, director of the Biblioteca Pública e Arquivo Distrital de Ponta Delgada.

I especially wish to thank my friends in Terceira, Dr. Manuel C. Baptista de Lima, director of the Biblioteca Pública e Arquivo Distrital de Angra do Heroísmo, and Senhor Emanuel Félix, the Terceiran poet and director of the museum at Angra. I am also indebted, in a general way, to the staffs of the Arquivo Nacional da Tôrre do Tombo, the Biblioteca Nacional de Lisboa, the Biblioteca Pública e Arquivo Distrital de Évora, and the Arquivo Distrital do Funchal.

Finally, coming closer to home, I wish to thank Mr. Frederick Hall, of the Newberry Library in Chicago, for much support over the years. The existence of the William B. Greenlee Collection at Newberry, and the general research strength of the Joseph Regenstein Library at the University of Chicago, greatly facilitate work in Portuguese history in the city of Chicago. To the American Council of Learned Societies, I am indebted for a timely grant-in-aid in 1969; and I am similarly indebted to my own institution, the University of Chicago, for various forms of direct and indirect assistance.

Intellectually I owe much, in a general way, to Professor Donald F. Lach of Chicago, who introduced me to Portuguese imperial and maritime history, and specifically (as far as this book is concerned), to Professor Francis M. Rogers of Harvard University, who gave the manuscript a very careful reading. Professor Rogers, out of his deep and personal knowledge of the Portuguese islands, made a large number of helpful suggestions and corrections, almost all of which I adopted. To him I am most grateful; but I alone bear the responsibility for the contents of this book and for any errors that are in it.

1
Introduction: The Importance
of Islands

Small islands situated in the midst of seas and oceans, remote from the continental land masses, often possess a high importance in communications, navigation, and strategy — an importance out of all relation to their size and resources. Mere location endows such islands with crucial advantages. The Azores, for instance, strategically located in the central North Atlantic, have supplied long-distance shipping with vital services for five hundred years. In the twentieth century the assistance of these islands has been extended to aircraft as well. Indeed, in 1939, the first regular commercial air service between the United States and Europe was established by way of the Azores.[1]

The military and strategic importance of islands is also illustrated by the Azores, which provided bases for the Allied powers during both

---

1. The flying boats or "clippers" (Boeing 314 series) of Pan American Airways landed on the sea channel at Horta in Fayal. Of the round-trip survey flight between America and Europe made by the *Yankee Clipper* in March and April of 1939, Burr W. Leyson wrote: "There was no incident on the flight and the entire operation assumed the character of routine" — see his *Wings around the World* (New York, 1948), p. 98. The first commercial flight began on 20 May 1939 by way of the New York-Bermuda-Azores-Lisbon route. For the Azores and aviation, see Francis M. Rogers, *Precision Astrolabe: Portuguese Navigators and Transoceanic Aviation* (Lisbon, 1971), and his "Os Açores: Plataforma no Atlântico," *Boletim da Academia Internacional da Cultura Portuguesa,* no. 2 (1966), pp. 193–209.

Today the islands of Terceira, São Miguel, Santa Maria, and Fayal all have modern airports. All are linked to one another by an inter-island air service, and most of them have direct flights to North America and Europe. An airport is also planned, or under construction, at Flores.

world wars. An examination of a map of the North Atlantic will reveal the command of communications given to the power that can control the Azorean islands. The islands of Terceira, São Miguel, and Fayal have all participated, at one time or another, in military operations of transport or supply, involving ships or aircraft – and even tiny Santa Maria, with but thirty-seven square miles of land, provided a site for an airport, and became a fuel-storage center, during World War II.[2]

In the exigencies of war, location can be more significant than size: a small hill can be coveted and fought for as if it were a whole mountain range, and a single islet, given the accident of location, can seem more desirable than an entire archipelago. The Pacific war of 1941–45 between the United States and Japan testified to the strategic functions of small and remote islands. In that far-spread conflict, the struggles that enveloped not only the large islands, such as Mindanao, Leyte, and New Guinea, but also such "flyspecks" as Midway and Iwo Jima define the peculiarly insular and maritime character of the war; and the very names of such islands as Wake, Tarawa, Guam, Guadalcanal, Kwajalein, Kiska, and Okinawa evoke memories of vast military operations.

The strategic importance of islands in times of warfare or international tension is, however, only a narrow aspect of the broad historical importance of islands as seen from the perspective of centuries. For three millennia or more, ever since the dawn of long-distance navigation, islands have been of central importance to commercial shipping. Before the development of mechanically propelled vessels and the emergence of instant radio communications, islands, along with the continental ports, were essential partners in the whole business of long-distance navigation and seaborne commerce. But with the recent revolution in transport and technology, the islands have been often bypassed, forgotten and relegated to a modest role in commerce and communications.

The diminishing status of islands can be illustrated, in a curious and indirect way, from the study of cartography. In modern maps of the Atlantic, where every piece of land is drawn to the same scale, Madeira and the Azores are but pinheads in the broad expanse of ocean; but in maps of the sixteenth and seventeenth centuries the islands appear monstrously swollen, enlarged out of all proportion to the continental land

2. Ponta Delgada (São Miguel) was a major Allied naval base during World War I. In World War II, although Portugal was not a belligerent, the British were allowed to build an air base at Lages on Terceira and made some use of the port at Horta (Fayal). The Lages base is still used by NATO, and the United States recently built harbor installations at Praia (Terceira).

masses. Indeed, in some of the world maps printed in the sixteenth century, the island of Madeira, one-fifth the size of Long Island, appears to rival in size the modern state of New York. In the old maps, the huge islands emphatically assert their presence in the mid-Atlantic and furnish graphic testimony to both the psychological and the practical significance of islands to men of former times.

Perhaps there are few persons today — other than maritime historians, yachtsmen who venture on the high seas in small sailing craft, and elderly seamen, if any still survive, able to recollect the days of "wooden ships and iron men" — who can appreciate the meaning of islands to the mariners of former ages. To be sure, the present-day navigator, whether at sea or in the air, may still welcome the sight of a mid-oceanic island, for it will provide a visual confirmation of his geographical position. Gyrocompasses, radar screens, intersecting radio beams, and automatic navigational systems may define a craft's position with effortless precision, but, to the human being in charge, the glimpse of a recognizable island, mountain, or beacon is welcome nevertheless, for seeing is still believing.

To the mariners of the seventeenth century the question of exact navigational position was vastly more difficult. Seventeenth-century pilots could ascertain latitude with fair accuracy, but finding longitude was a matter of guesswork. Transatlantic mariners always had to rely largely on dead reckoning, and for them a glimpse of an island, after weeks out of sight of land, was cause for rejoicing. Ships northward bound in the South Atlantic took the route which led past the islands of St. Helena and Ascension, both visible for great distances at sea. Merchantmen out of the South Atlantic or the west and bound for Europe often headed for the Azores, since the nine Azorean islands, spread out over 360 miles of sea, were targets virtually impossible to miss, and, when sighted, furnished immediate proof of geographical position. For many ships from Europe and bound for the South Atlantic or the West Indies, the Cape Verde Islands, some 400 miles off the coast of Senegal, fulfilled a similar function.

Besides the visual confirmation of geographical position, there were other reasons for seeking islands. Seventeenth-century ships, while yet in mid-journey, ran constantly short of beverages, victuals, nautical supplies, and even personnel. Most islands could supply at least food and water, and some could repair ships and furnish undermanned vessels with an extra hand or two. Sailors at St. Helena could fill their casks with fresh water, obtain citrus fruits to combat scurvy, and hunt the island's wild goats. The Cape Verdes made a regular business of providing passing vessels with salted meats. And the Azores could fill every need of even the most necessitous and crippled ships, from beverage wine and green vegetables to spars, sailcloth, cables, and lofty mainmasts.

Certain islands, in addition to serving as victualing stations and bases for ship maintenance, were also commercial centers in their own right. Islands could maintain a sound economy only if they developed valuable products that other countries found desirable. For instance, the Azorean island of São Miguel for several decades supplied the English textile industry with large quantities of pastel or woad, a blue dyestuff. Wine was the all-important and ineluctable commodity in the commerce of Madeira, the Canaries, and Pico-Fayal. Canary wines were marketed in all four of the continents that rim the Atlantic; and the wines of Madeira and Pico were once staple exports to the English plantations in North America and the West Indies.

Similarly, a number of the Azorean islands produced fairly large surpluses of wheat, which were shipped regularly to Lisbon, Madeira, and the Portuguese garrison towns in Morocco. The Cape Verdes, of all the Atlantic archipelagoes the one with the most precarious economy, had abundant stores of cheap salt. Many English ships outward bound to the West Indies, rather than take a direct route, would elect to sail by way of the Cape Verdes. Because of the patterns of wind and current, the Cape Verdes itinerary made good navigational sense. Moreover, the ships would be revictualed en route and would pick up a cargo of salt, which could be marketed at a fair profit in Newfoundland, New England, or the West Indies. Grains of Cape Verdean salt, after three long Atlantic voyages, might be found (along with the Newfoundland codfish which they seasoned and preserved) on the tables of Catholic households in Spain and Portugal.

Somewhat less important than the trade generated by island-produced commodities was the additional trade created by the islands as entrepôts of mainland merchandise. From time to time Madeira and the Azores sold chests of Brazilian sugar to English and French merchants. Small quantities of spices and other Eastern commodities, unloaded (usually clandestinely) from East Indiamen calling at the Azores, could be resold to other ships. In Madeira and the Azores textiles from Europe were sometimes transshipped to Africa or the Americas. And Santiago, most important of the Cape Verde Islands, aspired to be a major entrepôt in the slave trade; Spanish ships, in particular, sometimes preferred to pay a higher price for slaves in the islands, rather than hazard the difficulties and dangers of the disease-ridden African mainland.

All these trading activities, at the most active centers at least, also involved an intermixing and sometimes an interchange of persons. Some islands were not only multinational in population but also multiracial. The people of St. Helena (as of Hawaii in the Pacific) furnish an example of polyethnic and multiracial composition. In the Cape Verdes, similarly, the fusion of European and African produced a mulatto population. And at the three commercial towns in the Azores (Angra, Horta, and Ponta Delgada), as at Funchal in Madeira, there were English, Scottish, Irish, Dutch, Flemish, Italian, French, Spanish, and German residents, as well as New Englanders, Virginians, Brazilians, West Indians, and Africans.

Long exposure to international influences has given some of the islanders, particularly the upper classes in the port towns, a certain cosmopolitanism that is sometimes so culturally deep-rooted as to be almost instinctive and unconscious. In Funchal, for instance, certain "native" but non-Portuguese habits and attitudes strike one as being derived from the British, who for three and a half centuries have dominated the commercial life of Madeira. Moreover, both in Madeira and the Azores educated people are more likely to be able to speak English than their counterparts in Lisbon.

The movement of foreigners to the islands has been accompanied, and greatly surpassed, by the movement of islanders away from the islands. Overpopulation has been a chronic problem in most of the islands. In some, such as Madeira and São Miguel, the population has outstripped even very rich agricultural resources, while in the Cape Verdes, which are poorly watered, there never has been enough arable land to sustain more than a few people. In the seventeenth and eighteenth centuries the surplus population of Madeira and the Azores found employment in the king of Portugal's armies and navies and were an important element in the settlement and colonization of Brazil.

In the mid-twentieth century the islands still supply more than their share of Portugal's emigrants. Official policy encourages emigration to Angola and other parts of Portugal's overseas empire, but Azoreans prefer to go to the United States or Canada, and Madeirans have a predilection for Venezuela, Brazil, and the Netherlands Antilles. The Cape Verdeans have traditionally found occupations on the mainland of Portuguese Guinea, where they predominate in the middle and lower ranks of the bureaucracy. They have also served aboard the ships of many nations, and, partly for that reason, there are pockets of Cape Verdean immigrants in widely scattered places.

The ethnic and cultural influence of immigrant Azoreans, Madeirans, and Cape Verdeans on scores of communities in the Atlantic world is a subject that is diverse, complex, and largely unstudied. It is also a subject that is beyond the scope of this book, which is concerned not with the foreign peregrinations of the islanders but with the islands themselves — particularly with their role in seventeenth-century transatlantic navigation and commerce, before nineteenth-century technology revolutionized oceanic navigation and reduced the activity and consequence of the islands.

The thesis developed in the following pages is that the mid-Atlantic islands, in the days of sailing ships, played an important, an influential, and, in certain areas and times, even an indispensable and vital role in oceanic trade, transport, and communications. In a sense this book has a small subject, since the islands, although widely scattered, have altogether only 2,755 square miles of land area (which is considerably less than the state of Connecticut), and in total have never supported as many as 850,000 people at once. Yet the implications of this study are far-reaching, for the islands stood at the center of a spider web of shipping routes whose threads reached to all the maritime communities along the Atlantic coasts of four continents.

The thousands of ships that plied these routes carried not only goods but people; not only seamen but passengers, and the human cargoes of slaves. The transatlantic movement was not only commercial and economic but also social and personal. The islands were the geographical heart of this traffic, and through the narrow aperture of insular activity can be glimpsed broad vistas of intercontinental communication.

It is in this spirit, of examining the minutiae of insular detail while not neglecting broad historical and geographical dimensions, that this study hopefully proceeds. Ultimately, the importance of the mid-Atlantic islands in the seventeenth century derived from the great nations and peoples of the distant continental land masses which they served.

2
The Thrust into the Atlantic and the Development of the Islands

The fifteenth-century European thrust into the Atlantic was a movement of momentous import that had the result, eventually, of placing every part of the world in potential communication with every other part of the world. Many peoples contributed to commercial navigation in the Middle Ages — peoples such as the Scandinavians, Germans, Lowlanders, Scots, Irish, English, French, Berbers, and Arabs — but it was the Iberians and the Italians, and among them particularly the Portuguese, who led the way to new waters.

The new Atlantic world of seas and islands began to emerge with the Franco-Castilian colonization of Lanzarote, in the Canaries, in 1402, and with the Portuguese settlement of Madeira in 1425. The Madeiran venture in particular was a truly pioneering effort, occurring in virgin terrain, and was remarkably successful.

Credit for the imaginative Madeiran enterprise belongs properly to Prince Henry of Portugal, often called "the Navigator," and to his followers. It is not known when Prince Henry's mariners first reconnoitered Madeira, nor who they were, nor if they actually did so. But these matters are of no great importance. What is important is that a young gentleman and soldier, João Gonçalves, styled "Zarco" (the blue-eyed), having little or no money or property, persuaded his master, Prince Henry, to permit the colonization of Madeira and to finance the venture.[1] Zarco led a party of colonists to the main island in 1425. Near

1. In 1460, the year of his death, Prince Henry officially stated that he had ordered the settlement of Madeira thirty-five years previously, that is, in 1425. The dates 1418–20, given by many writers, seem to be too early and are inconsistent with the prince's own declaration; but there is some evidence in favor of

the middle of the south shore, he landed on a pebbly beach where three *ribeiras*, or streams, nearly converge and discharge their waters into the sea. Here, where there is a small stretch of almost level land, he burned away the brush and began to construct a settlement that the colonists called Funchal (the name came from the fennel plant, *funcho*, that grew in the vicinity).

Four or five miles to the west of Funchal, along the coast, there is an outcrop of rocks that extends an arm into the sea, in a peculiar fashion, creating a sheltered harbor suitable for fishing boats and other small craft. Here Zarco came across a group of large seals (in Portuguese, *lobo marinho*) and named the place Câmara de Lobos (chamber of wolves). At an early date, possibly even before the foundation of Funchal, Zarco established a settlement here, and identified himself with this location to such an extent that he added its name to his own, thus: João Gonçalves ("Zarco") da Câmara de Lobos.

Another early settlement was at Machico, located in a pleasant valley in the extreme east of the island, about a dozen miles northeast of Funchal. Machico may have been founded by Tristão Vaz Teixeira, whose name is associated with that area. A settlement was also planted on the neighboring island of Porto Santo, which is only nine miles long and has inadequate supplies of timber and water but is less rugged than Madeira. The Porto Santo settlement probably started a number of years after the foundation of Funchal, and its most active colonist was a certain Bartolomeu Perestrelo.[2] The three Desertas (Chão, Deserta Grande, and

---

1427; see Duarte Leite, *História dos descobrimentos,* 2 vols. (Lisbon, 1958-60), 1: 273. I assume that Zarco was a young man in his late twenties in 1425 and that he died ca. 1467, or later, in his seventies; see "Quando morreu Zarco?" in João Cabral do Nascimento, *Apontamentos de história insular* (Funchal, 1927), pp. 51-56; and Manuel Juvenal Pita Ferreira, "A morte de Zargo – 1480?" *Arquipélago da Madeira* (Funchal, 1959), pp. 397-402. The appellation "Zarco" was the Iberian version of the name, or nickname, "Al-azrak," borne by more than one prominent North African leader and derived from the Arabic *azrac,* "he of the blue eyes"; see *Chronicle of James of Aragon,* 2 vols. (London, 1883), 2: 475, n. 1."Zarco" was probably unconnected with the inelegant Spanish and Portuguese term *zargo,* meaning "wall-eyed" or "squint-eyed," although some writers insist on using "Zargo."

2. Bartolomeu Perestrelo (d. ca. 1457) was a younger son of Filippo Pallastrelli of Piacenza, Italy. Filippo entered the service of Princess Leonor, daughter of Ferdinand I of Aragon, who in 1428 married Prince Edward (Duarte), later king of Portugal (1433-38). Bartolomeu's daughter, Filipa Moniz de Perestrelo (d. ca. 1485), married Christopher Columbus in Lisbon and was the mother of Diego Colón. Prospero Peragallo, "Cenni intorno alla colonia italiana in Portogallo," *Miscellanea di Storia Italiana,* year 40, ser. iii, 9 (Turin, 1904): 432. Samuel Eliot Morison, *Admiral of the Ocean Sea,* 2 vols. (Boston, 1942), 1: 49-52.

Bugio), being small, arid, waterless, and difficult of access, were left unpopulated and even today are uninhabited.

The hierarchy of legal authority in the Madeiras during the years 1425–40 is not very clear, although Zarco seems to have acted as de facto governor. In 1440 Tristão Vaz obtained the titles of *donatário* ("donatory," or lord proprietor) and captain of Machico, which made him independent of Zarco. Similarly, in 1446, Prince Henry (overlord of the islands since 1433) conferred on Perestrelo the captaincy of Porto Santo. In 1450 Zarco became captain-donatory of Funchal.[3]

The island of Madeira was thus split between Zarco and Tristão Vaz, while Perestrelo kept the small island of Porto Santo. Zarco's captaincy included most of the south and southwest coast, while Tristão Vaz had jurisdiction over the entire north coast and the extreme east. The line of demarcation between the two captaincies ran east to west along the mountain peaks in the middle of the island, the two zones being roughly equal in area.

Although Funchal and Machico, as rival settlements, started on an equal footing, Funchal grew much faster than Machico. Funchal prospered because its anchorage offered better shelter for ships, it was more centrally located, and was the capital of a far richer captaincy. The captaincy of Machico remained undeveloped, because most of its territory comprised the wild, isolated, stormy, and exceptionally rugged north coast, which has almost no harbors. Today Funchal is a city of over 50,000 people, with 100,000 persons living in the immediate metropolitan area, while Machico is only a town of some 12,000.

The prosperity of Madeira after the middle years of the fifteenth century derived from the cultivation of sugarcane and the production of large amounts of excellent white sugar. In the late Middle Ages sugar was grown in Sicily, North Africa, the eastern Mediterranean, southern Spain, and in the Portuguese Algarve. Apparently the supply from all these places was not very great and prices were high. Sugarcane was introduced into Madeira, probably by the Genoese, and thrived there.[4]

3. Manuel Monteiro Velho Arruda, *Coleção de documentos relativos ao descobrimento dos Açores* (Ponta Delgada, 1932), p. cxxix.

4. According to João Lúcio de Azevedo, in Peres, ed., *História de Portugal*, 9 vols. (Barcelos, 1928–54), 3: 634, sugar sold in Sicily for 3 ducats per arroba in the mid-fifteenth century, or the equivalent of about 1$080 Portuguese réis, whereas an arroba of Madeiran sugar was sold in Rome in 1497, transportation costs included, for the equivalent of only $502 réis (for a definition of Portuguese weights and measures see Appendix III). The important role that the Genoese played in the plantation, processing, and marketing of Madeiran sugar in the fifteenth century is made clear in Peragallo, pp. 402, 405–6, 415–16, *et passim*.

The cane was, and still is, grown on narrow terraces clinging to the steep slopes of the hills and irrigated with water brought down from the mountain heights and distributed through an elaborate system of small conduits. Cultivation in Madeira is arduous. Draft animals cannot be used; everything must be done by hand. After 1443, slaves were imported from Africa to do the hardest work.

In the early days the cane was crushed at Madeira in inefficient hand presses. In 1452 a certain Diogo de Teive was authorized to build a mechanical *engenho,* or sugar mill, at Funchal, operated by a water-wheel. When Alvisi Cadamosto, a Venetian navigator in Prince Henry's service, visited Madeira in 1455, he found four settlements (Funchal, Machico, Câmara de Lobos, and Santa Cruz) capable, together, of raising eight hundred men-at-arms. Cadamosto was impressed with the thriving sugar production, which amounted to perhaps 1,600 arrobas (or 51,200 lbs.) per year. He wrote that the island produced considerable stores of wheat and that its wine was already good enough to be exported. The islanders also exported, to Portugal, fine furniture made from Madeiran woods.[5]

In 1456 the first shipment of Madeiran sugar was sent to England, and, during later years, considerable quantities went to Flanders. The exported sugar had been boiled only once and was very raw; most of the refining had to be done in the European sugar houses. The Madeiran cultivation was so successful, and the production so plentiful, that the price of sugar on European markets probably fell by about 50 percent between the years 1470 and 1500. The drop in prices alarmed the king of Portugal, who, in 1498, tried to support a price level by restricting exports; by the legislation of 1498, King Manuel I forbade the export

5. Richard H. Major, *Life of Prince Henry* (London, 1868), pp. 248–50; C.R. Beazley, *Prince Henry* (New York, 1904), pp. 264–65. Cadamosto's relation was first printed in Francanzano da Montalboddo, *Paesi nouamenti retrouati* (Vicenza, 1507), although it has usually been cited from the corrupt, but more accessible, version in G.B. Ramusio, *Navigationi et viaggi,* 3 vols. (Venice, 1550–59). The authentic text has been recently republished in António Brásio, *Monumenta missionaria Africana: Africa Ocidental,* ser. ii, 3 vols. (Lisbon, 1958–64), 1: 287–374. The best study of the Madeiran sugar trade during 1450–1600 is in Vitorino Magalhães Godinho, *Os descobrimentos e a economia mundial,* 3 pts. (Lisbon, 1963–68), 3: 419–56. Magalhães Godinho interprets Cadamosto's figure of 400 Italian cantaros (annual sugar production) as equivalent to 1,600 Portuguese arrobas (instead of 6,000 arrobas, as in earlier calculations). He estimated Madeiran production at 20,000 arrobas in 1470, 80,000 in 1490, 105,000 in 1494, and 144,000 in 1506; by the end of the sixteenth century, production had fallen to about 45,000.

of more than 120,000 arrobas (or 3,840,000 lbs.) of Madeiran sugar to foreign countries.[6]

Madeira, by the time Columbus sailed to the Americas, had become well integrated into the economies of Europe and Africa. The island was the prototype of that momentous and tragic social and economic system of sugar and slavery that was to be repeated, on a far larger scale, in the West Indies and Brazil. By 1500, when Madeira had reached only its seventy-fifth year of settlement, the island had become the world's greatest producer of sugar and, with its complex European and African connections, was also an important center for commercial shipping and navigation.

The development of the virgin territory of Madeira was, one may say, quite rapid; within two generations the colonists had seized upon their indispensable cash crop and had promoted it with astounding success. But what was true of Madeira was not true of the Azores. The settlement of the nine islands of the Azores was a lengthy, intermittent, and hesitant process, and in economic growth the islands lagged far behind Madeira.

According to Gaspar Frutuoso, who wrote his *Saudades da terra* during 1580–91 and who supposedly relied on the accounts of elderly Azoreans, the island of Santa Maria was discovered on 15 August 1432 by Gonçalo Velho Cabral. Unfortunately neither the date nor the person nor even the event can be proved to be correct. In fact, the evidence available indicates that the landing of Gonçalo Velho at Santa Maria in 1432, a story told and retold by many authors, is fictitious.

Frutuoso arrived at the exact date "15 August" by a backward deduction from the name of the island, Saint Mary, on the theory that the island was given this name because it was discovered on the principal feast day (the Assumption of the Virgin) honoring the mother of Christ. Following the same slippery line of reasoning, Frutuoso asserted that the island of São Miguel (Saint Michael) was "discovered" on 8 May 1444, on the day dedicated to the Archangel Michael. A venerable tradition among the islanders has it that São Miguel was first "discovered" in 1444 and that Santa Maria was "discovered" twelve years previously — hence Santa Maria "must" have been "discovered" on 15 August 1432. And, in 1932, great festivities commemorated the fifth centenary of this event — the fifth centenary of a myth!

---

6. Leite, I, 456–63; Edgar Prestage, *Portuguese Pioneers* (London, 1933), pp. 40–41.

For a myth it is, since the few scraps of contemporary documentary evidence that remain extant demolish these fine stories. The first piece of evidence comes from a map drawn by the Catalan cartographer Gabriel Vallseca, at Majorca in 1439, which shows eight islands presumed to be the Azores, and next to them is the legend: "These islands were found by Diego de Silues, pilot of the king of Portugal, in the year MCCCCXXVII [1427]."[7] Unfortunately nothing whatever is known about this Diogo de Silves or his voyage.

The second piece of documentary evidence is far more authoritative and reliable: it is a royal letter, dated 2 July 1439, authorizing Prince Henry to organize the settlement of the "seven islands of the Azores" on which, at some previous time, the prince had ordered the setting down of sheep.[8] This letter supports several conclusions. First of all, Frutuoso's statement about the "discovery" of São Miguel on 8 May 1444 is demonstrably false, and the statement that depends on it, that Santa Maria was "discovered" in 1432, by the calculation subtracting twelve years from 1444, must also be false. Second, by 1439 the Portuguese were familiar with seven of the islands — that is, all but the westernmost islands of Flores and Corvo, which are the most isolated, the stormiest, and, except as aids to navigation, the least significant of the Azores. Third, the Portuguese had already placed sheep on the islands to provide food for ships that might visit them. Fourth, the name Azores (Açores) was already in use.[9] And, last, the earliest efforts at colonization must have taken place after the letter of authorization, quite probably in 1440.

The colonization of Santa Maria and São Miguel, after they had been stocked with sheep during the 1430s, probably began in 1440 under the leadership of Gonçalo Velho Cabral, who was responsible directly to Prince Henry. Velho called himself "Friar" Gonçalo (Frei Gonçalo) and was a knight of the military Order of Christ, bound to a vow of celibacy, at a time when the members of the order still took their religious obli-

7. The original map is in the Biblioteca Central in Barcelona. There is a photograph of the map, and a lengthy discussion, in Damião Peres, *História dos descobrimentos,* 2d ed. (Coimbra, 1960), pp. 78–87.

8. Printed in Velho Arruda, p. 121 (and in many other books).

9. The name *Açores* derives from birds, the *milhafres* (kites), who still nest in most of the islands and were mistaken for *açores* (goshawks), whom they resemble. The birds of all the Portuguese islands, incidentally, have been thoroughly studied in D.A. and W.M. Bannerman, *Birds of the Atlantic Islands,* 4 vols. (Edinburgh, 1963–68).

gations seriously. Unlike Zarco, Velho seems to have been a man of means with substantial responsibilities in Portugal who could not devote his whole life to the Azorean colonization project.[10] Also unlike Zarco, Velho never became the captain or donatory of any island but had the title of *comendador* of Santa Maria and São Miguel, holding the properties in trust for his master, Prince Henry, who at some unknown date after 1440 became the official, if absentee, lord proprietor or donatory.

The central square of Ponta Delgada (capital of São Miguel) is called Praça Gonçalo Velho and is adorned with a statue of the "discoverer" of São Miguel. The square was built partly on land reclaimed from the sea by fill-in, in accordance with a plan of construction put into effect during the early 1940s.[11] The square and statue are thus very recent tributes to Velho, a man to whom the islanders owe perhaps much less than they think they do. For Velho did very little for São Miguel and nothing for Ponta Delgada. His proper sphere of activity was the small island of Santa Maria, and even there he may not have stayed very long.[12]

Santa Maria's western plain, with its scrub and grass vegetation, was easy to penetrate and could support considerable numbers of cattle, sheep, and goats. The lush, well-watered valleys in the central and eastern parts of the island were cultivated for grains and other crops. By the end of the 1440s Santa Maria was probably already exporting wheat to Portugal. As early as 1443 a royal decree suspended duties on imports from the Azores for a period of five years.[13]

The early development of the Azores was associated with two other factors: (1) the introduction of the caravel for long-distance Atlantic navigation; and (2) the Portuguese push down the West African coast. The two-masted, lateen-rigged, high-boarded caravel could sail close-hauled, six points off the wind, was fairly swift and nimble and could withstand the heavy pounding of the Atlantic seas. It was far better adapted to Atlantic navigation than the ships previously used in the

10. The collection of documents published by Aires de Sá, *Frei Gonçalo Velho*, 2 vols. (Lisbon, 1899–1900), while adding almost nothing to our knowledge of Velho's Azorean activities, does show the extent of Velho's responsibilities in Portugal.

11. A photograph showing the customshouse docks as they used to exist before the construction of the Praça Gonçalo Velho can be found in Luís de Vasconcelos, *Terra Nostra* (Lisbon, 1943), facing p. 80.

12. Velho Arruda, p. cxxxvi.

13. Ibid., p. 122.

Portuguese voyages.[14] The caravel made navigation to the Azores, and down the coast of Africa, cheap and practicable. The African voyages, which began to gather momentum during the years 1441–45, carried the Portuguese beyond Senegal and Cape Verde. From those latitudes ships on the return voyage, if they chose to stay close to Africa, had to battle strong headwinds. From Senegal and beyond the easiest route back to Europe was by way of the Azores, describing a great semicircle across the high seas of the Atlantic. The Azorean islands, in time, could hope to become the normal ports of call for ships making the return voyage from West Africa.

Yet whatever bright prospects the future might hold for the western islands, the immediate situation of the Azores in the middle years of the fifteenth century was far from satisfactory. Gonçalo Velho, having planted a small settlement at Santa Maria, departed for Portugal, where he spent the remainder of his days. Neither Velho nor Prince Henry paid much attention to the Azores, and the islands lacked the kind of leadership that Zarco provided in Madeira.

By 1450 a small settlement had been made at Povoação, on the south coast of São Miguel. Ten years later, when Prince Henry died and the islands passed into the hands of Prince Fernando, Henry's nephew, only a small group of settlers lived in São Miguel. Prince Fernando entrusted Santa Maria and São Miguel to João Soares, one of Velho's nephews, but Soares remained at Santa Maria and did nothing for São Miguel. In 1474 Soares sold São Miguel (but not Santa Maria) to Rui Gonçalves da Câmara, Zarco's second son, for the small sum of 2,000 cruzados and 4,000 arrobas of sugar. São Miguel was described at that time as "poorly utilized and little inhabited."[15]

Gonçalves da Câmara took charge of São Miguel with considerable gusto, and accelerated its development. By the year of his death, in 1497, the island had five official *vilas* (chartered, self-governing municipalities) — Ponta Delgada, Vila Franca do Campo, Ribeira Grande, Água de Pau, and Nordeste — and flourishing communities at Povoação and Lagôa. The island yielded bountiful harvests of wheat, and, before the

14. Peres, *Descobrimentos,* pp. 227–38, summarizes the main points concerning the earlier types of Portuguese ships (the *barca, barcha,* and *barinel*) and discusses the evolution of the caravel and the question of what routes were taken on the return voyage from West Africa. The *disadvantages* of the early caravel (because of the difficulty of changing the set of the sails), as well as its excellence for "windward work," are set forth in Morison, *Admiral,* 1: xxxvii–xliii.

15. Velho Arruda, p. cxliv.

end of the century, the blue-dye pastel plant (woad) had been introduced for cultivation. Pastel was to furnish the main support of the island's economy for a century and a half. The population increased rapidly during the sixteenth century until the island became almost overcrowded and began to provide emigrants for the Portuguese colonies and recruits for the king's armies and navies.

Santa Maria, once far ahead of São Miguel, soon fell behind. The smaller island became increasingly isolated, nearly self-supporting, and quite self-centered, and its only regular contact with the outside world was by way of the small boats that carried its surplus wheat to São Miguel for export. Its capital, Vila do Pôrto, remained small, hampered by its bad harbor and visited only occasionally by transoceanic ships.

Santa Maria, however, experienced a historic moment in February 1493, when Columbus stopped at the island on his way back from discovering America. The storm-tossed *Niña*, separated from the *Pinta* and in need of supplies, sent half her crew ashore. The sailors, in compliance with a vow made to the Virgin during a storm at sea, attended mass at the small chapel of Nossa Senhora dos Anjos at the northwest corner of the island. But the islanders were suspicious of these Castilian interlopers sailing about in "Portuguese" seas and suspected that they might have traded illegally in Portuguese Guinea. So the seamen were apprehended and detained ashore. Columbus — who wisely never left his ship — had to negotiate for the release of his men and, after several days, was no doubt glad to get away from Santa Maria.[16]

São Miguel, Santa Maria, and the rocks called the Formigas form the eastern group of Azores and today constitute a political unit known as the "autonomous district" of Ponta Delgada. To the northwest of São Miguel there are five islands — Terceira, Graciosa, São Jorge, Pico, and Fayal — which form the central group of the Azores. The nearest to São Miguel, some 75 nautical miles away and beyond the range of sight, is Terceira, called "Terceira" ("Third") because it was the third island to be colonized.[17]

---

16. The story is told fully, with considerable bias against the Portuguese, in Morison, *Admiral,* 1: 423–29.

17. In formal usage Terceira is sometimes called "Terceira de Jesus Cristo" — a lingering survival of the name "Jesus Christ" bestowed upon this island by Prince Henry. Four of Henry's pious names for the islands fell quickly into disuse: Pico was once "São Dinís" (possibly as an indirect homage to King Dinís of Portugal, founder of the Order of Christ), Fayal was "São Luís" (after the crusading St. Louis of France, one of Henry's favorite saints), Flores was "São Tomás" (after

The central Azores were probably reconnoitered during 1427 and after by the first Portuguese vessels that visited Santa Maria and São Miguel. Originally, the term Azores seems to have been applied only to the seven islands known to the seamen of the 1430s. The two western-most islands, Flores and Corvo — small, distant, and isolated in stormy seas — are no closer than about 130 nautical miles west-northwest of Fayal. Diogo de Teive, a Madeiran navigator and sugar merchant, prob-ably discovered Flores and Corvo in 1452.[18]

The colonization of the central and western islands took a very long time. Nothing significant had been done before the death of Prince Henry in 1460. The earliest colonizing ventures in Terceira are wrapped in obscurity; presumably they took place during the late 1450s and early 1460s. In 1474 the island was divided into two captaincies, cen-tered upon the two chief settlements of Angra and Praia. The earliest settlement, however, had been at a place called São Sebastião, midway between Angra and Praia. Of the larger islands, Terceira is the most cen-trally located and therefore in the best position to exercise political control over the others. Angra, its capital, was to become the chief political and ecclesiastical city in the Azores.

Prince Fernando, lord proprietor of the islands during the years 1460–70, recruited foreigners, particularly Flemish merchants and adventur-ers, for the development of the islands. The Flemish planted the first settlements in Terceira, and were wholly responsible for the initial colo-nization, during the late 1460s and early 1470s, of Fayal, Pico, and São Jorge. For three centuries thereafter on Dutch maps the Azores were called the "Flemish" Islands.

At the western edge of the central group, the twin islands of Fayal and Pico developed in a symbiotic economic relationship, and together constituted a center of commercial and maritime activity that rivaled Angra and Ponta Delgada in importance. Pico, dominated by its great active volcano over 7,700 feet high, produced the finest wine in the Azores, a wine that during the seventeenth and eighteenth centuries became a staple commodity in the North American and West Indian trades. But with no harbors, Pico had to send its produce in small boats across a narrow strait to the port of Horta in Fayal. Protected by moun-tains on two sides, Horta offered the only safe anchorage in the Azores.

St. Thomas à Becket, to whom was dedicated the chapel of the Order of Christ at Tomar), and Corvo was "Santa Iria" (the name of a local martyr at Tomar). Velho Arruda, pp. lxix, xci.

18. The date 1452 has sometimes been questioned, but I accept the reasoning supporting it in Peres, *Descobrimentos,* pp. 87–92.

It has occurred to many people that the Portuguese, having explored, mapped, and sent settlers to the Azores during the period 1427-52, were in an excellent position by the mid-1450s to send their caravels across the Atlantic to reach America and so might have anticipated the great Genoese mariner by some three or four decades. Yet, in truth, the elements of wind and sea current made westward navigation from the Azores impracticable. Any mariner attempting to sail due west from the vicinity of the Azores would have found his ship relentlessly opposed by the prevailing westerly winds.[19]

For many reasons the exploration of the Azores cannot be regarded as the beginning of Europe's westward movement toward the Americas; rather, the Azorean ventures marked the end of Europe's westward penetration in those latitudes. Any future westward probes were likely to come in waters either very far removed to the north, or very far removed to the south of the Azores. Except for vessels bound for the British, French, or Dutch West Indies, the Azores were not destined to become the first port of call for westward-bound ships, but rather the last port of call for homeward-bound European ships.

The Portuguese, instead of setting forth from the Azores into the great, unknown void of the central Atlantic, preferred to follow the far more enticing, safer, and already somewhat known coast of West Africa, which promised to lead to untold riches. Somewhere to the south lay the elusive and invisible sources of the gold that trickled in across the desert from the almost legendary Timbuktu, a city of euphonious and evocative name. As the caravels pushed ever closer to the mysterious "Gold Coast," there developed a trade in slaves, ivory, gold, and malagueta pepper which paid for the expeditions, and which made it unavoidable that more ships would come to those shores more often. A by-product of the maritime effort which created the Portuguese mercantile enterprise in West Africa was the discovery of the most promising "stepping stones" to the West Indies and South America — the Cape Verde islands. For the Cape Verde Islands, far more than the Azores, pointed the unsatisfied mariner toward the undiscovered West.

Cape Verde proper, continental Africa's westernmost protrusion into the Atlantic, now called Cap Vert, sticks out into the sea like a gigantic "sore thumb," at the end of a narrow peninsula some twenty miles long. The Portuguese mariner Dinis Dias first reached it in 1441. Boavista, the nearest island of the Cape Verde archipelago to the cape, is

19. "Owing to wind conditions in the North Atlantic, the Azores were of no use as 'stepping-stones' in an outward transatlantic voyage in days of sail." Morison, *Portuguese Voyages to America* (Cambridge, Mass., 1940), p. 15, n. 21.

still a considerable distance from it, over 300 miles to the west. The westernmost island, Santo Antão, is 458 miles from the African mainland. Since the islands are so far out to sea, and since the Portuguese were concerned with moving southward and south-southeastward from the cape (and not with looking for islands in the ocean to the west), the islands were not discovered until more than a decade after the cape had been reached.

Two Italians in Portuguese expeditions, acting independently of each other, share the credit for the initial discoveries. The Genoese Antonio da Noli probably discovered five islands (Sal, Boavista, Maio, Santiago, and Fogo) in July 1455. But ten months later, in May 1456, the Venetian Alvisi Cadamosto, ignorant of Noli's voyage, discovered once again the same group of islands.[20] A third navigator, the Portuguese Diogo Gomes, also claimed to have discovered the Cape Verdes, and said that Noli had robbed him of the credit for this feat. But the extant account of Gomes's voyage, a muddled version at second or third hand and written forty years after the events it purports to relate, seems only to indicate that Gomes could not have been in the Cape Verdes before 1458.[21]

The rival claims of Noli, Cadamosto, and Gomes have been much debated;[22] a document of 19 September 1462, however, officially credits Noli with the discovery of five[23] of the Cape Verdean islands, and it was Noli who was officially rewarded with the captaincy of one-half of Santiago island and who founded a settlement there.

The northwestern group of islands – containing Santo Antão, São Vicente, São Nicolau, and three smaller islands – was found by Diogo Afonso, Prince Fernando's squire, probably during December and January of 1461–62, although his voyage could have occurred a year ear-

20. In accordance with the line of reasoning adopted by Leite, 1: 281–85. For various other views, see Peres, pp. 189–205.

21. The case against the "claims" of Gomes is set forth at length and in detail in Peragallo, pp. 423–32.

22. In a course of lectures at the Universidade Técnica de Lisboa, the students must have been puzzled at the conflicting information received from their professors concerning the date of the discovery of the Cape Verdes. Joaquim Angélico de Jesus Guerra chose the year 1444; Oscar Barrata said between 1456 and 1460; Raquel Soeiro de Brito and Vasco Fortuna said "probably" 1460; João Ameal and José Júlio Gonçalves said "certainly" 1460; and the cautious António da Silva Rego said sometime before December 1460. Universidade Técnica de Lisboa, *Cabo Verde, Guiné, São Tomé e Príncipe: Curso de extensão universitária, ano lectivo de 1965–1966* (Lisbon, 1966), pp. 28, 69, 168, 505, 724, 928.

23. Peres, *Descobrimentos,* pp. 190–91.

lier.[24] This final event, which completed the discovery of all of the islands in the three Atlantic Portuguese archipelagoes, came shortly after the death of Prince Henry.

The two discoverers, Noli and Diogo Afonso, were given possession of the large island of Santiago; Noli became captain and donatory of the southern half, with his capital at Ribeira Grande, in the southwest, and Afonso received the northern half, with his capital at Alcatrazes, in the northwest. The pattern of Madeira, which had been divided into the two captaincies of Funchal and Machico, was here repeated. Again, as in Madeira, Genoese seamen and merchants, backed with Genoese capital, tried to turn Santiago into a rich sugar-producing area. Noli, who in his Portuguese expeditions used Genoese-built ships probably manned by Italian crews, arrived at Santiago in 1462, accompanied by his brother, Bartolomeo, and his nephew Raffaele da Noli, and founded the village of Ribeira Grande.[25]

Because of the aridity of the island, the difficulty of producing cash crops, the remoteness from Europe, and the lack of settlers, progress in Santiago was very slow. A charter of privileges issued by King Afonso V on 12 June 1466 mentions that the colonization of Santiago had begun four years before but that "because it is so far from our kingdoms, people do not want to go there and live, at their own expense, except with great liberties and exemptions."[26] The charter then went on to concede to Santiago free trade with the West African mainland, except at the island of Arguin, where the royal monopoly was maintained intact; it eliminated Lisbon tariffs on Cape Verdean imports and lifted customs duties on produce brought into Portugal from the Canaries, Madeira, or the Azores aboard Cape Verdean ships.

What emerged in Santiago was a plantation and pastoral economy run by slaves from Africa with a small group of white colonists acting as landlords, as exporters and importers, and as the civil and ecclesiastical authorities. Early documents on the Cape Verdes are scarce, but those that exist seem to mention many foreigners. For instance, in 1466, in a quarrel over a concubine, Bartolomeo da Noli murdered the seventy-year-old Franciscan friar Rogerio and then blamed the deed on Rogerio's colleague Friar Jaime; both friars were Catalans, although attached to a

24. Ibid., p. 205.

25. Cristiano José de Sena Barcelos, *Subsídios para a história de Cabo Verde*, 7 vols. (Lisbon, 1899–1913), 1: 21; Peragallo, pp. 424–25.

26. Sena Barcelos, 1: 21.

Lisbon convent.[27] Again, in 1469, when the king of Portugal let out a contract for the exploitation of the dye-yielding lichen called orchil (*urzela*), which is plentiful in the Cape Verdes, the contract went not to Portuguese merchants, but to the Castilian brothers Juan and Pedro de Lugo, who were permitted to send Castilian ships to Santiago.[28]

The facts concerning the considerable Castilian interest in and penetration of the seas around the Guinea coast in the fifteenth century were made clear in books published in the 1940s,[29] but have not always been appreciated. Even earlier, during the first decade of this century, the publication of the chronicle by Alonso de Palencia revealed that "the men of Palos [in Andalusia] knew of old the Guinea sea."[30] Palencia, who was historiographer to Queen Isabella of Castile, told the story of how the Castilians raided the Cape Verdes in 1476 during the Spanish-Portuguese war of 1475–79. Carlos de Valera, with twenty-five or thirty ships, attacked Ribeira Grande in Santiago and captured Antonio da Noli and most of his followers and brought them back to Europe.[31]

When the fleet arrived back in Andalusia early in 1477, Noli was held for a ransom of 1,000 Spanish gold *doblas*, which Genoese merchants were supposed to pay within four months. About that time, Enrique de Guzmán, duke of Medinasidonia, received the title of overlord of the Cape Verdes from the Castilian crown and thereafter evidently regarded Noli and his band as his own servants. Plainly the Spaniards were not yet prepared to surrender all claims to the Cape Verdes and the Guinea coast to the Portuguese – and would not be, at least until after the discovery of America. Eventually Ferdinand of Aragon ordered Noli's release, and Noli made his way to Portugal.[32]

What happened to Noli after 1477 is not known. Presumably he went back to Santiago and was living there when he died, either late in 1496 or early in 1497. His titles to the captaincy were transmitted through his daughter, Branca de Aguiar, to his son-in-law, Jorge Correa de Sousa. The other captain in Santiago, Diogo Afonso of Alcatrazes, died in 1473, when his rights were transferred to his nephew, Rodrigo Afonso.[33]

27. Ibid., pp. 28–29.
28. Ibid., pp. 33–34.
29. That is, John W. Blake, *Europeans in West Africa,* 2 vols. (London, 1942), and Florentino Perez Embid, *Descubrimientos en el Atlántico* (Seville, 1948).
30. Alonso de Palencia, *Cronica de Enrique IV*, 5 vols. (Madrid, 1904–9), 4: 213.
31. Ibid.; Embid, pp. 201–6; Blake, 1: 217–24.
32. Ibid.
33. Sena Barcelos, 1: 36–37, 51–53; Brásio, 1: 521, 279–80.

But it seems that neither Diogo nor Rodrigo Afonso ever lived in Santiago, and the ill-located hamlet of Alcatrazes never prospered.

The Castilian raid in 1476 must have halted the economic development of Santiago for several years. The Castilians carried away every inhabitant they could find, both black and white, the blacks to be sold as slaves, and the whites to be held for ransom. The sugar enterprise started by the Genoese never developed very far. In 1508 Santiago produced a mere 4,000 arrobas (128,000 lbs.) of sugar, compared with an annual production of 70,000 in Madeira and 20,000 in the Azores.[34] Sugarcane was to prosper in Portugal's equatorial island of São Tomé, off the Gabon coast, but it fared less well in the Cape Verdes, where the cane was used mostly for the production of rum — an item of some importance in the West African slave trade.

The extreme uncertainty of rainfall made it unlikely that the Cape Verdes would ever produce cash crops in great quantities. The earliest and most successful crop was cotton, introduced from West Africa and largely sold there. First the cotton was sold in bulk; but later, by the end of the sixteenth century, African weavers brought into the islands as slaves were producing high-quality cotton textiles that were marketed on the Guinea coast. Other Cape Verdean products were less significant. Bay salt, laid down by the sea, was freely available in the islands of Maio, Boavista, and Sal — yet it was not really sold as an export, but was merely picked up, almost for nothing, by passing vessels which landed crewmen on the nearly deserted "salt islands." Orchil, hides, goatskins, salted goatmeat, live donkeys and horses, and a little rice and maize complete the short list of Cape Verdean exports, most of which were exported in very small number or quantity.

In 1515 there were only eighty households in Ribeira Grande and only twenty-five in Alcatrazes.[35] Even so, the island of Santiago was important — important for its connection with the African coast and important because of its vital function as a supplier of ships. The proximity of the Cape Verdes to the African coast, offshore from Senegal and only some 500 miles from the land the Portuguese called Guiné, suggested that the islanders should play a major role in West African

34. *Archivo dos Açores* 3 (Ponta Delgada, 1881): 201. Frédéric Mauro, *Portugal et l'Atlantique* (Paris, 1960), p. 190. Magalhães Godinho (2: 430), however, puts Madeiran production during the years 1504–8 at over 140,000 arrobas per annum.

35. Orlando Ribeiro, *Aspectos e problemas da expansão portuguesa* (Lisbon, 1962), p. 144.

trade. This idea was undoubtedly present at the time the first settlements arose in Santiago, for the islanders' involvement with Africa was immediate, extensive, and of far-reaching consequence.

The Cape Verdes, immune to attacks from black Africa, provided a logical base for Portuguese expansion in the Gulf of Guinea; and since the Portuguese stockades, trading posts, and mission stations – weakly scattered along a hostile coast 2,500 miles long – were often in precarious circumstances, the islands provided reinforcements for the coastal positions in emergencies and were a place of refuge for persons expelled from Guiné by hostile Africans. The islands, which became the seat of a bishopric, also served as an ecclesiastical center from which to dispatch missionaries to the mainland.

The islanders were able, to some extent, to exploit their position off the African mainland; but they were also able to derive economic benefits from their crucial geographical situation at the crossroads of several routes for transatlantic shipping. In the words of an American visitor to the islands, written about 1859: "The Cape Verd Islands ... have been long and favorably known to the seafaring and commercial men of Europe and America, as a half-way house, or caravanserai of the seas, between the ports of Europe and South America, and those of America and Africa."[36]

The islanders could at least supply passing ships with salted goatmeat and water and always hoped that a little trade might be transacted as well. The Cape Verdeans catered to European ships bound for South America, Southwest Africa, and the Indian Ocean – and also to ships out of West Africa bound for the West Indies and North America. The islands also serviced ships following a complicated but very common route from Europe to the Cape Verdes, to the West Indies, to North America, and thence back to Europe.

Even after the days of sailing ships were over and steamships came into their own, the islands continued to assist shippers and merchants in an essential way. The port of Mindelo, on São Vicente, became a major coaling station. For instance, in 1890, a total of 156 ships unloaded 657,633,588 metric tons of coal at Mindelo. The port was visited by 2,264 ships, having a gross tonnage of over 4.25 million, and carrying 343,907 persons.[37]

36. Charles W. Thomas, *Adventures and Observations on the West Coast of Africa* (New York, 1860), p. 327.

37. Ernesto J. de Carvalho, *Colónias portuguezas,* 2d ed. (Lisbon, 1903), pp. 17, 26–27.

The three island groups – the Madeiras, Azores, and Cape Verdes – explored and colonized by the Portuguese in the fifteenth century, have many things in common. They all possess a distinctly oceanic position. They are all volcanic in origin, generally of rugged topography, and usually with high rocky cliffs where the islands rise from the sea; some have very high peaks. Almost all are lacking in good natural harbors.

All the islands were uninhabited when the Portuguese arrived. All were virgin lands, to be colonized "from scratch." All served, even if unwittingly, as laboratories, wherein the Portuguese developed colonial structures – with economic, social, political, and ecclesiastical features – that were to be applied on a much wider basis in Brazil, Angola, Mozambique, and elsewhere.

Yet in many other respects the archipelagoes differ widely from one another. Climatically there are enormous differences between the Azores and the Cape Verdes. The strong North Atlantic westerlies turn the Azores into places with much rain and mist, supporting a rich luxuriance of green vegetation; whereas the bone-dry northeasterlies from the Saharan deserts turn many of the Cape Verdes into parched wastelands much of the time. The island of Madeira, with its complicated "microclimates" and barren patches of "rain shadow," warmer than the Azores and cooler than the Cape Verdes, falls somewhere between the other two.

Racially and culturally the Azores and the Cape Verdes also differ markedly. The Portuguese-speaking, deeply Christian peasant peoples of the Azores, derived mostly from white-skinned European stock, have little in common with the creole-speaking, formerly semipagan, African population that was once predominant in the Cape Verdes. The Madeiras, in these respects, although they have had a strong infusion of African blood, are much closer to the Azores than to the Cape Verdes.

The Portuguese mid-Atlantic islands obviously derive their major social and cultural characteristics from the Eurasian and African continents that lie to the east of them; but the true function and destiny of the islands, as nodal points in the great web of interoceanic shipping routes, did not emerge until after the discovery and development of the American continents to the west of them. The Cape Verdes pointed the way west, but unfortunately the Portuguese overlords of the islands were more interested in going south and east, toward the fabled riches of India. If Columbus had been in the Portuguese service, he might have set out westward from the Cape Verdes, instead of from the Spanish Canaries, and made his American landfall in the convenient waters of the Lesser Antilles, instead of in the dangerous Bahamas. Yet the Columbian voyage itself eventually made possible the opening up of the more practicable Cape Verdean route to the West Indies. For four centuries the Cape Verdes exploited their position as the logical stopover point for ships in mid-journey between the Old World and the New.

Vasco da Gama, on his historic journey to India, spent a week in the Cape Verdes in 1497. It was the first of many such stopovers for ships on their way to the East. On his return voyage from discovering the Americas, Columbus made an involuntary stopover in the Azores. Again, it was the first of thousands of such stopovers for ships returning to Europe from the Americas. The British colonizing ventures in North America and the West Indies brought the Azores, Madeira, and the Cape Verdes into the complicated patterns of the maritime commerce of the English "plantations." The Azorean link with New England was particularly important and did not begin to weaken until the twentieth century. The whalers of New England employed large contingents of Azorean and Cape Verdean seamen.

In truth, the three mid-oceanic Portuguese archipelagoes derive their special character from all four of the continents that rim the Atlantic Ocean. The fifteenth-century Iberian thrust into the Atlantic brought about the utilization of the islands. The growing of special island products, and the evolution of the West African trade, enhanced the economic significance of the archipelagoes. But the true oceanic and intercontinental mission of the islands, as the nuclei of transoceanic shipping, was not realized until after the development of the communities on the shores of North and South America during the sixteenth and seventeenth centuries.

3
Madeira and Its Wine Trade

In Madeira men are both the masters and the slaves of their environment. Masters because they have succeeded in dominating the ungratefully precipitous terrain and forcing it to support them; yet they remain slaves because they cannot escape the pervasive tyranny of the island's geography. In Madeira, far more than in most places, geographical circumstances determine human function.

Madeira is a small island, only 286 square miles. Today this tiny piece of volcanic real estate, comprising the upper portions of a mountain peak that rises from the abyssal deep-sea floor, has a population of about 266,000 persons — which means that the population density runs to 930 persons per square mile and that Madeira is more crowded than the flat and fertile Netherlands. This population density is all the more striking when it is considered that about one-third of the island is barely inhabited or inhabitable and that the bulk of the population is to be found packed in along the south shore, clinging like ants to the steep slopes.

This population struggles to grow enough to feed itself. In Madeira agriculture is carried on at great cost in human effort. Massive erosion, the difficulty of collecting water and controlling its distribution, and the abrupt, rugged terrain make cultivation of the soil a truly penitential labor. There are very few "fields" in Madeira; crops are grown mostly on terraces, or *poios* — not the wide terraces of hill cultivation on the continent, but often mere ledges, sometimes only about twenty inches wide. On the south coast no patch of fertile soil, no matter how difficult of access, is left uncultivated.[1]

---

1. Many of the remarks in the initial sections of this chapter are based more upon personal observation than upon reading. Detailed geographical information about Madeira can be found in Orlando Ribeiro, *L'Île de Madère* (Lisbon, 1949).

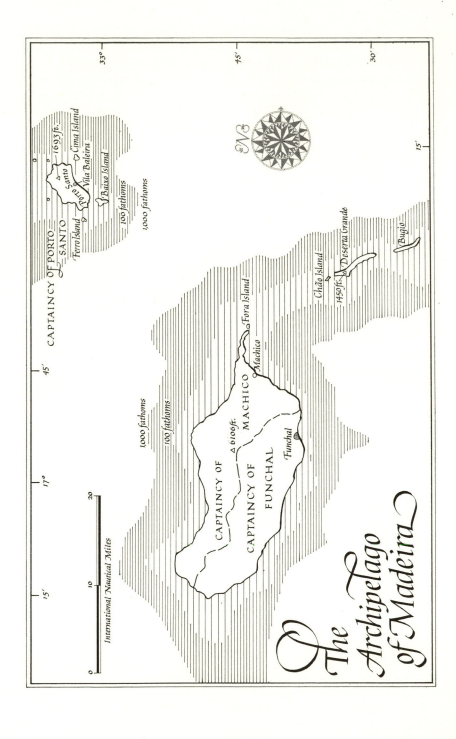

The Archipelago of Madeira

CAPTAINCY OF PORTO SANTO

Porto Santo
Ferro Island
Vila Baleira
Cima Island
1695 ft.
Baixo Island
100 fathoms
1,000 fathoms

Chão Island
1450 ft.
Deserta Grande
Bugio

Fora Island
Machico
Funchal
△ 6106 ft.
CAPTAINCY OF MACHICO
CAPTAINCY OF FUNCHAL

1,000 fathoms
100 fathoms

33°
45'
30'
15'
45'
17°
15'

International Nautical Miles
0   10   20

A hard-driven, exploited peasantry, who have to surrender a large portion of their crops to absentee landlords,[2] maintain their *poios* with simple tools, doing everything by hand. Machinery and animal traction are useless on the steep hillsides and narrow ledges. If a peasant keeps a cow, as many do, for the milk and manure, the animal rarely leaves the small cowshed and spends her life penned in. Most peasant families live in small cottages, right in the middle of their *poios,* with the crops growing almost to the walls.

Usually various kinds of crops are cultivated at the same time, and always there is room for a bed of flowers. The yield per acre is very high, and, partly as a consequence, holdings are small. The primitive conditions of cultivation make it difficult for a peasant family to look after more than a moderate amount of land, and in some places inheritance customs encourage subdivision. Holdings run to as small as 100 square meters, which is less than one-fortieth of an acre, but the average property is considerably larger than that.

Before the construction of the carriage roads, the peasant lived and died on his hillside; his only excursions were to the local church and market, which, although usually only two or three miles away, involved backbreaking ascents and descents. If he had to make a longer journey,

---

See also Fernando Augusto da Silva, *Elucidário madeirense,* 3 vols. (Funchal, 1940–46); and his *Dicionário corográfico do arquipélago da Madeira* (Funchal, 1934). In English, the Peace Handbooks of the British Foreign Office, although dated, still contain much pertinent information; see *Portuguese Possessions: Azores and Madeira* (London, 1920), pp. 9–22, 37–51. W.H. Koebel, *Madeira* (London, 1909), provides much general information (and misinformation) and – like the Ribeiro work cited above – includes many photographs, which give a clearer impression of the terrain than any verbal description. The older travel guides, such as A. Samler Brown, *Madeira and the Canary Islands, with the Azores,* 6th ed. (London, 1901), despite the limitations of the genre, contain much fuller information than current publications of the same type. For historians, the old records of travelers have some importance; see, for instance, Thomas, pp. 409–79; and John Adams Dix, *Winter in Madeira,* 4th ed. (New York, 1851), pp. 2–202. Another good guide to Madeira, Wilhelm Hartnack, *Madeira: Landeskunde einer Insel* (Hamburg, 1930), furnishes the most extensive bibliography (pp. 154–77) and can be supplemented by the bibliography in Mauro, pp. xi–liv.

2. In the land-tenure system of Madeira, often loosely referred to as the *bemfeitoria,* the landlords own the land and the water rights, but the tenant farmer owns the buildings, walls, trees, paved walks, etc. The sharecroppers turn over from one-third to one-half of their crops to the proprietors. If a peasant is evicted, he has to be reimbursed for all the improvements (*bemfeitorias*), such as houses, walls, trees, he has made, or grown, and left on the land, but, in practice, eviction is rare and tenure secure. For a full discussion, see Ribeiro, *Madère,* pp. 79–83.

27

it was usually because of some unpleasant necessity, such as having to carry goatskins full of raw wine to a winery, or to a small local port. Religious festivals provided the chief outlets for communal amusement.

Until the twentieth century, the many agricultural communities of Madeira have lived more or less in isolation from one another. There has always been small-boat traffic between Funchal and the nine or ten tiny coves (*calhetas*) along the south shore, but communication inland from these coves has been, until recently, very difficult. Small-boat communication with the two or three treacherous "harbors" of the north shore depends on weather and the condition of the sea and has rarely been free from hazard. In the seventeenth century there were no highways in the island; only three or four mule tracks or trails connected the north with the south and the east with the west and they required ascents from sea level to as high as 4,600 feet. As late as 1917 there were only two stretches of paved carriage road in Madeira, one linking Funchal with Câmara de Lobos and the second extending four miles east of Funchal in the direction of Caniço.[3] Only since 1952, with the opening of a tunnel between Seixal and Porto Moniz, has it been possible for wheeled traffic to make a complete circuit of the island. The irregular terrain "stretches" mileage: a journey of ten miles seems to require the time and effort of a journey five or six times that length in continental Portugal.

The scattered, self-contained, and self-supporting communities along the cold, wet, and windy north shore have lived, through the centuries, in isolation from the south shore. There has always been communication between Funchal and the two or three major market centers of the north, but this has had little effect on most of the agricultural communities of the north, which lie trapped in their separate valleys, surrounded by steep rocky walls. The northern communities are inbred to the point of biological danger; they are said to be more Negroid than the southern communities; and they speak in strange accents which the people of Funchal affect not to understand.

Agriculturally the north shore differs somewhat from the south. The north has much more Indian corn than the south but does not grow sugarcane, bananas, and the tropical fruits (avocados, guavas, pineapples, mangoes, papayas, and loquats) that can be found below the 600-foot level on the south shore. Wheat, other cereals, and vines grow plentifully on both coasts. On both sides of the island agricultural produce and

3. *Port. Poss.: Azores and Madeira*, p. 37.

plant life fall into distinctly different zones, depending upon altitude. Between 1,800 and 2,500 feet there are temperate fruit trees, vegetables, cereals, pasture land, and forest; but the bananas, sugarcane, and vines of lower altitudes are not to be found there. Above 2,500 feet the terrain becomes increasingly barren and windswept.[4]

The lands of the north and the south meet, as it were, at the top of the mountain mass. Slightly to the west of the center of the island there is a large, wet, foggy plateau, the Paúl da Serra, three and a half miles long by nearly two miles wide — the greatest extent of level land on the island, but so situated as to be nearly useless. To the center and east there are high peaks (*encumeadas*) from which can be discerned, at the same time, the *Mar do Norte* (North Sea) and the *Mar do Sul* (South Sea). These expressions, *Mar do Norte* and *Mar do Sul*, used by the common people, suggest that the two coastlines front upon different worlds, and illustrate the psychic distance that exists between the communities on the two shores.

Everywhere on the island the control and distribution of water is of vital importance. Much of the rock, though by no means all, is soft and crumbly, and rains and streams speedily eat into it. Massive erosion has created spectacular scenery; deep gorges and ravines divide neighboring villages from one another and impede communications. Nature labors to reduce the island to sea level and bury it under the waves. The peasant working on his terraces uses, canalizes, and guides the water to prevent the soil from being washed away. Long lines of retaining walls, punctuated by many holes to allow drainage, prop up the hillsides. At intervals along the tops and sides of the mountains, long stretches of horizontal water courses or conduits (*levadas*), hewn from the living rock or constructed of stone and cement, collect the rainwater and prevent a rapid runoff. Without using reservoirs or dams, the miles of conduits or *levadas* trap the water, store it for a short time, and control its distribution. Erosion is thereby diminished, and the danger of landslides reduced.

Although the rainfall in Madeira is fairly adequate to support cultivation, the runoff is rapid, the distribution erratic, and there are dry places where there is a "rain-shadow" effect. In these circumstances irrigation is essential for intensive cultivation. The "collection" *levadas* that gird the mountains trap and accumulate the water; the "distributing" *levadas*, built at an angle to the collection conduits, carry the water down the mountainsides, sometimes in a sharp precipitous rush of white water.

4. Ibid., pp. 41–42.

An intricate system of open conduits, tunnels (*furadas*), and branch courses (*lanços*) conveys the water downwards, with gravity doing all the work of propulsion (pumps are unnecessary), and makes possible what is supposed to be an equitable distribution.

The largest of the *levadas*, bordered with trees and flowers, also serve as pleasant footpaths across considerable sections of the island. The longest *levadas* are about 50 miles in length, and the system as a whole has an estimated 700 kilometers (435 miles) of major conduits. The most ambitious tunneling and canalizing projects, which had the object of conveying the water surplus on the north slopes to the parched south side, date from 1836, but the water-distribution method itself is far older, with origins in the fifteenth and sixteenth centuries.[5] In 1949 the *levadas* could deliver an estimated 45,960 gallons of water per minute, on an average, which is over 2.75 million gallons per hour; improvements and additions now being undertaken, or planned, will bring this total to nearly 4 million gallons per hour.[6]

Water quotas, rigidly allocated by practice and tradition, and fiercely argued over, determine land values and are regarded as an integral part of a property. An intricate series of local, customary, and communal laws, riddled with anomalies, governs the distribution of water. Some *levadas* are owned by the state, others are communally owned, and others belong to private persons. Officials known as *levadeiros* are in charge of water distribution; a powerful personage, the "judge of the *levadas*" (*juiz das levadas*), resolves disputes over water rights and is himself paid, not in money, but in additional water quotas.[7]

At the bottom of the water-distribution system stands the humble peasant in his terraces, with his own shallow dirt ditches running parallel to the rows of planted crops. In one particular irrigation season, running from May to September, he may receive water only four or five times, or even less often. At whatever hour his water comes, be it night or day, he stands ready in his terraces, with all the members of his family, armed with buckets and utensils, ready to make the most rapid and best possible distribution of the precious liquid. And if (though God

5. The Genoese settler, Raffaele Cattaneo (d. 1540), who earned high praise from Frutuoso (Funchal ed. [1873], p. 78), built a long *levada* at Machico to irrigate his cane; Peragallo, p. 401.

6. My description of the *levadas* derives partly from personal observation, and partly from Ribeiro, *Madère,* pp. 69–79. The gallons-per-hour statistics are converted from the metric estimates cited by him, p. 71.

7. Ribeiro, *Madère,* pp. 75–76.

forbid!) the water should be insufficient, his is the difficult decision, to pick and choose among his crops, giving the water to some and allowing the rest to perish.

On the well-watered north shore, the supply is usually ample and water distribution is less dramatic. But the north shore suffers from other physical problems, not the least of which is the mountain barrier that separates it from, and cuts off access to, the commercial capital of Funchal. The prosperity of the island's agricultural communities has always depended, to an extent, on proximity to the international marketing center of Funchal. The closer to Funchal, the less difficult the transport of agricultural produce, the higher the prices paid for such produce, and the lower the cost of imported necessities. In the seventeenth century there was intensive use of the land in and around Funchal, and the immediate vicinity of the city accounted for much of the wine production of the island. Vineyards even grew within the city limits.[8]

In the seventeenth century wine replaced sugar as Madeira's chief export. The Madeiran sugar trade began to decline after 1570, when the cheaper and better-refined Brazilian product appeared in quantity in European markets. Madeira production figures for the years 1581–86 show the following six-year totals: white sugar, 50,050 arrobas (1,601,600 lbs.); muscavado sugar, 55,045 arrobas (1,761,440 lbs.); third-grade sugars, 113,235 arrobas (3,623,520 lbs.); making a total of 218,330 arrobas (6,986,560 lbs.).[9] These figures average out at only 36,388 arrobas (1,164,416 lbs.) per annum; by the end of the century production probably fell short of 45,000 arrobas, even in good years – a far cry from the maximum figure of 150,000 that had once been attained. The island had thirty-nine *engenhos,* or sugar mills, of which only three were on the north shore (at Faial and Porto da Cruz); of the thirty-six mills on the south shore, twelve were in the Funchal and Câmara de Lobos area, six were at Machico, and six in the vicinity of Vila Nova de Calheta, in the west.[10] Machico exported some of its own produce directly, but the rest was marketed through Funchal.

The chief difficulties confronting the Madeiran sugarcane growers were erosion, soil exhaustion, expense of irrigation, and destruction caused by rats. Also slave laborers were expensive to purchase and in short

8. See the map showing crop distribution in Madeira at the end of the sixteenth century, in Ribeiro, *Madère,* p. 54; also reproduced in Mauro, p. 184.

9. Magalhães Godinho, 3: 432, 437.

10. Mauro, pp. 184, 186.

supply, and insects and plant diseases ravaged the cane. The Brazilian planters enjoyed every advantage over their Madeiran rivals except one − the distance from the European market. The Brazilian colonies had a seemingly endless supply of fertile land; their climate was much better suited than that of Madeira for the growth of sugarcane; the land was level and there was no need for terraced farming; the Brazilians had a somewhat easier access to the African slave marts; and Brazilian sugar-refining technology soon outstripped the crude processes of the Madeiran *engenhos*. Sun-dried Brazilian white crystal sugar was the finest in the Atlantic trade and the most efficiently and cheaply refined; the Madeirans never admitted this but continued to boast that "the sugar of Madeira is the best that is known to exist in the world."[11]

The single and most crucial advantage enjoyed by the Brazilian product was its low price. In the 1580s an arroba of white sugar cost 1$800 réis in Madeira, while in Brazil it cost $800 or less. The records of the Jesuit-owned Engenho Sergipe do Conde, in Bahia, show that during the years 1622–53, even in the depreciated currency of the seventeenth century, the cost of one arroba of white sugar never rose as high as 1$800 réis, and sometimes fell as low as $740, $550, and $470 réis.[12]

The massive competition from Brazil forced painful adjustments on the insular economy. The hard-pressed Madeiran planters hoped that Lisbon would limit Brazilian sugar imports by decree and guarantee to Madeiran sugar a fixed quota in the Portuguese market. In a general meeting held at Funchal on 28 January 1623 over fifty people (including the *fidalgos,* the chief Portuguese merchants, and members of the city chamber) signed a memorandum addressed to the king requesting a legally guaranteed outlet for Madeiran sugar exports.[13] But the Lisbon merchant community, and the government, for very good reasons, opposed any preferential treatment for the island's sugar, since Brazilian sugar had replaced Eastern spices as the most lucrative item in the Portuguese colonial trade and the crown derived large revenues from the tariffs on Brazilian commerce.

The kings of Portugal (who from 1580 to 1640 were the kings of Spain − Philip II, Philip III, and Philip IV) did agree to prohibit all ships from unloading Brazilian sugar in Madeira; they forbade Madeiran ship-owners to acquire sugar in Brazil for resale in Madeira; and they set

11. António Cordeiro, *História insulana,* 2 vols. (Lisbon, 1866), 1: 104.
12. *Engenho Sergipe do Conde: Livro de Contas, 1622–1653* (Rio de Janeiro, 1956), p. xi; Mauro, p. 188.
13. Arq. Dist. Funchal, "Livro de Vereações, ano 1623," fols. 10–12.

penalties for any traders who labeled or represented Brazilian sugar as Madeiran sugar.[14] The intent of this legislation, perhaps, was not so much to aid the Madeiran planters as to make sure that all Brazilian sugar went to Portugal, where heavy import and re-export duties would be collected, instead of having the sugar diverted to an entrepôt trade in the islands.

In truth, not everyone in Madeira was opposed to the entry of Brazilian sugar. The officials of the municipal chamber of Funchal complained regularly about the arrival of illegal sugar cargoes, but it does not appear that they did much to stop the trade with Brazil. At a chamber meeting on 18 October 1605 three officials declared that to their certain knowledge over four hundred chests of Brazilian sugar had been recently unloaded contrary to the king's express decrees,[15] but the blistering denunciations seemed to have been *pro forma* and for the record. The city officials, the Madeiran planters, and the king's laws to the contrary notwithstanding, there were Madeiran merchants and even *engenho* owners who profited from the traffic in Brazilian sugar. The merchants purchased Brazilian sugar chests and resold them to foreign ships. And the mill owners, or some of them, brought low-grade Brazilian sugars very cheaply and processed them to produce finer types that could be sold for an expensive price.

The Madeiran sugar trade, as distinct from the entrepôt traffic in the Brazilian commodity, went through various stages of collapse and recovery. During the last two decades of the sixteenth century the naval war, begun by the Dutch sea-beggars and the English sea-dogs against Spanish and Portuguese shipping, damaged the Brazil trade and indirectly benefited the Madeiran product. But the Anglo-Spanish peace of 1604, and the twelve-year Dutch-Spanish truce of 1609–21, opened the sea lanes to the Americas and gave Brazil a position of unchallenged superiority in the Atlantic sugar trade. The ravages to the Madeiran cane plants by parasites, during and before the year 1610, and the closing of many *engenhos*,[16] also contributed to this result.

By 1620 the trade in Madeiran sugar, though still continuing, had greatly declined. On 22 February 1620 the Funchal chamber affirmed, once again, that no one was allowed to buy sugar in the island for purposes of reselling it — a measure that was aimed against Brazilian sugar

14. Ibid., "Vereações 1603," fols. 49–52; "1618," fol. 39; "1620," fol. 16; Mauro, p. 188.
15. Arq. Dist. Funchal, "Vereações 1605," fol. 68.
16. Mauro, p. 188.

imports.[17] Late that year the chamber ordered the English merchant William Ray to secure special permission, from the city officials themselves, before embarking any more Brazilian sugar, on pain of a fine of 90 cruzados (36$000 réis or about £26) and condemnation to two years of banishment in Africa. A Portuguese merchant, Francisco Dias, received a similar order but was threatened with a fine of only 50 cruzados and told that no more Brazilian sugar could be exported until the entire Madeiran crop had been sold.[18]

In 1621 the resumption of the Dutch-Spanish war again brought hardships to the Brazilian sugar trade. Dutch enmity was directed against their old enemies, the Spaniards, but their aggressions overseas hurt not so much the Spaniards as the Portuguese. The Dutch attacked Bahia in 1624 and conquered Pernambuco, the richest Brazilian sugar province, in 1630.[19] Dutch privateers captured many ships engaged in the Brazil trade. These circumstances gave the Madeiran planters one more opportunity to recover a portion of the Portuguese market. By the mid-1630s there were signs of a revival of Madeiran sugar production.

Brazilian sugar, nonetheless, continued to dominate the Atlantic markets, and to arrive in Madeira for re-export. The Lisbon Treasury Council (*Conselho da Fazenda*) ordered the customshouse of Funchal not to admit into the harbor any ships from Brazil, unless the ships had been forced into Madeira by stress of weather or by the actions of pirates or privateers. By this order of 14 June 1638, before any unloading of sugar could take place, the customs officers had to investigate and then compile written reports (*autos*) explaining a ship's arrival at Madeira. Duties collected had to be entered into a special book, and the amounts regularly reported to Lisbon.[20]

The stringent rules regarding the admission of sugar ships to Funchal – rules which were commonplace in the Portuguese maritime trade – failed, as usual, to stop the entry of ships. Storm damage, leaks, shortages of supplies, illness, death, short-handed crews, and flights from or skirmishes with pirates and privateers – these were normal occurrences for ships engaged in the transatlantic trade. Any combination of such occurrences could be used by a ship's master to explain why his vessel could not proceed to her destination, and why she had been "forced

17. Arq. Dist. Funchal, "Vereações 1620," fol. 16.

18. Ibid., fols. 52, 56.

19. See Charles R. Boxer, *The Dutch in Brazil, 1624-1654* (Oxford, 1957).

20. Tombo, Arq. do Funchal, Codex 40, fols. 88–89. See the Bibliography for an explanation of this collection and its codex numbers.

into" Funchal. Officials ashore were in a poor situation to contradict, even if they had wished to, the written depositions of the master and his officers testifying that the ship had no choice but to make for the nearest friendly port. And therefore the customshouse at Funchal kept many ledger books marked "Livros para os direitos dos assucares do Brasil de navios derotados" ("Books for the duties of sugars of Brazil from derouted ships").

One such ledger, for the year 1640, listed five ships[21] "driven into" Funchal that unloaded 972 chests of sugar (with perhaps over 750,000 lbs.). Apart from some privileged people who paid only half duty or who were exempt from paying any duties at all, the merchants paid $100 réis for each arroba of imported panel sugar (the lowest grade), and $240 for each arroba of muscavado or white sugar. The records reported the unloading of 332 chests of panel, 93 of white, 17 of muscavado, and 530 of "white and muscavado" with the respective quantities of each left unspecified.[22] The astonishingly large quantity of coarse, raw panel sugar (many European merchants refused to deal in this commodity at all), and the probably large amount of muscavado hidden under the "white and muscavado" category, indicate that low-grade sugars were being imported for reprocessing at Madeiran *engenhos,* with a view to re-exporting the refined product at a large profit.

In addition to the sugars, the five ships from Brazil unloaded 220 hides (with a wholesale value of 79$200 réis, according to the customshouse valuation), an estimated 258 arrobas of tobacco (valued at 516$000), and 233 arrobas of raw cotton (valued at 214$360). The duties on the sugar, hides, tobacco, and cotton amounted to 4:451$360 réis (equivalent to about £3,230).[23]

After the recovery of Portuguese independence from Spain (in December 1640), Madeira was given the right to send a limited number of ships directly to Brazil. During the 1650s Brazilian sugar was unloaded at Fun-

21. They were: *Nossa Senhora do Rosário e Santo António,* probably out of Bahia, which began unloading on 12 April 1640; the flyboat *Nossa Senhora do Rosário,* out of Bahia and probably Madeiran-owned, 13 July; the caravel *Santo António,* out of Bahia, 14 August; the flyboat *Nossa Senhora da Ajuda,* 17 September; and *Nossa Senhora do Rosário,* out of Maranhão, 8 November.

22. These figures are my additions of the daily entries in the ledgers of Tombo, Arq. do Funchal, Codex 40.

23. My calculations from the same codex, except that the grand total of money collected in customs for the whole year is indicated on fol. 82, calculated by the customs officers themselves. For various other figures derived from the same source, see Mauro, p. 229.

chal without going through any special procedures.[24] Legislation grant-
ing tax rebates for the building of new sugar mills, although designed to
assist the Brazilian planters whose *engenhos* had been destroyed in the
warfare with the Dutch, benefited the Madeiran mill owners as well. In
Madeira, as in Brazil, the owners were accused of letting their old mills
fall to ruins so that they could benefit from the tax advantages given to
those who built new *engenhos*.[25]

During the years 1635–60 the trade in Madeira-grown sugar experienced a small boom. But in 1654 the Dutch were driven out of Brazil,
and the rich *fazendas* of Pernambuco began to produce again. In 1657
the merchants of Madeira signed a contract, duly published in the streets
of Funchal, that all sugar shipments exported from Madeira must contain at least 50 percent of island-grown sugar.[26] A ratio of 50:50 between Brazilian and Madeiran sugars was prescribed, and Brazilian sugars
were not supposed to be refined in Madeira. These measures benefited
the growers rather than the middlemen and merchants and were probably not rigorously observed.

Beginning in the 1660s, the invasion of the European markets by
West Indian planters undermined both the Brazilian and the Madeiran
sugar trades. English, Dutch, and French competitors, with enormous
sugar supplies from the West Indies, cut off the Portuguese planters
from many old markets. By the end of the century Brazil was only one
of many competing sources of supply, and the Madeiran product had
shrunk into insignificance. Measures such as the ordinance of 1683,
which did not come into effect until 15 October 1688, reducing the
amounts of sugar collected as a tax on the Madeiran mills from one-
fifth (*quinto*) of an *engenho*'s production to one-eighth (*oitavo*), came
too late.[27] The treasury and customs officer (Luís Moniz da Silva) at
Calheta, a *vila* at the center of a once thriving sugar-production area,
reported a total of only 29 arrobas and 21 libras (or 928 lbs.) in sugar
collected from the *engenhos* in his area during a period of seventeen
years (1689–1705).[28] This means that, if the customs duty was fully
collected, the production of sugar in the Calheta area at the end of the
seventeenth century had been reduced to an annual average of only 14
arrobas — a ludicrous quantity.

24. Tombo, Arq. do Funchal, Codex 1232, fols. 20, 23–24.
25. Ibid., fol. 6.
26. Arq. Dist. Funchal, "Vereações 1657," fol. 5.
27. Tombo, Arq. do Funchal, Codex 35, fol. 2.
28. Ibid., fol. 35.

Sugarcane, nonetheless, continued to be grown in both Brazil and Madeira. At the beginning of the nineteenth century, before the coffee boom, sugar was still Brazil's most valuable export. In Madeira, the cane, benefited by extraordinary protectionist legislation, remained one of the chief crops. In the years before World War I, when a ton of raw sugarcane sold in Cuba for U.S. $1.75, the officially supported Madeiran price, equivalent to U.S. $16.00, was more than nine times that amount.[29] Today much of the Madeiran cane, however inefficiently grown and expensive, is used in the manufacture of a poor-quality rum that is locally consumed. To protect this unattractive alcoholic beverage, all Portuguese brandy, which is generally of high quality and usually cheap, is rigidly excluded from the island.

As the international trade in sugar dwindled, the trade in wines took its place. Today the wines of Madeira stand, with port and sherry, among the elite dessert wines and need fear comparison with no wine of their class. Like the sherries, madeira offers a full range of types, including dryish *sercial,* sweet *malmsey,* well-balanced *boal,* and aromatic *verdelho,* and each of these types,[30] like the different sherries, is excellent in its way. And like port, madeira ages well in both cask and bottle, the best vintages improving decade by decade with seemingly no terminal limit to their mellowing maturity. In a recent work a wine historian described tasting a 170-year-old madeira – a Câmara de Lobos 1789, aged 111 years in wood, 50 in demijohn, and 9 in the bottle – and said that "it was glory on the palate and in the nose."[31]

It was with reference to a vintage madeira that the respected oenologist George Saintsbury remarked: "I know of no wine of its class that can beat Madeira when at its best; the very finest sherries of the luscious kind . . . cannot touch it."[32] Besides their ability to outlive the three-score-and-ten life span of man and still grow better, the finest

29. *Port. Poss.: Azores and Madeira,* p. 44. The enterprising Englishman William Hinton (1817–1904), who established the first modern sugar-refining factory at Madeira in 1845, and his son Harry Hinton (1857–1948), were granted an official monopoly for sugar production in Madeira in 1895, on condition that they paid 16 escudos per ton for all raw cane supplied to them. The monopoly contract was much criticized in Lisbon and was eventually suppressed in 1919. W. Hinton and Sons, nonetheless, continued to dominate the sugar business of Madeira.

30. *Sercial, boal,* malmsey (or *malvasia*), and *verdelho* all derive their names from grape varietals. There are two or three other types of wine, mostly locally consumed, that are of less importance.

31. Herbert Warner Allen, *History of Wine* (London, 1961), p. 237.

32. *Notes on a Cellar-Book,* 3d ed. (London, 1921), p. 24.

madeiras have other qualities that make them robust and nearly inde-
structible. Madeiras do not spoil in hot weather; heat actually ripens
and improves them, and a passage in the hold of a sailing ship, through
burning tropical waters, results in a better wine. Madeiras do not mind
being moved about, transported by ship or cart, and no amount of rough
handling will damage them; quite the contrary, the more madeira is
banged about, the better it tastes. Thus it was that the nineteenth-
century Englishman demanded that his madeira be imported, not directly from the island, but by way of the West Indies or Brazil, where
it would benefit from the hot and agitated tropical passage; and the true
connoisseur, heedless of cost, insisted that the wine must arrive at his
table by way of the East Indies, after undergoing four passages through
the tropics on a voyage of over 26,000 miles.[33]

Finally, madeira wine is exceptionally resistant to the multitude of
micro-organisms that enter a wine when it is exposed to contact with
the air.[34] Madeira survives when left in the cask, fights off the yeasts
that would convert it to vinegar, and resists vinous decay. Even direct
exposure to oxygen by the removal of the bung does not seem to damage the wine.

The hardihood of madeira, and its heat-resistant characteristics, gave
the seventeenth-century product remarkable advantages over many other
popular European wines, which, as a general rule, required quick bot-
tling, gentle handling, and constantly cool temperatures. In the seventeenth century madeira became – along with the Azorean wines of Pico-
Fayal, which were also heat-resistant – perhaps the most important
beverage wine consumed in tropical America. And even beyond tropical America, in England's North American plantations, madeira had
become a staple commodity by the end of the century.

33. Cyrus Redding, *History and Description of Modern Wines,* 3d ed. (London,
1860), p. 267. The transportation of one pipe of wine from Madeira to England
direct, during the first half of the nineteenth century, cost 20s. to 25s. per pipe,
whereas transport via the West Indies cost £4 4s., via Brazil £5 or £6, and via the
East Indies £7 and up.

34. "No one, I think, has ever satisfactorily explained how it is that Madeira
can be with impunity exposed to all the microbes which find their way through
the staves of a cask and to an unrationed dose of the oxygen, which is the prime
cause of vinous senile decay." Allen, p. 232. Seventeenth-century madeira, however, was less hardy than the modern varieties, for there were numerous instances
of madeira wines turning sour in the West Indies; see *Calendar of State Papers,
Colonial Series, America and West Indies, 1675-1676* (London, 1893), p. 428.

The wine which figured so prominently in the cargoes of many America-bound ships was a far different product from the madeiras of today. The modern types, in all their varieties, and especially the vintage wines, have their origins in the last decades of the eighteenth century, although the devastating nineteenth-century plagues of oidium and phylloxera intervened between the eighteenth-century product and that of today, forcing changes in the types of grapes cultivated.[35] It is probably true to say that today's vintage madeiras are not greatly different from the pre-oidium vintage madeiras of before 1850, a few bottles of which are still available for consumption; but it is probably also true that the madeiras of the 1840s had little in common with the plain red beverage wine of the 1650s.

The earlier wine, exported to the Americas by the hundreds of pipes, was an ordinary beverage wine, vintaged in September, racked clear in January, shipped out in the spring or later, and ready for immediate consumption on arrival at its destination. "The majority of this wine was drunk before it was more than a year old."[36] In the middle of the seventeenth century the islanders classified this general wine into two broad types: superior (*vinhos melhores*) and inferior (*vinhos mais baixos*). The superior wines were shipped primarily to Brazil and Portugal, while the inferior types were sent to Barbados and the English plantations. In 1650 the Madeira customshouse placed a value of 8$000 réis (£4) per pipe, wholesale at Funchal, for the superior wines, which were to pay customs duties of $888 réis (about 8s. 10d.) per pipe when exported by foreigners; and a value of 6$000 (or £3) per pipe for the inferior wines, which were to pay duties of $666 (or 6s. 8d.) per pipe.[37]

Later in the century the customshouse made no distinction between inferior and superior wines but charged a single duty for all types of

35. Oidium is a vine mildew or fungus that destroyed almost all the vines in Madeira shortly after its appearance on the island in 1852. Within a decade the blight was brought under control and the vineyards began to recover. In 1873 most vines were again destroyed, this time by the grape phylloxera, or *Phylloxera vastatrix,* plant lice native to the United States. The recovery of the vines after the 1873 disaster was very slow and was made possible only by the planting of phylloxera-resistant American vines, with the surviving Madeiran varietals grafted to them. By the first decade of this century, great vintages were once again being produced. Of a post-phylloxera *verdelho* 1910, Allen wrote (p. 263) that it was "so fine that it might have justified Virgil's cry, *Redeunt Saturnia regna, The Golden Age returns.*"

36. William Bolton, *Letters* (London, 1928), p. 17.

37. Tombo, Arq. do Funchal, Codex 1233, fol. 74.

beverage wine. Nor, by the 1670s, was there any distinction between the Brazilian and the English colonial markets, for the English plantations imported the best madeira available. In 1682 the customs officials evaluated all beverage wines at 12$000 réis (under £4 10s.) per pipe, with duties set at 1$333.[38] The difference between the price level of 1650 (8$000 for superior wines) and that of 1682 (12$000) can be almost fully accounted for by the debasements, or devaluations, of Portuguese coinage that took place in 1663 (a reduction of 25 percent in silver content) and 1668 (a further reduction of 10 percent in silver content).[39] By the end of the century, however, the customshouse had increased its valuation to the level of 18$000 per pipe (£6 6s.), with duties set at 2$000 (or 14s.).[40]

The *câmara*, or municipal chamber, of Funchal established the prices which the vintners had to pay the grape growers for their wines. The *vereadores*, or aldermen, met in the middle of October of each year, after the grapes had been harvested and pressed, and set the prices to be paid for the must, or the wine as it emerged from the wine press, measured in pipes containing 27 almudes (or 136 English wine gallons), which were 2 almudes (or slightly over 10 gallons) larger than the standard Lisbon pipe of 25 almudes. The aldermen distinguished between the wines coming from grapes grown on the lower slopes (*meias terras para baixo*, "from the middle lands down"), and the wines from grapes grown on the upper slopes (*meias terras para cima*, "from the middle lands up"). The wines from the lower slopes were priced slightly higher than those from the upper slopes.

In 1625 the wine growers petitioned the chamber of Funchal asking that no price be set on the 1625 wines, because the harvest had been unusually poor and had yielded less than one-half the normal quantity of wine. The aldermen denied the request for a free-market price, but raised the prices to 5$000 réis (or £3 17s.) per pipe for the upper slope

38. Ibid., Codex 1506, fol. 91.
39. Mauro, pp. lvii–lviii.
40. Tombo, Arq. do Funchal, Codex 1234, fol. 110. The high valuation set in January 1699 referred, of course, to the 1698 vintage, which had been exceptionally small; but the valuation of 18$000 réis per pipe was still well below what the wines eventually sold for, once they had matured. Bolton paid about 26$000 per pipe for wines of the 1698 vintage in May 1699. This compares with the 16$000 he had paid for 1695 wines, 18$000 for 1696 wines, and with the 20$000 to 23$000 he had paid for 1697 wines (another small vintage year). Bolton, pp. 28, 65, 98, 108, and 137.

wines, and 6$000 (or £4 12s. 6d.) for lower-slope wines.[41] The price difference between the two types of wine was 1$000, or 20 percent of the price of the upper-slope wine.

Forty-two years later, in 1667, the wine growers received only 6$500 (or £2 12s.) for the upper-slope wine, and only 7$000 (or £2 16s.) for the lower-slope wine.[42] As there had been three coin debasements (1641, 1643, and 1663) since 1625, the growers of 1667 actually received about one-third less silver for their pipes than the growers of 1625. In 1667 the price differential between the upper- and lower-slope wines came to only $500 réis, or less than 8 percent of the price of upper-slope wine. After 1667 the distinction in price between the two wines was abolished, and the aldermen set a single price to be paid to the growers for all ordinary beverage wine.

During the 1670s, in spite of a further coin debasement that had taken place in 1668, the price paid to the growers remained depressed. In 1671 the price was 6$500 per pipe, in 1675 it was 7$800, and in 1676 it was 6$000.[43] These prices seem to indicate overproduction, or low demand, or poor-quality vintages, or exploitation of the grape growers by the aldermen and merchants of Funchal — or, more probably, a combination of these factors. During the 1680s, conditions improved for the growers, and the aldermen allowed increases of 30 percent in the wine price, bringing in an extra 2$000 to the growers per pipe. The prices permitted during the five-year period 1680–84 ran as follows: 8$500, 9$000, 8$500, 8$000, and 10$000 — averaging 8$800 per pipe (compared with the 1670s average of 6$766).[44]

The fixing of higher price levels did not of itself mean that the growers collected more money. Since the aldermen reacted, although rather slowly, to the market factors of supply and demand, the highest prices usually occurred when the yield from the vintage was exceptionally low. The growers might collect a higher price per pipe only to suffer a loss in overall income, because of the small quantities of wine available for sale.

During the last two decades of the seventeenth century there was a healthy increase in the prices paid for wine, in the Funchal market, at all levels. Aside from the exceptional increase, such as that of 1699,

41. Arq. Dist. Funchal, "Vereações 1625," fol. 66.
42. Ibid., "1667," fol. 19.
43. Ibid., "1671," fol. 24; "1675," fol. 17; and "1676," fol. 45.
44. Ibid., "1680," fol. 29; "1681," fol. 22; "1682," fol. 20; "1683," fol. 16; and "1684," fol. 21.

which reflected the low-yield vintage of 1698, the underlying price trends seemed to be strong, irrespective of vintage yields. The opening up of new markets in the English American colonies, with their steadily rising demands, gave reliable support to the Madeiran wine economy, which formerly had depended almost exclusively on the Portuguese colonial markets.

In December of 1697 the English merchant William Bolton (d. 1722), one of the busiest wine traders in Funchal, noted that during a seventeen-day period no fewer than eleven ships had picked up wine cargoes in Madeira, ten of them British-owned ships bound for the English plantations.[45] These included one ship for Barbados with 150 pipes of madeira, three for Jamaica with 310 pipes, two for Boston with 130 pipes, one for Nevis with 45, and one for Antigua with 60 – a total of eight ships with 695 pipes (or about 100,000 gallons). Bolton did not specify the quantities carried by two other plantation-bound ships.

During the following weeks, even with the winter weather, another fourteen ships took on wine cargoes, and a representative of the firm of W. Bolton and Company complained that "if ships continue to come in this manner, we shal not buy wine at any price."[46] The price paid, in February 1698, was an unheard-of 20$000 réis (or £7) per pipe, ashore, not including wharfage and loading fees. Yet the merchants probably little suspected that, two years later, in the spring of 1700, they would be paying up to 30$000 (or £10 10s.) for wines that were still green.[47]

The price set by the Funchal aldermen every autumn for the raw juice of the grape was the price the growers, willy-nilly, had to accept. The vintners and merchants, some of whom usually served as aldermen, were interested in holding down the prices paid to the growers. The customshouse estimate of wine values, made every January, was arrived at after a formal consultation with representatives of the merchants and was the basis for establishing the duties to be collected on wine exported by foreigners, or loaded aboard foreign ships. The wine shippers, naturally enough, wanted the customs valuations to be as low as possible, and they were usually able to persuade the customs officers, who sometimes were themselves merchants, to set lower price estimates than the vintage actually sold for, once it had matured. The difference between the price paid to the growers and the customs valuation was on

45. Bolton, p. 91.
46. Ibid., p. 98.
47. Ibid., pp. 164, 172.

the order of 25 or 30 percent, or more. For instance, with the wines of the 1681 vintage, the growers received 9$000 réis per pipe, and the customs valuation was set at 12$000 réis, 30 percent higher.[48] The actual wholesale market price for these wines, when matured, was probably from 15$000 to 18$000.

All that has been said thus far about seventeenth-century Madeiran wines concerns the common beverage wine of the island, most of which was designed to be drunk as plain red table wine. The quality wines of the island, the exquisite malmseys, although of far more interest to connoisseurs and wine historians, were much less important commercially. The grapes for the sweet but rich and well-balanced dessert wines came from the best vineyards, were picked only when already overripe, and were pressed with great care.[49] Although it is commonly affirmed that true vintage wines, aside from those of classical times, were a discovery or rediscovery of the middle or late eighteenth century and were made possible by laying on their sides sealed glass bottles of improved design, there existed in Madeira, over one hundred years earlier, a quantity of "old wine," which apparently lay in cask for two, three, or more years before being sold. This "old wine" was probably choice malmsey, which unlike the Continental wines did not deteriorate on exposure to air and which vintners held off the market while awaiting a better price or allowed to stand from simple laziness or negligence, unwittingly creating true vintage wine or something very like it.

Gaspar Frutuoso, a sixteenth-century resident of São Miguel in the Azores, declared that Madeiran malmsey was "the best wine to be found in the Universe."[50] With this opinion, the foreign merchants of Funchal may have been inclined to concur, for malmsey never lacked for buyers. The limited quantities of "old wines" that appeared on the market were quickly purchased and shipped to wealthy and discerning consumers, scattered in the Americas from Boston to Rio de Janeiro.

The customshouse of Funchal placed a higher valuation on malmsey than on the other wines (see table 1). If one expects wine prices to increase steadily year by year, then the evaluations for the year 1687, which show a drop of one-third in the price of ordinary wine when compared with the 1682 evaluation, may come as a surprise. The low valua-

---

48. Arq. Dist. Funchal, "Vereações 1681," fol. 22; Tombo, Arq. do Funchal, Codex 1506, fol. 91.

49. Bolton, p. 17.

50. Quoted in the article "Madeira" in the *Grande enciclopédia portuguesa e brasileira* 15 (Lisbon, n.d.): 835.

TABLE 1

Official Customshouse Prices and Export Duties
of Wine Products at Funchal* (in réis per pipe)

Product	1650		1682		1687		1699	
	Price	Duty	Price	Duty	Price	Duty	Price	Duty
Beverage wines:								
Inferior type	6$000	$666						
Superior type	8$000	$888						
All types			12$000	1$333	8$000	$888	18$000	2$000
Malmsey	9$000	1$000	14$000	1$444	10$000	1$111	24$000	2$666
Brandy	20$000	2$220	24$000	2$666	20$000	2$222	40$000	4$444
Vinegar	3$600	$400	6$000	$666	4$000	$444	6$000	$666

*Tombo, Arq. do Funchal, Codices 1233, fol. 74; 1506, fol. 91; 1507, fols. 132–33; 1234, fol. 110.

tions for 1687 prove that the customshouse, to some extent, responded to downward, as well as upward, price changes in the market. Yet despite the low rates set in 1687, the underlying tendency was toward higher prices. The valuations for 1699, when compared with those of 1687, show a dramatic increase: beverage wine rose, in terms of sterling (at an exchange rate of 1$000 = 7s.), from £2 16s. to £6 16s. — an increase of 125 percent; and malmsey went up from £3 10s. to £8 8s. — an increase of 140 percent. Yet the increase in the 1699 valuations, when seen in terms of the levels of 1682, was less startling: in seventeen years (1682-99) the price of beverage wine went up 50 percent and that of malmsey about 71.5 percent.

Always it should be remembered that the customshouse evaluations were arrived at during the month of January, before the wines of the previous year's vintage were fit to drink, and that the actual prices per pipe, paid by the exporters in the spring, ran from 20 to 40 percent higher than the evaluations.

Malmsey comprised only a small fraction of total wine exports. The Funchal customshouse register of exports for the year 1650 shows that duties were paid on 2,405 pipes of wine, of which 1,540 pipes were superior wines, 778 pipes inferior wines, and only 87 pipes were malmsey.[51] Thus, in quantity, malmsey made up only 3.6 percent of the total shipments in 1650 and, in value, not more than about 5 or 6 percent. Yet malmsey was to enjoy a great future during the eighteenth century, when it grew steadily in price, export value, and in consumer preference. By the end of the seventeenth century, there were already signs of the growing importance of malmsey. On 15 April 1699, for instance, William Bolton loaded 158 pipes of malmsey aboard the *Castile Frigate* and paid duties of 421$228 réis (£147 8s. 7d.); this one shipment, which might eventually have filled about 75,000 one-quart bottles of wine, exceeded by more than 80 percent all the recorded malmsey shipments in 1650.[52]

Before the middle of the seventeenth century, Brazil was the island's most important wine market. In Brazil, madeira, because of its resistance to heat and spoilage, was preferred to all other Portuguese wines, which often arrived in poor condition.[53] Officials at Salvador da Bahia, the capital of Brazil, claimed that their own community consumed be-

51. Ibid., Codex 1233 (sum of all entries, by my calculations).
52. Ibid., Codex 1234, fol. 23.
53. *Consulta* 19 May 1651 and attached papers, AHU, Bahia, Caixa V.

tween 2,500 and 3,000 pipes of wine per year (during the 1650s), in addition to the amounts required by the other Brazilian settlements, but they were obviously exaggerating.[54] Madeiran wine exports to Brazil were damaged by the long war with the Netherlands (1624–54); yet, during the first five months of 1645, when a truce was in effect between Portugal and Holland, it is reported that 4,243.5 pipes of madeira were sent to Brazil.[55] Certainly the long-term trend was toward a greater and greater demand for Madeiran wines in the Brazilian colonies.

The Brazilian market, however, was not the most important one after about 1660. The British expansion in the West Indies, particularly after the conquest of Jamaica in 1655, created a significant new market for heat-resistant wines; and the Dutch, established at tiny Curaçao since 1634, also imported small quantities of madeira. Similarly, the madeira wine merchants profited from the growth and prosperity of New England, New York, Pennsylvania, and Virginia, all of which imported large quantities of Madeiran and Azorean wines. A numerous, well-established, and influential class of English merchants living at Funchal promoted the consumption of Madeiran wines in the English plantations. They were not successful, however, in getting their compatriots in England to drink the island's wines, even though the wines from the nearby Canaries were a staple in the London market. England did not import madeira, in significant quantities, until the middle of the eighteenth century and later, and then only by way of the clumsy West Indies or East Indies routes, which gave the wines a chance to mature on a long tropical passage.

The total volume of the island's wine exports is hard to estimate. The older historians, and the casual foreign visitors to the island, who spoke of a total wine production of 25,000 pipes per year, with exports of 10,000 pipes and up, are not to be trusted. The customs registers for 1650 show that 2,405 pipes of wine paid export duty at Funchal. The registers for the first nine months of 1682 show an outflow of 3,410 pipes; if the monthly average for nine months is calculated on a twelve-month basis, this would mean that 4,546 pipes were shipped at Funchal.

54. See papers attached to *consulta* 17 July 1653, AHU, Bahia, Caixa VI; Rio de Janeiro, Biblioteca Nacional, *Documentos históricos* 4 (Rio de Janeiro, 1928): 229–30. The Bahia settlers exaggerated their wine requirements in order to force the General Company of Brazil (the sole legal supplier of wine) to supply much more wine for the Brazilian market, which would bring down the price in Bahia; but the company preferred to undersupply Brazil, and keep wine prices high.

55. Mauro, p. 356; AHU, Codex 13, fols. 345–46.

For the month of January 1687 the registers show exports of 423 pipes; a risky multiplication of this figure by twelve months would yield a highly speculative total of 5,076 pipes exported in 1687. Finally, the registers for 1699, show total exports of 5,483 pipes.[56]

These figures and estimates of annual exports – 2,405, 4,549, 5,076, and 5,483 pipes, corresponding to the years 1650, 1682, 1687, and 1699 – are the irreducible minimum totals for wines exported by foreign merchants, and by Portuguese merchants aboard foreign ships, but they do not include the wines exported by Portuguese merchants aboard Portuguese ships. Thus the registers, for the most part, do not reflect the island's wine shipments to Brazil, although the 1650 wine total includes 1,011 pipes shipped aboard two Genoese vessels freighted by the General Company of Brazil. On 4 February 1699, William Bolton reported that there were four English ships at Funchal taking on wine for the West Indies and two large Portuguese ships loading 800 pipes for Brazil.[57] The customs register duly listed the English ships and their cargoes, but did not record the 800 pipes taken aboard the Portuguese ships, nor even the names of the ships, because their cargoes were not dutiable. Yet these 800 pipes, casually mentioned by Bolton, increase the total figure for the wine exports of 1699 from 5,483 pipes to 6,283 pipes.

To this figure of 6,283 pipes for 1699 must be added whatever other amounts went to Brazil but were not recorded. What then was the true total of wine exports for the year 1699 – 7,000 pipes? or more? The question cannot be answered with absolute accuracy, but an estimate of 7,500 pipes (based on the assumption that 2,000 pipes, at least, were sent to Brazil) would appear to be modest, reasonable, and defensible.

Calculations about the total wine exports of Madeira are full of uncertainties, and arithmetical conclusions concerning annual export averages may perhaps be mere guesswork. Yet, guesswork or not, taking full advantage of all available information, and subject always to the sovereign correction of further research, the figures in table 2 are suggested as conservative estimates of the wine exports from the islands of Madeira and Porto Santo. If there be weakness in these estimates, it is more likely to be exposed in the figures for the earlier period, for the years 1600–1639, than for the later years. There is much less hard informa-

56. My calculations derived from the addition of hundreds of separate entries in Tombo, Arq. do Funchal, Codices 1506, 1507, 1233, and 1234.

57. Bolton, p. 127.

TABLE 2

*Estimated Wine Exports from Madeira
and Porto Santo (in pipes)*

Years	Annual Average	Total
1600–1619	2,000	40,000
1620–39	2,500	50,000
1640–59	3,500	70,000
1660–79	5,000	100,000
1680–99	6,500	130,000
1600–1699	3,900	390,000

tion for the earlier years than for the later decades of the century, and the estimates for 1600–1639 may be either too high or too low. The smallness of the consumers' market (chiefly the underdeveloped, strife-ridden settlements of Brazil) during those years suggests, however, that wine exports were lower than they were after 1640. The opening of fresh markets in British America guaranteed a strong upward trend in exports during the last decades of the century.

To persons unfamiliar with wine measurements an annual export total of 5,000 or 6,000 pipes may seem unimpressive; even the 7,500 pipes exported from Funchal in 1699 (according to my estimate) may seem a small-scale business. If we take the figure of 7,500 pipes and assume that 90 percent of these shipments reached American destinations (the rest being consumed in Lisbon or aboard ship, or lost at sea), then 6,750 pipes arrived in the Americas. If these 6,750 pipes had suffered (on average) a 10 percent loss of liquid volume through evaporation and leakage, then only 6,075 pipes would have been left when repoured. Yet these 6,075 pipes would still have filled over 3,050,000 one-quart bottles. If 3,050,000 bottles of madeira are prorated among the sparse settler populations of the American colonies on a per capita basis, it will be seen that the people of such places as New England, New York, Pennsylvania, Virginia, Maryland, Bermuda, Barbados, Jamaica, Antigua, Curaçao, Pernambuco, Bahia, Rio de Janeiro, and elsewhere, consumed respectable quantities of the island's celebrated wines. Considering the small populations of the British and Portuguese colonies, the Madeira wine trade, even if modest by general European standards, was an important business in the Americas.

For the merchants, there were good possibilities for making profits in the Madeira-Americas wine trade. In 1650, for instance, when wine sold at about 10$000 réis per pipe delivered aboard at Funchal, the price per pipe of madeira at Bahia, Brazil, was at least 35$000 (the Brazil Company sold at 40$000 in 1650 on the Brazilian market). The economics of a wine shipment of 100 pipes from Funchal to Bahia in 1650 would have begun with the cost of the wine delivered aboard, 1:000$000, to which would be added the Funchal tax of $888 per pipe, or 88$800, and a freight charge of 2$000 per pipe, or 200$000, making the expenses from Funchal total 1:288$800. An assumption might then be made that 10 percent of the shipment would be lost through evaporation and leakage — for example, in 1654, of 1,012 pipes of wine sent to Bahia, only 892 pipes were left when repoured,[58] a loss of nearly 12 percent in liquid volume. Thus only 90 pipes would reach Bahia.

The wine tariff at Bahia was exceptionally high — 7$500 réis per pipe — so that 90 pipes would have paid 675$000; this amount, added to the above expenses, would come to 1:963$800 in total expenses (about £982 in sterling). The 90 pipes would then be sold at 35$000 per pipe, with the purchaser paying for the small unloading charges, and the seller would collect 3:150$000 (or £1,575). The balance sheet would then stand as follows: the total sum received at Bahia, 3:150$000 (£1,575), less the total expenses, 1:963$800, leaving a gross profit of 1:186$200 (£593). A gross profit of 1:186$200 réis on an outlay of 1:963$800 represented a return of 60 percent on the capital invested, which was not very much considering the heavy risks taken in the transatlantic passage. And from that gross profit would have to be deducted marine insurance costs, warehousing charges, and other fixed overhead expenses.

Fortunately the merchants had ways of increasing this profit margin. A Portuguese merchant shipping wines to Brazil aboard Portuguese ships was not required to pay export tariffs at Funchal; this would have saved a Portuguese merchant the sum of 88$800 on a 100-pipe shipment to Brazil in 1650. Moreover the freight charge of 2$000 per pipe represents a maximum charge; a merchant who owned his own ship, or who owned a share of a ship, could bring that charge down to as low as $500 or $600 per pipe. With these reductions in costs the gross return on investment, in the above transaction, might have come to 82 percent. And as for the high Bahia tariffs, which were imposed on Portuguese and foreigners alike, there was always the possibility of requiring the purchaser to pay the customshouse charges.

58. Senate chamber of Bahia to John IV, 29 January 1655, AHU, Bahia, Caixa VI.

Yet the main profit factor has yet to be mentioned: the profit on the return cargo. It was the likelihood of a double profit, from both the outward and the return voyages, that made the Atlantic trade highly attractive to the venturesome. The merchant who sold 90 pipes of madeira wine in Bahia for 3:150$000 réis would immediately purchase a cargo of sugar with the money, or else exchange his wine directly for sugar, with no cash involved.

At a price of 1$400 réis per arroba of white sugar — which was an average price paid for white sugar in Bahia in 1650 — the merchant, for his 3:150$000 réis, would have purchased about 112 chests of sugar, containing 2,250 arrobas, or 72,000 pounds. This cargo would then be taken to Lisbon, where import and re-export fees had to be paid, and then might be taken, perhaps, to London, where new customs charges would be paid, and then the sugar sold, wholesale, at about 15d. per pound. In London, the merchant would finally have received £4,500 sterling, after an initial investment of probably well under £1,000 for the madeira wine. The difference between these two figures — even after the customs charges in Lisbon and London, freight charges, warehousing, marine insurance, dock fees, and loading and unloading expenses have been deducted — explains the profit potential in the Madeira-Brazil-Europe trade.

The profit possibilities in the trade between Madeira and the British West Indies can be roughly expressed in the following two figures: in 1696 one pipe of madeira wine cost £5 5s. (or 15$000 réis), delivered aboard ship at Funchal free of all customs and loading charges, and sold in Barbados for £17 per pipe. The economics of the business, in the shipment of one hundred pipes of wine from Madeira to Barbados in 1696, would therefore have begun with the cost of the wine delivered aboard, £525 (15$000), to which would be added the freight charge of 15s. per pipe, £75, making the total expenses £600. With evaporation and leakage losses of 10 percent, there would have been 90 pipes left for sale in Barbados at £17 per pipe, and they would have fetched a total of £1,530. The balance sheet would have been as follows: the sum received at Barbados, £1,530, less expenses, £600, leaving a gross profit of £930. This gross profit would represent a return of 155 percent on the capital invested.

Yet the actual profit potential of the wine trade with the West Indies was greater than these figures suggest. The trade was entirely in the hands of English merchants of Funchal, who bought their wine cargoes with the proceeds from the sale of English textiles and other imported commodities (salted fish, pickled herring, English manufactures, Azorean wheat, etc.), and who therefore had usually turned a profit before purchasing the wine. The wine ships could go directly to the West Indies, or else sail by way of the Cape Verdes, taking on some salt at Maio and padding the profit margins. In the West Indies they could load sugar, molasses, and rum. The return voyage might be directly back to Europe, or else by way of New England, where some of the West Indian commodities might be exchanged for Newfoundland salted codfish and New England fish oil, lumber, and pipe staves (a low-profit item, but essential in the making of the madeira wine butts). A single voyage around the grand circle of North Atlantic maritime commerce could accumulate the mounting profits of many different transactions. A series of successful voyages could turn a merchant of modest means into a wealthy man.

Yet in the harsh world of North Atlantic commerce, success seldom came easily, and failure was often an imminent possibility. Sailing ships were but fragile instruments in an immensely harsh world of wind and water. Ships could be lost with men and cargo and leave not a single trace. Every voyage was an adventure, every departure a gamble with the relentless ocean, and each new venture a blind reassertion of human optimism.

In addition to the dangers from the elements, there were the dangers from man himself. Pirates and privateers were the plague of seventeenth-century commerce. From their residences on the heights around Funchal the merchants could see the dark shapes of the pirate ships from Sallee (Salé in Morocco, immediately north of present-day Rabat) lurking off the Madeira roads, awaiting their next victim. Sallee, the home of a relentless and successful group of Muslim pirates, aided by Christian renegades, was unfortunately only 500 miles from Madeira, and every ship to the island had to run the gauntlet of seagoing bandits.

Warfare among the major European powers added immeasurably to the risks of the sea. In times of war the seas would swarm with Biscayan and Dunkirk privateers, with Dutch "capers" (Dutch *kaper*, privateer) and Spanish "picaroons" (Spanish *picaro,* rogue), and, indeed, with English and French privateering craft of every description. The merchantmen, sailing in groups of five and six for safety, could still be surprised by a larger and more powerful enemy squadron; or they might encounter weaker ships and apprehend them. Thus every merchant ship became both hunter and hunted, and the prospect of general ruin hung over maritime commerce.

Lastly, the merchants had to deal with the ever present perils of human greed and graft — with corrupt partners and cheating associates, with dishonest seamen, and with embezzling agents in distant places. A merchant who was supremely prudent, who made the wisest choices, the best investments, and the most astute calculation of his risks, might have overcome all the perils of seventeenth-century maritime commerce and grown extremely wealthy — but even he would have required a large measure of plain good luck.

The island of Madeira was a pawn, helplessly dependent on the uncertainties of sea trade; yet it was a pawn with certain magnetic powers of attraction. Whatever the losses to storms and pirates, whatever the misadventures and the shipwrecks, ships still came to the island to take aboard the casks of wine and convey them to the hurricane-tormented waters of the West Indies. The regularity, persistent growth, and enormous volume of transatlantic shipping in the days of sail are matters touched by the miraculous, matters which speak eloquently of ordinary human tenacity and courage. Innumerable acts of unrecorded and unself-conscious heroism guaranteed the continuation of intercontinental commerce.

Madeira had its magnetically desirable product, the island's great wines made from the grapes grown with such difficulty by an industrious peasantry on narrow terraces on the steep-sloped mountains, nourished by volcanic soil, and watered with loving care through a costly and complicated irrigation system. The wine was itself a miracle — the inexplicable product of a hundred variables of soil, climate, rainfall, irrigation, altitude, obliquity of terrain, grape varietals, time of harvesting, method of handling, and so forth. The hardihood of the wine, its love of movement and of heat, and its resistance to air-borne organic contaminants gave it special advantages over other competitive wines.

The excellence of the wine and its durable character do not themselves explain the existence of the Madeira trade. The geographical position of the island, located on the main route for ships outward bound from Europe to tropical America, helps to account for the origin and nature of the Madeira-Americas wine trade. The steady growth of the settlements in Brazil, the British expansion in the West Indies, and the foundation and development of the English plantations in North America, all combined to give to the island's wines an increasing number of prosperous consumers.

Of central importance to the wine trade, the real heroes of the island's international commerce, were the merchants of Funchal (see the next

chapter) who found new markets for wine in Jamaica, Boston, and elsewhere, risked their ships on the wide ocean, provided the capital for the
transatlantic ventures, and made it possible for the islanders to earn the
money to buy essential imports. The Funchal merchants, particularly
the foreigners, greatly expanded sales beyond the narrow circles of Portuguese colonial commerce.

4
The Merchants of Funchal

The merchant community of Funchal was cosmopolitan in origin, international and transatlantic in outlook, and it maintained agents, factors, and correspondents in the seaports of four continents. Toward the end of the seventeenth century, judging from the Funchal customs registers of 1687, about eighty persons participated, to some extent or other, in the maritime commerce of Funchal. Of these eighty, more than one-half engaged in trading transactions that were infrequent, trivial, and of little value; these persons can probably be described as shopkeepers and retailers, rather than as merchant wholesalers. Some thirty other merchants accounted for most of the import-export business, and among them eight or nine of the wealthiest and most powerful controlled the major part of the island's maritime commerce. About two dozen merchants were foreigners, more than one-half of them English.

During the late 1680s the chief English merchants resident in Funchal were Obadiah Allen (the English vice consul), Henry Criton, George Fryer, Lawrence Gay, Samuel Hutchins, Matthew Matson, and Richard Miles. Their chief French rivals were Jacques Arnauld, Louis Caire, and Honoré Sauvaire (French consul). The principal Portuguese merchants whose names appear in the customs registers were Diogo Fernandes Branco, Martinho Gonçalves Correia, Mateus da Gama, Tomás Leite, Francisco Monteiro de Miranda, Gaspar Ferreira de Resende, and Matias Teixeira.[1]

Early in the century, there were fewer merchants and less business. In the year 1620 only about forty persons participated in the maritime

---

1. Tombo, Arq. do Funchal, Codex 1507.

commerce of Funchal, and less than half of them were very active. There were only about a dozen foreign merchants resident in Funchal, perhaps six of them Flemish, and the foreign merchant community as a whole did not have the importance it was later to acquire. The foreign merchants included the Englishmen William Crawford, Robert Willoughby, and William Ray, the Frenchman Raymond Biard (French consul and a lifelong resident of Funchal), the German Adrian Erspranger, and such Lowlanders as (to give them the Portuguese versions of their names) Francisco Guilherme, João Guilherme, Cornelis Selos, Adrião Nemi, and Maximiliano Vander; all these were somewhat overshadowed by their Portuguese associates and rivals. The foreigners shipped Madeira sugar to the Lowlands and elsewhere, but most of the lucrative Madeira-Brazil trade was probably in Portuguese hands.

Until the twentieth century, the English merchant community of Funchal was to occupy a pivotal position in the economy of Madeira. Isolated individuals of English, Scottish, and Irish extraction had lived in Madeira since the fifteenth century. The Scotsman John Drummond of Perth, said to have been the nephew of King Robert III of Scotland,[2] was the ancestor of numerous Drummonds who lived on the island during the fifteenth century and who later spread to the Azores. But it was not until the seventeenth century that the English merchants began to constitute a distinct community in Funchal.

The pioneer was Robert Willoughby, who arrived at Funchal about 1590, when he must have been a very young man. He was a strong Catholic, high in the esteem of the authorities in Lisbon and Madrid, who made him a knight of the Order of Christ.[3] The Portuguese called him "Roberto Velovi" (also "Velovit" and "Velovid" – all reasonable

---

2. This John Drummond covered up his tracks very well; the Scottish Drummonds knew only that he had disappeared somewhere on the Continent. Early in the sixteenth century, when the numerous Drummonds of Madeira became curious as to their ancestry and wished to find out if they were really related to the blood royal of Scotland, and thus entitled to the status of *fidalgos* in Portugal, they addressed an inquiry to Scotland. A letter from David, Lord Drummond, to Manuel Afonso Ferreira Drummond, dated at Drummond Castle, 1 December 1519, stated that, as far as could be determined in Scotland, the original Madeiran John Drummond was the youngest son of Sir John Drummond, Lord of Stobhall, Cargill, and Kynloch, the brother of Queen Annabella (1350?–1402), the brother of Queen Annabella (1350?–1402). Hence John Drummond was a nephew of Annabella and of her husband Robert III (1340?–1406), and a full cousin of her son, James I (1394–1437). The text of the letter can be found in William Drummond, *Genealogy of the House of Drummond* (Edinburgh, 1831), p. 94.

3. Cordeiro, 2: 388.

phonetic transcriptions of *Willoughby*) and there were other members of his family on the island. A certain Mary Willoughby was the wife and widow of the English merchant William Ray, who died sometime before October 1653; and Albans Willoughby ("Albanos Velovi") was an important merchant of Funchal during the years 1650–68. Robert Willoughby's name appears many times in customshouse records, although he was probably not as prosperous a merchant as his countryman William Ray. Willoughby died sometime in the early 1650s and was buried at the Franciscan convent in Funchal. An English translation of his Portuguese will and testament was proved at Canterbury in 1656.[4]

Although in Portuguese eyes Willoughby was a man of greater stature than William Ray, Ray (the "Guilherme Rei" of the Portuguese·records)[5] was probably a more important merchant. According to certain calculations made by Mauro in his *Portugal et l'Atlantique,*[6] the customs registers for 1620 show that Ray paid more duties that year for goods exported from Funchal than any other merchant, while Willoughby ranks ninth. The full list, with my emendations and additions, is given in table 3. The total amount of export taxes paid (and these figures are all as calculated by Mauro) came to 2:972$236 réis (a respectable £2,288 in sterling). The Funchal customshouse taxed dutiable exports at 11 percent of an officially established valuation. This means that the dutiable exports of the port of Funchal in 1620 were officially worth about 30:000$000. But since the official valuation usually underestimated the actual Funchal market price by about at least 20 percent, the true Funchal market value of dutiable exports in 1620 was something over 36:000$000 (or over £27,675).

Yet in order to understand all the above figures it is essential to realize that they *do not include the exports of Portuguese merchants aboard Portuguese ships*; the figures reflect only the exports by foreign merchants or those carried in foreign bottoms. This is one reason why the Portuguese merchants make so melancholy a showing on the above list of duties paid, because many of them exported nondutiable cargoes aboard

4. Tombo, Arq. do Funchal, Codex 1503; *Index to Wills Proved in the Prerogative Court of Canterbury* 7 (London, 1925): 580.

5. Another English merchant called William Ray, originally from London, lived at Ponta Delgada, São Miguel, Azores, during 1620. He married a Portuguese lady and left numerous descendants in the Azores; see Azevedo Soares, 2: 341–42. I do not know what the relationship was between William Ray of Funchal and William Ray of Ponta Delgada, but both were English Catholic merchants.

6. Mauro, p. 498.

TABLE 3

Customs Duties Paid by Funchal Merchants in 1620*
(in réis)

1.	William Ray (English)	592$284
2.	Guilherme Dinis (probably Flemish)	541$843
3.	Adrian Erspranger (German)	270$085
4.	Luís Gonçalves	262$000
5.	João Pintor	252$586
6.	Jacques Guilherme (Flemish)	201$713
7.	Robert Albert (French)	180$685
8.	Raymond Biard (French)	176$705
9.	Robert Willoughby (English)	149$335
10.	Cornelis Selos (Flemish)	118$422
11.	William Crawford (English)	85$696
12.	Jacques Matias (probably Flemish)	77$911
13.	Nicolas Hians (Janz? Flemish)	25$400
14.	Francisco Rodrigues Tavira	12$980
15.	João Hians (Janz? Flemish)	11$377
16.	João Rodrigues Tavira	8$503
17.	Francisco Gonçalves Silveira	4$345
18.	Gonçalves Rodrigues Jardim	$366

*Tombo, Arq. do Funchal, Codex 1503.

Portuguese ships and paid nothing, and therefore the cargoes were not entered on the customs books. Conversely, the foreign merchants, who handled the bulk of the trade with foreign ships, always figured prominently on such lists. And thus it was that the Englishman Ray led all the Portuguese with total tariff payments of 592$284 (or about £455).

Thirty years later William Ray was still an active trader in the Funchal markets. On 8 October 1647, at a time when there was the prospect of food shortages, the governor of Madeira and the senior officials and aldermen made a contract with Ray to supply Funchal with grain. He was supposed to obtain 300 moios (7,200 bushels) of wheat, wherever it could be found, at his own risk and credit, and bring it to the island within a time period of four months and fifteen days. The officials, in return, guaranteed him a high price of $300 réis per alqueire (about 1s. 10½d. per peck) for any wheat obtained.[7] In the Funchal customs registers of 1650, Ray's name still appeared with some frequency, although

7. Arq. Dist. Funchal, "Vereações 1647," fols. 22–23.

in amounts of commodities imported and exported he was clearly very far behind his English competitors Richard Pickford, Albans Willoughby, and George Pasmer, and also behind the outstanding Dutch merchant of Funchal, "Duarte Zormans," as the Portuguese called him. After 1651 Ray's name vanished from the records, and, on 3 October 1653, an official document mentioned that his wife, Mary Willoughby, was a widow.[8]

During the middle years of the century, Richard Pickford, who was active between 1638 and 1682, was the principal merchant, foreign or Portuguese, in Funchal. For decades Pickford occupied an enviable position at the heart of the Madeiran wine trade. Along with Pickford, in the middle and later years of the century, there are the names of such English merchants resident at Funchal as George Fryer (active during 1638-96), John Carter (1656-65), Obadiah Allen (1670?-1687), John Shattocke (1675-87), Samuel Hutchins (1677-87), Edward Potter (1682-98), Richard Richbell (1682-99), Samuel Brooking (1682-99), Matthew Matson (1687-94?), Richard Miles (1687-1710?), William Bolton (1695-1714), and Benjamin Hemming (1698-1715?).[9]

These are names worthy of being rescued from the near oblivion in which they now lie. William Bolton, it is true, has had a portion of his business correspondence published, and therefore is better known than the others, whose names exist, if at all, as misspelled appellations on the arcane family trees of the Madeiran genealogists — or as cryptic references in the calendars published by the Public Record Office of London. But neither the island genealogists nor the calendar editors had the knowledge to place these names in their proper context. And the books that treat more at large of the "British Factory" in Funchal — such as W.H. Koebel's *Madeira Old and New* and A. Samler Brown's informative guides — except for vague references to an influx of English merchants into Madeira after the marriage between King Charles II and the Portuguese Princess Catherine of Braganza in 1662, can offer no concrete facts about the English presence in Funchal preceding the establishment of the renowned Cossart, Gordon and Company (wine merchants), by Francis Newton and others, in 1745. From there the older writers proceed to a description of such better-known Anglo-Saxon in-

8. Tombo, Arq. do Funchal, Codex 1233, and Codex 1232, fol. 14; Mauro, pp. 498-99.
9. Among them, Fryer, Carter, Allen, and Hemming all served as English vice consuls of Madeira, usually under the authority of the English consul-general at Lisbon.

stitutions in Madeira as the celebrated and once powerful factory, the English church and cemetery, Blandy Brothers and Company, William Hinton and Company, and the deservedly famed hotels of William Reid.

There is no need, of course, to derogate from the accomplishments of Francis Newton, who labored in Funchal for sixty years (1745–1805); any man who finds a good wine and turns it into a great one has done much for the happiness of mankind. But Richard Pickford was surely Francis Newton's spiritual ancestor – and Newton built upon foundations that had been well established one hundred years and more before him.

The seventeenth-century English mercantile community of Funchal, whose growth, incidentally, had little to do with the marriage of Charles II and Catherine and much to do with the opening of English America, had certain large merits. By the middle of the century, it was no longer made up primarily of Catholic émigrés but included Protestants of various persuasions as well. Besides the orthodox Anglican merchants, the addition of Freegrace Bendall to the Funchal group at the end of the 1640s, with his Puritan name and New England connections, contributed a touch of Bostonian Calvinism to the Catholic atmosphere of Madeira.[10] The English merchants – Catholic, Anglican, Presbyterian, and Independent – besides their religious cosmopolitanism, were multilingual and multicultural, men of true "Atlantic" outlook, at home on two or three continents. They sent their ships to the farthest shores of Africa and of North, Central, and South America, and along with their colleagues in Lisbon, Cadiz, London, Amsterdam, Hamburg, and elsewhere, the men

---

10. Freegrace Bendall was evidently born in New England, and baptized at the First Church of Boston in 1635. His father, Edward Bendall, came to Massachusetts with Governor John Winthrop in 1630. Freegrace was apparently the eldest of a family which included another three sons (Hopedfor, Ephraim, and Restore), and two daughters (More Mercy and Reform). Freegrace was living in Funchal in 1649, while still an adolescent, probably serving as an apprentice merchant. He seems to have remained in Madeira until about 1665. In 1666 three of his daughters (Bridget, Elizabeth, and Anne) were baptized on the same day, at the Boston church, to which Freegrace was admitted to membership in 1668. He also had four sons (Pitford, More Mercy, Freegrace, and Scarlet). Although he resided in Boston for the rest of his life, he visited Madeira at least once, in 1672. On 9/19 November 1680 he was referred to as "the late" Freegrace Bendall, and his executors were engaged in selling his house and land in Massachusetts. *Records of the First Church of Boston,* 3 vols. (Boston, 1961), 1: 63, 279, 343; and 2: 347, 350, 355, 358; *Records of the Governor and Company of the Massachusetts Bay in New England* 5 (Boston, 1854): 296; *Aspinwall Notarial Records* (Boston, 1903), p. 375; *Records of the Suffolk County Court,* 2 vols. (Boston, 1933), 1: 121.

of Funchal contributed to the creation of the great Atlantic community.

Life for a merchant in Funchal was seldom easy. The unbroken history of the English commercial community at Funchal, from the 1620s to the 1970s, speaks eloquently of the Anglo-Saxon power to accommodate, to compromise, to persuade, and to persist. The Protestant merchant had to bear the weight of legislative discrimination and official disapproval; he had to endure public obloquy and petty insults; he was a pariah beyond the pale of decent Catholic society. The whole thrust of Portuguese social, political, and ecclesiastical institutions was directed toward identifying, and also, quite literally, killing, "heretics" and "apostates." And if, in an imperfect world and for reasons of general utility, a heretical foreign merchant were allowed to keep both his life and his faith, he was nonetheless made to feel, with repeated and painful sharpness, the awful anomaly of his position.

In various ways the English Catholic merchants – both at law and in official practice – enjoyed important advantages over their Protestant fellow countrymen, as well as more relaxed social relationships with the Portuguese, both male and female. Yet both Catholic and Protestant merchants, equally, had to endure on occasion enormous harassment from the municipal chamber of Funchal, which enjoyed wide powers over the commercial life of the city. During the first half of the seventeenth century, the municipal chamber of Funchal (*câmara municipal do Funchal*) consisted of six officials: two magistrates (*juizes ordinários*), three aldermen (*vereadores*), and a procurator (*procurador do conselho*; a kind of executive attorney for the chamber). Five of these men were selected, in a complicated ritual, on the first of January of every year; none could succeed himself, and none could be related by blood to any other member of the chamber; but the sixth man, the most junior of the aldermen, automatically became procurator for the following year (the post of procurator was apparently an unsought and burdensome obligation).[11]

The seats on the chamber were regularly monopolized by the six or seven leading families of Funchal. In spite of laws to the contrary, blood relatives often sat together – and sometimes were told to do so, by

11. There were numerous other minor officials who functioned under the *câmara,* or in association with it, including four elected representatives (*procuradores dos mesteres*) of the craft guilds. For information on the *câmaras* and how they worked, see Boxer, *Portuguese Society in the Tropics* (Madison, Wis., 1965), especially the preface.

direct order from the king. Occasionally, feuding families would struggle with one another for control of the chamber, but more often persons served on the chamber out of a sense of duty; and some had to be threatened by the governor with imprisonment before they would take their seats. After Portugal broke away from Spain in 1640, with the revolt of King John IV, some of the medieval traditions of the municipal chamber were disregarded. John IV began to appoint the aldermen every year by his direct decree (beginning in 1646 and 1647). At first the royal letter containing the new appointments was opened in January of every year, but eventually it began to arrive as late as June or July,[12] or not at all, and aldermen found themselves serving eighteen-month, and even twenty-four-month, terms. Another important change, beginning about 1647, was the appointment of one of the two magistrates as a *juiz de fora* (a kind of circuit judge), with greatly increased powers and a much heavier responsibility for districts outside of Funchal. The office of the second magistrate (*juiz ordinário*) seems to have fallen into abeyance.

The municipal chamber affected the merchants because it had direct responsibility for markets and shops, for weights and measures, and for the fixing of all prices for food and drink. The chamber also, on occasion, interfered with the movement of ships in the harbor; arrested, fined, and imprisoned sailors, captains, and merchants; and forbade merchants to sell certain goods, or — in the contrary case — compelled merchants to sell certain commodities, at specified places, in specified quantities, and at specified prices. A city chamber insensitive to the realities of the market place could make life very difficult for the merchants and, in fact, could make all normal trade impossible.

Of fundamental importance was the chamber's responsibility for keeping the city of Funchal and its environs supplied with food. Since the Madeiran agriculturalists concentrated narrowly on cash crops, such as sugarcane and grape vines, the island was a heavy importer of foodstuffs. Madeira was short of dairy products, meats, potatoes, maize, and cereals of all kinds, but the really critical item was wheat. There were well-inhabited areas of the island — such as the region from Caniço to Machico on the southeast coast, the Calheta area from Paúl do Mar to Madalena do Mar in the southwest, and Faial and Porto da Cruz in the northeast — where no cereals were grown at all. The Funchal area produced a small amount of wheat, far short of what the inhabitants con-

12. Arq. Dist. Funchal, "Vereações 1656," fol. 8; "1657," fol. 19.

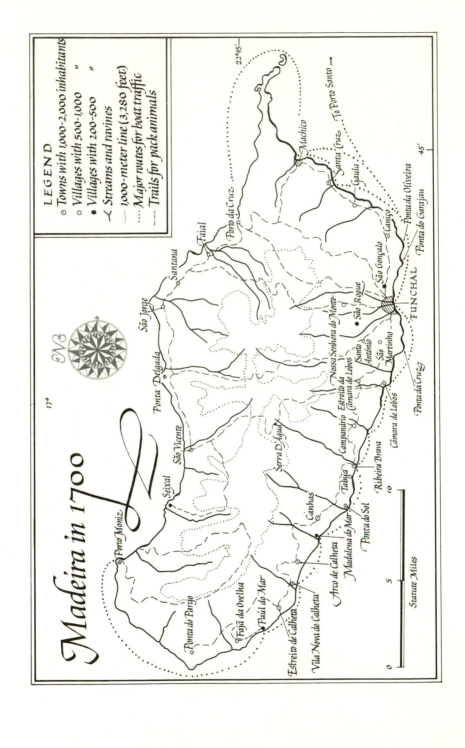

Madeira in 1700

Statute Miles

0   5   10

17°

22°45'

45'

Porto Moniz
Ponta do Pargo
Fajã da Ovelha
Paúl do Mar
Estreito de Calheta
Vila Nova de Calheta
Arco de Calheta
Madalena do Mar
Ponta do Sol
Canhas
Tábua
Ribeira Brava
Câmara de Lobos
Campanário
Estreito da Câmara de Lobos
Nossa Senhora do Monte
Santo António
São Martinho
São Roque
FUNCHAL
Ponta da Cruz
São Gonçalo
Caniço
Ponta da Oliveira
Ponta do Garajau
Gaula
Santa Cruz
To Porto Santo
Machico
Porto da Cruz
Faial
Santana
São Jorge
Ponta Delgada
São Vicente
Seixal
Serra D'Água

sumed. A few places, such as Ribeira Brava and Ponta do Sol on the south shore, and the north shore settlements of São Vicente, Ponta Delgada, São Jorge, and Santana, probably grew enough grain, when the harvest was good, to supply their own needs. The only area likely to produce a surplus of wheat was in the extreme west, in the districts of Porto Moniz, Ponta do Pargo, and Fajã da Ovelha, where grains were the only commercial crop. The western settlements occasionally shipped small quantities of wheat to Funchal by sea.[13]

Funchal's only reliable nearby source of wheat was the island of Porto Santo. This small, lonely, and defenseless island, a favorite target of attack for pirates and privateers, had attracted only about five or six hundred settlers by the end of the seventeenth century, and its population was never to grow very large. In spite of certain problems in obtaining a sufficient supply of water, the settlers were able to keep considerable numbers of cattle, sheep, goats, pigs, and horses, and to grow surpluses of wheat, barley, and rye.[14] Wheat was the most important cash crop; when the harvest was good, considerable quantities were exported to Funchal. Porto Santo could not supply all of Madeira's wheat deficit, or even half of it, but the news of a good harvest in Porto Santo always had a material effect on wheat prices in Funchal.

According to an authoritative report written at Funchal on 17 August 1757 by the governor and captain-general of Madeira, Manuel de Saldanha de Albuquerque, the island of Madeira, then thought to contain 80,000 persons, consumed 15 moios of wheat per day, which would add up to 5,475 moios (or 131,400 English bushels) per year. Of this amount, even when there was a good wheat harvest in the island, 4,000 moios (or 96,000 bushels) had to be imported, in addition to imports of maize.[15] In the middle of the eighteenth century, apparently, even in

13. Ribeiro, *Madère,* p. 54; Mauro, p. 184; Arq. Dist. Funchal, "Vereações 1669," fol. 15; "1681," fol. 15.

14. Henrique Henriques de Noronha, "Memorias seculares e eclesiasticas para a composição da historia da dioçesi do Funchal" (MS in the Arq. Dist. Ponta Delgada), fol. 127; Cordeiro, 1: 92–93. In the census of 1864 the island of Porto Santo had only 1,407 residents; in 1940 it had 2,701; in the 1950s, with an increase in tourism and the building of an airport, the population rose to about 3,500; *Anuário demográfico 1963,* p. lx. The grain question, in Portugal and the islands, is discussed in Magalhães Godinho, 3: 264–322. For a brief time, before 1470, Madeira was an exporter of grains, but serious wheat shortages developed in the mid-1470s. The first known imports of Azorean wheat to Madeira came in 1508. According to Magalhães Godinho (3: 286), Porto Santo was an important producer of barley, which was sold to the crown, to feed the king's horses.

15. AHU, Madeira, Caixa I, docs. 107–9.

good harvest years, Madeira grew only about one-quarter of its wheat needs.

Unfortunately the wheat-supply situation cannot be delineated with such precision for the seventeenth century. Reliable statistics on Madeiran wheat production, consumption, and importation are lacking.[16] From various lines of evidence, it would seem to be a fair inference that Madeira and Porto Santo together, in years of average harvest, supplied from one-third to one-half of the wheat needed on the island. In years of bumper wheat crops, up to two-thirds of the island's needs may have been met. But when the Porto Santo crop failed, the need for massive foreign imports became urgent.

During the first three decades of the seventeenth century, much of the wheat needed in Madeira came from the nearby Canary Islands, especially from the island of Lanzarote, which is less than 300 miles from Funchal. During the 1630s the supply from the Canaries began to falter, and, after Portugal rebelled against Spain on 1 December 1640, contacts between the Canaries and Madeira were broken off. The ensuing decades of war made it nearly impossible for Funchal to obtain wheat from the Canaries; yet, even if there had been no war, the supply of wheat from the Spanish islands could not have been relied on, because the Canaries ceased to produce surpluses of wheat and began to import it themselves.[17]

Another possible source of supply was the nearby coast of Muslim Africa. Unfortunately the Madeirans found it awkward to take advantage of the wheat supply from the "Barbary Coast," because the Portuguese waged perpetual war with the Moroccans. When the English ship *Phoenix* arrived at Funchal on 2 August 1623 with a wheat cargo from Morocco, the governor of Madeira arrested the master, Peter Blake, confined him to the fortress, and threatened to confiscate the cargo – all because the ship had traded with Portugal's enemies. Three days later the municipal chamber, more concerned with food supply than with ideology, protested the arrest and secured the release of the master and his cargo. The English merchant Richard Ellis duly put the "Barbary

16. But there is a wealth of information about wheat *prices* in the minute books of the Funchal chamber. These have been combed for information, and the statistics arranged in useful tables, by Mauro, pp. 324–28.

17. Arq. Dist. Funchal, "Vereações 1617," fols. 22, 30, 35; "1618," fols. 7, 10–11, 15, 22, 26; "1620," fol. 39; etc. George F. Steckley, "English Merchants in the Canaries, 1648–1661," M.A. thesis, University of Chicago, 1967, fols. 167, 279. For Azorean wheat shipments to the Canaries, see the next chapter.

wheat" on sale, and the chamber fixed its price at $180 réis per alqueire (about 1s. 10d. per peck).[18]

Occasionally English ships brought in small quantities of Barbary wheat (in 1624, 1627, and 1638) and were allowed to sell it undisturbed. Somewhat larger quantities were imported into Funchal from the same source during the years 1640–44,[19] but the supply from Morocco was never more than an occasional and incidental supplement to the island's needs.

In the early decades of the seventeenth century the Flemish merchants of Funchal imported considerable quantities of wheat from the Lowlands, but, after 1630, such shipments to Madeira were rare. France, England, and Ireland occasionally sent wheat to the island, but the supply from these European sources was never regular and dependable. The most important suppliers of wheat for Madeira were the islands of the Azores, particularly Terceira, São Miguel, and Santa Maria.

Wheat was a staple export from the Azores, and there was usually a fairly large surplus. Unfortunately Madeira had to share the Azorean supply with other Portuguese customers. The government of Lisbon, concerned about the provisioning of the garrison town of Mazagan in Morocco, insisted that Mazagan should have first call on the Azorean wheat supply. Furthermore, the city of Lisbon itself was heavily dependent on wheat imports, and, in times of scarcity, the Azoreans were instructed first to supply the capital and then the North African garrisons. The Madeirans came at the bottom of the list and had to scramble for whatever was left over. It was in vain that the islanders sought to have themselves included, with Lisbon and Mazagan, as a top priority market of strategic importance to Portugal; the most that Lisbon would allow was a weak decree, dated 1662, requiring the island of São Miguel to send two shiploads of wheat to Madeira every year, at a fair price.[20]

When the Azorean harvests were poor, Funchal faced the prospect of hunger. At such times the municipal chamber put strong pressures on the merchants. In 1647, when there was a wheat shortage, the chamber ordered the retailers not to sell more than one bag of wheat to any single person, on pain of being fined 2$000 réis if they did not obey. The chamber commandeered the English ship *Reformed*, consigned to the merchant Robert Downe, and forced her to go looking for 4,800 bush-

---

18. Arq. Dist. Funchal, "Vereações 1623," fols. 56–59, 64.
19. Ibid., "1640," fols. 15, 24; "1641," fol. 5; "1642," fol. 26; "1644," fol. 12.
20. AHU, Madeira, Caixa I, doc. 110 and attached papers.

els of wheat, "wherever it can be found," and to return within three months. The chamber guaranteed a price of $300 per alqueire for any wheat found, but if the master could find none, and brought back papers to prove it, then there would be no penalty (except of course that the shipowners would not be compensated for their loss of time and money).[21]

In April 1651 a French ship, on her way to Mazagan with 414 moios (9,936 bushels) of São Miguel wheat, touched at Funchal. Wheat cargoes for the garrison of Mazagan were sacrosanct and protected by the king's laws, yet nonetheless the Funchal chamber decided the Madeirans were entitled to one-quarter of the cargo and ordered the forcible unloading of 100 moios.[22]

During the years 1656–58 the books of the Funchal chamber record such actions as the following: the English merchant George Fryer was fined 4$000 for keeping quantities of pickled herring in his house (instead of in his shop); Richard Pickford and John Carter were forbidden to supply their ships with hardtack without the prior consent of the chamber; on 17 November 1657 all merchants had to declare under oath the quantities of wheat they were holding and were ordered to sell the same immediately; and in October 1658 the chamber forcibly unloaded two large Portuguese caravels, with cargoes for Lisbon (not foodstuffs), in order to compel the ships to go to the Azores looking for wheat (at the expense of the Funchal merchants, not the chamber), and when one of the captains refused, he was imprisoned with all his crew.[23]

The municipal chamber seemed to exercise almost unlimited powers over the movements of ships and the operations of the merchants. On 25 May 1680 the chamber notified the English consul, Obadiah Allen, that an English ship then in the harbor, with a cargo of salted meats, must unload the meats at Funchal, and must not leave without the chamber's permission — or the consul would have to pay a fine of 80$000 réis (£28). On 1 August 1680 a French ship, bound for Cadiz with a cargo of Canaries wheat but forced into Funchal by stress of weather, was compulsorily unloaded after the protesting captain had been jailed. On 19 July 1681 the chamber compelled a French ship, the *Marianne* of Bordeaux, to go to the Azores looking for wheat. The French consul, Honoré Sauvaire, entered a formal protest into the cham-

21. Arq. Dist. Funchal, "Vereações 1647," fols. 9, 21.
22. Ibid., "1651," fols. 14–16.
23. Ibid., "1656," fols. 12, 16; "1657," fol. 27; "1658," fols. 60–66.

ber's minute books, but to no avail — three weeks later the same thing happened to another French ship.[24]

In August 1682 the important English merchant Samuel Hutchins refused to allow his ship, the *Elizabeth*, to go to the Azores for wheat. The chamber promptly arrested Hutchins, the captain, and the crew. Consul Allen intervened to obtain the freedom of the English, but only after they had agreed to send the ship to the Azores. The usual formal protest was entered on the record, but the ship went to the Azores, found no wheat, and came back empty. As usual neither Hutchins nor the captain received a single penny from the chamber for their time and trouble.[25]

When three ships returned empty from the Azores, the chamber summoned all the English and French merchants and asked them to obtain wheat from wherever it could be found. No tariffs would be charged, and there would be no fixed price for the wheat, which could be sold at any price the merchants wanted. But the aldermen, unable to let the matter rest there, resorted to their customary threats: no ship, said the chamber, would be allowed to load wines at Funchal unless it had brought in wheat.[26] Since cargoes were arranged months ahead of time, and since it would have been many weeks before the merchants could inform their distant correspondents of any changes, the strict enforcement of this threat would have meant a serious disruption of business for a considerable period.

Merchants particularly objected to having their ships diverted to the Azores when they suspected that the Azoreans had no wheat to sell. The aldermen, who paid none of the costs, were always optimistic, but the merchants knew better. At times ships desiring wheat cargoes were turned away from the Azorean harbors at gun point — yet the aldermen persisted in forcing other ships to try their fortune too. The chamber compelled cooperation by threats, imprisonments, fines, and expropriations. Ship captains, having been forced to post heavy bonds or forced to leave half their cargo ashore, had no alternative but to go to the Azores and then return to Funchal. In times of scarcity it is a wonder that any ships put into Funchal at all.

One of the worst cases involved the captain of a Flemish ship from Rotterdam who had a cargo of rye for the Canaries; on 8 June 1683,

24. Ibid., "1680," fols. 19, 23; "1681," fol. 19.
25. Ibid., "1682," fols. 17–18.
26. Ibid.

after having been imprisoned for noncooperation, the captain was compelled to allow the unloading of his rye. The chamber entrusted the 3,168 bushels of rye to the Portuguese merchant Manuel Rodrigues, but since Rodrigues could not pay immediately for the purchase of the rye — the cost of which came to 1:504$800 réis (about £528) — the aldermen told the captain to proceed on his way to the Canaries, without cargo or capital, and return for his money in two months' time![27]

In spite of the problems involved in keeping Madeira supplied with foodstuffs, a number of merchants specialized in the wheat trade. Since the chamber controlled all food prices in Funchal, it was not possible for merchants importing wheat to make very large profits in the trade; but the profits were good enough, in normal times, to encourage them to remain in the business. Englishmen, both in the Azores and Madeira, were prominent in the wheat trade, as they were in other branches of island commerce. For instance, of twelve ships listed in the 1676 Funchal register of wheat shipments, six were English, three French, and three Portuguese.[28]

The letters of William Bolton and Company, written from Funchal during the last years of the seventeenth century, provide a clear picture of both the possibilities and the perils of the wheat trade. In a letter written on Christmas Day of 1695, Bolton remarked that wheat could be purchased in the Azores for 13$500 réis per moio, placed aboard with all charges paid, and sold in Madeira for the equivalent of 24$000 per moio.[29] Thus in December of 1695 the economics of a shipment of 100 moios (or 2,400 bushels) of wheat from the Azores to Madeira would have begun with the cost of the wheat delivered on board, 1:350$000, plus the freight charges of 3$000 per moio, or 300$000, making the total expenses 1:650$000 (£577). In Madeira, the merchant would have received 2:400$000 (£840), leaving, after deducting expenses, a gross profit of 750$000 (£263). This represented a fair profit margin, even after warehousing costs, dock fees, and other small charges had been deducted from the gross profit figure.

Yet the situation could change rapidly. Three weeks after reporting the current prices in the above letter, Bolton welcomed to Funchal his own ship, the *Angel*, which arrived on 15 January 1696 from Terceira with 100 moios of wheat, but he learned that the master had paid

---

27. Ibid., "1683," fols. 11–12.
28. Tombo, Arq. do Funchal, Codex 1505, fols. 1–21, 27.
29. Bolton, pp. 24–25.

15$000 per moio in the Azores (an increase of 1$500 from the price of the previous month), while the Funchal price had remained the same. This means that Bolton's gross profit was probably no more than 600$000 (£210). And these calculations assume the favorable freight charges of 3$000 per moio, whereas in midwinter, a master with a stout ship and a dry hold could demand, and receive, 6$000 and more per moio for taking wheat from the Azores to Madeira. Bolton, by owning shares in his own ships, cut his freight charges to a minimum; but another merchant, who might have had to pay freight of 6$000 per moio, on a shipment of 100 moios in January 1696, might have made a gross profit of only 300$000 réis (£105). After deduction of overhead and other fixed costs, little would have been left.[30]

The pattern of wheat prices in Funchal during the course of the year 1696 is instructive, and shows the disadvantages of trading in a small market that could be suddenly, and unexpectedly, oversupplied. At the end of May 1696 a Dublin ship had brought in wheat, butter, candles, salted beef, and herring and was loading 100 pipes of madeira for the West Indies. Early in June the Bristol sloop *Betty*, three weeks out of Youghal, Ireland, arrived in Funchal with butter, herring, and 50 moios of Irish wheat and loaded 50 pipes of wine for Antigua. Early in the summer the price of wheat in Funchal held steady at between $400 and $500 réis per alqueire, or 24$000 to 30$000 per moio (equivalent to between 7s. and 8s. 9d. per bushel). Ships with wheat arrived in normal numbers during the summer, until, in mid-September, four Dutch merchantmen from Flushing (Vlissingen) brought in such quantities of Azorean wheat that the price fell to $280 per alqueire, or 16$800 per moio (about 5s. per bushel). The price of 16$800 per moio was uncomfortably close to the Azorean prices of 13$500 and 15$000. In mid-October the Funchal price lay in the range of 16$800 to 18$000, and by the end of the following February, when the wheat price usually reached a peak, it was still only 21$000 per moio, less than it had been the previous summer.[31]

30. Ibid., p. 29; Arq. Dist. Funchal, "Vereações 1658," fols. 62–64.

31. Bolton, pp. 38–40, 49, 51, 65. The year 1696 was a difficult one for William Bolton in other ways. When one of his ships could not enter the harbor, because of a contrary wind, Bolton wanted to send out a small boat to her but needed prior permission from the governor of Madeira. On applying to the governor, he was told the governor was asleep and could not be disturbed. Since it was an emergency situation, he sent out a boat without authorization. The result was that on 11 July 1696, in Bolton's own words: "I was seized upon and putt into a

The Funchal wheat market went through irregular cycles of glut and scarcity. For the Madeirans, the best hope for relief from their recurrent food shortages came from the English colonies in North America. The New England plantations in particular, which had very few products to offer the transatlantic market, might one day become major suppliers of wheat and other foodstuffs for Madeira, Lisbon, and other grain-deficient areas. On 23 July 1688 the plantation-built brigantine *Supply* (30 tons) of Boston sailed directly for Madeira, from Boston, carrying not only the usual cargo of pipe staves and salted fish but also 240 bushels of wheat.[32] The ship was small, the wheat cargo (amounting to only 10 moios) trivial, but the initiative was important and the venture was to bear fruit. By the end of the century, the shipment of foodstuffs from the North American colonies to Madeira had become commonplace. For instance, during the course of a year, running from September 1699 to September 1700, Bolton commented on seven shiploads of provisions from the colonies to Funchal. These included: (1) a brigantine from Boston (September 1699) with wheat and Indian corn; (2) three brigantines from New England, one from New York, and one from Virginia – all in Funchal together during February 1700 – with cargoes of wheat, Indian corn, pease, and other products; and (3) a ketch from Pennsylvania (September 1700) with 150 moios, or 3,600 bushels, of Pennsylvania wheat.[33]

---

wett dungeon with my cheese [chaise] man where we remained 48 hours" (p. 41). Then he was dragged down to the beach, accompanied by the town mob: "You may guess what a multitude of neggros and mollottos and rable followed us in the prosesion; expected nothing but to have my Braines Beat out and was glad when I gott aboard" (p. 42). The governor, ordering Bolton to be deported within three hours, almost forced the merchant to sail aboard the frigate *Jersey*, bound for the West Indies. Instead, Bolton managed to get aboard a Dutch ship for Terceira, and from there took passage to Lisbon. He was unable to secure satisfaction or compensation from the dilatory Lisbon courts and was allowed back into Madeira, following an absence of over ten months, only after making profuse apologies to the governor. This episode illustrates the difficulties that confronted foreign merchants in Funchal, particularly at the hands of arbitrary governors, who were themselves often smugglers and usually the greatest transgressors of customs and treasury regulations, although Bolton himself was inclined to attach much of the blame to the machinations of his deadly English commercial rivals at Funchal, Richard Miles and Richard Richbell (Bolton, pp. 44, 74).

32. "Abstracts of English Shipping Records Relating to Massachusetts Ports, from original records in the Public Record Office, London, compiled for the Essex Institute, Salem, Massachusetts" (photostatic copy, in the University of Chicago Library, of an English typescript original; London, 1931), part I, fol. 110.

33. Bolton, pp. 144, 156, 179.

The circumstances favorable to the development of trade between Madeira and North America ran as follows: (1) Charles II in 1663 had specifically exempted the trade between the Portuguese islands and the English colonies from certain penalizing provisions in the Navigation Acts;[34] (2) the search in New England, and in some other northerly plantations, for locally produced marketable commodities; (3) Madeira's need for foodstuffs; and (4) the American thirst for Madeiran wines.

In the seventeenth century, New England was peculiarly short of locally produced merchantable exports. Pipe staves comprised one export staple, and timber (particularly in the form of great pine trunks to be used as ship masts) another. But pipe staves and timber had little value in relation to their large size and great weight, and, in international trade, neither could be considered a first-class commodity, since the profit ratio for them was too small. The sea, furnishing "fish oil" and some locally prepared salted fish, helped to compensate, to an extent, for the deficiencies in the products of the land. But still, the New Englanders had to scramble if they were to make their mark in transatlantic commerce. Boston became an important, but essentially parasitic, exchange market, trading in the commodities produced by other peoples. To Boston went a host of European products — textiles, manufactures, luxury goods, spices — and wines from the Atlantic islands and the Continent; and also to Boston went the products of the Americas — Newfoundland salted codfish, Virginian tobacco, West Indian sugar, rum, indigo, and molasses, and Tortugan salt. The New Englander, with not enough of his own products to occupy his attention, thus became the famed "Yankee trader" of the goods of others.

Like the Japanese of a later epoch, the "Yankee trader" became a great builder of ships and sent his vessels to the farthest seas, searching for new markets and probing for weaknesses in the economic amor of his competitors. By the mid-1670s the Yankees had already built 730 ships, and the Boston-Salem vicinity alone was turning out 12 new ships per year.[35]

Many of these plantation-built merchantmen were to make a specialty of the Madeiran and Azorean trades. The opening up of a Madeiran market for wheat and maize was a welcome initiative for the New Englanders, for it provided an outlet for home-grown produce. By the early

34. Ordinance 15 Car. 2, cap. 7 (1663): "Wines of the growth of Maderas, the Western Islands or Azores, may be carried [directly] from thence to any of the lands, islands, plantations, colonies, territories or places to his Majesty belonging, in Asia, Africa or America, in English built ships." Bolton, pp. 15–16.

35. *Cal. S.P., Colonial Ser., America 1675-76*, pp. 220–22, 464–66.

years of the eighteenth century, American competition had made it uneconomic for English Funchal merchants to import wheat from Cornwall and Devon.[36] Other American colonies followed New England's lead, and soon supplies of wheat, maize, and even rice (from the Carolinas) poured into Madeira from New York, Pennsylvania, Virginia, and other areas.

Besides wheat and maize, the other foodstuffs imported into Madeira included barley and rye, Newfoundland and New England salted codfish, English and Dutch pickled herring, English salted beef, Cape Verdean salted goatmeat, and English and Irish butter and cheese. From Portugal came salt, olives, olive oil, spices, cheese, sausages, and, on occasion, dried fruits.

The noncomestibles imported into Madeira included a wide variety of commodities and manufactures. There were metals (iron, lead, copper), materials for war (gunpowder, weapons, munitions), textiles and haberdashery (hats, ribbons, gloves, stockings, etc.), household articles (chinaware, kitchen utensils, mirrors, glassware, candles, furniture, etc.), ship supplies (pitch and tar, pine boards, masts, sailcloth, cordage, oakum, etc.), luxuries (silks, perfumes, ivory, jewelry, etc.), materials for cooperage (staves and hoops for tuns, pipes, hogsheads, and barrels), religious books and articles for religious devotions (from Lisbon), and such miscellaneous commodities as bottles, wax, leather, paper, tiles, whale oil, nails, tools, lumber, and plaster of Paris.

And in return, Madeira had little to offer except wines, wines, and more wines. By the end of the seventeenth century, madeira wine accounted for over 90 percent of the value of all exports. Brandy and vinegar exports were only of marginal importance. Island-grown sugar, a staple in international trade during the early years of the century, had become insignificant by the end of the century. The single most important new product developed by the Madeirans for the international trade during the last quarter of the century was "succatt" or succade (preserved candied fruit). There were "dry" preserves (heavily sugared "crystallized" fruit) and "wet" preserves (fruit preserved in a thick syrup), and various kinds of sugary confections. These were sent usually to France and the Netherlands. During the 1690s, succade was the second most valuable export, although a very distant second to wine, and its manufacture allowed the islanders to use up some of their excess supplies of home-grown sugar. Funchal also had a small business in re-

36. Bolton, p. 8.

exports, involving, first, the dispatching of Brazilian sugar to Europe, and, second, the transshipment of textiles and other manufactures to the Azores and Brazil.

In the export ledgers of the Funchal merchants, other than the Frenchmen shipping succade to France, wines overwhelmingly outnumbered all other entries; in their import ledgers, a wide and confusing variety of commodities jostled for space. Nonetheless, amid all the random diversity of imports, one article of trade clearly took pride of place: cloth. Cloth for the clothing of the inhabitants of Madeira was a repeated, an irreplaceable, and an essential import.

During the first three decades of the seventeenth century, Flemish and French merchants imported large quantities of textiles from the Lowlands and France; but, during the last half of this hundred-year period, most textiles came from England, aboard English ships, and most of the trade was handled by English merchants. The demand for English textiles in the Atlantic islands, not only in Madeira but also in the Azores and the Canaries, contributed materially to the development of the textile industry and the textile trade in a number of small English towns and ports. Tiny Topsham, downriver from Exeter in Devonshire, was, at times, an important trading partner of the Atlantic islands. Barnstaple, on the other side of Devon, was also a large supplier of textiles to the islands. Another steady supplier was Colchester, to the northeast of London. The ships from England to the islands were full of "pieces" of cloth — "Devon dozens," "Colchester bays" (baize), "Barnstaple bays," "perpetuanas," "says" and "kerseys," friezes and "frizados" — a rich variety with a now old-fashioned nomenclature.[37]

William Bolton in Funchal wanted his London correspondents and factors to send him nothing but good English textiles; instead, to his chagrin, he was constantly being sent hats, stockings, and haberdashery, butter and cheese, pipe staves and hoops, and other miscellany. In June

37. "Devon dozens" was the name of a "kersey" (or coarse woolen cloth) made in Devonshire; the "kerseys" were narrow cloths, woven from long wool and usually ribbed. The "bays" from Colchester and Barnstaple were somewhat finer and lighter than present-day baize, wider than kerseys, and much used for making habits for members of religious orders. "Say" was a cloth of fine texture, somewhat like serge. "Perpetuana" was a durable woolen cloth; "frieze" was a kind of coarse woolen cloth with a nap, usually on one side only; and "frizado" was a type of frieze. W.B. Stephens, *Seventeenth-Century Exeter* (Exeter, 1958), contains an interesting description of the evolution of the textile trade in one particular community that participated in the islands' commerce; see especially the tables on pp. 10, 26, 105, 110, 168, 173, 175–77.

1697 Bolton requested from London quantities of "madder black," Colchester bays, colored "Bockin," red and blue kerseys, perpetuanas, and "fine black says." In October 1697 he requested no more butter, cheese, and haberdashery.[38] One month later he raged at his London agents: "What goods were fitting to send must be madder black, Colchester bayes, kirsies, fine black sayes, long ells, etc., and not butter and cheese and hoopes and haberdashery and such like trash."[39] He said there was absolutely no profit in pipe hoops, which sold for only 9$000 réis per thousand. He wrote that the Irish supplied butter and cheese at a much cheaper rate than the butter and cheese from England.

Bolton's letters testify to the central importance of textiles for the English merchants of Funchal. He insisted that bays, says, kerseys, and perpetuanas "will never want sale one time or other" — and, unlike perishable commodities, textiles could be kept off the market until prices had risen. In April 1699 Bolton said that Madeira was glutted with goods; even the market for Colchester bays, "generally the best comodity we have in the country," was depressed. But, with a little care, the bolts of cloth could be kept in good condition, and disposed of at the right time.[40]

The ships that came from England with textiles often proceeded to the West Indies with pipes of wine. The exchange of textiles for wine, not by direct barter but in a two-way money transaction, was the commonest event in the commercial traffic of Funchal. The numbers of ships that comprised this traffic can be roughly estimated. The customs registers for 1682, 1687, and 1699 record shipping arrivals and departures, adding up to the following yearly totals: there were 87 ships in 1682, 72 ships in 1687, and 68 ships in 1699. The three registers added together yield a total of 227 ships, of which 142 (or 62.5 percent) were British (that is, ships belonging to subjects of the king of England, whether they were American, West Indian, Irish, or other), 51 (or 22.5 percent) were French, 21 (or 9.3 percent) were Portuguese, and the remaining 13 (or 5.7 percent) were Dutch.[41]

The annual average for these three years comes to 76 ships. Left out of these registers were the wheat ships, which from other customshouse records can be calculated as at least 12 ships per year, together with the

38. Bolton, pp. 79, 88. "Colored Bockin" refers to bays manufactured at Bocking, Essex. Madder is a plant that yields dyes of several colors.
39. Ibid., p. 90.
40. Ibid., pp. 74, 93, 133.
41. Tombo, Arq. do Funchal, Codices 1506, 1507, 2234.

Madeiran vessels in Brazilian commerce, and the Portuguese ships carrying nondutiable merchandise. The unrecorded Madeiran and Portuguese ships can be estimated, conservatively, at 1 per month, or 12 per year. The addition of 12 wheat ships, with another 12 unrecorded Portuguese ships, to the annual average of 76 recorded ships, makes a total of precisely 100 ships per year calling at Funchal. This would mean that a ship came into Funchal harbor every three or four days. A close reading of Bolton's correspondence indicates that ships arrived in groups of two, three, and four, but that the average, for the port of Funchal during the years 1695–1700, was probably a ship every three or four days.

The average of 100 ships per year was probably maintained during all of the forty-year period from 1660 through 1699 — which would mean that 4,000 ships loaded or unloaded cargo at Funchal during 1660-99. (This reckoning does not include ships which took on water and fresh fruits and vegetables while merely "passing by" the island; it includes only ships involved in Madeiran trade.) Yet it should be remembered that many of the ships in the trade, particularly the vessels that plied between the island and the English plantations, were very small, some no larger than 20 tons. Probably about 40 percent of the ships were under 100 tons; only about 25 percent of them ran to over 250 tons; while the remaining 35 percent fell somewhere between 100 and 250 tons. The total tonnage for any given year probably fell short of 16,000.[42]

The level of shipping activity for the years before 1660 is hard to estimate. The customs register for 1620 yields one solid statistic: 44 ships paid duties at Funchal during that year. This shows a level of activity, in dutiable commodities and involving foreign ships, of only about one-half of the level reached during the last decades of the century. The Funchal registers for 1650 show the presence of 38 ships, and there were, in addition, 5 English ships not recorded in the register, but known about from other sources, making a total of 43 ships. If this number is compared with the 1620 figure of 44, one might jump to the conclusion that there was no growth in traffic at Funchal between 1620 and 1650, but such a conclusion would be false.

---

42. These tonnage calculations refer to tonnage as reckoned in the seventeenth century, when a ship's length was multiplied by her breadth, the product then multiplied by her depth, and the result divided by an arbitrary figure. The tonnage figure thus obtained was an approximate calculation of the cubic volume of a vessel's hull; it had nothing to do, directly, with tons of cargo, with deadweight tons, or with water-displacement tonnage.

The year 1650 happens to be the year for which there is a customs register extant, but it was a miserable year for English and Portuguese shipping, which was completely disrupted by the Anglo-Portuguese naval war of June–December 1650, and the statistical total of 43 ships for the year 1650 must be interpreted in that light. Those 43 ships included 20 British ships, 11 French, 5 Dutch, 2 Portuguese, 2 Hamburger, 2 Genoese, and 1 unidentified foreign ship.[43] The British shipping owners, with less than half of the yearly total, had a lower percentage than usual. The customs register, because of the naval war, reveals prolonged stretches of inactivity. If it could be assumed that at least 17 ships, many of them English, were frightened away from Funchal by the war, then it could perhaps be stated that, if there had been no war, at least 60 ships would have traded in dutiable commodities at Funchal in 1650.

The register for 1650 proves that, even with six months of disruption, the level of international activity at Funchal equaled or surpassed the level of 1620. Finally, to both the 1620 and 1650 figures must be added the unrecorded ships — wheat ships, ships in the Brazil trade, and miscellaneous Portuguese ships — with nondutiable cargoes. A total estimate might be somewhat as follows: 60 ships trading at Funchal in 1620, 80 ships in 1650, and 100 ships an estimated annual average for 1660–99. These figures — 60, 80, 100 — seem to show a slow upward progression. Unfortunately, at the present state of knowledge, it is difficult to say much more about the statistics of shipping activity in Funchal during the prolonged period of 1600–1659.

By the end of the seventeenth century the ships trading with Madeira came from or went to England, Ireland, British North America, the British West Indies, and Bermuda within the British orbit; to Portugal, Brazil, and the Azores within the Portuguese orbit; and to the Netherlands and the French Atlantic ports. Subordinate and intermittent trading connections were maintained with the Canaries, Hamburg, Scotland, the French Mediterranean ports, the Dutch West Indies, the Cape Verdes, Guinea, Angola, and with the Portuguese and British East. Ships in the intercontinental and transatlantic trades greatly outnumbered those in the restricted Europe-Madeira-Azores circuit.

Apart from the ships trading with Madeira, there were large numbers of ships that sailed past Madeira while on their way to the West Indies,

43. Tombo, Arq. do Funchal, Codex 1233. Mauro, p. 499 ("Le trafic de Madère . . . n'a pas augmenté entre 1620 et 1650"), in interpreting the statistics in the customs register of 1650, failed to take into account the political situation.

the South Atlantic, or the East. Many a British, Portuguese, Dutch, and French admiral, governor, official, missionary, and savant, on his way to a colonial post, spent a day or two in Madeira. Others, less fortunate, sailed by, with only a seaward glimpse of the majestic island.

On 5 January 1699, Admiral John Benbow (1653–1702), bound for the West Indies with four warships, sailed into the Madeira roadstead. The stern admiral, whose courage was to become a legend after the tragic West Indies naval campaign of 1701–2, "sent his Pinnace ashore but would not stay for Wines or any Refreshments."[44] Benbow was only interested in dropping off and picking up mail, but in his company was a small vessel, the *Paramour*, commanded by the great English astronomer Edmund Halley (1656–1742), on his way to Barbados to study the variation of the compass. Although Benbow went on his way, Halley lingered for a few days to enjoy the hospitality of Funchal. Another person who chose to get to know Madeira was Sir William Norris, on his way to an important post in India, who kept the five-ship British India squadron waiting for one week, during March 1699, while Bolton entertained him at his home.[45]

The constant procession of visitors and ships kept Funchal alive and vital, filled with the latest information from four continents. The mercantile community, many of whose members were at home on both sides of the Atlantic, had particularly cosmopolitan members who brought the leaven of cross-cultural influences to the upper classes of Madeira. The small city of Funchal lay on the outer edges of European cultural consciousness, but the educated portion of its populace had a vision and a sense of the whole Atlantic world.

The Funchal merchants lived agreeably, in fine houses with luxuriant gardens and vineyards. The climate was nearly ideal, with cool summers, warm winters, and not too much rain. The wealthier merchants owned country estates, up the hillsides, where the air was bracing. They may have grumbled somewhat about the steep slopes and the backbreaking ascents and descents, but if they had any real complaints about the geographical setting, they concerned the precarious facilities for shipping in the harbor of Funchal.

The slight coastal indentation known as the Bay of Funchal contained no real harbor; it was nothing more than an open roadstead. Ships could anchor five or six hundred yards offshore in 15 to 20 fathoms of water,

44. Bolton, p. 124.
45. Ibid., pp. 124, 130.

with fairly good holding ground. They could also come in closer, in somewhat shallower water, if they wished to risk the weather. There was no dock or pier at Funchal; cargoes and passengers were landed by small boats on a pebbly beach. Unloading by lighter was normal in the seventeenth century, but the lighters at Madeira had to run onto a beach through the surf; when the surf ran high the boats could come crashing onto the beach, with boatmen, passengers, boats, merchandise, debris, and all, swirling around in a mass of foaming water.

Once ashore, passengers found that a strong wall separated the beach from the town, a wall built to discourage the attacks of pirates and enemies. Gateways through this wall led to the customshouse and to the governor's fortress-palace. Beyond these lay a network of narrow streets, paved with round slippery black pebbles, which led to the cathedral church and to a congested business and commercial center. Further up the slope was the large structure of the Jesuit church and college, which fronted on a spacious square.

In the Bay of Funchal ships were protected, by the mountain mass of the island itself, from all northerly winds blowing in a wide arc of 135 degrees from west-northwest to east-northeast. Westerly and easterly winds affected the ships but were not usually dangerous, but southerly winds were a mortal peril, especially if they came from due south. In a stiff south wind vessels had to slip their cables and claw off the shore and try to round the headlands of Ponta do Garajau and Ponta da Oliveira, some three miles to the east of the anchorage. Once past the Oliveira point the coastline turns sharply toward the northeast, allowing ships more sea room in a south wind. A westward escape, past the Ponta da Cruz, was even more troublesome, but had to be tried if the wind were from the south-southeast or the southeast.

Yet there were times when a sudden storm, with high winds, hit hard and fast from the south. On such occasions there was virtually no escape for ships anchored in the Funchal roadstead. This was as true for sailing ships in the nineteenth century as it had been in the seventeenth. In October 1842, during a sudden storm, all five ships in the roads were wrecked, including the British brig *Dart* and the American ship *Creole*.[46] Not until the mid-twentieth century, when a great mole and dock were pushed out into the deep water, allowing steamships to come alongside, did Funchal become a safe port.

46. Dix, pp. 36–37.

The harbor was just a dangerous roadstead, but to it came a swarm of ships, from many sections of the great Atlantic, bearing foodstuffs and manufactures. The same ships carried away wines, which were mostly bound for American destinations. Central to this process of profitable commercial intercourse were the sophisticated merchants of Funchal. Among them the English formed the wealthiest and most successful group. In spite of religious discrimination, and the needless harassment meted out to merchants by the aldermen of Funchal and other officials, the English persisted and prospered. The English and other merchants performed the essential task of making the island of Madeira a vital link in the great network of Atlantic commerce and communication.

5
The Maritime Commerce
of São Miguel

The island of São Miguel, dedicated to St. Michael the Archangel, consists of a long chain of volcanic cones and craters, some of them heavily eroded, rising from the abyssal sea floor. Its area of 288 square miles is almost exactly the same as Madeira's, but the slope of the land is much gentler than in Madeira and the terrain is less precipitous and rugged. In the mid-seventeenth century São Miguel, with 30,000 inhabitants, was as populous as Madeira, although its capital city of Ponta Delgada, with 7,000 residents, was smaller than Funchal, which probably had between 10,000 and 15,000. In 1646, São Miguel had 1 *cidade* (a chartered city), 5 *vilas* (towns with municipal chambers), 22 *lugares* (villages), 32 *freguesias* (parishes), 7,266 *fogos* (hearths or households), and 27,244 inhabitants, not counting priests and persons residing in religious institutions.[1]

---

1. Diogo das Chagas, "Espelho chrystalino," unpublished MS, written ca. 1646, in Arq. Dist. Ponta Delgada, pp. 172–74. There is a surprising wealth of demographic statistics for São Miguel for the period 1640–1720. Chagas is excellent for the years 1640 and 1646. Agostinho de Monte Alverne, *Crónicas da província de S. João Evangelista das Ilhas dos Açores,* 3 vols. (Ponta Delgada, 1960–62), 2: 20–21, 240, 297–98, 353, 385, has reliable statistics for ca. 1700. Somewhat harder to use is Cordeiro, 1: 176–93, with statistics on *vizinhos* (householders) in 1666; while Francisco de Chaves e Melo, *Descripção da Ilha de São Miguel* (Lisbon, 1723) – summarized in *Archivo dos Açores* 1: 200–224 – with figures for ca. 1720, consistently exaggerated the numbers of inhabitants. For geographical information on the island see Raquel Soeiro de Brito's excellent *Ilha de São Miguel* (Lisbon, 1955), with over one hundred charts, maps, and illustrations. Political history is covered in Francisco de Ataíde Machado, *História de São Miguel,* 3 vols. (Ponta Delgada, 1944-49).

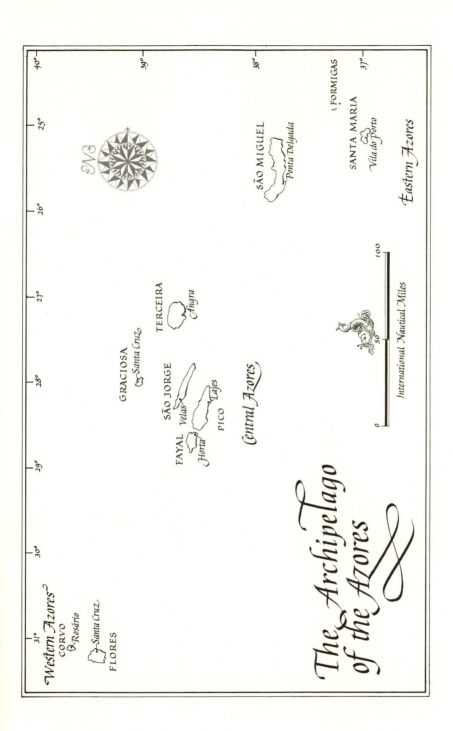

The Archipelago of the Azores

Western Azores
CORVO
Rosário
Santa Cruz
FLORES

GRACIOSA
Santa Cruz

TERCEIRA
Angra

SÃO JORGE
Velas
FAYAL
Horta
PICO
Lajes

Central Azores

SÃO MIGUEL
Ponta Delgada

FORMIGAS
SANTA MARIA
Vila do Porto

Eastern Azores

International Nautical Miles
0   50   100

31° 30° 29° 28° 27° 26° 25°

40° 39° 38° 37°

The names given to the towns and villages ran from the starkly simple Ponta Delgada (Slender Point), Ribeira Grande (Big Creek), Vila Franca (Free Town), Povoação (Settlement), Ribeira Sêca (Dry Creek), Lagôa (Lagoon), and Nordeste (Northeast) to the curious Rabo de Peixe (Fishtail), Fenais do Rabo de Peixe (Hay Fields of Fishtail), Rosto do Cão (Dog Face), and the enigmatic Água de Pau (Stick Water). Early in the sixteenth century Ponta Delgada was in a somewhat subordinate position to Vila Franca do Campo, a settlement that rivaled Ponta Delgada in size and exceeded it in prestige. But in 1552 Vila Franca was nearly totally destroyed and most of its inhabitants killed in a devastating earthquake. Except for a few houses in the western end, the town was swallowed by the earth and buried, leaving only a naked plain.[2]

Vila Franca never fully recovered from the catastrophe. Ponta Delgada, built on what is geologically the most stable area in the island, began to attract more people. The land around Ponta Delgada, particularly at the central "neck" of the island running from the capital to Rabo de Peixe, is relatively flat, or gently sloped, and was the easiest terrain to cultivate. Moreover, Ponta Delgada's harbor — actually a dangerous open roadstead — was neither better nor worse than Vila Franca's. Thus it was logical for Ponta Delgada to replace Vila Franca as the chief marketing center, the main port, and the focus of political and ecclesiastical activity. Ponta Delgada became an official *cidade* in 1546, while Vila Franca also lost out to another rival *vila*, the town of Ribeira Grande, which grew into an important center for the manufacture of linen, and thus Vila Franca dropped to third place.

In 1646 Ponta Delgada had 7,079 inhabitants, Ribeira Grande had 4,624, and Vila Franca only 2,598; another eight settlements — Rabo de Peixe, Povoação, Ribeira Sêca, the *vila* of Água de Pau, Fenais do Rabo de Peixe, Rosto do Cão, the *vila* of Lagôa, and the *vila* of Nordeste — had between 900 and 1,100 inhabitants apiece.[3] According to a description written about the year 1720, Ponta Delgada had 1,874 houses, 3 communities of male religious (Franciscans, Augustinians, and Jesuits), 4 nunneries, 3 religious sanctuaries (*recolhimentos*) for lay females, and 28 churches.[4] The ecclesiastical establishment maintained 82

2. See Monte Alverne, 2: 233–36, and other sources cited there.

3. Diogo das Chagas, pp. 173–74.

4. *Archivo dos Açores* 1: 200. Persons in religious orders comprised about 8 percent of the total population of Ponta Delgada; while in Rome itself, in 1644, such persons made up only 6.6 percent of the population (7,882 secular and religious clergy out of a total of 118,490 persons); Ludwig von Pastor, *History of the Popes* 30 (London, 1940): 374.

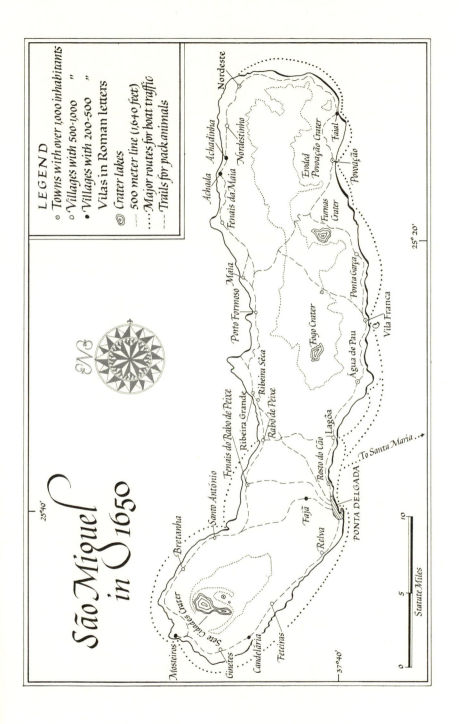

São Miguel
in 1650

LEGEND

⊙ Towns with over 1,000 inhabitants
○ Villages with 500-1,000   "
● Villages with 200-500   "
   Vilas in Roman letters
◎ Crater lakes
······ 500 meter line (1,640 feet)
····· Major routes for boat traffic
---- Trails for pack animals

Statute Miles

25°40'
25°20'
37°40'

Mosteiros
Ginetes
Candelária
Feteiras
Sete Cidades Crater
Bretanha
Santo António
Fajã
Relva
PONTA DELGADA
To Santa Maria
Fenais do Rabo de Peixe
Ribeira Grande
Rabo de Peixe
Ribeira Séca
Rosto do Cão
Lagôa
Porto Formoso
Maia
Fenais da Maia
Achada
Achadinha
Nordeste
Nordestinho
Eroded Povoação Crater
Faial
Povoação
Fogo Crater
Furnas Crater
Ponta Garça
Agua de Pau
Vila Franca

secular clergy, 92 male religious, and 489 nuns – a total of 663 persons in religious orders (out of an adult population of some 5,500), and the addition of the lay staff employed in the convents, and the women in the *recolhimentos*, probably increases that figure to around 1,200.

The swollen ecclesiastical establishments of the Azores can be illustrated by the Jesuits, who maintained three enormous colleges in Ponta Delgada, Angra, and Horta, with perhaps the three largest buildings in all of the Azores, with the exception of military installations. One out of every eight adults in Ponta Delgada was in religious orders, and probably about a third of the citizens made their living, directly or indirectly, from the religious foundations. From two-thirds to three-quarters of the royal revenues went to support the religious houses and churches, and to supply the needs of the long list of ecclesiastics on the rolls of the *filhos da folha* (sons of the payroll).

Supreme civil authority in the island of São Miguel was wielded by the hereditary counts of Vila Franca, who were descended from Rui Gonçalves da Câmara (d. 1522), second son of Zarco of Madeira. Rui Gonçalves had the misfortune to lose two sons, two daughters, a sister, and all his servants and slaves in the Vila Franca earthquake of 1522; he, his wife, and another son survived because they happened to be away from Vila Franca at the time.[5] Fifty-eight years later, in 1580, a descendant of his, also called Rui Gonçalves da Câmara, received the title of Count of Vila Franca. He was the father of Manuel da Câmara (d. 1619), second count of Vila Franca, and the grandfather of Rodrigo da Câmara (d. 1672), the third count.

The third count of Vila Franca was his family's seventh hereditary governor, donatory, and captain of São Miguel, and grand warden (*alcaide mor*) of the castle of São Brás (the chief fortress in Ponta Delgada). He maintained palatial establishments in both Lisbon and São Miguel, and enjoyed incomes from the island, paid in kind, amounting to 900 moios (21,600 bushels) of wheat – which at 6$000 réis per moio, in the 1630s, was worth 5:400$000 (equivalent to £4,150 in sterling). He also collected another 900$000 per year from his share of import and export tariffs, and from his share of taxes on agricultural produce and fisheries, and from incidental notary fees.[6]

This Dom Rodrigo da Câmara, third and last count of Vila Franca, was a hot-tempered, quarrelsome sensualist and pederast, who seduced

---

5. Monte Alverne, 2: 235.
6. Anselmo Braacamp Freire, *Conde de Villa Franca* (Lisbon, 1899), pp. 17–18.

young women and boys indiscriminately. The best that could be said for him, from the point of view of the islanders, was that he spent much time in São Miguel, was not, like other Portuguese donatories, an absentee landlord, and he contributed liberally to the island's religious foundations. He was arrested by the Inquisition on 26 May 1651, charged with homosexuality, confessed his faults, and spent the rest of his life in prison. He died on 30 April 1672 at a small lonely convent in remote Cape St. Vincent, after twenty-one years of confinement.[7]

The title of count of Vila Franca thus became infamous, and was suppressed. The last count's son, Manuel da Câmara (1630–73), a psychotic, was given the title of first count of Ribeira Grande, in 1672, shortly after the death of his father. And so the nouveau riche, upstart town of Ribeira Grande replaced old and luckless Vila Franca in the titles of the island's overlords.

The chief financial support for the counts of Vila Franca (or Ribeira Grande), the secular and religious clergy, and the royal officials derived from taxes that were collected on a very narrow basis. The bulk of the taxation fell on the shoulders of the peasants, who raised the *frutos da terra* (fruits of the land), the fishermen, who risked their lives in the treacherous Azorean seas, and the merchant importers and exporters, who invested their capital on the uncertain ventures of maritime commerce. These industrious persons – peasants, fishermen, and merchants – had to support the *fidalgos*, the bureaucrats, the soldiers, and the ecclesiastics.

To make the fiscal system work, so that the count proprietor and the others would receive their pensions and stipends and in order to earn the income necessary to pay for imports, it was essential that the island produce at least one desirable and reliable cash crop. From the long-range point of view, the commercial history of the island of São Miguel, with its tragicomic succession of booms and busts, has been a long search for a dependable cash crop. In the fifteenth century, there was a short flirtation with sugarcane, in direct imitation of the Madeiran venture; but the Azorean islands lacked the warm climate that sugarcane needs. Then, for over a century, pastel dye from the woad plant was the great money earner. But in the middle of the seventeenth century indigo imported from the Americas drove pastel off the market.

With the collapse of pastel, the islanders developed their wheat exports, raised more flax and began exporting linens, and tried to sell such

7. Ibid., pp. 37, 95, 107.

products as embroideries, bacon, broad beans, and barley. Yet there was not much progress until the eighteenth century, when exports of oranges saved the insular economy. In 1864 over 200 million oranges were sent to Britain alone; but in the 1890s the orange groves were devastated by parasites, and for fifty years no oranges were grown.[8] Once again the islanders looked for an agricultural staple, but never again really found one. They have grown sweet potatoes, yams, potatoes, grapes (producing a rather inferior wine), beetroot (for sugar), tea, peanuts, tobacco, cattails (for fibers), and other crops, but none of these has been of more than local importance. They have also gone in for fishing and whaling, have raised herds of cattle and flocks of sheep, and produced dairy products. The most recent export has been hothouse pineapples, marketed in Europe.

Pastel, oranges, and wheat have been the most successful cash crops raised on São Miguel. The woad plant (*Isatis tinctoria*), from which the pastel dyestuff is made, was introduced into the island from Toulouse, France, probably during the 1490s. It was cultivated until the 1680s (the last recorded exports of pastel were in 1685), and therefore was grown for almost two hundred years. The pastel trade was important, however, for only about a century (1550-1650), and its most prosperous phase lasted barely fifty years (1580-1630).

Pastel was a very common dye in the Middle Ages and had been used in Italy since the tenth century. Italy, Germany, Spain, France, and England all produced pastel in the sixteenth century, and the Azorean product faced heavy competition. Azorean pastel, nonetheless, made headway in English, Flemish, and French markets, and Azorean sources indicate that, about the 1580s, some 60,000 Portuguese quintals of pastel were exported per year, with a value of 160,000 cruzados (or 64:000$000 réis, equivalent to 1$067 per quintal).[9] This figure of 60,000 quintals, one suspects, represented the high-water mark of the pastel export trade, although there are those who claim, on the basis of perhaps inadequate evidence, that the island of São Miguel alone produced 100,000 quintals of pastel during its heyday.[10]

8. Soeiro de Brito, pp. 74-75.
9. Helder de Sousa Lima, "Os Açores na economia atlântica," dissertation, University of Lisbon, 1960, fol. 61.
10. Francisco Carreiro da Costa, "Cultura do pastel nos Açores," *Boletim da Comissão Reguladora dos Cereais do Arquipélago dos Açores,* no. 4 (Ponta Delgada, 1946).

In France, where woad cultivation and the use of the dye survived into the middle of the nineteenth century, one acre of woad yielded between 13,350 and 19,500 pounds of raw leaves.[11] The leaves, which resemble lettuce, were dried, ground in a mill, wetted, sun-dried again, ground again to powder, rewetted, formed into cakes or large balls, and again dried. The process, which was an old and traditional one and followed in the Azores as elsewhere, took from six to eight weeks. In São Miguel the finished balls of paste weighed one Portuguese quintal (128 lbs.) each.[12]

In nineteenth-century France, 1,000 pounds of fresh woad leaves produced only 60 to 65 pounds of pastel paste, and thus, in the processes of grinding and refining, 93.5 to 94 percent of the weight of the original vegetable substance was lost. If the French statistics are applicable to São Miguel, it would mean that 2,000 pounds of fresh leaves were necessary to make one quintal of pastel; and if São Miguel exported 60,000 quintals of pastel, then the island must have produced at least 120,000,000 pounds of woad leaves. This amount of woad (again reckoning by the French figures) would have required 8,570 acres, or 28.5 percent of the estimated 30,000 acres (one-sixth of the island's surface) under cultivation. But if the annual production figure of 100,000 quintals for São Miguel is insisted on, then that would mean, by the same reckoning, that 200,000,000 pounds of woad were produced, on 14,285 acres, occupying 47.5 percent of the estimated acreage under cultivation. If that much land had been given over to woad, it would seem that the food supply of the island might have been endangered.[13]

It was unfortunate for the Azoreans that the islands' pastel trade came into its own precisely at the time that the Spaniards began supplying Europe with Central American indigo. Guatemalan and Honduran indigo, once it was produced in quantity, created a crisis for the inferior pastel dye, and woad cultivation fell off everywhere. Export statistics for São Miguel pastel during the year 1620 (the first year in the seventeenth century for which reliable statistics are available) show that the island's pastel trade was still healthy, although it had probably declined

11. Figures adapted from the informative article, "Pastel," in *La Grande Encyclopédie* 26: 69–70.

12. Cordeiro, 1: 278; Soeiro de Brito, p. 72.

13. According to Ataíde Machado, 1: 262, in the latter half of the sixteenth century the cultivators of São Miguel were asked to plant no more than one-third of the cultivated areas with woad, because excessive use of land for woad threatened the food supply.

since the end of the sixteenth century. In 1620 a total of 46 ships imported or exported dutiable merchandise at the port of Ponta Delgada, including 35 ships that loaded the sum of 41,590 quintals of pastel, or the equivalent of 5,323,520 pounds of blue dyestuff.[14]

In 1620 the English took the lion's share of São Miguel dyestuff for use in coloring English textiles. During that year, 28 English ships carried away 26,981 quintals of pastel (or 64.9 percent of total pastel exports), 3 Dutch and Flemish ships loaded 8,018 quintals (or 19.3 percent), and 4 French ships took 6,591 quintals (or 15.8 percent). Only 3 ships loaded wheat, according to the customshouse records, and they took only 472 moios (or 11,328 bushels). Of the 46 ships calling at Ponta Delgada, 35 (or 69.5 percent) were British, and they brought in by far the greater share of the island's imports. The most valuable import, as was common in the Azorean trade, was cloth, and most of it came from England. In 1620 the island took in textiles to the amount of 2,523 *peças* ("pieces" or bolts), 12,308 *varas*, and 19,377 *covados.* The 12,308 varas and 19,377 covados add up to an equivalent of 28,658 yards of textiles.[15]

The Azorean islands and the English textile towns, in the early years of the seventeenth century, enjoyed a mutually beneficial trading relationship: the islanders bought English textiles, and the cloth manufacturers bought Azorean pastel. It was, of course, an unequal partnership, since the trade was far more important to the islands than to the English; the Atlantic islands were a small market, yet, for two or three English towns and ports, in the days when the Dutch offered relentless competition in all branches of maritime commerce, it was a market worth defending. Statistics for the port of Exeter in 1624 show that Exeter sent 10 ships to the Azores (8 of them to São Miguel), 8 to the Canary Islands, and 3 to Madeira (out of a total of 94 outward-bound ships) and that these ships carried to the islands 3,383 pieces of "Devon dozens," 237 of perpetuanas, 292 of "Barnstaple bays," 563 of "Dunsters," and 104 of "Taunton cottons" (which were really woolens).[16] Although France was far and away the most important market for Exeter textiles, more important than all other export markets combined, the statistics show that the islands were the second most important market in 1624 and that they absorbed more Exeter textiles than all of Spain. Also there were 152 ships which carried imports to Exeter in

14. Arq. Dist. Ponta Delgada, "Livros da Alfândega – Ano 1620."
15. Ibid. For information on these measures see Appendix III.
16. Stephens, pp. 10, 168.

TABLE 4

*Pastel Exports from São Miguel**

Year	Ships (Total)	Ships Loading Pastel	Pastel Loaded (quintals)
1620	46	35	41,590
1633	?	23	24,610
1639†	45	25	22,294
1640	31	10	8,731
1646	28	15	26,237
1648	31	13	14,338
1669	21	7	7,707
1676	56	3	2,817
1686	26	0	0
1694	18	0	0

*Compiled from Arq. Dist. Ponta Delgada, "Livros da Alfândega," Anos 1620, 1633, 1639, 1640, 1646, 1648, 1669, 1686, 1694.
† Partly estimated.

1624, of which 21 came from the Atlantic islands, including 13 from the Azores, 5 from Madeira, and 3 from the Canaries. The ships from the islands brought in 3,112 hundredweight of sugar, 302 tons of pastel (probably most of it from São Miguel), and 12 hundredweight of ginger.[17]

Unfortunately for the Azoreans the declining demand for pastel brought an end to the partnership with the English textile merchants. The available statistics for the port of Ponta Delgada show a dramatic decline in pastel exports, and then a slow death, until the trade was entirely extinguished (see table 4). Thus pastel exports from São Miguel shrank from a late sixteenth-century high of 60,000 quintals per year, to 40,000 quintals during the 1620s to below 25,000 during the 1630s, to below 20,000 in the 1640s, to below 10,000 in the 1660s, and finally to under 5,000 quintals per year in the 1670s.

The last reference to pastel exports comes in the customshouse records of 1685.[18] The 1686 customs registers do not mention pastel, and,

17. Ibid., pp. 168, 173.
18. Arq. Dist. Ponta Delgada, "Livros da Alfândega – Ano 1676." This register contains addenda, with a new foliation, with tax records for the years 1685-91: "Folha da Feitoria," fol. 3

TABLE 5

*Pastel Dyestuff Imported by Exeter**

Year	English Long Tons	Portuguese Quintals
1624	302	5,285
1636	111	1,942.5
1638	84	1,470
1647	25	437.5
1666	33	577.5
1676	0	0

*Adapted from W.B. Stephens, *Seventeenth-Century Exeter* (Exeter, 1958), pp. 173, 175–77.

unlike all previous registers, do not even have a special section devoted to recording pastel exports (instead there is a special place for recording wheat exports). There was also, of course, a steep decline in the price of pastel. At the end of the sixteenth century a Portuguese quintal of pastel sold at Ponta Delgada for about 1$200 réis; the highest price paid in the sixteenth century was said to have been 2$000 per quintal. In 1620 the average price for good quality pastel was $800 per quintal. By 1685 the price had fallen to $250. Since Portuguese currency was debased several times during the mid-seventeenth century, the ratio between the 1620 and the 1685 prices can be better understood if expressed in sterling: the 1620 price was equivalent to 12s. 4d. per quintal, and that of 1685 equivalent to 1s. 9d.

The available figures for Exeter imports of Azorean pastel complement the Ponta Delgada registers, and confirm the demise of the trade (see table 5). The Jesuit António Cordeiro, who lived at Terceira at the time of the collapse of the pastel business, wrote that the pastel trade was killed by the heavy taxes imposed by the king of Portugal.[19] The taxes were indeed heavy; Father Manuel Luís Maldonado, a contemporary of Cordeiro, said that the taxes imposed on pastel ran up to 28 percent.[20] First of all, 13 percent of all pastel was collected, in kind, at the source of production; then at dockside the customshouse collected another 13 percent, also in kind. On the amount actually loaded, a further 2 percent *ad valorem* duty was paid in money.

19. Cordeiro, 1: 279.
20. Sousa Lima, p. 65.

This means that when a manufacturer made 100 quintals of pastel, the treasury took 13 quintals, leaving 87 quintals to be exported; of the 87 quintals arriving at dockside, the customs took a further 13 percent, or 11.31 quintals, leaving the exporter with 75.69 quintals loaded aboard, on which he paid a further 2 percent money tax. The king's treasury and customs thus "confiscated" 24.31 percent of all pastel produced, or almost one-quarter, which was then sold at auction, chiefly to the merchant exporters.

This was the system of taxation in effect during the 1630s and later. In the 1620s taxation had been less onerous, for then the exporters merely declared, under oath, the total value of their pastel shipment and paid a 10 percent tax on that value, without losing part of their cargo. A more punitive system of taxation was imposed later, when pastel was already of declining importance. Thus the product that needed all possible support was, instead, penalized, once again confirming the self-defeating tendencies of Portuguese fiscal policy. As Cordeiro remarked about the extinction of the pastel trade, quoting a Spanish proverb, "Quien todo lo quiere, todo lo pierde"[21] (meaning, roughly, "He who goes after everything, loses everything").

Yet Cordeiro to the contrary, taxes did not kill the commerce in pastel; heavy taxes, of course, hurt the commerce, but even if all taxes had been removed, Azorean pastel could not have been saved. When the Spaniards brought over from the Americas large quantities of cheap indigo — a dyestuff that had been known and used since antiquity — nothing could have saved São Miguel's pastel. For the essential dye constituent of woad, *indigotin*, is chemically identical with the *indigotin* of indigo; but woad is an inefficient, low-yielding, and, compared with indigo, relatively expensive source for indigotin, while indigo is a more efficient, higher-yielding, and cheaper source. The fact that woad and indigo both produce blue or bluish dyes is somewhat unimportant; but the fact that their active ingredients were chemically similar meant that indigo would inevitably drive out woad. Different dyes bond differently with different textiles. A dye that works well with wool, may not bond with cotton or linen; one that holds fast to cotton fibers, may be useless for woolens; and so forth. Hence three or four dyes producing approximately the same color may all flourish together on the market, provided they are chemically different and each has a special use for a particular kind of textile. But if two dyestuffs producing the same color or colors are chemically identical, as are pastel and indigo, and are used for pre-

---

21. Cordeiro, 1: 279.

Chapter Five

TABLE 6

*Estimated Exportable Surplus of Wheat in
Five Azorean Islands in 1621**

Island	Moios	Bushels
São Miguel	3,500	84,000
Terceira	2,500	60,000
Graciosa	1,000	24,000
Fayal	800	19,200
Santa Maria	400	9,600
Total	8,200	196,800

*Adapted from Frédéric Mauro, *Le Portugal et l'Atlantique au XVIIe siècle* (Paris, 1960), p. 315.

cisely the same textiles, then the cheaper and more efficient dye will drive out the other.

Central American indigo shipments to Europe rose from an average of 21,529 pounds per year during 1577–88 to an average of 300,660 pounds per year during 1608–14. Shipments of indigo in 1620 ran to 451,800 pounds, and in 1643 to 1,250,660 pounds. At the same time the price of indigo fell from an average of 500 maravedís per pound in the 1580s, to 400 during 1606-16, and finally to only 150 in the 1630s.[22] In May 1651 it was reported that London had enough indigo on hand to meet all anticipated needs for the next five or six years.[23] Perhaps only the traditional attachment of certain English dyers to pastel enabled the Azoreans to continue to export small quantities of pastel until as late as 1685.

With the collapse of pastel, the inhabitants of São Miguel, in order to pay for essential imports, such as textiles and manufactures, had to develop other export staples. The most important alternative exports were wheat and linens. According to treasury estimates made in 1621, in years of good harvest, five islands were capable of exporting a total of nearly 200,000 bushels of wheat (see table 6). But that estimate came early in the century, at a time when much of the land in São Miguel (and some in Terceira) was turned over to pastel cultivation.

22. Huguette and Pierre Chaunu, *Séville et l'Atlantique,* 8 vols. (Paris, 1955–60), 6: 988–90, 1050–51.
23. Steckley, fol. 109.

92

TABLE 7

Wheat Production in the Azores in 1680*
(in moios)

Island	Production	Estimated Consumption (1/3 moio per head)	Surplus or (Deficit)
São Miguel	18,880	11,000	7,880
Terceira	10,850	8,000	2,850
Fayal	2,390	3,000	(–610)
Santa Maria	2,000 est.	800	1,200
Graciosa	1,630	1,800	(–170)
São Jorge	1,560	2,700	(–1,140)
Pico	1,230	1,200	30
Flores	1,000?	1,000	
Corvo	500?	160	340
Total	40,040	29,660	10,380[†]

*Arq. Dist. Évora, Codex CXIII/2–28, fols. 7–8. Santa Maria production estimate derived from Cordeiro, 1:169. Estimates of per capita consumption are based on population figures derived from Maldonado, fols. 270, 339, 341–42; and Cordeiro, 2:327–32.
[†] Net exportable surplus, with deficits subtracted.

Some sixty years later, in 1680, after the collapse of pastel, a calculation may be made of wheat production in all the islands, derived from tax records and other information (see table 7). The statistics for 1680 reveal three major exporters of wheat (São Miguel, Terceira, and Santa Maria), and one major importer (São Jorge), and this pattern can be shown to have been fairly constant throughout the century. Fayal evidently had a weak harvest in 1680, for Fayal was usually a small exporter. Graciosa, by 1680, had replaced wheat with barley and consequently was an exporter of barley and sometimes had to import small quantities of wheat. Not much is known about the exact amounts of wheat produced in Flores and Corvo, but Flores seems to have been usually self-sufficient, and Corvo was a small-scale exporter. Some Corvo wheat even went to Madeira.

The total São Miguel wheat production, in 1680, of 18,880 moios (453,120 bushels) was unusually high, representing 47 percent of the Azorean total, and indicated an exceptional yield of perhaps as much as

TABLE 8

Wheat Production in the Azores in 1701*
(in moios)

Island	Production	Estimated Consumption	Surplus or (Deficit)
São Miguel	13,234	11,000	2,234
Terceira	12,232	8,000	4,232
Fayal	3,053	3,000	53
Santa Maria	2,000?	800	1,200
São Jorge	1,645	2,700	(-1,055)
Pico	1,441	1,200	241
Graciosa	1,194	1,800	(-606)
Flores	1,000?	1,000	
Corvo	500?	160	340
Total	36,299	29,660	6,639[†]

*Calculated from statistics in *Archivo dos Açores,* 1:499.
[†] Net exportable surplus, with deficits subtracted.

25 or 30 bushels per acre. In 1680 São Miguel contributed 64 percent of the gross surplus, and 76 percent of the net Azorean exportable surplus. Normally a good harvest of São Miguel fell somewhat below 15,000 moios (360,000 bushels), and left less than 4,000 moios (96,000 bushels) available for export.

Estimates of Azorean wheat production for the year 1701 provide figures that can be compared with those for 1680 (see table 8). The 1701 estimates show the same three major exporters, and the same major importer, as the 1680 figures. Graciosa, with only 1,194 moios of wheat probably had to import some; in 1701 Graciosa produced 2,057 moios (49,368 bushels) of barley,[24] which had become its main crop. Fayal was self-supporting. As usual, not much was known about Flores and Corvo.

The 1701 figures for São Miguel show a 30 percent drop in production compared with 1680. São Miguel accounted for 36 percent of total production, 27 percent of the gross surplus, and 34 percent of the net Azorean surplus. Although São Miguel grew more wheat than Terceira, it had less to export, for its larger population consumed more of the

24. *Archivo dos Açores,* 1: 499.

TABLE 9

*Wheat Exports from São Miguel**

Year	Ships Loading Wheat	Wheat Cargoes (moios)	Average Price per moio	Estimated Value of Cargoes at Ponta Delgada Prices	
				Réis	£ Sterling
1620	3	472	6$000	2:832$000	2,175
1639[†]	19	2,505	6$000	15:030$000	11,530
1640	15	3,355.5	6$000	20:133$000	15,462
1646	8	2,145.5	6$000	12:873$000	6,436
1648	5	2,290.5	15$000	34:357$500	17,179
1669	9	1,867.5	6$600	12:325$500	4,314
1676	45	4,737.5	6$600	31:267$500	10,944
1686[†]	18	1,342	9$000	12:078$000	4,227
1694	9	2,687.5	8$580	23:058$750	7,686
Total	131	21,403	—	163:955$250	79,953
Average	15	2,377	7$753	18:217$250	8,883

*From the customs registers in Arq. Dist. Ponta Delgada.
[†] Includes estimates for certain missing months.

crop. This result is based on the assumption that the Azorean population consumed nearly 20 alqueires (8 bushels) of wheat per capita, per
year; although this is low in relation to the citizens of Lisbon, who may
have consumed 27 or 28 alqueires,[25] it may be too high an estimate for
the Azores, where among the peasantry, particularly those in São Miguel, maize was replacing wheat as the main item in the diet. Furthermore there is evidence that even in years of shortage and hunger, the
islands exported grain; for the wheat was exported shortly after the
autumn harvest, in large quantities, and by the time shortages developed
during the following winter and spring, it was too late. Legal attempts
to compel the storage of wheat, in quantities adequate for all future
needs, had little effect.

Customs registers give us a precise picture of São Miguel wheat exports to Madeira, Lisbon, and other distant places, during nine scattered
years of the seventeenth century (see table 9). From tax returns for
1640 it is even possible to estimate the wheat production of each of

25. Magalhães Godinho, 2: 351.

TABLE 10

São Miguel Wheat Production in 1640*

			Estimated Value	
District	Moios	(Bushels)	Réis	£ Sterling
1. Ribeira Grande	2,300	(55,200)	13:800$000	9,430
2. Relva to Ponta Delgada (west)	1,950	(46,800)	11:700$000	7,995
3. Rabo de Peixe to Fenais da Luz	1,710	(41,040)	10:260$000	7,011
4. Mosteiros to Feteira	1,210	(29,040)	7:260$000	4,961
5. Bretanha	1,150	(27,600)	6:900$000	4,715
6. Ponta Delgada (east) to (Rosto do Cão?)	1,140	(27,360)	6:840$000	4,674
7. Vila Franca do Campo	880	(21,120)	5:280$000	3,608
8. Achada to Fenais	750	(18,000)	4:500$000	3,075
9. Maia to Porto Formoso	620	(14,880)	3:720$000	2,542
10. Lagoa	605	(14,520)	3:630$000	2,481
11. Nordeste	600	(14,400)	3:600$000	2,460
12. Água de Pau	445	(10,680)	2:670$000	1,825
13. Povoação to Faial	440	(10,560)	2:640$000	1,804
Total	13,800	(331,200)	82:800$000	56,581

*Calculated from tax returns in the customs register for 1640 in the Arq. Dist. Ponta Delgada. The above estimated values are based on an average price of 6$000 réis per moio. The sterling equivalencies are calculated on the basis of 1$000 = 13s. 8d. (a ratio which, three years later, changed to 1$000 = 10s.).

thirteen districts in São Miguel (see table 10). Certain elements in table 9 require clarification. First of all, the table does not include any exports of wheat from São Miguel to other islands in the Azores; hence total exports were higher than indicated. Second, the "average price" per moio of wheat is an arbitrary determination, a conservative estimate, that gives a rough indication of overall values at Ponta Delgada. Real prices at Ponta Delgada varied enormously according to the season of the year, the age and quality of the wheat, and supply and demand. Third, because of the successive debasements of Portuguese silver coinage, the figures expressed in sterling equivalents are more useful than those in réis. For instance, the 1676 figure of 31:262$500, when compared with the 1640 figure of 20:133$000, shows an increase in the value of wheat shipments of 11:129$500; yet in terms of stable sterling currency, the actual value had declined by £4,518.

The figures do not show any very close correlation between the numbers of ships loading wheat and the amounts taken. The five ships loading in 1648 took more wheat than the nineteen ships loaded in 1639. The five ships of 1648 took an average of 458 moios each, while the forty-five ships of 1676 took only 105 moios each. The circumstances in 1648 were very special: the harvest of 1647 failed, both in Terceira and São Miguel, and wheat prices in January 1648 rose to 24$000 réis per moio. Terceira imported foodstuffs from Graciosa and elsewhere; and vessels from Madeira seeking wheat at São Miguel were turned away. On 27 June 1648 the chamber of Ponta Delgada forbade all export of wheat. No wheat left São Miguel until the middle of September, and then only probably because of direct orders from the king of Portugal, who commanded that supplies be sent to Lisbon and to the garrison towns in North Africa. Between 12 September and 8 October 1648 two ships loaded for North Africa and two for Lisbon; on 24 December a fifth ship loaded for North Africa. These ships took as much as they could and paid whatever they had to (estimated in the table at 15$000 per moio).[26] The island of Madeira was left to its own devices.

Small boats carried much wheat in the busy inter-island trade. São Jorge, and sometimes other islands, had to be supplied with wheat. Small islands with a surplus had to market their wheat in the larger islands. Graciosa sent her barley to Terceira, and Corvo made use of the port of Horta, in Fayal. Santa Maria, especially, with a large wheat crop (reputed to be the finest wheat in the Azores) was not regularly visited by ships in the international trade, and marketed much of her surplus through Ponta Delgada.

Santa Maria was a commercial satellite of São Miguel: Ponta Delgada was the marketing place for Santa Marian wheat, orchil dyestuff, pottery clays, earthenwares, and cheese; and from Ponta Delgada went the textiles and manufactures required in Santa Maria. In 1646 the small island had one *vila* (town), four *lugares* (villages), four parishes, and 2,373 inhabitants. The town of Vila do Porto boasted a Franciscan convent, a nunnery, and an *igreja matriz* (mother church) with a vicar and a curate (assisted by six other salaried persons) and 1,700 communi-

---

26. Francisco Ferreira Drummond, *Annaes da Ilha Terceira,* 4 vols. (Angra, 1850–64), 2: 95; Mauro, p. 317.

cants.[27] The town is built on a rise overlooking a small bay, where there is a cramped beach suitable for unloading small boats. There is no real harbor; ships must stand out about three-quarters of a mile offshore, exposed to every wind, anchored in 15 to 20 fathoms of water, with a good sandy bottom for holding. São Miguel, less than 44 nautical miles away, can be seen easily from Santa Maria, and contact between the two islands by way of sailing boats was a matter of hours.

Santa Marian wheat, although largely marketed through Ponta Delgada, does not seem to appear in the Ponta Delgada customs registers; presumably the customs were paid at Santa Maria. The wheat loaded at Ponta Delgada went primarily to Madeira, the Canaries, Portugal, and Portuguese North Africa; shipments to other places, such as France, the Netherlands, and England, were very rare. In times of scarcity the Portuguese government demanded that the needs of Lisbon, the capital, be given absolute priority over all other customers. Next to Lisbon, the requirements of the North African garrison towns, engaged in war with the Moors, must be met.

While the wheat trade enabled São Miguel, in part, to pay her way, the ordinary citizen of Ponta Delgada looked upon wheat exports with a jaundiced eye. The greater the quantity of wheat exported, the higher the price of bread. Too great a volume of wheat exports during the autumn might mean bread shortages during the following winter. Some serious bread riots took place on this island during the seventeenth century. In February 1643, during a shortage, when the caravel *São Boaventura* was taking on wheat for Lisbon, the populace of Ponta Delgada rioted and prevented further loading. The mob ripped open the sacks, spilled the wheat, dumped sacks in the sea, and stole or destroyed many bushels; with "stones, swords, weapons, and cudgels" they drove back the warehouse guards and committed "great madnesses and excesses."[28]

The bread revolts of March 1695, which swept the whole island, were more serious and had overtones of social revolution. On 21 March 1695 the populace rioted and forced the municipal government of Ponta Delgada to agree to sell wheat "forever" at a price of $120 per alqueire (equivalent to 7$200 per moio), instead of $200 per alqueire (equivalent to 12$000 per moio), which was the price then prevailing. The officials also agreed to sell maize to the "people" at not more than $080

27. Diogo das Chagas, p. 155; Monte Alverne, 1: 86–87; Cordeiro, 1: 143–46.
28. Sousa Lima, fol. 150.

per alqueire, and salt at no more than $080 per alqueire.[29] The movement for lower food prices quickly spread to other towns and villages. In Água de Pau a rebel leader, Manuel Pacheco, seized control of the town for one month. But the count of Ribeira Grande raised a force of *fidalgos* and retainers, moved into Água de Pau, and arrested Pacheco. One by one the revolts were crushed, but the unrest continued. The count agreed to ban all exports of wheat until the island's needs had been met; he agreed to hold 200 moios of wheat in reserve for emergencies; and set the price at $180 per alqueire.

In mid-July two frigates of the *Armada Real*, with two hundred soldiers, and a high judicial officer to conduct an investigation, arrived at Ponta Delgada. The rebels were punished and the people beaten into submission. The unfortunate islanders were even compelled to raise new taxes to pay for the expedition.[30]

The high prices of the 1690s caught the people by surprise and they rebelled, but the merchants saw the matter in a different light. For decades the prices of Azorean wheat had been depressed in relation to the prices which had prevailed during the first half of the century. Wheat had been a very poor business during the 1660s, 1670s, and 1680s, and the international commerce of Ponta Delgada had suffered because of it. The debasement of the Portuguese coinage, in part, concealed the drop in prices, particularly from the ignorant. The wheat that sold at 9$000 per moio (equivalent to £3 3s.) in the 1690s was actually cheaper than the wheat that had sold at 6$000 (equivalent to £4 12s. 3d.) in the 1630s. The movement toward higher prices during the years 1690–1709 was a partial return to the stable and firm price levels that had prevailed, much of the time, during the period 1600–1640.

The introduction of American corn relieved the lower classes from their dependence on wheat. The maize plant fared well on the island's volcanic soils and tolerated the rain and dampness better than the wheat. By the end of the century, maize and yams fed the peasantry, while wheat was a cash crop destined for the townspeople and for export. Maize was also exported in small quantities to Madeira. The first maize exports show up in the customs register of 1676, which indicates shipments amounting to 77 moios (1,848 bushels). In 1686, 478 moios and

29. Monte Alverne, 2: 437–38; Julião Soares de Azevedo, "Os Açores e o comércio do Norte no final do séc. XVII," *Boletim do Arq. Dist. Angra,* 2 (1952–53): 33–34.

30. Monte Alverne, 2: 438.

51 alqueires (11,492 bushels) were exported; but the register for 1694 shows only a trivial total of 4 moios and 20 alqueires (104 bushels) of maize cargoes.

Other foodstuffs were exported in small amounts. Broad beans (*favas*) appear in every register from 1640 onward, with the maximum recorded exports of 32 moios and 38 alqueires (783 bushels) coming in 1676. Tiny quantities of island-grown sugar were shipped in 1640, 1646, and 1669. Barley is seen first in the 1646 register and appears in every subsequent register, but in small amounts, the maximum being 67.5 moios (1,620 bushels) in 1669. The island also shipped out pork products, including salted pork, salted hog carcasses, and sides of bacon; a total of 321 sides of bacon appears in the 1686 register. Lastly, wheat was sometimes exported as flour – most curiously in May 1676, when three English ships bound for Newfoundland took on small quantities. Richard Huchenson supplied the *Felicity* with 3 moios of flour, John Stone sold another 3 moios to the *Gift*, and William Chamberlin shipped 3.5 moios aboard the pinnace *John.* These three ships, thus supplied by three different English merchants of Ponta Delgada, proceeded to Fayal, there to pick up Pico wines before continuing to the Newfoundland fisheries.[31]

São Miguel's exports of foodstuffs, other than wheat, although curiously varied, were economically insignificant. After the disappearance of pastel, flax products, next to wheat, provided the only export staple. São Miguel flax was exported in the following ways: (1) as *pedras de linho* or linen fiber after hackling (that is, after being separated, combed, disentangled, and smoothed, with the aid of a spiked board called a "rougher"), sold in sheaves of dressed flax weighing eight pounds each; (2) as low-quality tow cloth (*pano de estopa*), made from short or broken fibers; (3) as common linen cloth (*pano de linho ordinário*); (4) as good quality cloth for napkins (*pano de guardanapos*); and (5) as fine quality linen for tablecloths (*pano de toalhas de mesa*). Other products derived from the flax plant – such as linen thread, linseeds, and linseed oil – were exported only in negligible quantities.

The busy town of Ribeira Grande was the center of the linen industry, as well as the chief marketing point for wheat and broad beans. In 1646 the town had 4,624 inhabitants, including 40 shoemakers, 30 tailors, 2 surgeons, 1 physician, and 1 apothecary. The town is said to have produced 5,000 *pedras de linho* per year – that is, the equivalent of

---

31. Arq. Dist. Ponta Delgada, "Livros da Alfândega – Ano 1676," fol. 61.

TABLE 11

São Miguel Exports of Flax Fibers and Tow Cloth*

Year	Flax Fibers (pedras de linho)	Tow Cloth (varas)
1639	500	0
1640	979	394
1646	40	0
1648	243	424
1669	26	0
1676	0	2,228
1686	53.5	38
1694	5	4,820
Total	1,846.5	7,904
Average per year	231	988
Total in English measures	14,772 lbs.	9,465 yards
Average per year in English measures	1,848 lbs.	1,183 yards

*Based on customs registers in Arq. Dist. Ponta Delgada.

40,000 pounds in dressed flax fibers — which kept over two hundred male weavers busy at their looms making the various kinds of linen textiles. The annual income from linens came to over 16:000$000 réis (£8,000). Ribeira Grande is situated on the rugged north coast, on cliffs overlooking the sea, and it has no harbor. Its communications with other towns, particularly with the port of Ponta Delgada, were by horse and mule. In the 1640s, according to eyewitness accounts, one hundred pack animals arrived, and one hundred left, every day, carrying merchandise.[32]

The extant customs registers show the levels of export of flax fibers and tow cloth (see table 11). Flax fibers and tow cloth were commodities of limited value, with little profit potential; far more profitable were the exports of quality linens (see table 12).

32. Diogo das Chagas, p. 192.

TABLE 12
São Miguel Linen Exports*
(in varas)

Year	Common Linen Cloth	Cloth for Napkins	Cloth for Tablecloths
1639	1,000	0	0
1640	9,944	0	0
1646	6,486	28	24
1648	4,415	50	24
1669	5,936	899	635
1676	2,189	364	141
1686[†]	2,304	107	91
1694	16,189	661	4,282
Total	48,463	2,109	5,197
Average per year	6,058	264	650
Total in English measures	58,034 yards	2,526 yards	6,223 yards
Average per year in English measures	7,254 yards	316 yards	778 yards

*Based on customs registers in Arq. Dist. Ponta Delgada.
[†] Includes estimates for three missing months.

The 1639–40 export figures show that these two years account for over 80 percent of the shipments of flax fibers, a low-profit item, while no high-grade napkin and tablecloth linens were exported at that time. Linen-cloth exports were a fairly modest enterprise until about the year 1694; judging from eight random years of statistics, the linen export business did not come into its own until the last decade of the century. In tables 11 and 12 the year 1694, surprisingly, accounts for 32 percent of the eight-year total of exports of cloth for napkins, for 34 percent of the exports of common linen, for 61 percent of tow-cloth exports, and for an astonishing 83 percent of the high-grade linen tablecloth exports.

For purposes of estimating taxes to be paid, the customshouse of Ponta Delgada set a standard evaluation for each of the different types of linen. These evaluations suffered very little change during the period

TABLE 13

The Value of São Miguel Linen Exports
(Eight Scattered Years Combined)*

Type of Cloth	Varas	Yards	Per Vara	Total
Tow cloth	7,904	9,465	$050	395$200
Ordinary cloth	47,887	57,345	$085	4:070$395
Napkin cloth	2,082	2,493	$100	208$200
Table cloth	5,174	6,196	$250	1:293$000
Total	63,047	75,499	–	5:967$295

*Based on customs registers in Arq. Dist. Ponta Delgada.

1640–94 and were set at what seems to have been a very low rate. The customs officers evaluated tow cloth at $050 réis per vara (about 3.5d. per yard). Ordinary linen cloth was set at $070 per vara, but a higher grade of the same cloth (*pano curado*, or "cured" cloth) went for $100 per vara. Cloth for napkins was set at $100 per vara (about 7d. per yard). Linen for tablecloths was set at $250 per vara (about 1s. 6d. per yard). Flax fiber was set at $500 for each *pedra de linho* (about 3s. for 8 lbs.).

At these very low customshouse rates the value of the total linen exports from São Miguel, during the eight years for which there are registers, is unimpressive. The total amount of linen-cloth exports, and their value as determined by the customshouse price levels, can be seen in table 13. The sum of 5:967$295 réis, which expresses the complete value of the cloth trade, in customshouse terms, for a period of eight scattered years, is equivalent to only £2,089 in sterling (at the exchange rates prevailing during 1668–1700).

The number of ships which loaded linens was very small (see table 14). The chief market for São Miguel linens was in Portugal, and the second important market was in Madeira and the Canaries. Ships carrying linens to Portugal, Madeira, and the Canaries made up 70 percent of the total number of ships engaged in this traffic. The English, for a while, interested themselves in exporting linens to England, but there were no exports in that direction recorded before 1646 or after 1669. Exports to other places were fortuitous and negligible. It is probably true to say that, outside of the Canaries, where the merchants could push the linens as an adjunct to the Azorean wheat shipments, and outside the protected

TABLE 14

Ships in the São Miguel Linen Trade*

Destination	1639	1640	1646	1648	1669	1676	1686	1694	Total
Portugal	1	5	1	1	2	0	7	2	19
England	0	0	4	3	2	0	0	0	9
Madeira	0	0	1	1	1	0	1	3	7
Canaries	1	1	0	0	2	0	0	3	7
Newfoundland	0	0	0	0	0	1	1	0	2
North Africa	0	0	0	1	0	0	0	0	1
Brazil	0	0	0	1	0	0	0	0	1
France	0	0	0	0	0	1	0	0	1
Total	2	6	6	7	7	2	9	8	47

*Based on customs registers in Arq. Dist. Ponta Delgada.

TABLE 15

São Miguel Shipments of Pastel, Wheat, and Linens

Year	Ships Loading Pastel	Ships Loading Wheat	Ships Loading Linens	Total
1620	35	3	0	38
1639	25*	19*	2	46*
1640	10	15	6	31
1646	15	8	6	29
1648	13	5	7	25
1669	7	9	7	23
1676	3	45	2	50
1686	0	18*	9	27*
1694	0	9	8	17
Total	108	131	47	286

*Estimated.

markets within the Portuguese domains, the linens of São Miguel could not compete with the old and well-established linen centers of Europe, located in the Lowlands, Scotland, Ireland, France, and elsewhere.

In the overall pattern of São Miguel trade during the seventeenth century, linens ran a poor third behind pastel and wheat in numbers of shipments (see table 15).

Over the course of the century, the island's trade suffered strong dislocations. Originally, during the first decades of the century, São Miguel was closely linked to England, to English textiles, and to English shipping. In 1620 more than a dozen English merchants lived at Ponta Delgada and busied themselves with the exchange of pastel for English textiles and manufactures. Among the names filling the pages of the customs registers of 1620 were John Ellis, Richard Langford, Thomas Precost, William Ray, Henry Walker, and others. The decline of the pastel trade undermined the position of the English, although not very quickly, for the decline was gradual. In 1640 there were still a dozen English merchants at Ponta Delgada, including Matthew Goodwin, Philip Palgrave, Robert Potter, John Searchfield, and Christopher Williams, but they had begun to shift the direction of their ventures. English ships still came to São Miguel, but now half of them left, not for England with pastel, but for Madeira and the Canaries with wheat, as the Englishmen tried to compensate for their pastel losses by engaging heavily in inter-island commerce.

The people of São Miguel grew wheat where they had grown woad, tried to augment their trade with Madeira and the Canaries, attempted to push other products, such as broad beans, and entertained hopes of a bright future for their linens, particularly in Portuguese markets. But Portugal's revolt against Spain, on 1 December 1640, and the quarter-of-a-century of war which followed, killed the trade with the Canaries, while the pastel commerce, instead of recovering from its slump, nearly disappeared after the 1650s. The English merchant community at Ponta Delgada slowly dwindled. The customs register for 1669 seems to contain the names of only seven English residents — John Chamberlin, William Chamberlin, Peter Goodwin, Richard Huchenson, John Stone, Christopher Williams, and one other of uncertain name — and of these it should be mentioned that Williams and the two Chamberlins were well-entrenched English Catholics, very Portuguese in manner, with Portuguese wives and close associations with the best families of São Miguel, while Huchenson served as factor for the king of Portugal[33] and was a lifelong resident (1638–77?) of the Azores.

Only ten English ships called at Ponta Delgada during 1669. The customs register of 1676 seems to promise a renewal of extensive trading activities by the English in São Miguel, for forty-two English ships touched at Ponta Delgada in 1676. But a close look reveals that few of these ships came directly from England, and only three of them took Azorean products back to England; almost all were consigned to Madeira and the Canaries. São Miguel's trade with Europe (apart from Portugal) was in a state of collapse; of the fifty-six ships listed on the records, only five were bound for European ports, while 41 were bound for Madeira or the Canaries.

The final customs registers, for 1686 and 1694, show much change and considerable decline. The resident English merchants numbered, perhaps, no more than three: John Chamberlin, Samuel Hoper, and John Stone — and of these, Chamberlin died in 1694, and Stone sometime before, leaving only Hoper, who was the English vice consul and spent much of his time in Terceira.[34] The level of shipping had dropped

33. *Archivo dos Açores,* 8: 176–79.

34. Ernesto do Canto and Carlos Machado, "Livro de genealogias" (manuscript in Arq. Dist. Ponta Delgada), p. 66; Arq. Dist. Ponta Delgada, "Livros de Alfândega — Ano 1676" (which contains a section written in Chamberlain's own hand,

to almost one-half, with only eighteen ships per year. Only six English ships called at Ponta Delgada in 1686, and only three in 1694. But eleven French ships came in during both those years, and for the first time in the century the French became more important than the English in the commerce of São Miguel.

During the 1690s, the French merchants Christophe Bressan, Jean Bressan, and Bernard Fartoat (French consul) transacted more business than the English. In spite of this, the French ventures were not very promising. For the French ships brought from Lisbon a miscellany of manufactured items, all of them re-exports, with a few standard Portuguese products (salt, spices, olive oil) as well, and then loaded mostly wheat, consigned to Madeira, Lisbon, and the Canaries. The catalog of miscellaneous articles exported from São Miguel in 1694 seems to indicate a frantic search for negotiable commodities. The long and curious list includes (besides wheat and linens) bacon, salted pork, salted hog carcasses, barley, maize, broad beans, linseed oil, vinegar, São Miguel wine, re-exported Pico wine, brandy, biscuits, sumac, and tallow candles — but all in small quantities. The one bright spot in the picture was the export of linen, which seemed to be gaining ground in Portugal.

An overview of the international maritime commerce of São Miguel is presented in tables 16, 17, and 18. The customshouse records reveal little of the intra-Azorean commerce, which was very important to São Miguel; the charts *do* show some of the movements of foreign ships between São Miguel and Terceira, but none of the movements of Azorean vessels, which were far more significant. Portuguese shipping is also underrepresented in the customs registers; the ships that Ponta Delgada sent to Brazil, at least one per year, do not figure in the registers. Nondutiable cargoes, particularly those loaded to the account of the king of Portugal, were seldom mentioned.

The foreign trade of São Miguel, nonetheless, is accurately mirrored in the customshouse books; and the transactions in which foreign merchants took part are minutely described. The last two registers show a noticeable decline in the island's maritime commerce, and the replacement of English influence by French influence. Yet the position of English and French in São Miguel at the end of the century was not representative of the balance of commercial forces between the two in the Azores as a whole. In the very year 1686, when only six English ships

---

for he was the royal *feitor*); "1686," fol. 1; Arq. Dist. Angra, Câmara de Angra, Registo Geral, Livro no. III, fols. 339–40; Sousa Lima, fol. 205.

TABLE 16
Number and Nationality of Ships at São Miguel*

Nationality	1620	1639†	1640	1646	1648	1669	1676	1686†	1694	Total
British	32	23	25	19	16	10	42	6	3	176
French	4	0	0	2	3	1	7	11	11	39
Dutch/Flemish	4	0	0	4	8	7	1	1	2	27
Portuguese	6	3	2	3	3	3	2	0	0	22
Spanish	0	0	1	0	0	0	4	0	2	7
Hamburger	0	1	1	1	1	0	0	0	0	4
Unidentified	0	1	3	0	0	0	0	0	0	4
Total	46	28†	32	29	31	21	56	18†	18	279

*Based on customs registers in Arq. Dist. Ponta Delgada.
† Slightly incomplete.

TABLE 17

Provenance of Ships Arriving at São Miguel*

Place of Origin	1620	1639[†]	1640	1646	1648	1669	1676	1686[†]	1694	Total
England	20	13	10	12	6	3	0	3	1	68
Portugal	6	0	6	7	7	2	1	7	5	41
Canaries	5	3	2	0	0	5	16	0	2	33
Madeira	3	1	1	2	1	0	3	3	2	16
Terceira	3	0	4	3	4	0	0	0	0	14
Netherlands	0	0	0	2	5	2	0	0	2	11
France	2	0	0	1	0	0	2	0	4	9
New England	0	0	0	1	1	1	1	0	0	4
Fayal	0	0	2	0	0	0	0	0	0	2
North Africa	0	0	0	0	2	0	0	0	0	2
Spain	0	0	1	0	1	0	0	0	0	2
Brazil	0	0	0	0	0	2	0	0	0	2
Santa Maria	0	0	0	0	1	0	0	0	0	1
Unrecorded	7	11	6	1	3	6	33	5	2	74
Total	46	28[†]	32	29	31	21	56	18[†]	18	279

*Based on customs registers in Arq. Dist. Ponta Delgada.
[†] Slightly incomplete.

TABLE 18

Destination of Ships Departing from São Miguel*

Destination	1620	1639†	1640	1646	1648	1669	1676	1686†	1694	Total
England	28	16	11	13	7	4	3	0	2	84
Canaries	2	3	6	0	0	7	27	0	3	48
Madeira	1	4	3	2	2	1	14	3	4	34
Portugal	0	2	6	2	2	2	0	10	3	27
Netherlands	2	0	0	2	4	4	1	0	0	13
North Africa	0	1	0	3	3	0	1	0	0	8
France	4	0	0	0	0	0	2	0	2	8
Terceira	0	0	1	2	4	0	0	0	0	7
Newfoundland	0	0	0	0	0	0	4	1	0	5
Santa Maria	0	0	0	0	1	0	0	0	0	1
Brazil	0	0	0	0	1	0	0	0	0	1
Barbados	0	0	0	0	0	0	1	0	0	1
Unrecorded	9	2	5	5	7	3	3	4	4	42
Total	46	28†	32	29	31	21	56	18†	18	279

*Based on customs registers in Arq. Dist. Ponta Delgada.
†Slightly incomplete.

touched at Ponta Delgada, the French consul at Fayal, Jean d'Harriague, wrote a report from Horta saying that only a few French ships called at Fayal in the course of a year, while the English sent 70 or 80 ships a year to load Pico wines for the Americas.[35]

The truth was that, during the last decades of the century, the port of Horta in Fayal was the great entrepôt for Anglo-Portuguese commerce in the Azores, while São Miguel became a backwater. The island of São Miguel, although the largest and most populous in the Azores, suffered from her geographical position. Within the archipelago, São Miguel was too far east to be the normal center of political, military, and ecclesiastical authority in the islands. Terceira, well placed in the middle of the group, asserted a natural leadership. The bishop of the Azores, to the eternal mortification of Ponta Delgada, had, and still has, his see at Angra on Terceira; the largest military garrison in the Azores was also at Angra (to the great relief of the taxpayers of São Miguel); and the king's ships from India, on their return voyage, were refitted at Angra, not at Ponta Delgada.

In addition, São Miguel was far from the normal routes of shipping going from the Americas to Europe. The logical stopping place for ships outward bound from the Americas was the port of Horta, the only safe anchorage in all the Azores. Even the little island of Flores was more frequently visited by ships on transatlantic crossings than was São Miguel. In these circumstances São Miguel had to have a coveted product — one that would draw the ships and merchants from far and wide. In the eighteenth century, oranges were the coveted product that drew the traders to the island.

Despite the disadvantages of location, and the bewildering fluctuations of maritime trade, the island had certain reliable assets. First, São Miguel was self-supporting in foodstuffs. In Madeira, and in other islands, a loss of trade could result in hunger for the people, but in São Miguel it might only cause a shortage of luxuries. Second, the island produced its own linen, a serviceable textile with many uses; lack of English woolens and cottons would not mean that the people had to go about naked or in rags. Third, the island could always ship foodstuffs to São Jorge and Pico, which lacked grains, and could exploit promising commercial opportunities within the Azores group itself. Today São Miguel pays its way, in part, by selling tea, beer, cigarettes, bricks, tiles, ceramics, and dairy produce to its sister islands.

35. Soares de Azevedo, 2: 31–32.

In the seventeenth century São Miguel had very little to do with trans-atlantic commerce, in the strict sense; the island's commercial relations were with Europe, Africa, and the other islands. Within that sphere, after the collapse of the pastel trade, the island's role was small. Fortunately for the islanders, São Miguel was a storehouse of food, and they could survive, fairly comfortably, with only a modest level of international trading activity.

6
Terceira, the Heart of the Azores

São Miguel and Santa Maria, neighboring islands visible to each other, live in their own world, somewhat aside from the major shipping routes, like a planet and its satellite on a distant course. To the northwest, 74 miles from São Miguel, out of sight beyond the horizon, lies the island of Terceira, São Miguel's chief rival in the Azores. Terceira is an oval-shaped island, not much more than half the size of São Miguel, with a population today of only 78,000 people, less than half that of São Miguel.

Terceira, of simple name, the "Third" island (formerly "The Third Island of Our Lord Jesus Christ" — Ilha Terceira do Nosso Senhor Jesus Cristo), today lags behind São Miguel in population, wealth, industrialization, commerce, agricultural production, and in harbor facilities, but in the past it has overshadowed São Miguel in political, military, and ecclesiastical importance, as the logical geographical capital of the archipelago. Its chief town, Angra do Heroísmo, today a quaint place with 17,000 residents, contains elaborate monuments of its past greatness. Its common people, who enjoy a little more prosperity and comfort than do the downtrodden peasants of São Miguel,[1] consider themselves superior to the inhabitants of São Miguel and think of their island as by far the more fortunate of the two.

---

1. About the unfortunate peasantry of São Miguel, Soeiro de Brito had this to say (p. 169): "The great majority of the population own no goods; their standard of living is very low, and most of these people live without hygiene and without comfort, in cramped houses, poorly fed and poorly dressed, always uncertain about what tomorrow will bring, for during the last fifty years things have only become worse."

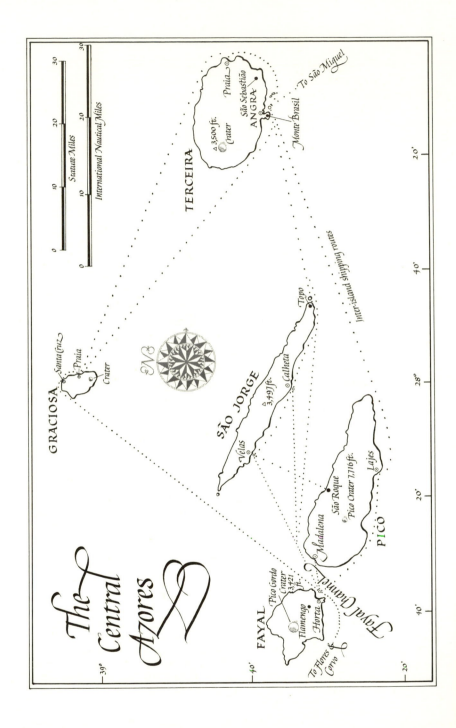

The Central Azores

Statute Miles
International Nautical Miles

GRACIOSA
Santa Cruz
Praia
Crater

TERCEIRA
Praia
São Sebastião
ANGRA
△ 3,500 ft. Crater
Monte Brasil
To São Miguel

SÃO JORGE
Topo
Calheta
3,491 ft.
Velas

Inter-island shipping routes

FAYAL
Pico Gordo Crater 3,421 ft.
Flamengo
Horta
To Flores & Corvo

Fayal Channel

PICO
Madalena
São Roque
Pico Crater 7,716 ft.
Lajes

39°
40'
28°
20'
40'
20'
40'
20'

Historically, through the centuries, Terceira has been the scene of some major political events, as a battleground where kings of Portugal have been made and unmade. It was at Terceira that Prince António, Prior of Crato, failed at last to make good his claim to the Portuguese crown (1580–83), and lost to the ships and men of the all-conquering Philip II. Philip, angered by the opposition of the Terceirans, built an enormous fortress outside Angra to overawe the town, assert control over the islands, and give himself a point of strength in the mid-Atlantic from which to support the Spanish silver ships. The fortress of St. Philip mounted 160 guns, had high walls of over 3,000 feet in length, cut off the peninsula separating Angra from Monte Brasil, and enclosed two hills and many acres of land containing ample supplies of water. In the somewhat ungrammatical words of a seventeenth-century Azorean: "In all of Europe there is not known to exist a fortress more unconquerable."[2]

When John IV led the revolt against Spain in December 1640, the first serious military conflict with the Spaniards took place, not in Portugal, but in Terceira. On 26 March 1641 the fortress of St. Philip opened fire on the town of Angra and the Spanish garrison was placed under siege. After eleven months and eleven days of siege, "unconquerable" or not, the fortress surrendered. King John, in gratitude, conferred on Angra the title of "Sempre Leal" (Ever Loyal), and the name of the fortress was changed to St. John the Baptist.[3]

2. "Não se sabe haver em toda a Europa Fortaleza mais inconquistavel," Cordeiro, 2: 39. The fullest history of Terceira is in the four-volume *Annaes da Ilha Terceira* by Drummond, who relied heavily on the unpublished manuscript "Fénix Angrense" (1710), by Manuel Luís Maldonado (b. Terceira 1645, d. 1711). Drummond's account does not supersede the "Fénix Angrense," which remains the best source for, and the best general narrative of, seventeenth-century Terceiran history. Alfredo da Silva Sampaio's *Memória sobre a Ilha Terceira* (Angra, 1904) is a compendium of information about the island, in all its aspects, with a historical summary (pp. 405–826). Campos de Azevedo Soares's *Nobiliário da Ilha Terceira*, a three-volume genealogical compilation, has the best general bibliography on Terceira (1: 20–28; 3: 17–24), listing some two hundred titles. There are also two periodicals, which appear very irregularly, that are of interest to historians: *Boletim do Instituto Histórico da Ilha Terceira* (published at Angra since 1943); and the *Boletim do Arq. Dist. Angra* (published at Angra since 1949). The defunct *Archivo dos Açores*, although primarily concerned with São Miguel, also has much information about Terceira.

3. Maldonado, section on years 1641–42, fols. 242–95. Drummond, 2: 1–71; Miguel Cristóvam de Araujo, "A Restauração na Ilha Terceira," *Boletim do Instituto Histórico da Ilha Terceira* 6 (1948): 38–116.

Some twenty-seven years later, Afonso VI, titular king of Portugal but ousted from power by his brother Prince Pedro, spent five years (1669–74) as a prisoner in the great fortress at Angra. Rumors that the Terceirans were becoming over fond of their imprisoned king, and were forming a party in his favor, induced Prince Pedro to bring his brother back to Portugal. Terceira was too dangerous a place for a prisoner of such high rank.[4]

Terceira had to wait another century and a half before the next royal visit and one final involvement with the high politics of Portugal. In the interim, in 1766, under the reformist regime of the marquis of Pombal, civil administration was "rationalized"; the antiquated, semifeudal privileges of the proprietary lords (*donatários*) and their captains were abolished; and the islands ceased to be autonomous captaincies but were all incorporated into a single captaincy-general (*Capitania Geral*), with headquarters at Angra. To the reformers in Lisbon, the creation of a single authority in the Azores appeared to be a logical step, but it went against the strong historical and psychological individualism of the islands. To the inhabitants of São Miguel and Fayal, in particular, it was intolerable to be under the control of a government located in Terceira.

During the 1820s, Terceira was again involved in the making and unmaking of kings. The island rallied to the cause of Pedro IV, ex-emperor of Brazil and leader of the liberal-constitutional forces in the struggle with his brother, Dom Miguel, titular king of Portugal and head of the ultraroyalist "Miguelistas." In 1829 the liberals won an important victory over the Miguelistas at Vila da Praia. In 1832 Pedro himself arrived in the Azores and made Terceira his headquarters, and thus Angra, for an all too brief season (from March until June 1832), could claim to be the de facto capital of the Portuguese Empire.[5]

From the Azores, Pedro IV sailed with an expedition to Portugal, and eventually drove Dom Miguel out of the kingdom. After peace had been reestablished, the simply and aptly named town of Praia (Beach; it is located on the only fair stretch of sandy beach in the Azores), scene of

---

4. Maldonado, who served as chaplain at the fortress of São João, left the best account of Afonso VI's imprisonment at Terceira; his clinical description of the pathological behavior of the unfortunate king, although largely unpublished, is especially valuable; "Fénix Angrense," sections on years 1669–74, fols. 239–55. The general circumstances involving Afonso VI are set forth in Peres, *História de Portugal* 6: 108–18.

5. Peres, *História de Portugal* 7: 189–91.

the catastrophic defeat of the Miguelistas, was renamed Praia da Vitória (Victory Beach) and graced with the title Muito Notável (Most Notable). The equally simply named Angra (meaning "bay" or "anchorage") was given the title of Sempre Constante (Ever Constant), to add to its Sempre Leal (Ever Loyal), and pretentiously renamed Angra do Heroísmo (Bay of Heroism). And lastly, Dom Pedro's chief servant, António José de Sousa, marquis of Vila Flor, was honored with the new title of duke of Terceira.

These inflated titles that were applied to the new duchy of Terceira — with plain Praia becoming "victorious" and "notable," and simple Angra becoming "heroic" and "ever constant" — coincided with an actual decline in the island's political influence. In 1832 the sixty-six-year-old captaincy-general was abolished by Pedro IV. In 1836 the civil administration of the Azores was reorganized into three districts, with three coequal and autonomous capitals at Angra, Ponta Delgada, and Horta. The District of Angra included Graciosa and São Jorge; that of Ponta Delgada included Santa Maria; and that of Horta all the remaining islands (Fayal, Pico, Flores, and Corvo). The new system, which is still in effect, was more in accord with historical, economic, and psychological realities.

In the seventeenth century Angra was a slightly more populous, and a much more prestigious city, than Ponta Delgada, and probably, after the collapse of the pastel trade, a busier port, although the island of Terceira, as a whole, was less populous, less productive, and less wealthy than São Miguel. Angra, although founded later than Ponta Delgada, was always a step ahead. In 1478 Angra became an official *vila*, but Ponta Delgada had to wait until 1499. In 1533 Angra became an official *cidade*, while Ponta Delgada did not attain this status until 1546. Most important of all, in 1533, Angra acquired a bishop, a cathedral chapter and staff, and became the ecclesiastical headquarters of the Azores.

The building of the cathedral was begun in 1570 and not completed until 1700, and the total cost, according to contemporary estimates, ran to over 200,000 cruzados (about £40,000). At the end of the seventeenth century the cathedral staff of eighty persons included a dean, an archdeacon, several chaplains, twelve canons, four demi-prebendaries, a music director, and so forth, all the way down to altar boys, a bell ringer, and a man in charge of the church clock. The cathedral enjoyed an income of 711 moios (17,064 bushels) of wheat, paid in kind from the treasury wheat receipts, plus money amounting to 1:303$421 réis; at 10$000 per moio the wheat was worth 7:110$000, making a total income of 8:413$421 (about £2,700 in 1700).[6]

The Jesuits of Angra began building a church and college in 1637 to replace an older structure, and they evidently set out to exceed the cathedral in size and magnificence. The Jesuit college is an enormous and expensive building, its magnitude only partly concealed by a severe façade, done in the "Jesuit style." The Franciscans, not to be outdone, erected a huge convent during the years 1666–80. The Jesuits, who moved into their new college in 1651, kept making additions to it during the rest of the century. Furthermore, there were four other religious houses, including the enormous cloisters of São Gonçalo, with 179 residents, and the large nunnery of Esperança, with 90 Franciscan nuns and 60 other inmates.[7] Thus it happens that the small town of Angra contains architectural monuments whose size, grandeur, and artistry would be a credit to some cities in Europe with twenty times the population of Angra.

The total number of ecclesiastics and of people living in religious houses was 655 in 1700. The town had 2,162 householders, and 8,829 persons (apart from those in the religious houses, babes in arms, and foreigners). The total population was probably over 11,000.[8] The large and expensive religious institutions, containing consumers but not producers, created a heavy demand for goods and services, and for financial support. All the islands contributed, directly or indirectly, to the maintenance of the bishop and the cathedral chapter. Otherwise, most of the burden fell on the citizens of Terceira, who also had the great expense of supporting the garrison at the fortress of São João.

The small oval bay at Angra, formed by the protrusion of the volcanic mass of Monte Brasil into the sea, is only 700 yards wide at the mouth and only about 800 yards long. Superficially, it might look like an excellent harbor, but unfortunately the bay itself is extremely shallow, with rough water, and is nearly useless for shipping. Sailing ships of any size rarely even entered the Bay of Angra: just as the steamers and motor ships do today, the sailing vessels would drop anchor in 10 to 12 fathoms, at the mouth of the bay or slightly outside it. The anchorage has a sandy bottom with good holding ground, but all ships so anchored

6. Cordeiro, 2: 48–57; Maldonado, section called "Epitome da Ilha Terceira," fols. 114–17.

7. Ibid.

8. Cordeiro, 2: 21–23, 328; Maldonado, "Epitome," fols. 114, 117.

were exposed to winds from the south, southeast, and east. Unfortunately the southeast wind represented a mortal peril for sailing ships, turning the bay itself into a cul-de-sac from which no escape was possible. Cables cast ashore on both sides, at the foot of Monte Brasil and on the Angra side, together with sheet anchors, could sometimes save a sailing ship in an emergency, but cables over one thousand feet long were required, and the procedure was expensive, time-consuming, and troublesome, and often there was not enough warning.

The other alternative was to stay over a mile out, fully exposed to wind and sea, in 30 to 35 fathoms, with uncertain holding ground. The lighters which unloaded the ships found excellent shelter, along with other small craft, in a shallow inlet known as the Porto das Pipas, where a finger of land extending into the bay formed a natural breakwater. At the Porto das Pipas there was a shipbuilding yard for the construction of boats and of larger vessels of up to about 150 tons.

A deadly southeast wind, known as the *Carpinteiro* (Carpenter), often sprang up without much warning; masters would slip their cables and scramble frantically to get out of the harbor. A few hundred yards to windward lay salvation, but clawing off the headland of Monte Brasil was a difficult job, and sometimes two hundred yards might just as well have been two hundred miles. A common result was shipwreck, although usually all the men, and often much of the cargo, were saved. The Bay of Angra was a graveyard for many sailing ships.[9]

From the top of Monte Brasil, 585 feet high, lookouts could watch a wide expanse of sea and could discern the low shadow of the island of São Jorge, with the great mountain mass of Pico looming on the horizon. At the approach of a ship, signal flags from Monte Brasil would inform the town, often hours ahead of the vessel's arrival.[10] Once an-

9. Cordeiro, 2: 40; Edward Boid, *Description of the Azores* (London, 1835), p. 225. Boid, a sea captain who visited the islands in 1831-32, said that 5 or 6 vessels were lost at Angra every year and that, in the Azorean ports (p. 39), "all vessels are obliged to weigh and stand out immediately the wind sets on the land." Boid said that anywhere from 700 to 900 ships were engaged in the Azorean trade in the 1830s, but that they were almost all small vessels, and, indeed, had to be small, "on account of the total absence of any thing like a sheltered port or safe harbour." Maldonado has many details about ships lost at Angra and elsewhere in the Azores. On 12 February 1648, for instance, four ships were washed ashore at Angra in a storm (year 1648, fol. 148). Chaunu, 7: 122, lists 53 Spanish ships lost in the Azores during 1550-1650, including 30 lost at or near Terceira.

10. Emanuel Félix, *Angra no último quartel do século XVI* (Angra, 1970), p. 1, said that flag signals from Monte Brasil indicated whether a vessel was approach-

chored, ships were directly under the guns of Fort São Sebastião, a harbor fortification across the bay from the São João fortress. Foreign masters often found it irksome to have their ships under the control of the harbor, and, for that reason, many preferred the port of Ponta Delgada on São Miguel, where they could sail away at will.

The second port in Terceira was at Praia, on the eastern side of the island. Praia was an old town, an official *vila*, the head of a captaincy that embraced half the island (the other half was under the captaincy of Angra), and at one time had rivaled Angra in size and importance. By the end of the seventeenth century, Vila da Praia had fallen far behind and had only about 2,600 inhabitants, although it was still a fairly busy port, and maintained a royal customshouse with five officers. The port at Praia was no better than an open roadstead, exposed to all winds except westerlies and southwesterlies. At Praia there is a long curving beach of fine sand, forming a shallow half-moon, bounded by promontories at both ends, and about one and a half miles long. Sailing ships anchored 2,500 yards offshore, in 10 fathoms of water, with a sandy bottom; if the weather was uncertain, masters might choose to drop anchor twice as far offshore, in 20 fathoms, but there the bottom was rocky and the holding ground poor. The anchorage was fairly safe, except in storms and when there was an east wind. Even with the wind due east, there was more leeway than at Angra, and, for a weatherly ship, the chances of successfully clawing off the lee shore, to the north or south, were reasonably good.

After Angra and Praia, the most important settlement, officially at least, was the old and historic inland town of São Sebastião, which was legally a *vila*. In addition, there were sixteen villages on the island, none of them of any consequence. The population of Terceira about the year 1700 probably totaled over 21,000 persons, of whom one-half lived at Angra or in its vicinity.

The commercial history of Terceira, judging only by appearances, has mimicked that of São Miguel. When São Miguel made pastel, Terceira made pastel; when São Miguel grew oranges, Terceira grew oranges; when São Miguel traded in salted pork, so did Terceira. But usually Terceira, when trading in the same products, has come in a poor second to São Miguel in volume of production and value of exports. Yet the similarities in appearance were superficial, and the differences in the patterns of shipping, and in general commercial orientation, were fundamental.

---

ing from the east or the west, and an especially large flag was used if five or more ships were sighted at the same time.

First of all, Angra, far more than Ponta Delgada, had a brisk entrepôt trade with the other islands, bringing in, for instance, wine from Pico, wheat from Fayal, and barley from Graciosa, and exchanging these commodities for English and French textiles and manufactures and Portuguese olive oil and salt. Second, Angra was a normal port of call for Portuguese East Indiamen on their homeward journey; and the sugar ships homeward-bound from Brazil sometimes stopped at Angra as well. (Neither the East Indiamen nor the Brazilmen ever went to São Miguel, except in the most unusual circumstances.) Third, where São Miguel grew flax and traded in linens, Terceira grew grapes and attempted, usually unsuccessfully, to market its own wines. Lastly, Terceira depended on wheat as its one staple export to an extent not true of São Miguel, where other exports were preferred.

Angra's busy, inter-island entrepôt trade was conducted mostly, although not exclusively, in small boats. Just as Santa Maria was a satellite of São Miguel, so the island of Graciosa was commercially subordinate to Terceira. Graciosa is about 31 nautical miles west-northwest of Terceira; the distance from Angra to the port of Santa Cruz, Graciosa, by the shortest sea route, is about 48 nautical miles — a sail of from ten to twenty hours in favorable weather. Graciosa does not have the high forbidding cliffs that surround the other islands; its appearance from the sea is soft and pleasant. As the Scottish lady Janet Schaw remarked, while on a journey from Edinburgh to Antigua in 1774, Graciosa "deserves its name, for never did my eyes behold so beautiful a spot."[11]

Graciosa is only about 23.5 square miles in area, but since almost all of the soil was put to use for cultivation and pasturage, the island could support a considerable population and still produce a surplus for export. Today Graciosa has 8,760 inhabitants, or 373 persons per square mile; but at the close of the seventeenth century there were already 5,620 inhabitants, or 239 per square mile. It had two *vilas* — Santa Cruz and Praia — one village, four parishes, and one Franciscan convent. The capital, Santa Cruz, is well laid out and spacious, and it suggests a larger and more populous place than it actually is. In 1700 it had about 600 *vizinhos* (householders), with possibly 2,400 persons, and some thought it was worthy of being made a *cidade.* Its port was a dangerous, exposed roadstead, with a rocky bottom. The port of Praia was not much better.[12]

11. Janet Schaw, *Journal of a Lady of Quality,* 2d ed. (New Haven, Conn., 1934), p. 61.
12. Maldonado, year 1690, fol. 341; Cordeiro, 2: 246, 328; Boid, pp. 251–52.

Graciosa is much drier than the other islands, has never had any for-ests, and lacks streams. The inhabitants had to collect rainwater for their own use; fortunately there is a large volcanic cone that served as a nat-ural catchment basin. The island was critically short of wood and fuel; the peasants saved the chaff from the wheat, after it had been threshed, to use for fuel. During the course of the seventeenth century, barley replaced wheat as the leading crop. At the beginning of the century, wheat was much more important; during the middle decades of the cen-tury, wheat and barley were grown in equal amounts; by the year 1701, tax returns indicate that the taxable crop of wheat amounted to 1,192 moios (28,608 bushels), while the barley crop, at 2,020 moios (48,480 bushels) was nearly 70 percent larger.[13]

The barley crop rose progressively from 1,130 moios in 1682, to 1,456 moios in 1694, to over 2,000 moios in the first years of the 1700s. In barley production, with a crop of over 50,000 bushels at the turn of the century, Graciosa had no real rival in the Azores; São Miguel exported only a little, and Terceira even less. For their own consumption, the islanders raised fruits and vegetables, and kept cattle, hogs, and chickens. Father Manuel Luís Maldonado (1645–1711) of Terceira, who ought to have known, said that fresh meat was so abundant at Graciosa that it sold for $020 réis for 2 arratéis (about 3 English farthings per pound of meat).[14]

In the Azores barley sold at about half the price of wheat. In 1677, when wheat cost 8$400 per moio at Angra, barley went for about 4$400.[15] Graciosan barley and wheat was usually sent to Angra in small boats, and re-exported from there. For example, in September 1677, a Genoese ship, quaintly named "Noah's Ark" (*Arca de Noé*) in Portu-guese; *l'Arca di Noè* in Italian), arrived at Angra with orders from the Prince-Regent Dom Pedro commanding the lading of 450 moios (10,800

13. Sousa Lima, fols. 156–57; Maldonado, year 1690, fol. 341.

14. Maldonado, year 1690, fol. 341. Meat was cheap in the cattle-rich Azores; in 1648, even after the failure of the wheat harvest of 1647 brought pressure on food prices, meat sold at Horta for $015 réis per arratel, or about 2¼d. per pound; see António Lourenço da Silveira Macedo, *História das quatro ilhas,* 3 vols. (Horta, 1871), 1: 165.

15. Maldonado, year 1661, fol. 188. At customshouse auctions at Angra in 1668 and 1669, Graciosa barley went for 2$500 réis per moio, and for 2$750 in 1670, while wheat sold for between 6$000 and 8$000; Arq. Dist. Angra, Capitania Geral, Livro no. 238, fols. 33–34, 40–41, 52. But the customshouse barley may have been old barley, and auction bids were often artificially low, because of col-lusion among the merchants.

bushels) of wheat and 200 moios (4,800 bushels) of barley for Lisbon, to the account of the royal treasury; the comptroller of the treasury at Angra immediately dispatched five boats to Graciosa to pick up the barley.[16]

Occasionally Graciosa participated directly in the European trade, without the help of Terceira. In 1601, for instance, the caravel *Nossa Senhora da Boa Viagem* loaded 60 moios (1,440 bushels) of wheat at Santa Cruz, Graciosa, and took it to Viana do Castelo in Portugal. The *Nossa Senhora da Guia,* in 1616, picked up twice that quantity of wheat and barley, directly at Graciosa, in a shipment consigned for Lisbon.[17] The usual pattern, nonetheless, was for Graciosan exports (and imports) to be transshipped at Angra, thus contributing to the volume of business transacted at the Terceiran capital.

The Terceirans also maintained boat traffic with the islands of São Jorge, Pico, and Fayal. Porto das Velas, principal town and harbor in the long, cigar-shaped island of São Jorge, is 53 nautical miles from Angra by the shortest sea route. Velas, which is only 21 nautical miles from Horta, the leading port in the Azores at the end of the seventeenth century, maintained much more frequent commercial contacts with Horta than with Angra, but Angra, nonetheless, was an important secondary market for the wines of São Jorge, and from Angra, São Jorge received products sent from Lisbon, such as salt, olives, olive oil, Portuguese haberdashery, and earthenware. São Jorge also imported wheat directly from Terceira.

Boats from Angra also went to the dangerous little anchorage at Lajes, on the island of Pico, to pick up wines. Pico's most intensive commercial relations were, of course, with its inseparable "twin," the island of Fayal, which, at the closest point across the Fayal Channel, is only 3.25 nautical miles away. But Pico also kept up, through Lajes, communication with Angra, which is 55 nautical miles away by the shortest sea route, and imported wheat from Terceira and São Miguel.

The single most important inter-island trading route, other than the one-hour ferry passage from Horta to Madalena across the Fayal Channel, ran between Horta and Angra. Horta, with its busy transatlantic commerce, was the emporium for goods from North America, the West

16. The boats came back with only 185 moios of barley, but the ship could not wait for more, and was sent back to Portugal; Maldonado, year 1661, fols. 188–89. The Lisbon government treated barley as a strategic commodity, for it was used to feed the king's cavalry horses; Magalhães Godinho, 2: 286.

17. Sousa Lima, fols. 108–9.

Indies, Brazil, and the East. From Horta the Terceirans could acquire Newfoundland salted codfish, New England fish oil and lumber, Brazilian sugar and tobacco, and, occasionally, Asian spices, silks, porcelain, and other luxury goods. From Angra to Horta went European textiles and manufactures, Portuguese produce, foodstuffs, and an endless parade of officials. The distance between Angra and Horta, by the shortest sea route, is 70 nautical miles; in theory, a good sailer could have covered that distance in fourteen hours or less, but, in practice, the passage sometimes took a whole week.

The small-boat traffic with the various islands probably contributed as much to the volume of business at Angra as the large ships from foreign ports, but without the large ships there would have been much less for the small boats to carry. The largest and most interesting ships that called at Angra regularly were the Portuguese East Indiamen. The great Portuguese galleons and carracks in the India trade, sometimes running up to 2,000 tons, usually arrived at the Azores in very poor condition. Portugal's trade with the East, a royal monopoly encrusted with obsolete traditions and crippled by built-in inefficiencies, was conducted with reckless improvidence. Carracks left Goa in unseaworthy condition, having been negligently cleaned and serviced, critically overloaded, with too many people and too few supplies, and under the command of incompetent personnel. Many were lost on the voyage, particularly in the vicinity of the Cape of Good Hope. As the great ships neared the Azores, often crippled by storms and with half the crew dead and the rest at the extremity of their strength, they were set upon by pirates and privateers. Quick assistance from the islanders was their only hope of salvation.

The king of Portugal maintained at Angra an official, known as the *Provedor das Naus da India* (Purveyor to the India Ships), whose special responsibility was the protection, the repairing, and the supplying of ships from India. For this purpose the treasury at Angra kept a warehouse with naval stores, weapons, munitions, and provisions. The *provedor* was empowered to buy supplies in the king's name, to hire Azoreans to serve as soldiers and sailors aboard the East Indiamen, and to charter other ships, whether Portuguese or foreign, to supply the Indiamen with an armed escort while on their passage to Lisbon. Another official, a "guardian" of the India ships, was stationed at Horta in Fayal, and his task was to provide emergency assistance to the Indiamen when they were first sighted off the Azores, to supply them with immediate essentials, and to speed them on their way to Angra with whatever reinforcements and escorts he could muster. Indiamen were not encouraged to linger too long in the Fayal Channel, because pirates and privateers had been known to seize ships while they lay at anchor before Horta, since the straits were open and difficult to police from the shore.

The procedures for assisting the richly laden ships from India can be illustrated by what happened in 1649. On 14 July 1649, at 6:00 p.m., a ship's longboat pulled in at Horta with a letter for the captain-major of Fayal. The letter had been written the previous day by Gasper Pereira dos Reis, captain of the *Santo André*, informing the Fayal authorities of the approach of his galleon from India. The galleon had left India on 19 January 1647 — thirty months before her appearance at Horta — in the company of the galleons *São João Baptista* and *Sacramento* and of the carrack *Atalaia*. The *Atalaia* and *Sacramento* were both wrecked near the Cape of Good Hope, and the other two ships retired to Mozambique. On resuming the journey, the *Santo André* became separated from the *São João Baptista*, which finally put in at Bahia, where she spent sixteen months. As was characteristic of the Portuguese Indiamen of that day, out of four great ships, only one reached European waters, and she was not destined to get to Portugal.[18]

As soon as Horta received word of the approach of the galleon, a dispatch boat was sent to Angra. Since privateers had been sighted off the Azores, there was considerable apprehension about the safety of the East Indiaman. At Horta, the authorities chartered a Dutch ship of fourteen guns and an English vessel with eight guns as makeshift escorts for the galleon, which anchored off Horta while awaiting help from Angra. At Terceira, the *provedor* João do Canto e Castro chartered a three-hundred-ton English ship from London with twenty guns and went aboard her himself as commander of the expedition. He also chartered two French vessels with eight guns apiece. The three ships sailed from Angra on 1 August and reached Horta on 3 August. The Dutch and English vessels at Horta were then added to the squadron, and the five foreign escort vessels convoyed the East Indiaman from Horta to Angra, in a slow, troublesome, ten-day journey, plagued by headwinds.[19] Two or three privateers, probably Zeelanders or Dunkirkers, circled the convoy but dared not attack.

At Angra the officials decided to unload the twenty-six-year-old galleon, because of danger from the weather. The unloading of the rich

18. Maldonado, year 1649, fols. 149–50.
19. Ibid., fols. 150–51.

cargo of cinnamon at Angra was a direct violation of royal decrees and was permissible only on grounds of urgent necessity.[20] On this occasion, Lisbon gave retroactive approval to the unloading, even though it was painfully aware that Eastern cargoes mysteriously diminished when landed at unscheduled ports. The treasury at Lisbon chartered two large, well-gunned English ships and sent them to Angra, along with two fighting ships from the *Armada Real.* One of the king's ships was sunk by a privateer, with the loss of almost ninety men, but the other three reached Angra at the end of November 1649.

The cinnamon cargo was then divided into three parts and carefully loaded aboard the galleon and the two English ships, in equal amounts. The ships sailed at a late hour on 15 December. The two English ships and the Portuguese man-of-war safely entered the Tagus on 1 January 1650, but the galleon dropped anchor outside the river, and was forced to put to sea again when a storm blew up. The winter storm raged fiercely, the galleon was old and unseaworthy, and the master felt he had no alternative but to seek shelter in the rias of Galicia. He made for the ria at Vigo, where the Spaniards, at war with Portugal, seized ship and cargo. Thus the galleon was lost, but two-thirds of the cargo had been brought to Lisbon in the English ships.[21]

The support given the East Indiamen in the Azores was an important factor in the preservation of Portugal's maritime connections with the East. British, Dutch, and French East Indiamen had not the use of any such convenient base in the mid-Atlantic. Except for a certain amount of smuggling that may have occurred, however, the visits of the East Indiamen were of little commercial importance to the Azores, since the Eastern cargoes, by law, had all to be brought to Lisbon. Eastern spices were then reimported into the Azores from Portugal. Moreover, the Portuguese Eastern trade declined greatly by the end of the seventeenth century, when pinnaces, advice boats, and other small vessels often replaced the gigantic carracks and galleons of former years. These ships, and probably some of the foreign East Indiamen as well, brought in carved ivories, Chinese porcelains, and other *objets d'art,* which can still

20. The officials had to draw up a formal report, justifying the unloading, in the course of which they cited precedents for their action, including the unloading of the galleons *Batalha* at Angra in 1629 and *São Felipe* in 1630. The cargoes were afterwards reloaded, and both these ships were safely convoyed to Lisbon. Maldonado, year 1649, fols. 151–52; an inventory of the *Santo André*'s cargo is on fols. 153–54. Discussed also in Drummond, 2: 100–101.

21. Maldonado, year 1649, fols. 154–55.

be found in rich collections in the Azores. And artistic influences from Luso-India affected furniture design in the islands.[22]

From an economic standpoint, the relationship between the islands and Brazil was more significant than their relations with the East. In the seventeenth century Brazil imported wines, flour, olive oil, salted codfish, textiles, and manufactures; it exported primarily sugar (making up 90 percent of the value of total exports, and most of the sugar was high-quality, well-refined white sugar), followed distantly by brazilwood (for its red dye), hides, and tobacco. The Azoreans sent Pico wines, São Miguel and Terceira flour, and Newfoundland codfish to Brazil and brought back sugar. The Brazilian sugar trade — until the West Indian competition began to take its toll in the 1660s and 1670s — occupied between 80 and 120 ships every year, of which some 8 to 12 ships were Madeiran-owned, and some 6 to 10 were Azorean-owned.

In 1649 the monopolistic General Company of the State of Brazil (*Companhia Geral do Estado do Brasil*) was founded, with exclusive rights over the shipping of wines, olive oil, flour, and salted fish to Brazil and with a monopoly on the extraction of brazilwood, which had formerly been a royal monopoly. Moreover a convoy system was formed (shipping losses to Dutch and Dunkirker privateers had been enormous), and merchants had to send their ships out with the Brazil Company's annual or semiannual fleets and return in convoy, paying a convoy fee (*avaria*) to the company for the protection afforded by its warships.[23]

The merchants of the Azores and Madeira were allowed seven months in which to buy shares in the company. The company's monopoly over wines, flour, and salted fish affected the staples in the Azorean trade with Brazil; and the requirement of sailing in convoy meant that Azorean vessels had to go to Brazil by way of Lisbon, depart only at the times specified by the company's directors, and pay extra for the "privilege." The Madeiran and Azorean merchants wanted to be exempted from these restrictions but were not listened to. Some of the island merchants may have joined the company and shipped their products through

22. Eastern objects can be found in the public museums at Angra and Ponta Delgada. Francisco Ernesto de Oliveira Martins, an avid collector of antiques and of painting and sculpture, has a remarkable private collection at Angra, with many objects of Asian origin.

23. There is a full-length study of the Brazil Company by Gustavo de Freitas, "Companhia Geral do Comércio do Brasil," *Revista de História* 2 (São Paulo, 1951): 307–28; 3 (1951): 85–110, 313–44.

it, but there is not much information on this point; at any event, offi-cials in the islands continued to complain about the Brazil Company.

In Terceira, on 6 November 1652, the municipal chambers of Angra, Praia, and São Sebastião held a joint meeting and decided to send a rep-resentative to Lisbon to protest the company's monopoly over the sup-ply of flour and wine to Brazil.[24] By that time King John IV was ready to listen to the islanders: a royal decree of 19 November 1652 permitted Madeira to send two ships, and the Azores three ships, to Brazil every year with flour and wine, outside of the Brazil Company, but in the company's convoys.[25] The Azores, however, were not supposed to send more than 400 pipes of wine or more than 2,000 arrobas (64,000 lbs.) of flour.

This decree of exemption created a class of ships known as the *navios do privilégio* (ships of the privilege). The decree allowed the Azores to send three ships per year, without specifying what islands could send what ships; but as interpreted at Angra, politically powerful Terceira allocated two ships to itself, one to São Miguel, and none at all to Fayal and Pico. Pico wine (whose port of outlet was Horta), nonetheless, was the most important single commodity in the Brazil-bound cargoes, but had to be transshipped to Angra, and sometimes to Ponta Delgada, by small boats. Horta was left out in the cold until 1670, when a decree dated 4 June permitted Fayal to send one ship with wines to Brazil every year,[26] thus bringing to four the annual number of *navios do privi-légio*. In that year, 1670, with Portugal at peace with all her old enemies, the irksome restriction concerning sailing in convoys, particularly in connection with the return voyage from Brazil, was lifted, and the is-land ships could sail to Brazil when they pleased.[27]

Some extant records of shipping licenses for the *navios do privilégio* for the years 1671-77, after which records become fragmentary and intermittent, indicate that Terceira, and probably the other islands as well, took the fullest advantage of the exemptions granted by the decree

24. Arq. Dist. Angra, Câmara de Angra, Registo Geral, Livro III, fols. 24–25.
25. Ibid., fol. 30; Sousa Lima, fols. 126–27; Drummond, 2: 121.
26. Silveira Macedo, 1: 416–17.
27. Long before 1670, the convoy system from Portugal to Brazil had broken down, although convoys on the return voyage were kept up until the end of the Spanish war in 1668. Upon petition, shipmasters were routinely exempted from sailing in convoy on the outward journey, although Lisbon usually insisted that ships sail in squadrons of four, five, or six vessels. The decree of free navigation in 1670 simply made it unnecessary for shipowners to petition for special licenses.

of 1652. The ships employed in the trade were sometimes Azorean-built vessels, but more often were ships purchased from Dutch and English owners. They ranged in size from 130 to 200 tons, although a few were larger.[28] If maximum use was made of the trading privileges, then the Azores sent out three ships per year during the period 1653–70, and four per year during 1671–99, making a total of 170 ships sent to Brazil during the years 1653–99. Any other direct trading with Brazil must have taken place through the Brazil Company, and its extent and volume is not known.

There was also indirect trading with Brazil, which was sometimes considerable and at other times negligible. First there were the *navios derrotados* (derouted ships) – Brazilmen bound for Lisbon that were "forced" to unload their sugar at Horta or Angra because of stress of weather or some other reason. Second, there were occasionally Brazilmen which stopped at Azorean ports while on their way home to Portugal. The most dramatic stopover came in 1656, when a huge fleet of 107 sugar ships, under the command of Captain-General Francisco de Brito Freire, spent twenty-seven days at Angra, 4 June to 1 July, thereby driving up food prices in Terceira.[29] The circumstances of this visit were very special: a powerful fleet from Cromwellian England menaced the port of

---

28. The names of the Terceiran *navios do privilégio*, insofar as they are known, run as follows: the 200-ton flyboat *São Miguel* (made the voyage to Brazil in 1670), formerly an English ship; the 140-ton flyboat *São José* (1670 and 1671), formerly Dutch; the 140-ton flyboat *Nossa Senhora do Rosário e São Francisco* (1671), formerly Dutch; the 300-ton *nau* (large ship) *Nossa Senhora de Penha de França* (1672), formerly Dutch; the pinnace *Jesús, Maria, José* (1672, 1673, and 1674), built at Terceira; the 125-ton *Santa Helena* (1673); the 130-ton *São Francisco Xavier* (1674), formerly Dutch; the flyboat *Nossa Senhora da Penha de França e São Francisco Xavier* (1675); the Terceiran-built, 100-ton *Nossa Senhora da Esperança e Santo António* (1675); the *Santa Catarina* (1676); the 300-ton *nau Corpo Santo e Almas* (1676); the Terceiran-built pinnace *Santo António e Almas* (1677); the 100-ton pinnace *São João e Almas* (1677); the *Nossa Senhora do Pilar* (1678); the *Espírito Santo e Almas* (1681); the *Jesús, Maria, José* (1694); the flyboat *Nossa Senhora da Conceição* (1694); the flyboat *Jesús, Maria, José* (1696, 1697, and 1700), formerly English; and the *Santo António de Flores* (1699). Extracted from the records of the Angra *câmara* in the Arq. Dist. Angra, by Sousa Lima, fols. 130–33. See Soares de Azevedo, "Relações comerciais da Ilha Terceira com o Brasil no século XVII," *Boletim do Instituto Histórico da Ilha Terceira* 4 (1946): 39–64, with the texts of official documents.

29. Francisco de Brito Freire, *Relação da viagem que fez ao Estado do Brazil a armada da Cõpanhia, anno 1655* (Lisbon, 1657); Maldonado, year 1656, fols. 169–70; Drummond, 2: 130–31.

Lisbon, and Brito Freire was detained at Angra until the coast of Portugal was clear.

Official policy discouraged Brazilmen from stopping in the Azores or Madeira when on the return voyage. At times commanders were instructed to avoid even coming within sight of the islands. Since Azorean harbors were dangerous and unreliable, Azorean seas often stormy, and the whole area swarming with European privateers and Moroccan pirates, the Lisbon authorities had plausible reasons for thus denying the islanders a more active role in the lucrative Portugal-Brazil trade. But the most important reason was fiscal: by forcing all ships to leave from Lisbon and return to Lisbon, without visiting ports of call en route, the king of Portugal made certain that the royal customshouse of Lisbon squeezed the maximum amount of revenue out of the Brazilmen.

Official restrictions, however, were not always observed. In June 1663 no fewer than eleven ships unloaded four thousand chests of sugar at Angra. This is an enormous amount of sugar, probably equivalent to over three million pounds and was obviously intended for re-export. Customs duties on these cargoes came to 42:000$000 réis (£21,000), a very large sum; Lisbon may have compelled the Terceiran officials to remit most of this money to Portugal.[30] Toward the end of the century, the rules governing the Brazilian trade seem to have been more strictly enforced. Father Maldonado, writing during the period 1705–10, remarked that no Brazilmen had visited Angra for over twenty years.[31]

In the direct trade between the Azores and Brazil, the most important article exported from the islands was wine. The Brazilian settlements consumed prodigious quantities of wine from Portugal, Madeira, and the Azores — and, indeed, were officially encouraged to do so, since the tariff on wine imports was the principal means of raising revenue to pay for the large garrisons that fought off Dutch and French invaders, and the Indians. The Azorean wine sent to Brazil was probably almost always from Pico or São Jorge. Many of the islands produced at least a little wine, but most of it was not of good enough quality to sell on the international market. In general quality of the wines produced, the islands ranked roughly as follows: (1) Pico, (2) São Jorge, (3) Graciosa, (4) Terceira, (5) Fayal, and (6) São Miguel. Only Pico wine — known in the Americas as "Fayal wine" — and São Jorge wine were of an acceptable international standard.

30. Maldonado, year 1664, fol. 219.
31. Ibid.

According to records from the city of Angra for the year 1693, the taverns sold 1,463 oversized Azorean pipes of wine (Angra pipes contained 495 liters of wine, or the equivalent of 130 English wine gallons, instead of the standard Lisbon pipe measure of 477 liters, equivalent to 126 gallons) at the rate of $050 réis per canada (or 11$250 per pipe), and collected a total sum of 16:458$750 (£5,280). In addition, it was claimed that the landed proprietors, great houses, convents, etc., consumed another 1,500 pipes or more, making for a total consumption on the island of 3,000 pipes per year.[32] Exports from Angra were said to run at a level of 2,000 pipes per year. If all of this wine came from Terceira, then the island produced 5,000 pipes per year; but one suspects that almost all the exports, and some of the wine consumed at Angra, was Pico wine. The landed proprietors and the inmates of the wealthier and more worldly convents probably drank something better than the Terceiran product.[33]

Wine was grown at Terceira, as in Pico, under conditions of great adversity; indeed, one wonders why the Azoreans troubled to grow grape vines at all. The wetness and coolness of the climate, the relentless wind, and the salt from the sea spray make the Azores unsuitable for grape cultivation. Nonetheless the grapes are still raised, surrounded by walls for protection and warmth and growing virtually from the bare rock of lava flows known as *biscoitos*. Seemingly with little need for ordinary soil, the plant draws its sustenance directly from the crumbly black rocks, and the rocks grow warm in the heat of the sun and help to keep the vines warm. The walls are usually built in squares (in Terceira), or else arranged in semicircles (especially at Pico), and are very close together, creating an intricate patchwork quilt of tiny vineyards. In Pico this curious system produced a unique and distinctive wine which was

32. Sousa Lima, fols. 170–71; *Arquivo dos Açores* 4: 134.

33. The judgment of the quality of wine is a subjective matter, complicated by local pride; and there are not lacking local boosters who affirm that Terceiran wine is one of the world's excellent beverages. Yet travelers seldom thought highly of Terceira wine, and Portuguese ships taking on wine for the *Armada Real* always insisted on obtaining Pico and São Jorge wines (Arq. Dist. Angra, Livros da Capitania Geral, Livro 118, fol. 19). The *câmara* at Praia, and probably that of Angra as well, distinguished between *vinhos da terra* (Terceiran wines), to be sold in taverns at $040 réis per canada, and outside wines, to be sold at $050 per canada; see Drummond, 2: 223. The action of the Praia chamber proves that Terceirans drank imported wines, probably from Pico and São Jorge, and hints that those who could afford them preferred them.

TABLE 19

Estimated Wheat Production in Terceira

Year	Moios	Bushels
1634	8,020	192,480
1635	8,259	198,216
1636	8,025	192,600
1637	7,797	187,128
1638	7,562	181,488
1639	7,929	190,296
1640	7,949	190,776
1641	8,093	194,232
1642	10,249	245,976
1643	13,360	320,640
1652	7,864	188,736
1656	13,277	318,648
1664*	13,223	317,352
1665*	13,223	317,352
1666*	13,223	317,352
1667*	13,223	317,352
1680	10,850	260,400
1693	12,952	310,848
1701	12,232	293,568
Total	197,310	4,735,440
Annual		
Average	10,385	249,234

*Total figures for four years (1664–67) converted into annual averages.

once widely esteemed. In Terceira the lava-cultivated grapes made beverages that have never been more than of local interest.

Despite the efforts of the Terceirans to boost their wines, wine remained of minor importance in the sea trade of Angra. The one indispensable and reliable Terceiran export was wheat. On the basis of tax returns, estimates may be made of the annual production of wheat at Terceira (see table 19).[34] These figures, calculated by multiplying treas-

34. Arq. Dist. Angra, Livros da Capitania Geral, Livro 118, fols. 29–30, 41–42, 144–45, 162, 284, and Câmara de Angra, Registo Geral, Livro III, fol. 337; Sousa Lima, fols. 112–13; Silva Sampaio, p. 346; Arq. Dist. Évora, Codex CXIII/2–28, fols. 7–8.

ury wheat receipts by a factor of ten, represent minimum production estimates; actual production was certainly greater, by perhaps as much as 20 percent. The total production of wheat at Terceira during the seventeenth century may have come to about 1,250,000 moios, or 30 million bushels.

The volume of wheat exports from Terceira probably came to between 1,000 and 6,000 moios per year, depending on the harvest. The annual yield seems to have increased from a level of about 9,000 moios during the 1630s, to an average figure of over 14,000 after the midcentury. This increase of 5,000 moios, unaccompanied by any such dramatic increase in the number of Terceiran consumers, must have meant that substantially greater amounts of wheat were available for export.

The consumers of Terceira, like those of São Miguel, did not favor a high level of wheat exports, because of the effect on food prices. The interests of the ordinary townsmen and of the merchant exporters were in conflict. After a chorus of complaints from Azoreans at the end of the sixteenth century, a royal letter issued by King Philip III of Spain on 22 May 1603 decreed that royal officials, in every island, should see to it that no wheat whatever was exported until three needs had been fully satisfied: (1) the needs of military garrisons, especially the large Spanish garrison at Fort St. Philip in Angra; (2) the needs of the inhabitants of the island; and (3) the agriculturalists' needs for seeds for replanting.[35] In order to allow enough time for accurate estimates to be made of the requirements of the population, no wheat was to be exported, not even from one island to another, for a period of three months after the harvest.

The inconvenience and impracticality of this measure angered the merchants. It would mean that even bumper crops of wheat would have to be stored for three months before being sold. This would have been awkward and expensive, raising costs for the merchants while possibly lowering the prices (three-month-old wheat might sell for less than fresh wheat). Moreover, the three-month delay would mean that ships would have to wait until late in the year for their ladings, picking up cargoes in the winter, when Azorean seas were at their stormiest.

The municipal chambers of the Azores immediately suggested that reserves of wheat, fully adequate to all anticipated needs, could be set aside during a one-month period, from 15 July to 15 August every year, and that after 15 August wheat should be exported freely.[36] The crown

35. Drummond, 1: 411–12.
36. Ibid.

officials gave way under the pressure of the municipal chambers and came up with a face-saving formula which permitted the chambers, between the dates of 15 July and 20 August of each year, to set a flexible time period during which exports would be forbidden and during which the size of the harvest could be determined and the necessary reserves of wheat set aside. In practice, the new procedures probably resulted in no improvement over the old.

There were years, of course, when the Terceira harvest failed. In 1648, for instance, Terceira had to import wheat; and in the mid-1690s, there were shortages and high prices, leading to public riots.[37] Yet, as a general rule, wheat was the most abundant agricultural commodity in Terceira, and the most important export, both in volume and in value.

The international trade of Angra, principally involving the exchange of wheat for textiles and manufactures, occupied a numerous community of merchants, including many foreigners. The French had strong interests in Azorean commerce dating from the mid-sixteenth century. Huguenot merchants resident in the Azores kept up a brisk trade with La Rochelle. Jacques de Labat, French vice consul at Angra (1671-76), was a Rochelais and one of the five or six most important merchants of Terceira. His brother Gédéon de Labat served as vice consul of Fayal (appointed in 1679), and another brother, Bernabé de Labat, resided in the Netherlands. Other important French merchants at Angra during the last quarter of the seventeenth century were Jean-Ange Nègre, long-term French vice consul (1676-1716), Louis de la Ronde (another Rochelais, related to Jacques de la Ronde of La Rochelle), Hermigio Nolette, and Antoine Sieuvre (appointed French vice consul in 1716, but resident at Angra since before 1679).[38]

During the last half of the seventeenth century, the French at Angra, and also the Dutch, were outnumbered by the English, who handled a far larger volume of trade than any other foreign merchant group. The English merchant community, which had once numbered about eight persons, increased to twelve or fifteen by the end of the century. The wealthiest English merchants of the period 1650-75 were William Searchfield (English vice consul, 1638-58), John Mallory, and Timothy Townsend. Richard Huchenson of Ponta Delgada also spent some time at Angra during the 1660s. Townsend, whose brother Michael was a

37. Mauro, p. 317; Soares de Azevedo, "Açores e o Norte," 2: 33-34.
38. Soares de Azevedo, "Açores e o Norte," and his "Nota e documentos sobre o comércio de La Rochelle com a Terceira no século XVII," *Boletim do Arq. Dist. Angra* 6 (1948): 1-23.

merchant of Oporto, was an English Catholic married to Helena de Figueiredo of Terceira. Two of his sons, Timothy and John (known in Terceira as Timoteu Tonsen de Figueiredo and João Tonsen de Figueiredo), became merchants at Angra.[39]

After 1675 the most prominent English merchants of Terceira were William Fisher (d. 1714), a Catholic, married to Apolónia da Cruz Tavares and progenitor of numerous Fishers whose male line was extinguished in 1822 but whose descendants by female lines still live in the Azores; James Stone, married to Joan Mallory, daughter of the above-named John Mallory, and designated English consul at Terceira in 1703; Andrew White; and John Crooke. There was considerable intermarriage among the descendants of the English. For instance, James Stone's grandson, who was John Mallory's great-grandson, married a Townsend — and two male descendants of William Fisher married two female descendants of John Chamberlin of Ponta Delgada. The most successful English line was that established by William Street of London, who emigrated to Fayal at the end of the seventeenth century and whose descendants became governors of Pico and Fayal and eventually noblemen in the kingdom of Portugal (counts of Carnide).[40]

The foreign merchants, whose ships and seamen, and whose own persons were frequently subject to arbitrary harassment by Portuguese officials, required the protection of vice consuls. The Azorean vice consuls (English, French, and Dutch, primarily) usually received their patents of appointment from consuls resident in Lisbon. The French kept vice consuls at Horta, Angra, and Ponta Delgada. In the 1690s Jean d'Harriague was French (and Genoese) vice consul at Angra, Jean-Ange Nègre served at Angra, and Bernard Fartoat at Ponta Delgada. The English sometimes put Angra and Ponta Delgada under one consul; at the end of the century Samuel Hoper covered both Angra and Ponta Delgada, while John Whytton served at Fayal.[41]

The same person could serve as consul for various nations. The champion accumulator of vice consulships was Abram Vogullar, Dutch vice consul at Angra in 1681, who also represented Sweden, Spain, Denmark,

39. Campos de Castro de Azevedo Soares, 2: 381.

40. Ibid.; Marcelino Lima, pp. 283, 599–601; Arq. Dist. Ponta Delgada, "Livro de Genealogias," pp. 38, 65–66.

41. Sousa Lima, fols. 199–205; Soares de Azevedo, "Açores e o Norte"; Arq. Dist. Angra, Câmara de Angra, Registo Geral, Livro III, fols. 90, 202, 300, 339–40, 342; Marcelino Lima, p. 715; Arq. Dist. Ponta Delgada, "Livros da Alfândega — Ano 1694," fols. 9, 64.

and Hamburg[42] — nations with little business in the Azores. The consuls raised revenues from their own ships and merchants. The English collected 12$000 réis for each English ship loading in the Azores, and 9$000 from each vessel that unloaded but did not take on cargo. The French charged their ships 1$000 apiece and levied a tax of 0.5 percent on the value of all goods loaded and unloaded.[43]

The port of Angra, as the political nerve center of the Azores, was the place with the most consuls. Angra was also the heart of a network of small-boat communications that kept all the islands in the Azores in touch with one another. The small boats added substantial volume to the entrepôt trade of Angra. Angra, along with Praia, also attracted considerable numbers of foreign ships. The large wheat surpluses regularly produced in Terceira were the heart and soul of the island's international commerce. The island of Terceira, in addition, victualed and watered the Portuguese East Indiamen, and supplied them with seamen, soldiers, and armed escorts. Brazilmen were also, on occasion, revictualed and protected. The island was in touch with distant shores in the North and South Atlantic; the Terceirans traded directly with Brazil, and welcomed the codfish ships from Newfoundland and the New Englanders with their fish oil, pipe staves, and timbers. From the perspectives of maritime commerce, the picture of seventeenth-century Terceira is one of bustle, enterprise, energy, and movement.

Today Terceira is ignored by most of the ships that ply the North Atlantic; but in the seventeenth century the proud city of Angra, with its great monuments, attracted vessels from all parts, and was one of the nodal points of Atlantic maritime commerce.

42. Sousa Lima, fol. 204; Arq. Dist. Angra, Câmara de Angra, Registo Geral, Livro III, fol. 300.
43. Sousa Lima, fols. 202, 205.

7

Pico-Fayal and the Trade with
the American Plantations

The great volcano of Pico (Peak) rises from the abyssal sea floor, some 17,000 feet high, but only 7,715 feet are above water; its crater, which is snow-capped several months of the year, emits thin wisps of smoke; and the whole massive mountain, rising most unexpectedly from the depths of the mid-Atlantic, broods over and dominates the Western Azores. The "Peak" of Pico constitutes by itself most of the land mass of the western and central parts of the 30-mile-long island, with its 167 square miles of area. To the east a long narrow ridge, pockmarked with craters and crater lakes, forms the eastern extremity of the island.

The great peak, across the narrow Fayal Channel, dominates the picturesque town of Horta, today the capital of the four islands (Fayal, Pico, Flores, and Corvo) comprising the autonomous district of Horta, and formerly the greatest entrepôt, emporium, and victualing and fueling station between Europe and North America. The Fayal Channel is shallow, and the two islands, geologically, form a single land mass. Historically and economically, Fayal and Pico are twin islands, and the expression "Pico-Fayal," or "Fayal-Pico," makes good historical and geographical sense. As Father Maldonado phrased it, "Fayal would not be what it is without Pico, nor would Pico amount to anything without Fayal, and thus these islands, being two, are yet considered as a single island."[1]

---

1. Maldonado, year 1672, fol. 270. Very few books deal with the western Azores. The only full-length historical work is Silveira Macedo's three-volume *História das quatro ilhas* (Horta, 1871). This hard-to-find work is an earnest, old-

The small island of Fayal consists essentially of a single extinct volcano, the Pico Gordo (Fat Peak), which rises only to 3,421 feet but which has an immense volcanic crater over a mile wide and 400 feet deep. The island is seismically unstable. In April 1672 a fiery volcano sprang up in the western end of the island, and a subsequent earthquake, followed by heavy ash falls and fires, caused extensive damage to agriculture, pastures, and to certain villages.[2] The same general area was the scene of the volcanic and seismic disturbances of 1957–58. A submarine volcano off the western coast erupted on 27 September 1957, creating an immense column of vapor and a short-lived islet. The eruption continued for two months and drowned the western coast of Fayal with ashes, which in some places reached a thickness of over 30 feet and caused the disappearance of the tiny fishing village of Comprido. After two months of ash falls, there followed a great eruption of molten lava; this was succeeded on 13 May 1958 by an earthquake.[3]

The configuration of the Bay of Horta and the Fayal Channel is such as to provide protection for sailing vessels in the harbor, with two possible exits in times of storm. The place is also very scenic. As an English visitor remarked in 1839, Horta's "situation is the best that could have been chosen, both for commerce and natural beauty."[4] The Fayal Channel is shielded from most winds by Pico and by the hills behind Horta.

------

fashioned, year-by-year chronicle, wretchedly printed on local presses, devoted almost exclusively to Fayal (the title promised coverage of Pico, Flores, and Corvo as well), with almost no information on economic topics. As usual there is a full-scale genealogical study available: Marcelino Lima's careful *Famílias Faialenses* (Horta, 1922). The general histories of the Azores, whether in manuscript or in print, have little to say about Pico-Fayal. The archives in Lisbon, Ponta Delgada, and Angra contain almost nothing dealing with Pico-Fayal. The beginning of archival research on Pico-Fayal awaits the opening of a district archive at Horta, which has been promised for the last twenty years or more. Many records of the *câmara* of Horta are extant, and no doubt contain valuable information. Fortunately the published records of colonial New England and the American eastern seaboard are full of references to "Fyall" and to "Fyall wine," and furnish one important approach to the commercial history of Horta. There are also a number of fine descriptions of Fayal by nineteenth-century American travelers; Thomas W. Higginson's sympathetic and penetrating essay, "Fayal and the Portuguese," in *Atlantic Essays* (Boston, 1882), pp. 227–68, is particularly informative.

2. Silveira Macedo, 1: 184.

3. Frederico Machado, *Actividades vulcânicas da Ilha do Faial, 1957–1958* (Lisbon, 1959).

4. Joseph Bullar and Henry Bullar, *Winter in the Azores,* 2 vols. (London, 1841), 1: 299.

Shipping at anchor in Horta harbor is exposed to southerly and south-southwest winds, but these are not usually dangerous and, moreover, are moderated by currents in the channel. The one dangerous wind is a southeasterly gale; in such a gale a vessel could slip her cables, sail north-by-east until past Ribeirinha point, and then turn northwestward into smooth water on the leeward side of the island.[5]

The currents in the channel create a cross-sea, and ships at anchor could roll considerably, but without danger. The anchorage itself, in front of Horta, in 18 to 25 fathoms, is excellent, with fine holding ground. The volcanic protrusion of Monte da Guia, which extends eight-tenths of a mile into the channel, creates a shelter for small boats at Porto Pim, immediately to the south of Horta. To the north of Horta there is another modest harbor used by small boats, at Praia do Almoxarife. In the seventeenth century, foreigners were not allowed to unload at Pim or Praia, except in emergencies, but had to use the main port at Horta.[6]

The *vila* of Horta consisted, in the seventeenth century, of one long street curving around the bay. The town, together with the neighboring settlements of Ribeira dos Flamengos and Praia do Almoxarife, was sacked by Sir Walter Raleigh in 1597. The English set the town on fire and burned down the four largest churches. The islanders, carrying all their portable valuables, fled to the hills, and the English soldiers and seamen complained about the lack of plunder.[7] Horta at that time was small and had little commerce. The islanders soon rebuilt their houses and erected a wall at the seashore to afford better protection against any future raids. (This wall was severely damaged by a great storm on 20 November 1669, but it was subsequently repaired.) The island's militia was raised to a total strength of twenty companies, and, in 1650, Horta received permission to maintain a company of regular troops, with a captain, an ensign, a sergeant, and one hundred men.[8]

The history of Horta in the seventeenth century is the story of the evolution of a quiet settlement, with a small trade, into a busy, booming mid-Atlantic seaport at the center of a complex network of shipping routes. Like Madeira, Horta developed in association with the American plantations; the growth and prosperity of the English settlements in the West Indies and North America called into being the transatlantic com-

5. Boid, p. 263.
6. Soares de Azevedo, "Açores e o Norte," 2: 38.
7. Southey, 4: 85–89; Drummond, 1: 389; Monte Alverne, 2: 287.
8. Silveira Macedo, 1: 170.

merce of Pico-Fayal. The codfish ships on their way from Newfoundland to Europe called at Horta; the outward-bound ships for the West
Indies called at Horta; the ships from New England and New York, on
their way to England, or to Madeira, put in at Horta. Ships from the
South Atlantic, from Angola, Brazil, and the East, stopped at Horta.
The sheer volume and diversity of shipping created irresistible pressures
toward commercial development. Horta became the great victualer, wa-
terer, repairer, and supplier of ships. Thanks to Pico, with her fine wines,
Horta had a quality product with which to load the Newfoundlanders,
the New Englanders, and the West Indiamen. In return Horta unloaded
pipe staves, salted codfish, timber, nautical supplies, English textiles,
and European manufactures.

The town of Horta, responding to the stimulus of increased shipping,
grew larger and added a new district, Vila Nova. On 16 June 1670 the
municipal chamber of Horta, conscious of the growing importance of
the locality, petitioned the crown to have the *vila* raised to the status
of a *cidade*. The aldermen cited as their reasons for the change the
existence, at Horta, of three convents, two nunneries, three parishes,
and a mother church staffed by a vicar, two curates, a priest-treasurer,
and eight beneficed clergy. In the Azores, of course, municipal prestige
was measured by the number of religious and priests, and the number
of churches and convents, of which a community could boast. The number of religious institutions at Horta, while not overwhelming by the
standards of Angra or Funchal, was fairly impressive. In addition, the
aldermen pointed to the fact that Fayal maintained twenty companies
of militia, plus a company of regular troops; and, lastly, the aldermen
cited the "frequency with which ships come to Horta to trade."[9]

Such petitions were in vain, for Lisbon repeatedly rejected them,
thinking that Horta was too insignificant to become a *cidade*. Father
Maldonado disagreed, and asserted that Horta was more worthy of becoming a *cidade* than many a decaying settlement in the Portuguese Empire that already bore that title.[10] The population concentrated in the
vicinity of Horta, from Praia do Almoxarife to Porto Pim, probably
came to between four and five thousand souls, although Horta itself, in
1700, was said to have only 500 householders, or about 2,250 persons.
The island's total population came to 9,403. Besides Horta there were

9. Ibid., 1: 414–15.
10. Maldonado, year 1672, fol. 270: Horta "pudera ser Cidade sem enveja de
muitas de ultramar que o são."

nine other settlements in Fayal, all *lugares* (or villages). Thus Horta, which became a *vila* in 1498, was denied the status of *cidade* until the nineteenth century, when a decree dated 4 July 1833 raised it to that long-coveted position.[11]

If the islanders felt that they were the victims of official neglect, they nonetheless could console themselves, by the end of the seventeenth century, with the thought that, *vila* or *cidade*, the town of Horta had a greater commerce than proud Angra, and one with more international ramifications. Moreover, the Jesuits were good for the morale of the townsmen, making Horta the center of their impressive Azorean operations. One would not imagine that the Jesuits, having built a very large college at Ponta Delgada and a gigantic structure (now serving as the government headquarters) at Angra, would turn around and build an even larger church and college at Horta, but that is precisely what they did. The islanders attracted them by giving them a large legacy to be used for a college. The first Jesuits arrived in 1641, and work on the enormous church and college began in 1680. The church measured 387 feet in length and was still incomplete in 1759, when the Jesuit order was suppressed in Portugal.[12]

The only exportable product produced in quantity at Fayal was wheat. Close-by Pico and São Jorge were chronically short of grain and provided a steady and accessible market for Fayal's wheat surpluses. Some wheat was also exported directly to Madeira and Lisbon. Judging by the wheat prices set by the municipal chamber at Horta, Fayal's wheat harvests were consistently good; bad years seem to have been rare. The chamber set wheat prices in units of *vintens* (small silver coins worth $020 réis each) per alqueires (equivalent to 1.5 English pecks). During the entire period from 1655 to 1693 wheat sold at Horta, retail, for either 6 or 7 vintens per alqueire — that is, for $120 or $140 réis — except for the years 1656, 1658, 1659, and 1671, when there were lows of $100 (indicating abundance), and except for the year 1667, when there was a high price of $160 (indicating scarcity).[13] After 1693 the wheat prices set by the chamber reflected the same forces of inflation and scarcity that influenced wheat prices in São Miguel and Terceira in

11. Cordeiro, 2: 268, 329; Silveira Macedo, 2: 121.

12. Silveira Macedo, 1: 131–32; 3: 16. After the expulsion of the Jesuits, the church was taken over by the secular clergy, who turned it into the "mother church" (*igreja matriz*) of the island; the enormous college became the governor's residence and the seat of the municipal government, which it still is.

13. Silveira Macedo, 3: 171–75.

TABLE 20

Wheat Prices at Horta,1694–1704*

Year	Réis per Alqueire
1694	$200
1695	$200
1696	$140
1697	$240
1698	$240
1699	$240
1700	$240
1701	$240
1702	$240
1703	$200
1704	$200

*Based on António da Silveira Macedo, *História das quatro ilhas,* 3 vols. (Horta, 1871), 3:171–75.

the mid-1690s (see table 20), rising to a high of $240. In 1705, curiously enough, wheat prices returned to their old level of $140 réis. The prices of $140 and $240 were equivalent, in English terms, to lows of 2s. 3d. per bushel and highs of 3s. 10d.

In addition to wheat, Fayal attempted to produce its own wines. Here it imitated Pico, planting the same grape stock, in the same type of soil, in the same type of locations, and at the same times – but the result was vastly different, and it was universally acknowledged that Fayal wine was poor in quality. The islanders had to content themselves with the thought that, everywhere in English America, the good wines of Pico were always called "Fyall" or "Fiall" wines.

Almost all the wine exported at Horta was either Pico or São Jorge wine. The pipes of Pico wine were loaded aboard boats at a small landing place at Madalena and carried to Horta, a distance of about four-and-a-half nautical miles. According to the Terceiran Jesuit António Cordeiro, who completed his book on the islands in 1716, the whole island of Pico had only 820 householders (*vizinhos*), or perhaps 3,700 persons. There were two *vilas*, both small, and five villages. Lajes, on the south coast, with a cove offering shelter for small boats, had only 200 house-holds, and São Roque on the north coast, had only 150 households.[14]

All the settlements on Pico lay at or near the sea, along the coastal periphery; they were linked by donkey trails that circled the island but did not cross it. Nowhere on the island was there the semblance of a harbor; the coves and landing places were dangerous, even for small boats. Pico was absolutely isolated from international shipping, and wholly dependent on the neighboring port of Horta. In the Fayal Chan-nel, boatmen of exceptional daring and skill maintained daily commu-nication between Horta and Madalena, in almost all kinds of weather.

Horta also kept up small-boat communications with São Jorge, Flores, and Corvo. The island of São Jorge is separated from Pico by the São Jorge Channel, and runs almost exactly parallel to the north coast of Pico, at a distance of about eleven nautical miles. The channel is deep, registering over 700 fathoms at the midpoint between the two islands. São Jorge has a cigar-shaped configuration, and consists of a single, very straight and narrow mountain range, with only the peaks and upper slopes appearing above the water.

In 1703 São Jorge had a population of 8,239 persons.[15] The island had three *vilas* (Velas, Topo, and Calheta) and five villages, all on the south coast facing the sea and usually built on small patches of level ground (called *fajãs*), either tucked between hills or on ledges extending into the sea. The mountain range rises steeply behind and around the settlements, making communication by land very difficult. The town of Velas in the western part of the island has a good anchorage and a ser-viceable quay and sometimes attracted Portuguese caravels and small foreign vessels. Its main commerce, however, was by way of small boats to nearby Horta, by which it was in almost daily communication with Fayal. On the other hand the *vila* of Topo, which had a small landing place and was situated in the eastern extremity of the island, was much closer to Angra than to Horta and therefore exported its products to Terceira. The third *vila*, Calheta, about midway between Velas and Topo, had a small cove offering shelter for boats.

14. Cordeiro, 2: 329. But Cordeiro may have based his figures on Frutuoso (see *Livro Sexto*, 1963 ed., pp. 288–305), whose estimates relate to the 1580s period; indeed, Cordeiro's figures are hardly greater than Frutuoso's. By my cal-culations, Pico had over 8,000 inhabitants in 1700.
15. Maldonado, year 1703, fol. 339.

The island boasted two Franciscan convents, one nunnery, and nine parish churches. Its wheat harvest amounted to only about 1,500 moios (36,000 bushels) per year, insufficient to meet the island's needs, and São Jorge had to import grain. The islanders kept large herds of cattle, and produced the best dairy products in the Azores. The distinctive and excellent cheese of São Jorge is deservedly renowned. The most reliable cash exports were wine and brandy, which were sent to New England, the West Indies, and Newfoundland (all by way of Horta), and also to Terceira and Portugal. São Jorge wine, particularly in the eighteenth century, was often mixed with Pico wine.[16]

São Jorge, Pico, Fayal, Terceira, and Graciosa — at one time all fairly comfortable and prosperous islands — are close together and can be seen from one another. Far out to the west, far beyond the range of vision, lie the two lonely Azorean outposts of Flores and Corvo, keeping each other company in the wildest and windiest stretch of ocean in the whole Azores. Flores is nearly 120 miles from Fayal. The journey from Horta to Flores could be accomplished, by sail, in two or three days. In 1839 John and Henry Bullar, traveling on the *Flor do Faial*, "the dullest sailer afloat in the Atlantic," made the crossing from Horta to Santa Cruz, Flores, in sixty-six hours.[17] Normally, small-boat traffic between Fayal and the westermost islands was maintained during the summer months only.

Flores is actually farther from Fayal than Pico is from São Miguel. Flores and Corvo lay, therefore, on the outer periphery of Azorean consciousness. Yet the endearing and friendly inhabitants of these remote islands — who have contributed so many seamen to American ships, and who have sent their sons to toil in the factories of New England — these inhabitants saw many a ship stop at their island to pick up food and water. As great a number of ships passed Flores as any other Azorean island, although most did not stop and almost none transacted any business there. Others, however, made Flores a frequent and a favorite calling place.

The attractions of Flores to ships on the long, stormy journey from North America to Europe are fairly obvious. Masters who were weary of being tossed about on mountainous seas liked to sail around to the lee coast of Flores, where there were four or five excellent sheltered anchorages, with good holding ground and gentle sea. There the scurvied

16. Ibid.
17. Bullar, 2: 49–55.

crew would feast on fresh fruits and vegetables and take aboard ample supplies of excellent Flores water. Such victualing services formed an important part of the island's economic activities.

The constant procession of transatlantic shipping opened new perspectives for the inhabitants of Flores and Corvo. The men of these islands, unlike the land-bound peasants of São Miguel and Terceira, had the sea in their blood and felt the call to serve aboard the great ships. The young male, leaving wife and children behind him, would sign up on a foreign vessel, seek out and find a land — such as Hawaii or New England or Brazil — with greater opportunities than his own and then send for his family when he had accumulated sufficient money. But, having left their island home, the emigrants would never forget it and would sometimes return in old age.

Flores, with its 55 square miles of area, is eight times the size of tiny Corvo, which has only 6.7 square miles. At the end of the seventeenth century Flores had 938 households and a population of 3,239.[18] The island had two *vilas* (Santa Cruz and Lajes) and four villages, and rejoiced in one Franciscan convent and six parish churches. It had good anchorages, but no real port; at the main town, Santa Cruz, the harbor was dangerous, its rocky bottom a poor holding ground.[19] Fortunately there were better anchorages elsewhere along the east coast, and it was merely a question of the boats and lighters from Santa Cruz sailing or rowing a few miles farther to attend to the needs of a visiting ship.

Flores kept cattle, pigs, and sheep. Salted beef and pork were sold to visiting ships. The sheep supplied wool, which was woven into a coarse and very cheap cloth and sold to the poorest classes in Terceira. The island had ample supplies of timber, which found a good market in some of the other islands that had few trees. There are scattered indications in the shipping records for the early part of the seventeenth century that Flores was once a regular exporter of wheat, although Maldonado and Cordeiro, writing early in the next century, do not mention any wheat at Flores.

Just as Flores was dependent on the boat traffic from Horta, so Corvo depended on Flores. Corvo has two small anchorages but no harbors and was rarely visited by ships of any kind. If a ship had to stop at these islands, it would obviously head for Flores rather than Corvo. The distance between the islands is only 9.5 nautical miles at the closest point,

18. Maldonado, year 1692, fol. 342.
19. Boid, p. 321.

but the seas are so stormy that communications were often cut off for weeks at a time; boat traffic almost ceased during the winter months. The population at the end of the seventeenth century numbered about 500 persons; today there are about 680 persons living there. The maximum number of inhabitants, early in the nineteenth century, was about 900. The island had no *vilas* and only one *lugar* (village), called Rosário, but by favor of Dom Pedro IV, in 1832, this tiny settlement was officially designated a *vila* (town), with the name Vila Nova do Corvo. Today this *vila* consists of about 180 houses grouped around a small church. Many houses have two floors, with the lower floor reserved for farm animals, an arrangement commonly found in the peasant houses in North Portugal.[20]

The island itself consists mainly of one large extinct volcano, rising to 2,548 feet. A donkey trip to the old crater – which contains a lake with nine rocks that are supposed to resemble, by their arrangement, a map of the nine islands of the Azores – is the only "excursion" available to whatever tourists have been curious enough to venture so far. The inhabitants, all of whom are related by blood to one another, live like "one big happy family." There seem to be no landlords and no tenants; every farmer owns his own land; and few doors have any locks. The ordinary agriculturalist has more freedom in Corvo than elsewhere in the Azores.

Corvo is commercially insignificant, since it is really only a village serviced by Flores. In the seventeenth century Flores had a fairly important function as a victualer of transatlantic ships and enjoyed a little commerce of its own; but both Flores and Corvo, along with Pico and São Jorge, were commercial appendages attached to the great port of Horta. The dependence of all these islands on the maritime trade of Horta became obvious during the last decades of the nineteenth century, when the commerce of Horta began to diminish. While, on the one hand, the plagues of oidium and phylloxera destroyed the Pico vines and ended a wine trade that has never subsequently been revived, on the other hand, the advent of the steamship altered the old sailing routes and eliminated the need to revictual while in midpassage.

Table 21 shows population statistics for the five westernmost islands, with estimates for the year 1700, with the returns from 1864 (the first census) and 1920 (the census low point), and ending with the figures

---

20. Francisco Carreiro da Costa, *Açores* (Lisbon, 1967), pp. 57–58. There is a charming description of the people of Corvo in Bullar, 2: 62–78.

TABLE 21

Demographic Trends in the Western Azores

Island	1700*	1864[†]	1920[†]	1960[†]
Pico	8,000	27,537	20,176	21,626
Fayal	9,000	26,104	18,996	20,343
São Jorge	5,400	17,862	13,364	15,701
Flores	3,000	10,463	6,662	6,556
Corvo	500	881	661	669
Total	25,900	82,847	59,859	64,895

*Estimated.
[†]From census returns in the *Anuário demográfico 1963*, p. lx.

for the census of 1960. Between 1864 and 1920 all five islands lost population, the loss in numbers coming to about 28 percent of the total for 1864. Since 1920 there has been a slow and slight gain in population. The stabilization of population levels in these islands during the last four decades has been achieved only because of United States immigration restrictions and because of new Portuguese laws and procedures making emigration difficult.

The fundamental strength of the port of Horta lay in its geographical position and in its access to Pico wine. The old wines of Pico are hard to describe; since no bottles of the pre-oidium vintages seem to have survived, the wine is somewhat of a mystery to oenologists. The vineyards of Pico have been neglected for decades, many of them completely abandoned, although in recent years there has been a revival of winemaking. The wines made today, mostly sweetish dessert wines, somewhat like but inferior to ordinary Madeiran malmsey, may have only an uncertain relationship to the pre-oidium vintages. Moreover the pre-oidium vintages of 1750–1850, which had brandy additives and were artificially heated, may have been very unlike the seventeenth-century wines, which were not so treated.

The Scotswoman Janet Schaw, no fool in matters of food and drink, wrote in her diary, when passing through the Azores in 1774, that Fayal was "famous thro' the West Indies and America for its wine, which is a sort of weak Madeira," although much better than Canary wine.[21] A

21. Schaw, p. 64.

poor man's madeira, somewhat weaker and half the price of the Funchal product, may well have been a good description of ordinary Pico wine. Thomas Ashe, who visited the Azores in 1810, said that Pico produced five thousand pipes of wine per year, although eight to ten thousand pipes were exported from Horta in a good year, that these wines found their best market in the West Indies, and that the wine itself was of the color and flavor of inferior madeira and cost half the price.[22] Another Englishman, Captain Boid, who visited Horta in 1832, correctly distinguished between ordinary Pico wine and the sweet *vinho passado* (a malmsey type), and estimated the annual production at 25,000 casks (equivalent to 6,250 pipes).[23] A few years later, the physician Joseph Bullar, who sailed to Fayal in 1839, described the heated, *estufa* wine of Pico as "an execrable liquor, hot, fiery and intoxicating," which looked like brown sherry but which at its best was "not altogether an unpalatable liquor."[24] He said *estufa* wine was exported in great quantities to America and Britain, and was sometimes fraudulently sold in England under the name of "sherry." Bullar thought that *vinho passado* was a pleasant, sweet wine; and he also described various experiments in Pico to make a sparkling white wine, which had produced, he said, a moderately good, "hock type" beverage.[25]

The travelers Schaw, Ashe, Boid, and Bullar, writing between 1774 and 1839, were describing pre-oidium wines that had evolved considerably from the type of wines sold in the seventeenth century. The practice of adding brandy to the wine, to fortify it and prevent spoilage, was unknown in the seventeenth century in the Azores and Madeira and was apparently devised by the English vintners of Oporto in the eighteenth century. The Oporto winemakers, who were fiercely criticized for "polluting" the wine with brandy, were endeavoring futilely to create a high-quality table wine; by accident they evolved one of the world's great dessert wines. The practice of adding brandy to wine then spread to Madeira and Pico. In the Azores, brandies of São Jorge were added to the raw Pico wines, about five months after the harvesting and pressing, with very good results — but not in the seventeenth century.[26]

22. Ashe, p. 296.
23. Boid, pp. 302–4.
24. Bullar, 1: 339–40.
25. Ibid. See also Redding, p. 268.
26. The best account of the pre-oidium Pico vintages is in Ernesto Rebelo, "As uvas: Ilha do Pico," *Archivo dos Açores* 7: 65–75. For brandy addition and the *estufa* system see Allen, p. 233 *et passim*.

The other eighteenth-century practice, that of heating the wines, was also unknown. It evolved, apparently, in Madeira, in an attempt to re-produce artificially the effects of hot tropical weather on the madeiran beverage. The *vinho de estufa* (a "hothouse" wine) was kept in hot rooms heated by stoves; both Pico and Madeira wines acquired interest-ing characteristics during this process – but again this was not practiced during the seventeenth century.

The older authors speak of only two types of Pico wine: *vinho comum* and *vinho passado*, "common wine" and "passed wine," the latter refer-ring to wine made from grapes that had "passed" their prime. *Vinho comum* was almost certainly an ordinary red table wine made from *ver-delho* grapes, which had been introduced from Madeira. This wine shared certain characteristics with madeira, particularly its capacity to improve with heat, although it is supposed to have had a completely different taste and aroma. *Vinho passado* was a high-quality sweet wine, made from grapes that had been allowed to shrivel, thus concentrating their essential flavors and sugars, in accordance with an age-old process used in the Rhineland and elsewhere.

The grapes of Pico grew in the northern and western sections of the island, particularly in the district around Madalena; lava cultivation was very common;[27] the vines were protected from the wind by tall, semi-circular walls. The climate of Pico is warmer and less humid than that of the other islands; with the same grapes and using the same methods in the same types of soil, but with a different climate, cool and humid Fayal could only produce a wine that was weak and had no bouquet. In the nineteenth century there were at least a dozen grape varietals growing in Pico's vineyards – including *boal, terrantez, alicante, tinta* (or *tent,* producing a dark wine used only for coloring purposes), *mus-catel,* etc. – but *verdelho* was more important than all the others com-bined. After the invasions of oidium and phylloxera, Californian varie-tals were introduced to strengthen the stock, but the wines of Pico never recovered properly.[28]

Cordeiro believed that the *vinho passado* of Pico was as good as the malmsey of Madeira, which it may have resembled.[29] More important is the view of the merchant Jean d'Harriague, French consul at Horta, who, without overly committing himself, declared in an official report

27. How a stretch of barren lava can be turned into a garden is explained in Ashe, pp. 63–71. See also Bullar, 1: 337; Rebelo, 7: 72; and Soeiro de Brito, p. 75.
28. Rebelo, 7: 74–75.
29. Cordeiro, 2: 295.

(26 November 1686) that Pico wine, if it is well selected, is such that "there are those of the opinion that it surpasses in goodness the wines of the Canaries, Madeira and Málaga."[30] The demand for Pico wines in the West Indies, North America, and even in Europe testified to its desirability; one reason for the demand was probably because of the cheapness of the wine, and another (in hot climates) was because of its heat-resistant characteristics. Whether the connoisseur would have ranked the best Pico wines in the same class as the best wines of Madeira, the Canaries, and Málaga is another question.

The supply of wine from Pico was usually ample. Maldonado wrote that 15,000 pipes were produced in a normal year, and that bumper harvests yielded 30,000 pipes in 1649 and almost 40,000 in 1658,[31] but these figures seem inflated. Another source says that Pico, in 1649, produced over 8,000 pipes[32] – a figure that cannot be reconciled with Maldonado's 30,000 pipes.[33] In any event, in 1649 wine was so abundant in Pico that there were shortages of pipes and casks, the price of must (newly pressed wine) fell to $300 réis (or 3s.) per pipe, while the officially set tavern price skidded to $012 per canada – or the equivalent, in English terms, of less than one penny for one quart of wine. The year 1658 was even better; the tavern price at Horta was probably $010 or less per canada, and at Angra the wines of Pico and São Jorge were set at between $024 and $032 per canada, while the *vinho da terra*, of Terceiran origin, went for $010 per canada.[34]

Maldonado also speaks of shortages, especially in the years 1662–63, when wine had to be imported into the Azores from Madeira, and the tavern price at Angra jumped to $080 per canada,[35] which was still only sixpence per quart. The maximum wine production of Pico, Maldonado to the contrary, was probably not much over 12,000 pipes per year, and the average production probably came to less than 10,000. Since the population of Pico-Fayal was small, the bulk of this wine was destined for export, particularly to the other islands, to Portugal, and to the Americas.

30. Soares de Azevedo, "Açores e o Norte," 2: 39.
31. Maldonado, year 1672, fol. 270; 1649, fol. 148; 1658, fol. 177.
32. Silveira Macedo, 1: 168.
33. Maldonado clearly wrote "30,000" pipes, but Drummond, 2: 99, conscious of the difficulties and borrowing directly from Maldonado, chose to transcribe it as "3,000" pipes, a figure that is obviously too small.
34. Silveira Macedo, 1: 165, 168; Drummond, 2: 99; Maldonado, year 1649, fol. 148; 1658, fol. 177.
35. Maldonado, year 1658, fol. 177.

Early in the seventeenth century, Pico and São Jorge wines were sent to Brazil directly, although some of the wines remitted to Portugal were probably re-exported to Brazil as well. In the middle years of the century other markets opened up, particularly in the English plantations in the Americas. Maldonado also speaks of a market for Pico wines in "Northern Europe," meaning Europe north of the Pyrenees. Corroboration for this statement can be found in a curious document drawn up by Estácio Machado de Utra, notary at the Horta customshouse, at the request of the French consul at Angra, Jean-Ange Nègre, and notarized at Angra on 2 March 1680. Nègre, who hated the Huguenot brothers Labat, wanted to prove that the Labats traded with the enemies of France (the Netherlands, Flanders, Hamburg, Denmark, and Spain) while France was at war, during 1672–78. So Nègre secured a statement which showed that Gédéon de Labat, merchant at Horta, between 12 February 1672 and 21 November 1678, dispatched fifteen ships to enemy ports, and these ships carried a total of 454.5 pipes of Pico wine. Of the fifteen ships, eight went to Amsterdam, three to other Lowland ports, three to Hamburg, and one to Cadiz. Of the 454.5 pipes taken, 96 were *vinho passado* and 358.5 were *vinho comum.*[36]

Since this report reflected only the activities of one single merchant, in a time of general war, and was restricted to listing shipments to certain specified "enemy" countries, the total of 454.5 pipes — enough to fill over 225,000 one-quart bottles — is impressive. The wines taken included not only the cheap *vinho comum*, which conceivably could have been mixed with more expensive "sack" from the Canaries and Málaga and sold under another label, but also the higher grade *vinho passado*, which may have commanded a market of its own. Although there are other scattered references to shipments of wine to Europe, particularly to the Netherlands, there is insufficient evidence with which to construct a general picture of Horta's wine trade with Europe. Nègre's spiteful little report on the Labats, providentially preserved in a French archive,[37] gives us only a tantalizing glimpse of a wine trade whose very existence is somewhat surprising.

Fayal's shipments of wine to New England were certainly more important than the exports to Europe. Fragmentary shipping records for the port of Boston, covering parts of the years 1686–88, give some idea of the movements of Madeira and Pico wines in one area of the North

---

36. Soares de Azevedo, "Açores e o Norte," 2: 35–38; Sousa Lima, fol. 172.
37. Paris, Archives Nationales, Affaires Étrangères, "Fonds des consulats," B1 487 (Consulat de Horta).

TABLE 22

Boston Imports of Island Wines, 1686–88*

Month and Year	Ship Arrivals			Amounts of Wine Imported (pipes)		
	From Madeira	From Fayal	Total Ships	Madeira Wine	Pico Wine	Total Wines
May–Sept. 1686	2	3	5	110	191	301
Oct.–Dec. 1687	1	1	2	27	61.75	88.75
Jan.–Oct. 1688	2	6	8	129.50	168.75	298.25
Total	5	10	15	266.50	421.50	688

*Compiled from "Abstracts of English Shipping Records Relating to Massachusetts Ports" (typescript prepared for the Essex Institute, Salem, Mass., from papers at the Public Record Office, London, in 1931; photostatic copy at the University of Chicago Library), fols. 4–6, 77–92, 128–72.

American trade (see table 22). Records from these three years actually cover only about eighteen months. During those eighteen months they show twice as many ships arriving from Fayal as from Madeira, with almost twice as much Pico wine as madeira. Some of the Pico wine — including at least one shipment of 85 pipes aboard the 60-ton Bristol ship *Welcome,* which arrived in Boston on 10 August 1686 (New Style) — was "Presader" wine (*vinho passado*).[38]

Since Boston was perhaps still in its infancy in the 1680s and was only one of several American ports (in 1671, for instance, the as yet undeveloped colony of New Hampshire was said to import 300 tuns, or 600 pipes, of wines and brandy per year)[39] and considering that these records cover only a brief period, the total import of 688 pipes is fairly impressive. The 688 pipes would have filled 345,000 one-quart bottles — which is eloquent testimony to the thirst of the settlers. Some of this

38. Ibid., fol. 6.
39. *Cal. S.P., Colonial Ser., America and West Indies, 1669–1674* (London, 1889), p. 294.

TABLE 23

Wine Ships Leaving Boston, 1686–88*

Month and Year	To Madeira	To Fayal	To American Ports with Madeira Wine	To American Ports with Pico Wine	Total
May–Sept. 1686	2	0	3	0	5
Apr.–Oct. 1687	7	1	7	0	15
Apr.–Oct. 1688	4	1	14	7	26
Total	13	2	24	7	46

*Compiled from "Abstracts of English Shipping Records Relating to Massachusetts Ports," fols. 22–76, 93–127.

wine, however, was destined not for local consumption but for re-export. The same records show Boston sending ships back to Madeira and Fayal, for more wine, and also dispatching small quantities of wine, aboard many ships, to a large variety of American destinations, from New York to Curaçao (see table 23). The ships with madeira wine went to Rhode Island, New York, Maryland, Antigua, and Montserrat, although the favorite destinations were Pennsylvania, Virginia, and Bermuda; the ships with Pico wines went to Pennsylvania, Maryland, Virginia, Bermuda, and Curaçao. Some ships carried both Pico and Madeiran wines.

The records show only two ships leaving Boston and giving Fayal as their destination. These were the Boston-owned, English-built, forty-ton bark *Bachelor's Adventure*, which left Boston in April 1687 with lumber, salted fish, and thirty-six barrels of train oil (oil from whale blubber); and the Boston-owned, plantation-built, twenty-ton ketch *Adventure*, which left in June 1688 with lumber, provisions, eight barrels of train oil, and half a ton of New England iron.[40] These two may have been on a back-and-forth trade between Horta and Boston, though this type of route was not very common in the transatlantic trade. There

40. Ibid., fols. 44, 100.

were, of course, many other ships that went to Horta from Boston during these years, but their destination was usually given as London or some other English port. In fact, every ship from Boston bound for Europe had the opportunity, and some incentive, for calling at Horta.

Transatlantic shipping in the seventeenth century followed no simple pattern; except for the fact that no ship could sail against wind and current, for it was physically impossible to do so, ships went in almost every imaginable direction. Simplified generalizations, such as the shopworn and perilous formula of the "triangular trade," distort rather than illuminate the movements of shipping. Seventeenth-century shipping routes were neither triangular nor square nor yet pentagonal — they were multifaceted, intricate, unexpected, and capricious. Yet there were certain "trunk lines" followed by hundreds of ships: one of these ran from North America to England, another from Newfoundland to Iberia, and a third from England to the West Indies. The great port of Horta was a nodal point on all three of these routes — a collection point for the timber ships of New England, for codfish ships, and for outward-bound West Indiamen — and a logical entrepôt for exchange and transshipment.

The French consul at Fayal reported, in 1686, that "the English do a great business here," and that seventy or eighty ships traded annually at Horta, from England and New England.[41] This was not an exaggeration, but rather an understatement; for instance, in one particular day during May 1699, there were twenty ships loading wine and brandy at Horta.[42] The codfish trade involved many nations and many interests. By the middle of the seventeenth century, after the contraction of Portuguese and Spanish efforts in Newfoundland, the English and French divided the large and lucrative trade in salted fish. The development of New England led to an extensive American involvement, and Boston became an important entrepôt for the reshipment of salted fish.[43]

The great market for codfish lay in Spain and Portugal, with certain Mediterranean areas, the Azores, Madeira, the Canaries, and Portuguese North Africa constituting subsidiary markets. Brazil, also, was a major importer, but all codfish for Brazil had to be taken to Lisbon first. The Azores lay directly athwart the routes from Newfoundland and New England to the Iberian, the insular, and the Mediterranean markets. Thus it was that Horta became a rendezvous point for codfish ships, with fish

41. Soares de Azevedo, "Açores e o Norte," 2: 39.
42. Bolton, p. 138.
43. See R.G. Lounsbury, *The British Fishery at Newfoundland* (New Haven, Conn., 1934), pp. 23–31; and H.A. Innes, *The Cod Fisheries* (New Haven, Conn., 1940), p. 118.

being unloaded at Fayal for the island's own use and also for transshipment to the other islands. In return, the Newfoundlanders loaded Pico wine and São Jorge brandy, particularly the latter, which found ready consumers among the hardworking and hard drinking fishermen of lonely Newfoundland.

The salted fish sent to Boston was transshipped to various destinations. Unlike the Newfoundland ships, which carried only codfish, the New Englandmen carried mixed cargoes to Europe, with codfish, timber, cereals, pipe staves, and fish oil offering greater opportunities for trading and profit, because of their diversity. The mixed cargoes afforded splendid opportunities for commercial transactions in Horta. Like Madeira, Pico-Fayal depended on New England for the staves used in making the wine casks; and, as in Madeira, the New Englanders loaded wines. The connection between New England and Pico-Fayal, however, was much closer, both psychologically and economically, than the connection between New England and Madeira. There developed between the Yankees and the Azoreans, in the seventeenth century, a voluminous interchange of commodities, and a certain psychic rapport, that was not to be broken until the collapse of the Yankee whaling ventures in the nineteenth century.

Another important aspect of the Pico-Fayal trade in wines involved the West Indies. A procession of ships bound for the West Indies from England unloaded textiles and manufactures at Horta and took on wines. In the British West Indies the only imports that paid customs duties were beer, wine, and spirits. In Jamaica, in 1672, beer paid 30s. per tun, wine 5s. per tun, and brandy 1s. per gallon.[44] It is quite probable that import duties paid on Madeiran and Pico wines and brandy raised the greater portion of the public revenues in the British West Indies. The English were far more active in carrying Azorean wines to the West Indies than any other nation, although the Dutch and French also participated. French merchants were not supposed to take Azorean wines to the French West Indies, but they sometimes did so. In 1671, for instance, the Rochelais ship *Philippe* took on 180 pipes of Pico wine at Horta, consigned to the West Indies.[45]

The growth of trading and victualing at Horta was directly related to the expansion of British interests in the Americas. The English intrusion in the Guianas and the Lesser Antilles, and the English seizure of

44. *Cal. S.P., Colonial Ser., America and the West Indies,1669–1674*, pp. 304, 326.
45. Soares de Azevedo, "Comércio de La Rochelle," 6: 21.

Jamaica (1655), removed areas from the Spanish-directed Cadiz-Canaries trading axis and brought them into the London-Boston axis, in which Madeira and the Azores occupied a more important position. The wines of Pico and Madeira could not penetrate Spanish colonial markets, but they were welcomed in the English colonies. The aggressive English moves in 1664 into New York, New Jersey, and Delaware, and the gradual English settlement of Maine and the Carolinas, created new markets and augmented the volume of shipping and trade. The greater the number of ships on the England-Americas routes, the greater the prosperity of Pico-Fayal.

Trading and shipping activities at Horta intensified, therefore, after the middle of the century. The precise volume can only be guessed at; probably, in the 1690s, between 300 and 600 ships put in at Horta every year, of which only about 75 to 130 loaded or unloaded cargoes — the rest came to the Fayal Channel for water, victuals, shelter, and repairs. In the eighteenth century, after 1715, when the Spanish wars ended, shipping at Horta continued to grow. The crude newssheets of eighteenth-century Boston and New York contain many references to ships coming from and going to the "Western Isles," and their columns of advertisements list many sales of "Fyall" wines.

An international community of merchants handled the brisk commerce of Horta. During the 1640s there were probably twenty resident English merchants, including Samuel Andrews, John Gard, Nathaniel Long, James Neale, William Pennicott, Augustine Walker, John Wilson, and others. James Neale, who lived at Horta at certain times, had close connections with New England, and sailed across the Atlantic several times.[46] The French and Dutch also had small groups of resident merchants.

The close of the seventeenth century saw the emergence of Horta as the first port in the Azores, and it was destined to play a great role in the international commerce of the eighteenth and nineteenth centuries, only to fall, at last, into a prolonged slumber. Geography conferred on Horta a position of priceless advantage. Nearby Pico produced the indispensable staple product. Three satellite islands depended on Pico-Fayal, and helped to fatten the commerce of all. The growth and development of British and French America brought the potentialities of the mid-Atlantic position to full realization. The possession of a safe harbor, unique in the Azores, gave Horta most of the trump cards in its competition with Angra and Ponta Delgada for international shipping.

46. Aspinwall Notarial Records, pp. 110, 243, 260.

The nine islands of the Azores possess three ancient and historic ports. Three international ports are quite a few for islands as small as the Azores. At the end of the seventeenth century, Horta was well launched on its great career as the busiest center for mid-Atlantic shipping. Angra, at the heart of the internal Azorean communications network, sending small boats to the other islands, having surplus wheat for export — and blessed with a monopoly of the higher political and ecclesiastical positions — maintained a steady and active inter-island and international trade. Ponta Delgada, at the turn of the century, was in a state of transition, with its pastel trade only a memory and its orange trade only a glimmer on the horizon of the future. In another few decades, with its orange ships arriving by the dozen, it would be ready to challenge Horta as the premier port in the islands. In the meantime, the patient inhabitants of São Miguel made do with exports of wheat, linens, salted pork, and odds and ends.

The three ports, which lived in a relationship with one another that, in different areas, was both competitive and cooperative, showed curious differences in their patterns of trade. Angra was the most heavily involved in the purely Portuguese trade with Lisbon, and with the inter-island trade. It was also a refuge for Portuguese East Indiamen. Ponta Delgada was tied to Madeira, the Canaries, France, and England. Horta, the most cosmopolitan, was preeminent in the transatlantic sphere. Of the three, Horta was the best symbol of the importance of the Azores to the Atlantic sailing ships of a bygone day.

8
The Cape Verdes:
Crossroads of the Atlantic

The accident of geographical location confers on the Cape Verdean archipelago its central importance for the history of transatlantic shipping. The pattern of North Atlantic winds made it likely that every European sailing ship, outward bound to destinations in the South Atlantic or in Eastern seas, would pass through the vicinity of the Cape Verdes. Also ships from Europe to the West Indies, or between Africa and the Americas, followed routes that took them, at times, through Cape Verdean waters. The hazards and mishaps that arose from the very nature of long-distance navigation under sail dictated that a certain proportion of those ships passing through the archipelago's seas would find it desirable, even essential, to put in at a Cape Verdean port to procure beverages, victuals, or nautical supplies, or to undertake indispensable repairs. Necessitous and crippled ships depended on the islands; and the islands too, because they needed so many things from the outside world, depended on the ships. The islands and the ships supported and complemented one another.

The archipelago enjoyed a superb geographical position, at the very crossroads of the Atlantic, where wind and current brought together the ships of Europe, Africa, the West Indies, and North and South America. But, unfortunately, this excellent geographical position also brings with it a poor climate, of desert-like dryness. Of the ten major islands in the Cape Verdean group, five (São Vicente, Sal, Maio, Boavista, and Santa Luzia) are arid wastelands, largely without vegetation. The other five islands (Santiago, Fogo, Brava, São Nicolau, and Santo Antão) depend on a short and capricious rainy season that, all too commonly, produces very little precipitation. Unlike Madeira and the Azores, the Cape Verdes

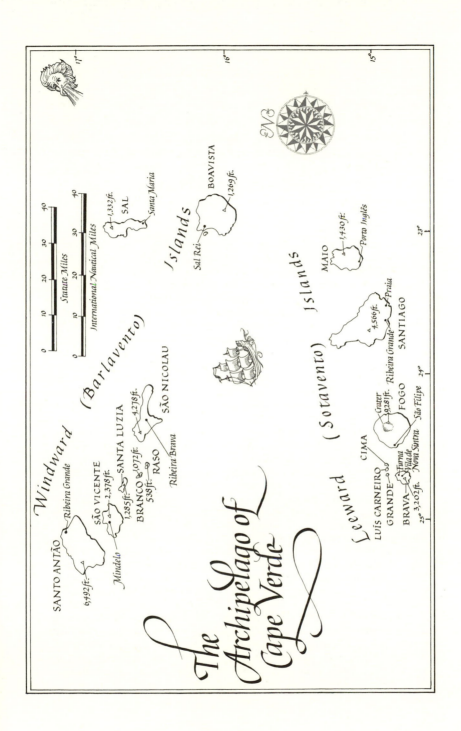

The Archipelago of Cape Verde

Windward (Barlavento) Islands

SANTO ANTÃO
6,492 ft.
Ribeira Grande
Mindelo
SÃO VICENTE
2,378 ft.
SANTA LUZIA
1,285 ft.
BRANCO
538 ft.
1,072 ft.
RASO
SÃO NICOLAU
4,278 ft.
Ribeira Brava

SAL
1,332 ft.
Santa Maria

BOAVISTA
1,269 ft.
Sal Rei

MAIO
1,430 ft.
Porto Inglês

Leeward (Sotavento) Islands

CIMA
LUÍS CARNEIRO
GRANDE
BRAVA
3,202 ft.
Turra
Vila de
Nova Sintra
FOGO
Crater
9,281 ft.
São Filipe
SANTIAGO
Ribeira Grande
Praia
4,566 ft.

Statute Miles
0 10 20 30 40

International Nautical Miles
0 10 20 30 40

17°
16°
15°
23°
24°
25°

have not supplied the Atlantic trade with crops of great quantity and value.[1]

Prior to the nineteenth century, cash crops (such as sugarcane and indigo) did not yield great returns. The one agricultural product of some significance in trade was *cotton*, which was grown by slaves and woven into a fine-quality striped cloth that was once marketed along the West African coast and in Brazil. There was also one nonagricultural plant product – the dye-yielding lichen called orchil (*urzela* in Portuguese), which was collected in mountainous areas, processed, and exported.

1. The literature on the Cape Verdes is limited but lively. The best introduction to the islands in English is Archibald Lyall, *Black and White Make Brown* (London, 1938). Two geographical monographs in Portuguese – Ilídio do Amaral, *Santiago de Cabo Verde* (Lisbon, 1964), and Orlando Ribeiro, *Ilha do Fogo* (Lisbon, 1954), both profusely illustrated – give comprehensive coverage to those two islands. Various nineteenth-century travel accounts, memoirs, and geographical studies are well worth reading and contain much historical material: Joseph Corry, *Observations upon the Windward Coast of Africa* (London, 1807); João de Andrade Corvo, *Estudos sobre as províncias ultramarinas,* 2 vols. (Lisbon, 1833); José Conrado Carlos de Chelmicki, *Corografia Cabo-Verdiana,* 2 vols. (Lisbon, 1841); Horatio Bridge, *Journal of an African Cruiser* (London, 1845); José Maria de Sousa Monteiro, *Diccionario geographico* (Lisbon, 1850); Charles W. Thomas, *Adventures and Observations on the West Coast of Africa* (New York, 1860); Francisco Travassos Valdez, *Six Years of a Traveller's Life in Western Africa,* 2 vols. (London, 1861); and Alfred B. Ellis, *West African Islands* (London, 1845). The last-named author borrowed extensively from Horatio Bridge, without acknowledgment. A much earlier traveler, William Dampier, *Voyages,* 4 vols. (London, 1729), 1: 65–78, and 3: 10–28, visited the Cape Verdes at least four times (1670, 1683, 1699, and 1703), and knew the lesser islands very well.

Most useful of all is Cristiano José de Sena Barcelos, *Subsídios para a história de Cabo Verde e Guiné,* 7 vols. (Lisbon/Coimbra, 1899–1913), a massive compilation of factual materials, in strict chronological order. Other documents can be found printed in António Brásio, *Monumenta Missionaria Africana: África Ocidental,* pt. II, vols. 1–3 (Lisbon, 1958–64). Other pertinent materials include: António Mendes Corrêa, *Ultramar Português,* vol. 2: *Ilhas de Cabo Verde* (Lisbon, 1954), with summaries in French and English; Universidade Técnica de Lisboa, *Cabo Verde, Guiné, São Tomé e Príncipe: Curso de extensão universitária, ano lectivo de 1965-1966* (Lisbon, 1965?), a collection of lectures; João Cesário de Lacerda, *Relatório do Governo Geral de Cabo Verde* (Lisbon, 1901), a governor's official report; Álvaro Lereno, *Subsídios para a história da moeda em Cabo Verde* (Lisbon, 1942), a monograph on coinage; and Norman Araujo, *Study of Cape Verdean Literature* (Chestnut Hill, Mass., 1966), a critical survey of literary movements, with a good bibliography. For further bibliography, and a long analysis of the question of Cape Verdean identity, see Manuel Ferreira, *Aventura crioula* (Lisbon, 1967).

From the animal realm, the chief exports were horses, donkeys, goats, and cattle, which were either exported alive, or else killed to furnish hides, pelts, and cured and salted meats. The mineral world yielded one important product: bay salt. The salt was sea-deposited in the bleak and windblown islands of Maio, Boavista, and Sal and was easily obtained.

Cotton, orchil, domesticated animals, hides, pelts, salted meats, and salt round out the meager list of Cape Verdean products in the seventeenth-century Atlantic trade. Setting aside the slave trade, which was perhaps the most lucrative commercial activity in the archipelago,[2] it will be seen that fleets of ships could have passed through Cape Verdean waters without necessarily generating a heavy volume of commercial transactions. The lack of enticing and lucrative insular products meant that, from the perspective of general Atlantic navigation, the islands were significant chiefly as the suppliers of ships, not as great trading stations.

The main function of the Cape Verdes, therefore, was purely maritime, and such a function is well illustrated by the coaling and fueling activities of the port of Mindelo since the year 1850. The harbor of Porto Grande at Mindelo, on the island of São Vicente, has the best anchorage in the Cape Verdes. It consists of a wide, well-sheltered bay formed by a sunken volcanic crater, where ships could anchor from a third of a mile to a mile or more offshore, in 5 to 14 fathoms of water, with a sandy bottom and good holding ground, and protected from most winds. Although the waters in the bay are sometimes ruffled, the anchorage is the safest and most convenient of all the anchorages in the Portuguese Atlantic islands.[3]

The island of São Vicente, which contains this fine harbor, although of fair size (88 square miles in area), is "a completely desert island with no running water, no vegetation, no countryside and no peasantry."[4] Because of its coal dumps, soot, and dust, the long-suffering British residents of Mindelo referred to it as the "cinder-heap."

Until the middle of the nineteenth century, the harbor was little used. In 1838 the Englishman John Lewis established the first small coal deposit at Mindelo, for the refueling of British East Indiamen.[5] In 1850

2. See chap. 9, below.
3. Mendes Corrêa, p. 17; *Port. Poss.: Cape Verde*, pp. 14–15; Lyall, pp. 75–78. U.S. Hydrographic Office, Chart 5720, 2d ed. (Washington, 1951), has a detailed map of the harbor at Mindelo, based on a Portuguese chart of 1946.
4. Lyall, p. 26.
5. Ibid., p. 78.

TABLE 24

Shipping at Mindelo, 1875–98*

Years	Number of Ships	Annual Average
1875–78	1,122	281
1879–82	2,587	647
1883–86	3,596	899
1887–90	5,745	1,436
1891–94	3,681	920
1895–98	5,321	1,330
Total	22,052	919

*Adapted from statistics in João Cesário de Lacerda, *Relatório do Governo Geral de Cabo Verde* (Lisbon, 1901), pp. 33–34.

the important Royal Mail Steam Packet Company was authorized and even encouraged, by promises of tariff exemptions, to build its own coaling facilities and jetty for servicing ships on the England-Brazil run, and several other shipping or coaling companies followed suit.[6] In 1855 an American visitor described Mindelo as "a collection of small stone huts, surrounded by hills and valleys that are the very emblems of barrenness."[7] But the village grew rapidly; in 1858 it was raised to the status of *vila* (town), and twenty-one years later, with a population of 3,300 persons, it was formally designated a *cidade* (city). By the year 1867 nearly one thousand ships called at the Cape Verdes, with Porto Grande at Mindelo accounting for most of the tonnage.[8]

The opening of the Suez Canal, in 1869, diverted many ships away from the Cape Verdes and diminished the activity of the port, but Mindelo gradually recovered. Table 24 shows the quadrennial movement of transoceanic shipping (inter-island traffic excluded) at Mindelo during

6. That is, the Patent Fuel Company (in 1851); John Rendall and Company (1852); Visger and Miller (1853); McLeod and Martin (1858); Cory Brothers and Company (1875); Wilson, Son and Company (1885); and the St. Vincent Coaling Company (1896). Sena Barcelos, 5: 157, 222, 250; and 6: 5, 170–71; *Colóquios Cabo-Verdianos*, p. 8.

7. Thomas, p. 331.

8. *Colóquios Cabo-Verdianos*, p. 8.

TABLE 25

Ships at Mindelo in 1898 by Nationality*

Nationality	Number of Ships	Tonnage
1. British	913	1,768,482
2. German	254	478,980
3. Italian	133	251,617
4. Portuguese	76	128,130
5. Spanish	18	57,775
6. French	31	47,837
7. Argentine	10	46,290
8. Norwegian	13	19,319
9. Austrian	8	16,342
10. Brazilian	16	13,590
11. Other	31	31,106
Total	1,503	2,859,468

*Lacerda, *Relatório*, p. 77.

the years 1875 to 1898. In 1898 a total of 1,802 ships, with a tonnage of 3,146,325 tons and carrying 89,992 seamen, called at the archipelago.[9] Over 1,500 of these ships, belonging to eighteen different nationalities, and accounting for over 90 percent of the above tonnage, put in at Mindelo (see table 25). Yet this very large number of ships, averaging out to more than four vessels every single day, did not generate much commercial activity at Mindelo. For the ships purchased almost nothing except coal and water.

The coal, of which a constant reserve of 34,000 tons was maintained (with 5,000 tons always kept immediately available aboard lighters), came from Wales, was unloaded from coal ships to lighters, and, if customs regulations had permitted, might have been reloaded aboard other ships directly from the lighter, without ever touching land.[10] Like the coal, the expensive water sold at Mindelo did not come from Mindelo, or from any part of the island of São Vicente, but had to be imported from the adjacent island of Santo Antão. São Vicente endures a truly

9. Lacerda, pp. 74–77.
10. *Port. Poss.: Cape Verde*, p. 15.

Saharan climate; during a twelve-year period, for instance, from 1894 to 1905, Mindelo recorded a total rainfall of only slightly over 20 inches — an average of less than 1.7 inches of rain per year.[11] When rain did fall, it came all at once, in a few showers that quickly drained into the ground and ran off into the sea. In these circumstances, water was brought from Tarrafal in the neighboring island of Santo Antão, and a tank holding 100,000 gallons was kept filled in the harbor for the supply of ships, but the price charged for this water was very high.

High-priced water, anchorage fees, and coal taxes[12] were the few devices through which the Cape Verdeans tried to make money from the ships that tarried briefly at Porto Grande. The port was a great asset to Atlantic shipping, but the islanders derived surprisingly few benefits from it. The moving and hauling of coal required the services of numerous persons — chiefly women, who did most of the heavy work in São Vicente; but the coaling business as such was largely in the hands of foreigners, who also absorbed the profits.

Aside from the business of ship supply, commercial activities in the great harbor were always marginal and precarious, and often immoral or illegal. Whenever a ship came in, it was quickly surrounded by small boats. Ignoring the many sharks in the water, divers would dive in after the small coins tossed into the sea by the bemused sailors or passengers. A horde of peddlers, making a precarious living from selling fruits, sweets, and island curios, would try to gain the deck. Others would buy cigarettes and tobacco, to be smuggled ashore and resold, defrauding the Portuguese customs. The passenger or seaman who ventured ashore found himself assailed by a small army of beggars, pimps, prostitutes, and vagabonds — not to mention the importunate *secretários,* the self-appointed all-purpose guides, messenger boys, and procurers who at-

11. Mendes Corrêa, p. 65.
12. English sources record frequent complaints about the high price of water at Mindelo but do not give the actual figures. At Praia, in 1839, the installation of a new water pipeline reduced the price of water from 4s. 4d. to 1s. 8d. per cask. In 1852, at dry Boavista, one shilling fetched only 18 gallons of water. At an earlier time, in 1696, Ribeira Grande in Santiago charged $100 réis (or nearly 8d.) per pipe for good fresh water. More recently, in 1956, Mindelo sold 54,886 metric tons of water for 2,091,000 Portuguese *escudos,* which, by my calculations, would run to U.S.$135 for 100 metric tons (containing roughly 26,400 gallons). The coal tax at Mindelo was $100 réis per ton in 1854, which was raised to $300 in 1880. Anchorage fees ran to 3$000 for a 100-ton ship, 6$000 for a 200-ton ship, and so forth, at a rate of $030 per ton. Sena Barcelos, 2: 132; 5: 260; 6: 5; Travassos Valdez, *Six Years,* 1: 72, 103; *Colóquios Cabo-Verdianos,* p. 166; *Port. Poss.: Cape Verde,* p. 15.

tached themselves to the luckless visitor with undiscourageable enthusiasm; one such *secretário* might even earn his "wages," or tip, by keeping other *secretários,* beggars, and panderers at bay.[13]

Only the very thirsty, or the lascivious, could have found Mindelo attractive. Alfred B. Ellis, who was overcharged and cheated at Mindelo in 1873, described it as "perhaps the most wretched and immoral town that I have ever seen."[14] It was too small, dreary, and provincial — and all too lacking in amenities — to draw much money out of the pockets of its hurried visitors. Yet if the dingy drinking establishments and bordellos did but a trifling business, that business still sufficed to keep alive thousands of poverty-stricken Cape Verdeans. And the sordid traffic in prostitution had long-lasting consequences, for São Vicente became a racial crossroads of random genetic types. Down the streets of Mindelo walked persons of many races and many racial mixtures.

In order to extract whatever profit they could from the Mindelo ships, the Portuguese authorities embarked on the ill-advised policy of placing high tariffs on the coal. This drove away many ships, as did the lack of adequate piers and docks. Ships which had once called at Mindelo were lured to the Canary Islands and Casablanca, and especially to neighboring Dakar,[15] where the French built good harbor facilities. The competition from rival ports began to be felt most keenly precisely at the time when the worldwide depression of the 1930s reduced shipping activity, and when the technological shift from coal to oil, from the steamship to the motor ship, caused problems at all coaling stations. In 1912 a total of 1,707 ships called at Porto Grande; in 1929 the number was 1,363, and by 1933 it had fallen to 586.[16] In 1937 the Portuguese government moved to lower the tariffs on coal, but this action came twenty or thirty years too late, when oil was displacing coal[17] as a shipping fuel (see table 26).

13. All of which is well described in Lyall, pp. 26–27, 80–82.

14. Ellis, p. 128.

15. On Dakar as a bunkering port, in rivalry with Mindelo, see B.S. Hoyle and D. Hilling, eds., *Seaports and Development in Tropical Africa* (London, 1970), pp. 43–45.

16. Lyall, p. 127.

17. The change from coal to oil greatly reduced the number of jobs at the Mindelo docks (because oil refueling, in contrast to coal, required few hands and was nearly automatic), and thus damaged the fragile economy of Mindelo. Since the mid-1950s the port has recovered somewhat and has begun to attract more ships. Recent improvements in the docking facilities, combined with the closings of the Suez Canal, have helped to divert more ships to Mindelo.

TABLE 26

Sales of Coal and Oil at Mindelo, 1927–32 and 1952–57*

Year	Coal Sold at Mindelo (in metric tons)	Oil Sold at Mindelo (in metric tons)
1927	305,500	32,811
1928	234,300	66,509
1929	262,800	141,938
1930	153,200	123,899
1931	120,500	125,549
1932	70,000	203,000
Six-year total	1,146,300	693,706
1952	10,200	362,098
1953	4,200	465,143
1954	3,300	701,935
1955	2,400	447,583
1956	5,200	440,662
1957	1,200	537,929
Six-year total	26,500	2,955,350

*Adapted from *Colóquios Cabo-Verdianos* (Lisbon, 1959), pp. 164–65.

In the seventeenth century, as in the nineteenth and twentieth centuries, ship supply, rather than the buying and selling of voluminous cargoes, was the principal service rendered by the Cape Verdes to Atlantic commerce and navigation. In the nineteenth century the chief article supplied to ships was coal and the port was in São Vicente; in the seventeenth century the chief articles were victuals, beverages, and ship's stores, and the ports were in the island of Santiago — but the principle was the same. As early as 1512 a letter from the settlers at the capital city of Ribeira Grande claimed that Santiago "already has a large concourse of ships which come to trade, and is a great port of call for the king's carracks and vessels, and also for ships from São Tomé and Príncipe, and those that come from the ports of Brazil and Mina and all parts of Guiné." The settlers remarked that when ships arrived at Santiago in a distressed condition, "without supplies and manpower, they are repaired and provided with everything, as happened to Afonso de

Albuquerque who came from India in his carrack *Santiago*, and Alfredo Barreto in the carrack *Santa Marta*, who lacked money and seamen, and who received everything and proceeded to Lisbon, which they reached."[18]

Although the letter speaks of assisting Portuguese East Indiamen on the return to Europe, it was more common for such ships to call at the Cape Verdes on the outward, rather than on the return, voyage. For instance the governor of India, Nuno da Cunha, with a powerful armada, put in at Santiago in April 1528 while on his way to the East.[19] And again, although the letter mentions the "ports of Brazil," there were no settlements in Brazil in 1512 and therefore ships to that area were few; yet when such settlements emerged, the islands furnished them with assistance. When Martim Afonso de Sousa set out from Lisbon on 3 December 1530, with five ships, on the first officially sponsored effort to plant a permanent colony on the coast of Brazil, the officials of Santiago were ordered to supply him with all necessities, up to the value of 300 cruzados. The farm animals and livestock which were taken to São Vicente (the Brazilian settlement he founded in 1532) probably came from Santiago. The sugarcane that was first harvested in São Vicente in 1533 – possibly planted by the Genoese brothers Francesco, Giuseppe, and Paolo Adorno – came from the Cape Verdes or Madeira, or from both places.[20]

The islands continued to assist all ships to Brazil, particularly after the foundation of the Brazilian capital city, Salvador da Bahia, with a resident governor-general, in 1549. Santiago supplied Bahia with oxen, cows, horses, mares, sheep, goats, and with sugarcane and rice shoots.[21] When the first bishop of Bahia, Pero Fernandes Sardinha, was on his way to Brazil, he stopped at Santiago in April 1552, confirmed five or six hundred persons, and reported to Portugal that "we were at this island for four days, during which time I felt that this land was richer in money than in virtue."[22] One century later, Santiago gave a generous welcome to the celebrated Jesuit preacher, missionary, and diplomat, Father António Vieira, who was on his way to Brazil. Vieira arrived aboard the pirate-pursued and storm-tossed caravel, *Nossa Senhora das*

18. Sena Barcelos, 1: 69.
19. Ibid., p. 94.
20. Brásio, 2: 216–17; Peragallo, pp. 387–88; Peres, *História de Portugal,* 3: 636; 4: 153–59.
21. Ribeiro, *Aspectos e problemas,* p. 135.
22. Brásio, 2: 441.

Candeias, in the company of several merchantmen bound for Pernambuco, on Saturday, 21 December 1652. The next day, which was Christmas Sunday, he preached at the cathedral of Ribeira Grande, was well received, and came away with a good impression of the Cape Verdeans.[23]

The experiences of Sardinha in 1552 and Vieira in 1652, separated by one hundred years, were normal and routine, and were shared by thousands of others on the Portugal-Brazil voyage during stopovers in the Cape Verdes. The islands were also a frequent port of call for ships bound from Europe to the West Indies and to Newfoundland. These included Portuguese and Spanish slavers, English, French, and Dutch West Indiamen in the slaves-and-sugar trade, and English codfishers picking up Cape Verdean salt.

In its early days Santiago served as a point of collection and diffusion, transmitting animals and plants from one continent to another. To Brazil, from Santiago, went rice, sugarcane, African yams, and the domesticated animals of the Old World. In the other direction, the Cape Verdeans imported from Brazil the plant that soon became the chief source of food for the islands — Brazilian maize; this maize, in turn, the Cape Verdeans took to the coast of West Africa, where in some places it became a staple. Brazilian manioc plants were also introduced into Africa by way of the Cape Verdes.[24]

This transoceanic transmittal of vital food-bearing plants, dramatic though it was, lasted but a few short years; once a certain amount of diffusion had taken place, it was self-perpetuating — and the Cape Verdes settled down to their proper, but humdrum, function of ship supply. The islanders found in the processes of revictualing their most vital service to Atlantic navigation, and the essential products involved were dried and salted meats, particularly salted goatmeat, an article of consumption that may not be to the modern taste, but which was, given the agricultural and climatic restrictions of the island situation, an ideal product for the Cape Verdes to produce — ideal because the goat was the only domesticated animal that could thrive on the meager scrub pasturages of the islands, and salt was the only important Cape Verdean mineral product. Raising goats and extracting salt, virtually the sole economic activities on several islands, cost the Cape Verdeans little or nothing; and producing salted goatmeat was simple and cheap. The prepara-

23. Arq. Dist. Évora, Codex CXV/2-13, fols. 324–25; Vieira, *Cartas* 1 (Lisbon, 1925): 295.
24. Ribeiro, *Aspectos e problemas*, pp. 153–54; Amaral, p. 180.

tion of dried meat, making use of the hot Cape Verdean sun, was likewise simple and cheap.

The islands could also supply beef, pork, and small quantities of lamb and mutton, in dried and salted forms, but these meat products were in shorter supply and were much more expensive than goatmeat. When the Palatine princes Rupert and Maurice, in their ill-advised and semipiratical attempt to keep alive the Royalist cause of the exiled Charles II of England, sailed about the Cape Verdean and West African seas in search of prizes during the months from February to May of 1652, their six or seven ships put in at Santiago, Boavista, and Maio in quest of supplies.[25] In return for hides, leather, paper, beads, ironware, and other objects, the princes received 2,000 arrobas of dried goatmeat and 230 arrobas of dried beef.[26] In this particular revictualing operation, the quantity of goatmeat exceeded that of beef by a ratio of almost nine to one, and this furnishes some idea of the comparative importance of goatmeat in relation to beef and of how the islands could supply much more of one commodity than the other. In all, counting both goatmeat and beef, the Cape Verdeans furnished the Palatine princes with 2,230 arrobas of meat — a respectable quantity which, in modern English terms, came to the equivalent of over 70,000 pounds.

Although at times there were heavy demands from ships for Cape Verdean meats, it seems that usually the ability of the islands to supply goatmeat exceeded the capacity or desire of visiting seamen to purchase it. There was consequently a surplus which was exported to Madeira and Brazil. The island of Madeira, chronically short of cereals, dairy products, and meat, was forced to import heavy quantities of various foodstuffs, including salted meat and fish. Although it is impossible to determine the quantity of meat sent from the Cape Verdes to Madeira (since salted and dried meats paid no import duties, they were not recorded in the customshouse registers), the extant minute books of the Funchal aldermen are full of references to *chacinas do Cabe Verde* (preserved meats from Cape Verde), which were almost certainly goatmeat. The minute books of 1618 and 1623, for example, record several large shipments of Cape Verdean meat, samples of which were shown to the

25. For a full explanation of Prince Rupert's muddled expedition of 1651–53, see B.E.G. Warburton, *Memoirs of Prince Rupert,* 3 vols. (London, 1849), 3: 351–70; and R.C. Anderson, "Royalists at Sea, 1651–1653," *Mariner's Mirror* 21 (1935): 78–83.

26. "Memorial de matalotagem" (copy dated 9 July 1652) in AHU, Cabo Verde, Caixa II; Warburton, 3: 541.

aldermen, who set a retail price of $012 réis (a little more than 2d.) per pound, a price so low as to place the humble commodity within the reach of almost every purse.[27]

If the retail price of salted goatmeat at Funchal between 1610 and 1640 was only $012 réis per pound, this means that the wholesale export price in the Cape Verdes could not have been more than about $005 or $006 per pound – a value so low, in relation to bulk and to time spent in preparation and handling, as to make goatmeat a product of marginal profitability for producer and shipper alike. After the Portuguese devaluations of 1641 and 1643, which reduced the silver content of Portuguese coins by about 43 percent, the merchants at Funchal raised the price of Cape Verdean meats but were fined by the aldermen for doing so. By 1655 the aldermen were forced to approve a price level of $025 réis per pound – which in terms of sterling was only 3d. per pound, and therefore not much of a real increase on the 1618 price of 2¼d. – but there are indications in the minute books that the merchants were still unhappy about prices.[28]

Facts about the export of Cape Verdean meats to Brazil are hard to find, but there is evidence here and there of fairly large shipments from Santiago to Bahia. In 1647, for instance, one ship carried 1,400 arrobas (equivalent to 44,800 lbs., or exactly 20 English long tons) of Cape Verdean meat to Bahia; yet records of this cargo are extant only because a complaint was made to Lisbon that 200 arrobas of the meat had been spoiled by sea water.[29]

Nonetheless the export of goatmeat, to whatever destinations, was less important than the use of such meat for the revictualing of ships. In the islands themselves, the flesh and milk of goats were staples of diet. Similarly, the characteristic Cape Verdean dairy products were goat butter and goat cheese, and not the butter and cheese derived from the cow. Furthermore the goat supplied another exported product – goatskins – which were sent abroad either as treated leather or as hairy pelts. During the nineteenth century a brisk trade in goatskins flourished between the Cape Verdes and New England. In 1840 goatskins sold in the islands

27. Arq. Dist. Funchal, "Vereações, 1618," fols. 27, 35; "1623," fols. 64–65.
28. Ibid., "1650," fol. 28; "1655," fol. 10; "1658," fol. 48.
29. Conselho Ultramarino *consulta*, 4 February 1648, AHU, Bahia, Caixa VI. Sun-dried meat, especially "jerked beef" (Portuguese *charque* or *carne sêca*), was part of the ordinary diet of the slaves and common people in the Brazilian Northeast; there are still today people in that area who prefer dried and salted meat to fresh meat.

for between $160 and $300 réis apiece, and could be disposed of in Boston for the equivalent of $600 réis each.[30] That is, if a merchant at Santiago bought 1,000 goatskins for $275 réis each, he would spend the equivalent of U.S.$220 and could hope to sell in New England for U.S. $660. Cape Verdean goatskins were still being sold in the United States during the first decades of the twentieth century.

The humble goat was therefore one of the pillars of the shaky Cape Verdean economy; yet such a reliance on the goat was itself a symptom of the poverty of the islands and speaks eloquently of the barrenness of the Cape Verdean environment. The goats, moreover, although they could be used as a means of extracting a small economic profit from a skimpy pasturage, only worsened the situation by doing further damage to the vegetation. For in the Cape Verdes the goats ran wild, unpenned, uncontrolled, and unchecked; indeed, in at least five of the islands (Boavista, Sal, Maio, Brava, and São Nicolau), goats were placed and allowed to run free before any humans settled at all.[31]

In addition to the dried and salted meats, acquired by purchase or barter and designed for the sustenance of the ordinary seamen of visiting ships, other food products of a more or less luxurious nature were acquired for the use of officers and passengers. The more privileged persons aboard obtained fresh meat, fish, cheese, butter, and eggs, and also live poultry (and the corn meal to feed them), so that during the voyage fresh eggs, or an occasional roast fowl, would be available. Visiting seamen, particularly those with some notion of the importance of good nutrition, especially to guard against scurvy, purchased fresh fruits and vegetables in the Cape Verdes. The islands apparently did not produce much in the way of leafy green vegetables but did grow ample quantities of sweet potatoes, yams, squashes, maize, and beans, and were well supplied with fruits, particularly the citrus fruits vital in the fight against scurvy.

The upper valley beyond the capital of Ribeira Grande, according to a sixteenth-century account, was planted with "vast groves . . . of oranges, cedars, lemons, pomegranates, figs of every kind, and . . . palms which

30. Chelmicki, 2: 359–60.
31. Brásio, 1: 741–44. In 1875 the Cape Verdean goat population was estimated at 80,000 head, but in 1878 at only 58,374; Andrade Corvo, 1: 55–56. In times of drought the number of animals has dropped drastically, only to recover again afterwards. No actual head count has ever been made, so that estimates of animal population are based on gross calculations. For recent estimates, see Amaral, pp. 289–90.

produce coconuts."[32] Other old sources mention many tropical fruits available in Santiago, fruits such as melons, plantains, limes, guavas, watermelons, bananas, prickly pears, custard apples, quinces, papayas, pineapples, and dates.[33]

Apart from revictualing, the Cape Verdean function of ship supply and ship support involved the furnishing of beverages, the sale of naval stores, and the repairing of ships. Of beverages, there was little more than water; there was no beer, and only small quantities of island-made wine. The normal seventeenth-century ship beverage, aside from beer, was made up of four or five parts water to one of wine, with the wine helping to preserve the water, which if left unmixed would soon turn bad. Not much water-and-wine beverage, if any, was made in the Cape Verdes, because most of the wine was imported and expensive.[34]

Naval stores, almost all of which had to be imported, were also scarce and expensive in the islands. The island imported quantities of timber, sailcloth, cordage, and pitch, and kept supplies on hand to sell, at a high price, to needy ships. Essential ship repairs could be carried out at Santaigo, if they were not too complicated; but the island had neither the facilities nor the skilled labor necessary for extensive overhauls or large-scale alterations. Ship construction, in Santiago, seems to have been limited to the small craft used for inter-island communication.

Most of the activities of victualing, watering, and ship maintenance were centered on the island of Santiago,[35] which is the largest, most

32. Blake, 1: 149.

33. Ligon, p. 11; Dampier, 3: 24; Thomas Salmon, *Modern History; or, the Present State of All Nations,* 3d ed., 3 vols. (London, 1746), 3: 93; Southey, 3: 178; A. Teixeira da Mota, *Cinco séculos de cartografia das Ilhas de Cabo Verde* (Lisbon, 1961), p. 12.

34. Wine from Madeira, the Canaries, and Portugal – and perhaps a little from Spain and the Azores – was one of the chief imports at Santiago. Santiago, Fogo, Brava, São Nicolau, Santo Antão, and possibly Boavista and Maio as well, all produced small quantities of wine, entirely consumed locally and probably of no great quality. Wine production was more important in the more isolated islands – such as Santo Antão and Brava – which had little trade and could not afford European wines, than in Santiago. Most of the islands also produced their own rum.

35. The Spanish spelling "Santiago" seems to be the preferred form in the islands, although the Portuguese spelling "São Tiago" (Saint James) was once common, particularly in official use. In the older documents the island of Santiago was usually called "Cabo Verde," while the town of Ribeira Grande was called "Santiago." The inhabitants of Santiago still, to this day, refer to their own island as "Cabo Verde" – or "Cáu Berde" in the creole – as if it were the mainland, while calling the other Cape Verdes simply "as Ilhas" (the Islands), and they will not admit the other islands to inclusion under the name "Cabo Verde."

TABLE 27

The Population of the Island of Santiago in 1572*
(by parishes)

Santa Catarina do Mato	2,400
Ribeira Grande	1,500
Antónia	1,050
São Domingos	950
São Lourenço dos Órgãos	650
Praia	500
Ribeira dos Flamengos	450
Tarrafal	250
Alcatrazes	250
Total	8,000

*A rough estimate calculated from figures for either *fogos* (hearths) or *almas* (souls) in António Brásio, *Monumenta Missionaria Africana: África Ocidental,* pt. II, 3 (Lisbon, 1964): 28–52. Figures raised by one-third to include uncounted slaves.

populous, and historically the most significant of the ten large islands in the archipelago. The Cape Verdes have never been oversupplied with riches, comforts, and amenities – but, historically speaking (prior to the emergence of the port of Mindelo after 1850), Santiago has absorbed the lion's share of the archipelago's improvements, benefits, and money. Already by 1572 the main island had two large settlements, Ribeira Grande and Praia, one fair-sized but scattered interior village, São Domingos (which Sir Francis Drake, in his 1585 raid, thought was worth attacking), and there were enough persons in the interior to form seven parishes. Ribeira Grande had perhaps 1,500 persons, Praia about 500, and approximately 6,000 persons lived in the interior and along the coasts, divided among seven parishes (see table 27). The interior population – comprised of slaves, freedmen, mulattoes, and a few white landlords – was scattered about the inland mountains and valleys, without forming towns or marketing centers of importance. Nor were there any other ports that could compete with Ribeira Grande and Praia. Even today the "big" villages of Tarrafal, Assomada, and Pedra Badejo are but shapeless agglomerations of small houses, with only one or two dusty streets, and perhaps one or two small public buildings or general stores to give them character and definition.[36]

36. See the charts and photographs in Amaral, and his discussion on pp. 247–53.

Ribeira Grande, founded by Antonio da Noli and his Genoese followers, was the first settlement in Santiago. The site was located on the
south coast, at a suitable anchorage, protected by the central range of
mountains, which rise to a maximum height of 4,566 feet, from the prevailing northeasterly and northerly winds. The consistency of direction
of these winds, together with their strength and regularity, probably induced the Genoese mariners to pick out the most leeward point on the
island for their settlement.[37] The leeward position, which obstructed
the wind, sometimes made sailing to the anchorage at Ribeira Grande
a tricky matter, and the anchorage itself has the general appearance of
an open roadstead, but the infrequency of southern and southwestern
winds (which blow only a few days during the months from July to
November), and the extreme infrequency of westerly winds, meant that
ships at anchor had much protection most of the time.

Captain William Dampier, indeed, annoyed at the rocky bottom and
poor holding ground, declared that the Ribeira Grande harbor was "one
of the worst that I have been in."[38] He contended that there was good
anchorage at only one point, where only three ships could anchor at a
time, and even then they would be dangerously close together. Yet the
anchorage at Ribeira Grande was safer than any in Madeira or the Azores
(except Horta), and, in relation to other mid-Atlantic island harbors,
was superior to most; even if an infrequent, but dangerous, south or
southwesterly wind should spring up, a ship at Ribeira Grande could
escape fairly easily by way of the northwest or by sailing due east.

The site, moreover, had other advantages, including a stony landing
beach and an ample supply of fresh water. Dampier himself admitted
that there was "good watering and good landing at any time; tho' the
Road be rocky and bad for ships."[39] The large stream that gave Ribeira
Grande (Big Creek) its name, ran down a narrow valley and, before
reaching the sea, formed a wide pool, which was damned at the mouth
by a maze of pebbles through which the water trickled out slowly to
the sea. The pool, which apparently never dried up and was not con-
taminated by the seawater, afforded an ample supply of fresh water for

37. Santiago wind patterns are examined minutely in Amaral, pp. 29–32. Old
descriptions of Santiago's climate agree at most points with modern studies, indicating that the climate – at least as far as droughts, seasonal rainfall, and wind
patterns are concerned – may not have changed much during the last five hundred
years.
38. Dampier, 3: 26.
39. Ibid., p. 23.

the town and for visiting ships. In addition, the site was easy to defend. Hills and cliffs overlooked and surrounded the town; when the heights were fortified, they commanded the landward and seaward approaches.

Ribeira Grande came of age suddenly, in 1533, when it was raised in rank from *vila* to *cidade* and when a papal bull made it the seat of a bishopric whose jurisdiction extended along the African coast from Gambia to Cape Palmas. The new diocese had a cathedral chapter that included a dean, an archdeacon, a choir director, a treasurer, a schoolmaster, and twelve canons, but no bishop was actually in residence at Santiago until 1550, and the cathedral building, whose construction was delayed for decades, was not actually finished until 1692.[40]

In 1572 the "city" of Ribeira Grande had 225 households,[41] divided among three separate districts, with a total population of perhaps 1,500 persons, many of them slaves. Its harbor was the normal port of call for all Portuguese ships outward bound to India and Brazil, and for many of the ships engaged in the African slave trade. Its chief drawback was its reputation for being unhealthy; during the rainy season (August to October), in particular, mortality was high at Ribeira Grande.

The chief challenge to the preeminence enjoyed by Ribeira Grande in Santiago, and throughout the Cape Verdes, came from the settlement known formally as the "Vila da Praia de Santa Maria." Praia (the name means "Beach") lay seven or eight miles to the east of Ribeira Grande and was built on a tableland or shelf of rock, with steep escarpments on all sides, situated on a small bay. The bay is about one-and-a-half miles wide at the mouth, with a length of about one mile. It offered good shelter for sailing ships — except during the short season of the year when the wind blew, occasionally, from the south and southeast — but, unfortunately, was filled with tricky shallows; most of the water in the bay is under five fathoms in depth, and much of it under three. Modern ships drawing a fair amount of water have to anchor very far out indeed, and hardly any of them can enter the bay at all; but seventeenth-century pinnaces and caravels could penetrate the bay and drop anchor in good holding ground, in 4 or 5 fathoms of water, some 550 yards from shore.[42]

40. Brásio, 3: 249–54; Sena Barcelos, 1: 104–6; 2: 104; Amaral, pp. 177–78; Mendes Corrêa, pp. 196–97.

41. Brásio, 3: 36.

42. U.S. Naval Oceanographic Office, Chart 5722, rev. ed. (Washington, 1968), includes an inset map of the harbor at Praia.

Small boats could touch shore at the wide sandy beach of Praia Grande, or at the small pebbly beach of Praia Negra. The sheltered bay and the landing beaches presented the Santiagoans with a military problem: unless Praia were strongly fortified, an enemy could land his forces there and then march overland and take Ribeira Grande from the rear. The difficulty was not one of mere theory, for this is precisely what Sir Francis Drake did in mid-November 1585. An English force of 1,000 men landed at Praia, marched overland to Ribeira Grande, but found the capital deserted because the inhabitants had fled to the interior mountains. Indeed, even under the most favorable circumstances, the Santiagoans would have had little chance against as formidable a force as came at them in 1585 — for Drake had 25 ships and 2,300 men.[43]

The Englishmen stayed two weeks but acquired little in the way of booty. Drake marched 600 men inland to the village of São Domingos, but found it too to be deserted and wisely proceeded no farther. When one of the English boys was killed and his body mutilated, probably by African slaves, Drake avenged himself by burning every house in Ribeira Grande, but spared the hospital building, the Santa Casa da Misericórdia.[44]

Unfortunately for Portugal, the union of the crowns of Spain and Portugal in 1580 made the Portuguese overseas territories fair game for the Dutch and English enemies of Spain, and isolated outposts, such as those in the Azores and the Cape Verdes, suffered assaults. After Drake's attack, the strong fortress of São Felipe was erected in Ribeira Grande and was built so as to provide some protection on the landward side of the town; and, in 1587, the Cape Verdes, for the first time, were placed under the control of a single governor or captain-general, a reform that was long overdue.

Some years later, measures were taken toward fortifying, improving, and populating the town of Praia and providing it with fiscal inspection and control. The port of Praia, left largely unsupervised, was undoubtedly a center for smuggling and, left undefended, was too attractive to would-be aggressors. Praia, early in the seventeenth century, had very few, if any, stone and brick buildings, but consisted of temporary structures, mostly mere shacks; and it was losing inhabitants to the city of Ribeira Grande. A decree issued at Lisbon on 14 August 1612 attempted

---

43. Southey, 3: 174, 177.
44. Ibid., pp. 179–80. The church attached to the hospital was then serving as the diocesan cathedral and as the residence of the cathedral chapter.

to put Praia on an equal footing with Ribeira Grande. It ordered all former residents of Praia to return there and build themselves houses "of stone and mortar and roofed with tiles";[45] it required all ships to put in at Praia, instead of Ribeira Grande, and to process their cargoes through the Praia customshouse; and it ordered the governor and the bishop to reside, alternately, at Ribeira Grande and at Praia.

The decree of 14 August 1612 may have had some effect in diverting shipping to Praia from Ribeira Grande, although this would probably have occurred even without official encouragement. Otherwise the 1612 decree had little result. Stone buildings were not constructed at Praia, nor did its population increase very much. Governors and bishops continued to reside at Ribeira Grande and paid little attention to Praia. In 1652 the command that governors and bishops should reside, alternately, at Praia and Ribeira Grande, and that ships were to use only the port of Praia, was emphatically repeated[46] — which is proof that the decree had not been and was not being observed.

The decree, moreover, had little or no effect on the growth of Praia in relation to Ribeira Grande. For instance, fifty years later, when António Galvão, governor of the Cape Verdes, visited Praia on 16 December 1663, he found it to be undeveloped, in an unhealthy location, and "with a port that is very small, full of shallows, and with very poor anchorages."[47] The governor's remarks on the port, however, reflected his bias in favor of Ribeira Grande and concerned only the extreme interior of the bay, near the landing beach; he himself admitted that there were good anchorages well offshore. The governor's preference for Ribeira Grande was shared by most officials; during the seventeenth century Ribeira Grande continued to be the ecclesiastical, judicial, administrative, and military center, while Praia remained a village of straw-thatched shacks, with only the customshouse and the harbor to give it any claims to distinction.[48]

Ribeira Grande reached its height during the years 1688–1705, when the energetic Franciscan friar, Vitoriano Portuense (also called Vitoriano do Porto), was bishop of Cape Verde. In 1693, owing entirely to the

45. Arq. Dist. Évora, Codex CXVI/2-10, fol. 17; AHU, Cabo Verde, Caixa I, doc. 15; Sena Barcelos, 1: 204.
46. Sena Barcelos, 2: 19.
47. AHU, Cabo Verde, Caixa III, doc. 485.
48. I stress this fact because, in a number of Portuguese accounts, the decline of Ribeira Grande has been traced back to the 1612 decree and hence unduly anticipated.

efforts of Bishop Vitoriano, the great cathedral building was at last completed. The cathedral had been started by the third bishop of Cape Verde, Francisco da Cruz, who died in 1574. After 1574, work on the building was sporadic and halfhearted, and construction funds were even diverted to other purposes. In 1676 the ambitious original plans were scaled down, and it was proposed to build a sanctuary of only 110 hand-breadths in length by 50 in width (that is, about 83 by 38 feet). But Bishop Vitoriano returned to the original design and carried it through to triumphant completion 160 years after the foundation of the diocese.[49] The cathedral chapter left its "temporary" quarters in the church of the hospital of Misericórdia and took up residence in its proper place. Today only ruins survive of the old cathedral, but those ruins, with their four-foot thick walls, testify to the fact that the cathedral of Ribeira Grande was the most splendid building ever erected in the Cape Verdes.

In 1694 Ribeira Grande had 327 households (an increase of 45 percent over the 225 households in 1572), with 1,885 communicants, who were divided into two parishes. The total population probably came to well over 2,000. In 1664 the militia of Santiago, divided between Ribeira Grande and Praia, came to 1,710 officers and men. In 1702 the total was 2,026. Three-quarters of the horses, firearms, equipment, and personnel were committed to the defense of Ribeira Grande, which left Praia too weakly supported. For instance Praia, in 1664, had only 398 officers and men to the capital's 1,312, and only 24 cavalrymen to the capital's 64, and again, in 1702, Praia had only 15 cannon whereas the capital had 80.[50]

The weakness of Praia was demonstrated in May 1712, when it was captured and sacked by a French force under Jacques Cassart. His ten ships flew Dutch and English flags, concealing their nationality. Cassart duplicated the tactics that Drake had used in 1585 and marched over-land to take Ribeira Grande from the rear. Ribeira Grande was much stronger on the landward side than it had been in 1585, but an excessive delay in calling out the militia, and the incompetence and cowardice of the Portuguese leaders, led to an ignominious surrender. The

49. Sena Barcelos, 2: 72–73, 99, 103–4, 174. In 1673 the bishop of Cape Verde, Fabião dos Reis, wanted to divert for his own use 4,000 cruzados (about £580) from the cathedral construction fund, since 6,000 cruzados (about £870) of the fund had already been diverted to the construction of the fortress of Cacheu on the Guiné coast; AHU, Cabo Verde, Caixa IV, *consulta* 12 October 1673.

50. Sena Barcelos, 2: 114, 168–69; AHU, Cabo Verde, Caixa III, doc. 494.

Santiagoans promised the French a large sum of money if they would spare Ribeira Grande, but when the money was not raised, the French helped themselves to whatever valuables they could find, including 8,000 cruzados in silver (about £105) from Misericórdia funds and all the brass cannon, and sailed away after a stay of eight days.[51]

After the French raid of 1712, official attention encouraged the growth and strengthening of Praia, while Ribeira Grande slowly began its long, disastrous decline — a decline which is so strongly apparent to the visitor in present-day Santiago. In 1735 the cathedral was reported to be in disrepair and the roof leaking. In 1754 a new bishop, Pedro Jacinto Valente, arrived at Santiago, but refused to live on the island or care for his cathedral. He spent only three weeks in Santiago and then sailed for São Nicolau, where he stayed eight months. Finally he went to the island of Santo Antão, where he spent the rest of his life, dying there in January 1774, nineteen years later.[52]

The bishop's sudden, perplexing, and permanent abandonment of his own cathedral signaled the beginning of the decline of Ribeira Grande. In 1770, when governor Joaquim Salema Saldanha Lobo transferred his capital to Praia, the process of depopulation was accelerated. In the nineteenth century the old capital, with its cathedral, fell into ruins; its very name vanished from common use, and Ribeira Grande became known only as Cidade Velha, the "Old City." In the meantime, Praia increased in size and importance, was raised to the rank of *cidade* in 1858, and reigned unchallenged over the island.[53]

In the seventeenth century none of the other islands in the archipelago could match Santiago in urban development, political importance, or in population resources. One or two of the other islands, nonetheless, had their own independent roles to play in the world of Atlantic commerce and navigation. The Cape Verdes, with reference to seventeenth-century trade, can be divided into three categories: (1) the agricultural islands

51. Sena Barcelos, 2: 188–204, 225; Charles de la Roncière, *Histoire de la marine française* 6 (Paris, 192?): 540–42; Arq. Dist. Évora, Codex CXVI/2-15, doc. 5.

52. Sena Barcelos, 3: 20–21. Bishop Valente, who probably abandoned Santiago because it was extremely unhealthy, erected the large church of Nossa Senhora do Rosário in the village of Ribeira Grande, at the northern end of the island of Santo Antão. Rosário, it seems, was intended to be the bishop's cathedral, but the transfer of the see to Santo Antão was never officially approved. Instead, sometime later, the see was transferred to São Nicolau, where it remained until the twentieth century. Today the bishop's seat is at Praia.

53. Sena Barcelos, 3: 51; Amaral, pp. 327–29.

(which included Fogo, Brava, Santo Antão, and São Nicolau, as well as Santiago); (2) the salt islands (Maio, Boavista, and Sal); and (3) the uninhabited, tradeless islands (São Vicente, Santa Luzia, and the islets of Branco and Raso).

Of the third group – the tradeless, barren, uninhabited, and all but "useless" islands, little need be said. These islands lie in a string, one after the other, in the fifty miles of sea that separate Santo Antão and São Nicolau. Lack of rain makes them inhospitable and bleak. São Vicente, as has been noted, was one day to enjoy a period of development and growth as the British "cinder-heap," but in the seventeenth century it was rarely visited and rarely mentioned. Santa Luzia, Branco, and Raso are small, arid, and forbidding, and remain uninhabited. They possess no harbors, and only the crudest of anchorages, and some of the passages between them are treacherous to sailing ships and have not been adequately charted.

The barren, uninhabited islands lack any importance for the seventeenth-century Atlantic world, yet they stand as fit symbols of an archipelago where even the greenest islands are touched by barrenness and drought. For the phrase "agricultural islands" must be understood in a very limited sense: the islands of Santiago, Fogo, Brava, and São Nicolau are "agricultural" only in comparison with the others, and the word must not conjure up visions of rolling fields of grain, or of groves of fruit trees. Agriculture in the Cape Verdes is strictly limited in time and place. Limited in time to a short season of a few months or weeks, and limited in place to a few cramped, less inhospitable locations, such as the banks of a small creek, an "oasis" around a well or spring, or the dew-touched slopes of a high mountain. Much of the volcanic soil, to be sure, is rich and fertile and requires no fertilizers, but without an adequate supply of water little can be done with it.

The island of Fogo, next to Santiago, is the most important of the agricultural islands. This well-named island ("Fogo" means "Fire") consists largely of the base and slopes and craters of a gigantic, active, and fiercesome volcano, twice as high and covering twice the area of Vesuvius. Since 1563 the volcano has erupted twenty-eight times, including the eruption of 1951.[54] It is higher than Pico in the Azores and, among the Atlantic islands, is exceeded in height only by Tenerife in the Canaries.

---

54. The only full-length study is in Ribeiro, *Fogo*, which is amply supplied with maps, charts, and excellent photographs. See also Mendes Corrêa, pp. 31–32, and Lyall, pp. 138–40.

Fogo was the second island in the Cape Verdes to be colonized. The earliest settlement came between 1480 and 1500, probably about the end of the 1480s. In 1572 the island had two parishes and a total of 240 hearths (*fogos*), indicating a population of perhaps about 1,200.[55] Fogo produced raw cotton, and also cotton cloth, which was shipped by small boat to Santiago and from there re-exported to Guiné and Brazil. Although the small-boat traffic between Santiago and Fogo may have been fairly brisk, Fogo felt isolated and neglected, was seldom visited by transoceanic ships except for an occasional English vessel, and was evidently regarded as a hardship post. Even Lisbon, in a decree issued in 1612, threatened the inhabitants of Santiago with a penalty of two years of exile in Fogo if they disobeyed certain commands.[56] Since Fogo is only 30 nautical miles to the west of Santiago, it appears that the psychological distance between the two islands was greater than the geographical and that the Santiagoans thought of a compulsory stay at Fogo as a kind of imprisonment.

The isolation of the island, and the cooperation of Portuguese renegades, contributed to the success of a Dutch attack on Fogo in 1655. For four days the Dutch plundered and destroyed at will, and a relief force from Santiago arrived too late.[57] When news of the attack reached Lisbon, together with the pleas from Fogo for more Portuguese settlers, King John IV ordered his judges to sentence convicts to exile in Fogo but reminded them that such a sentence was considered more severe than exile to Angola.[58] After the sack of 1655 the most effective assistance came from English ships; Fogo, although forbidden to supply foreign ships with anything more than food and water, nonetheless traded frequently with the English and continued to do so in spite of the reiterated prohibitions emanating from Santiago and Lisbon.[59]

Fogo's participation in seventeenth-century international navigation was limited and intermittent, but it never entirely ceased. In the nineteenth century, like its tiny neighbor Brava, Fogo had close relations with American whaling ships, supplied men for service aboard American vessels, and sent emigrants to Massachusetts. Yet the island itself lagged

55. Brásio, 1: 476; 3: 44, 53; Ribeiro, *Aspectos e problemas,* p. 137.
56. Arq. Dist. Évora, Codex CXVI/2-10, fol. 17.
57. AHU, Cabo Verde, Caixa III, *consulta* 12 June 1656; and Codex 15, fols. 231–32; Sena Barcelos, 2: 26.
58. Biblioteca da Ajuda, Codex 51-V-17, doc. 111.
59. AHU, Cabo Verde, Caixa III, doc. 449; Caixa IV, *consultas* 4 September 1670, 19 August 1673.

behind the outside world and was ignored by Santiago and Lisbon. When Lyall visited Fogo's capital of São Filipe in 1936 he found a town which, although occupying a larger area than the city of Praia, had no electric light or power, no refrigeration, no restaurants, no hotels or "pensions," and where small shaggy horses provided the only means of transportation.[60] The living circumstances of Praia in 1936, by contrast, were comparatively luxurious.

Fogo's closest neighbor is the tiny, but densely populated, island of Brava. Brava has only 25 square miles of surface, but in 1960 its population was 8,646, which means a population density of 346 persons per square mile.[61] Brava, far from being "wild," is the most intensively cultivated island in the Cape Verdes and possesses certain features unique in the archipelago. The island is a small, extinct volcano, greener and more moist than the other Cape Verdes, and has a charming "garden city" capital of Vila de Nova Sintra situated within the crater of the old volcano.

Its inhabitants are less Africanized than the other Cape Verdeans, contain a great proportion of men with pure white blood, and have kept up a long seafaring tradition. Like the Azoreans of Pico-Fayal, the men of Brava served aboard the New Bedford whalers, sent many emigrants to New England, and have themselves owned and manned sailing vessels that maintained regular connections between the United States and the Cape Verdes. The Bravans, as a group, are (or were) the most nautical, the most venturesome, the most Americanized, and the most cosmopolitan of the lower-class Cape Verdeans.[62]

Yet Brava is hardly ever mentioned in seventeenth-century records and was probably seldom visited by ships. Its main channel of communication with the outside world was by way of small-boat traffic to the neighboring island of Fogo, for the distance between Brava's quaint little port of Furna (which is actually a small volcanic crater) and the anchorage near São Filipe in Fogo is only about ten nautical miles. According to one account, Brava was settled sometime before 1545 by order of a certain João da Fonseca, who was its proprietor. The island's humidity and fertility probably made it attractive to farmers. A number of people were certainly living there in 1624, and by 1686, when it

60. Lyall, pp. 138–40.
61. Amaral, p. 375.
62. Lyall, pp. 64–65, 140–57.

was attacked by pirates and the royal *feitor*, or factor, was killed, it was probably a thriving agricultural community.[63] Brava, nonetheless, is of little or no importance for seventeenth-century Cape Verdean history.

The two remaining agricultural islands — Santo Antão and São Nicolau — both belong to the Windward Islands of the northwest, and both are very mountainous and rugged. Santo Antão, with 300 square miles of area, is the largest of the Cape Verdes after Santiago but suffers from serious disadvantages. It has virtually no road system and few means of interior communications. Its anchorages are few and poor, and the best one, at Tarrafal on the southwest, is far removed from the most promising agricultural areas, which are in the north. In the seventeenth century, moreover, the island was remote from the main Cape Verdean shipping nexus of Santiago-Maio-Fogo.

Information about the early history of Santo Antão is skimpy. It was first settled in 1548, but the community there remained ingrown and isolated. In 1732 the principal village, Ribeira Grande on the northern coast, was said to have sixteen streets and was given the status of *vila*.[64] The fact that bishop Valente chose to settle there in 1755 says something in its favor, although as late as 1869 the Portuguese minister of colonies remarked that "Santo Antão presented the appearance of an island that had only been discovered months ago."[65]

São Nicolau, like Santo Antão, is mountainous and rugged, but is far smaller and more arid. The island is saved by certain interior valleys, scarcely visible from the sea, that are green and well watered; the rest of the terrain is rock and sand. In 1595 the church at São Nicolau had only seventy communicants, and by 1619 was still too small to support a priest; the island may not have received a priest until 1677.[66] When Dampier visited the "mountainous barren island" in 1683, he was met

63. AHU, Cabo Verde, Caixa I, doc. 125; and Codex 489, fol. 53. Sena Barcelos, 1: 122; Ribeiro, *Aspectos e problemas*, p. 148. Those who think that Brava was first colonized by people from Fogo fleeing volcanic eruptions in the 1670s (Mendes Corrêa, p. 130), or that Brava was not settled until the end of the seventeenth century (*Cabo Verde: Curso de extensão*, p. 929), are mistaken. Yet Drake's mariners in 1578 saw no inhabitants at Brava, "one only hermit excepted," who cared for a small chapel; Francis Drake, *World Encompassed* (London, 1854), p. 25. Any settlement, however, would have been located in the well-watered valley inside the high crater, and therefore not visible from either sea or shore.

64. Sena Barcelos, 2: 265–67; Ribeiro, *Aspectos e problemas,* p. 148.

65. Andrade Corvo, p. 85.

66. Brásio, 3: 381; AHU, Cabo Verde, Caixa I, doc. 95.

by the "governor" (that is, the royal factor),[67] three or four well-dressed gentlemen, and twenty or thirty men in ragged garb. Dampier learned that there were over a hundred families on the island. He was pleasantly surprised by the greenness of the interior and by the vineyards and plantations. He commented on the wood available for fuel, on the considerable numbers of goats and donkeys, and on the quality of the island's wine, which he said "tasted much like *Madera.*"[68]

Dampier's party stayed at São Nicolau for five or six days, digging wells for water and careening their ships in the wide bay of São Jorge, for the island is so formed that its long eastern arm, and a sharp mountainous thrust to the south, combine to form the largest bay in the Cape Verdes. Careening (that is, laying a vessel on her side in order to clean and repair the bottom) is a dangerous operation, and would not have been attempted by Dampier had not the bay offered good protection from the wind. The main anchorage in the bay is off Porto da Preguiça, in 7 to 18 fathoms, with fair holding ground, from 150 to 350 yards offshore.[69] The sheltering bay, the safe anchorage, the availability of water, and the victuals obtainable from the interior valleys made São Nicolau a reasonably attractive port of call.

More important than the agricultural islands to transatlantic trade were the three salt islands of Maio, Sal, and Boavista, all situated to the east. The salt islands differ greatly from the agricultural islands because they are low-lying and flat (their highest elevation, on Maio, is only 1,430 feet), they are largely without vegetable cover, and they support very few people. Population densities in the salt islands are very low. Boavista, for instance, which with 240 square miles is the third largest of the Cape Verdes, reported only 3,309 inhabitants in the 1960 census, which gave it a population density of only 14 persons per square mile.

Historically speaking, Maio was the most important, the most populous, and the most frequented of the salt islands. Salt deposits are Maio's

67. The *feitor real* was the administrator in islands or outposts too small to have a governor, captain-major, captain, or a sergeant-major in command. He was usually appointed from among the principal merchants. He had special responsibility for collecting the king's revenues and looking after royal properties. He also served as the local magistrate, with jurisdiction over small disputes and petty crimes. The duties and privileges of the royal factor are explained in Luiz de Bivar Guerra, "Sindicância do desembargador Custódio de Matos," *Studia* (Lisbon), no. 2 (1958), pp. 198–272.

68. Dampier, 1: 74.

69. U.S. Navy Hydrographic Office, Chart 5720, 2d ed. (Washington, 1951).

most striking feature and its main, almost its only, source of wealth. An anonymous Portuguese account written between 1535 and 1550 stated that at Maio "there is a lake more than two leagues long, and wide in proportion, full of salt dried by the sun, enough to fill a thousand ships."[70] The "two leagues" of salt, "wide in proportion," was an exaggeration; Dampier said that the Maio salina was two miles long by half a mile wide,[71] and even today the largest salt-panning area is under four miles long, by not more than one and a quarter miles wide. But whatever the size of the salina, the salt was certainly available in nearly unbelievable quantities; Drake's men, in 1578, found "huge heaps of salt like drifts of snow, and most fine and perfect in nature, the aboundance whereof is such, and the daily increase so exceeding great that they serve all countryes and ilands about them, and is impossible to be consumed."[72]

"This salt is available to all, like the waters of the sea," wrote the anonymous Portuguese author, "and the subjects of the Kingdom of Portugal pay nothing at all for it"[73] — and neither did anyone else. Dampier noted that, at high tide, "the water which yields this salt, works in from out of the sea through a hole in the sand-bank"; and "it costs nothing but men's labour to rake it together, and wheel it out of the pond, except the carriage." The inhabitants of Maio received nothing for the salt itself; as Dampier remarked: "We don't pay them for their salt, but for the labour of themselves and their beasts in lading it — for which we give them victuals, some money, and old cloaths, *viz.* hats, shirts, and other cloaths."[74]

Salt-loading operations at Maio were efficient, prompt, and frequent, and they involved large quantities. From the salina the salt, in sacks, was loaded into panniers, which were carried by donkeys to the beach, where transfer from shore to ship was often made difficult by heavy swells. A flat-bottomed "frape-boat," of very special design and built strong enough to navigate the breakers, protected the salt from wetness. The boat was "all calk'd very tight,"[75] girded and bound with ropes, with a watertight storage bin of unusual construction rising from the deck. An anchor out to sea kept the stern constantly to the waves. Once

70. Blake, 1: 147.
71. Dampier, 3: 12.
72. Drake, p. 19.
73. Blake, 1: 147.
74. Dampier, pp. 12–13, 20.
75. Ibid., p. 13; Sena Barcelos, 2: 228–29.

conveyed safely through the waves and out to the calm waters of the roadstead, the salt was transferred to the ship's boats and then loaded aboard the ship herself.

Many ships called at Maio for salt, but it was hardly an attractive place in which to live. At the end of the fifteenth century, Maio, although only 14 nautical miles from Santiago, had no human settlers, only goats.[76] Visitors to the island were probably frequent, but permanent settlement was long delayed. When Drake visited the Cape Verdes in 1578 he found at Maio, not only salt and the ubiquitous goats, but also hens, coconuts, and fig trees; and "in the vallies and low ground, where little low cottages were built, were pleasant vineyards planted, bearing them ripe and most pleasant grapes."[77] This may indicate the beginning of serious colonization. The salt ships, which became ever more numerous during the course of the seventeenth century, stimulated Maio's development. At the end of the century, in 1699, when Dampier called at Maio he found 230 inhabitants, distributed among three villages, which he called Pinose (Pinoso), Lagôa, and St. John's (Ribeirão João), each with its own little church. The island grew figs, watermelons, pulse, cotton, and pumpkins, but fig trees were the only source of wood; guinea hens, goats, and donkeys were numerous, but cattle very few. Turtles were plentiful in season.

Dampier wrote that "the inhabitants of this island [Maio], even their governour and padres, are all Negro's, wool-pated like their African-neighbours; from whom 'tis like they are descended; tho' being subjects to the Portugueze, they have their religion and language." The "governor" (that is, factor) he described as "a very civil and sensible poor man."[78] It is curious that 237 years later, in 1936, Archibald Lyall visited Maio and saw much the same things that Dampier had recorded. Lyall was handsomely welcomed by a six-foot four-inch black administrator, António Évora, who owned the island, and showed him the landing place, the salt pans, the green patch at Lagôa, and the same scenes of desolation that Dampier had witnessed.[79] At Maio, few things change.

The other salt islands, Sal and Boavista, were less important in the seventeenth century, and less frequented by ships. To Lyall, the low, flat island of Sal was the most desolate of all; life there was made miserable by the relentless wind and the blowing sand, from which there

76. Brásio, 1: 742.
77. Drake, p. 20; Southey, 3: 122.
78. Dampier, 3: 16–20.
79. Lyall, pp. 64–65.

was no refuge and no escape.[80] At night the crabs scurried down the dusty street of the little village capital, aptly named Santa Maria das Dores (St. Mary of Sorrows). In the sixteenth century little happened at Sal, although goats were probably placed there. In 1624 a letter from the governor of Cape Verde indicated that four Dutch ships were at Sal, picking up salt, but there was no indication that the island was inhabited at that time.[81] When Dampier visited Sal in 1683 he paid much more attention to the island's striking flamingos than to the human residents, whom he said were only five or six men, and a poor "governor," from whom he purchased "about 20 bushels of salt for a few old cloaths."[82] Dampier's associate, Captain Cowley, in a separate narration, wrote that there were only four "officers" and one boy on the island, including a mulatto governor. "They are all black, but scorn to be counted any other than Portuguese; for if any man call them Negroes, they will be very angry, saying, that they are white Portuguese."[83] At the time of this visit, in 1683, no ship had touched at Sal for three years.

The large island of Boavista, the third of the salt islands, may have attracted some settlers during the sixteenth century; at least it was visited and goats were placed there. In 1619 its inhabitants, however, were described only as "hunters."[84] In 1677 Boavista received its first priest, and twenty years later, in 1697, a pirate craft considered the small settlement to be worth pillaging.[85] When Charles W. Thomas, chaplain to the U.S. Africa Squadron, visited the island in 1855, he found its salt supply ample but its inhabitants starving. "Fishing, salt-making, and going to funerals," wrote Thomas, "are the chief amusements and employments of the people."[86]

Although it has been claimed that Boavista produces some of the best salt in the Cape Verdes,[87] the island attracted fewer ships than Maio or Sal. Unfortunately for Boavista and its residents, the northern and eastern coasts of the island, strewn with rocks and shallows, are notoriously dangerous to navigation. Persistent and gusty northeasterly winds, combined with a strong current, drag unwary vessels to shipwreck on Boa-

80. Ibid., p. 68.
81. AHU, Cabo Verde, Caixa I, doc. 125.
82. Dampier, 1: 71.
83. Ibid., 4, pt. ii: 4.
84. AHU, Cabo Verde, Caixa I, doc. 95.
85. Sena Barcelos, 2: 66; AHU, Codex 489, fol. 138.
86. Thomas, p. 330.
87. Chelmicki, 2: 40.

vista's rocky shores. In addition, metallic deposits in the island's hills cause compass needles to be pulled astray, so that many ship captains, however cautious, have been deceived. Even the celebrated navigator Captain James Cook, while on his third and last voyage to the South Seas, narrowly escaped shipwreck at Boavista on 10 August 1776. In more recent times, during the ninety-five-year period from 1842 to 1936, the island has claimed sixty-three wrecks.[88]

As early as the 1620s English codfish ships, bound for the Newfoundland fisheries, called regularly at Maio and Sal for salt. Part of the English codfish fleet, in the early spring, would sail directly from the south-of-England ports to Newfoundland; but another part of the fleet, leaving late in January, would go by way of the Cape Verdes.[89] As the century progressed, the number of English ships collecting salt increased, and they included not only the codfish fleet, which put in at Maio and Sal early in the year, but also ordinary merchantmen on their way from Europe to the West Indies or North America, or plying between America and Africa, who called at the Cape Verdes at any season of the year.

When Prince Rupert raided the Cape Verdes in 1652 he captured three English ships at the salt islands and chased four others, who got away.[90] In 1683 Dampier noted that Maio was "a place much frequented by shipping for its great plenty of salt"; sixteen years later, in 1699, he wrote: "I stay'd at Mayo 6 days, and got 7 or 8 ton of salt aboard for my voyage: in which time there came also into this road several sail of merchants ships for salt; all bound with it for Newfoundland."[91] From the other side of the water, at the port of Boston, scraps of evidence indicate a considerable importation of Cape Verdean salt. For instance, on 3/13 August 1686, on the same day that the *Calais Merchant* sailed for London after having unloaded a cargo of Maio salt, the *Sarah Merchant* of Poole, England, came into Boston with more Maio salt.[92] But

88. Fontoura da Costa, p. 14, n. 22; Lyall, p. 66; Chelmicki, I, 51.

89. R.C. Anderson, ed., *Book of Examinations and Depositions 1622-1644*, 4 vols. (Southampton, 1929-36), 2: 72, 82, 69-70. The 1671 regulations determined that English codfish ships, proceeding to Newfoundland by way of Cape Verde, should not leave England before 15 January (or 25 January, New Style), and those sailing directly to Newfoundland were not to leave before 1 March (or 11 March, New Style); Ralph G. Lounsbury, *British Fishery at Newfoundland, 1634-1763* (New Haven, Conn., 1934), p. 130. For further information on the Newfoundland fisheries, see Harold A. Innes, *Cod Fisheries* (New Haven, Conn., 1940); for the salt trade in the Portuguese empire, see Mauro, pp. 259-77, 292-94.

90. Anderson, "Royalists at Sea, 1651-1653," *Mariner's Mirror* 21: 78-83.

91. Dampier, 1: 75, 3: 21.

92. Abstracts of English Shipping Records, pp. 4-5, 24, 34.

less salt came into New England from the Cape Verdes than from the Tortugas, or Salt Tortugas (the "Saltertooga" or "Saltertoodos" of the Boston shipping records), in the Bahamas. For instance, during a six-month period in 1688, a dozen ships from the Tortugas brought in over 700 tons of salt to Boston, while only one ship arrived from the Cape Verdes: the *Exchange of Poole*, which unloaded 12 frying pans, 4½ dozen worsted hose, and 70 tons of Maio salt.[93]

Newfoundland was a more important market for Cape Verdean salt than New England. Dampier estimated that a hundred English ships called at Maio every year, and, by the end of the century, the salt ships received the protection of the Royal Navy. In Dampier's words: "Our nation drives here [in Maio] a great trade for salt, and have commonly a man of war here for the guard of our ships and barks that come to take it in."[94] In 1713 a total of 110 salt ships called at Maio,[95] but this may have been a peak year. In the seventeenth century, the salt trade of Maio and Sal probably engaged about eighty ships per year.

The high volume of salt exports, however, did not generate much revenue for the Cape Verdes. Ships came to the Cape Verdes precisely because the salt was the cheapest obtainable. The men of Maio were supposed to charge 4 or 5 Spanish reales (that is, less than 1s. 6d.) for the transportation of every ten sacks of salt,[96] but this was paid mostly in cheap European goods, calculated according to their inflated value in the Cape Verdes. Thus a two-shilling hat could satisfy a six-shilling debt in the Cape Verdes. An English vessel loading 1,000 moios (or 24,000 bushels) of Maio salt could conceivably have paid no more than about £25 for the merchandise offered in exchange. Dampier, in 1699, took the process a step further: after acquiring about 8 tons of salt at a very cheap rate in Maio, he sailed to Ribeira Grande and exchanged part of the salt for the victuals he needed.[97]

Indeed, the Cape Verdeans gained much more from the indirect consequences of the salt trade than from the trade itself. Salt ships had to be victualed and watered and might be induced to buy or barter other commodities. Salt was free at Maio, but good fresh water cost $100 réis per pipe at Santiago.[98] Salt ships purchased water, salted goatmeat, and other victuals, and also bought donkeys to be carried to the West Indies.

93. Ibid., pp. 131–50.
94. Dampier, 3: 13.
95. Sena Barcelos, 2: 228.
96. Ibid.
97. Dampier, 3: 21.
98. Sena Barcelos, 2: 132.

TABLE 28

Annual Salt Production Capacity in the Cape Verdes (ca. 1850)*

Island	Cape Verdean Moios	Average Price per Moio	Total Value at Local Prices
Sal	5,000	21s.	£ 5,250
Boavista	2,500	7s.	£ 875
Maio	6,000	15s.	£ 4,500
Total	13,500	–	£ 10,625

*Compiled from Francisco Travassos Valdez, *Six Years of a Traveller's Life in Western Africa,* 2 vols. (London, 1861), 1:67, 74, 88.

In the seventeenth century Portugal forbade the sale of donkeys and other livestock to foreign ships in the Cape Verdes; in fact even the salt trade itself was technically illegal; but enforcement of these restrictive measures was infrequent, and in the end impossible.

Since Maio is very close to Santiago, and English ships loading salt in the roadstead of Porto Inglês could be seen from Santiago, the officials in Santiago could have made a much more vigorous effort at supervision and control of salt exports if they had so wished. Failure to pay attention to the affairs of Maio meant that the island, by default, fell largely under British control.

From the fifteenth century to the twentieth, salt has been the one Cape Verdean product that has been continuously and uninterruptedly in international trade. Table 28 shows the maximum annual salt production in the salt islands about the year 1850. The large differential in average prices, from 7s. at Boavista to 21s. at Sal, reflected differences in quality, purity, and processing; industrial procedures for purifying the salt were well developed only at Sal, while the Boavista product was of low quality and mixed with sand. The Cape Verdean moio, it should be noted, was three times as large as the Lisbon moio of 24 bushels, and therefore the above figure of 13,500 Cape Verdean moios represents 972,000 English bushels, or the equivalent of 30,375 English long tons. If the average ship cargo was 200 tons, then exports of 30,000 tons of salt would have required the services of 150 ships.

The main market for Cape Verdean salt, in the nineteenth century, was no longer Newfoundland, but Brazil. In 1891 salt exports reached an all-time high of 42,500 metric tons, but the imposition of a high protective tariff in Brazil killed off the Brazilian market. Exports fell to 2,471 metric tons in 1901 and then slowly recovered. During the five-year period 1953–57, salt exports averaged 19,560 metric tons, but at a price of U.S.$3.41 per ton, average annual income from salt exports came to only U.S.$66,700.[99]

Other important facets of Cape Verdean commerce — such as the slave trade, the cotton trade, and the trade with Guiné — are examined in the next chapter. Sugar and orchil were of minor importance in seventeenth-century commerce. Large quantities of high quality, inexpensive Brazilian sugar, after 1600, undermined the sugar trade of the Azores, Madeira, the Cape Verdes, and São Tomé; the tropical island of São Tomé alone survived among the Portuguese islands as an exporter of sugar in some volume. But in the Cape Verdes, as in Madeira, sugar continued to be important in local commerce, particularly for the manufacture of rum, some of which was sold in Guiné. Sugar is still today one of the chief crops in both Madeira and Santiago.

As for the dye-yielding lichen called orchil, which could be found in quantity in the more mountainous islands of the Cape Verdes, it was exported as early as 1469, when the Portuguese crown conceded to the Castilians Juan and Pero de Lugo the right to collect and export orchil from Santiago.[100] The trade in orchil was a royal monopoly, leased to merchants for a fixed term of years, in return for payment of a lump sum to the crown, with collection rights going to the merchant who bid the highest amount for the contract. In 1512 the contract sold for 55$550 réis per year. In the seventeenth century little mention is made of orchil in the extant records, which probably indicates a lack of interest in exploiting the large orchil resources. But in the eighteenth century, partly in response to the developing English textile trade, the demand for orchil greatly increased. The English firm of Philip Balesty and Company purchased a six-year contract, in force during 1745–51, which covered all the islands in the archipelagoes of Cape Verde, Azores, and Madeira, and for which they paid 60,000 cruzados (over £6,000).[101]

Orchil was prepared by grinding the lichen to powder, mixing it with stale urine, and then making it into a paste. The addition of quicklime produced good blue, violet, and purple dyes; or the addition of a solution of tin produced a fine scarlet dye. In the early nineteenth century

99. *Colóquios cabo-verdianos,* p. 152; Lacerda, p. 23; Mendes Corrêa, pp. 233–34.
100. Sena Barcelos, 1: 33–34.
101. Ibid., 2: 283–85; Blake, 1: 116.

orchil could be procured in the Cape Verdes for between 3$840 and 4$480 réis per quintal, and could be sold at Lisbon for up to 50$000; the enormous differential in these prices made it a valuable crown monopoly. In the 1830s orchil collection was still a thriving business, but the discovery of massive orchil growths in Angola and Mozambique, after 1837, destroyed the Cape Verdean market and greatly lowered the price.[102]

It is not known how much orchil was collected in the seventeenth century, or from where, or what ships were involved. The absence of statistics about orchil is but symptomatic of a similar absence in many other branches of Cape Verdean commerce and trade. But from what is known about Cape Verdean shipping, three generalizations seem to be possible: (1) more ships called at the Cape Verdes to be victualed and watered than for any other purpose; (2) of the ships that came to the Cape Verdes in search of a specific product, the salt ships outnumbered all others; and (3) ships that came to the Cape Verdes to trade in commodities other than salt were few, and from one-third to one-half of them were small craft engaged in the local Santiago-Guiné trade.

The victualing functions of the Cape Verdes were certainly considerable and may have involved over 150 ships in a good year and at least 50 ships in a poor one. For instance, the Portugal-Brazil sugar trade in the seventeenth century occupied from 40 to 150 ships per year, and most of those ships called at the Cape Verdes on the outward voyage. In May 1655 there were over 30 ships of the Brazil fleet at Santiago; in December 1649 there were more than 50, all at Santiago at the same time.[103] The English ships for victuals, unlike the sugar ships, did not arrive in squadrons or fleets, but in twos and threes; but they came in steadily and dependably, 5 or 6 ships per month, aside from the salt ships.

In the last half of the seventeenth century victualing might well be described as the true "commerce" of the Cape Verdes. It is possible that the value of the victuals bartered to ships rivaled the value of cotton exports; and victualing was probably a more dependable and regular commercial activity than the erratic slave trade. Victualing also engaged

102. Boid, pp. 312–13; Amaral, pp. 201–2; Chelmicki, 2: 96–103; Andrade Corvo, p. 54.
103. Francisco de Brito Freire, *Relação da viagem que fez ao Estado do Brazil a armada da Cõpanhia, anno 1655* (Lisbon, 1657), p. 32; "Relaçam dos sucessos da armada ao Estado do Brasil 1649," *Anais da Biblioteca Nacional do Rio de Janeiro* 20 (Rio de Janeiro, 1899): 159.

the common people of the islands in a very direct way; at Ribeira Grande, for instance, Dampier's seamen haggled with the marketwomen for chickens and maize, without the intervention of middlemen, factors, or merchants.

The salt ships, although numerous, running to perhaps between 30 and 90 ships per year, generated little real commercial movement in the islands, for reasons that have been set forth. The main interest the islanders had in the salt ships was, once again, as potential consumers of victuals, although the salt ships also purchased donkeys and other live-stock for transport to the West Indies.

As for the ships that came to the Cape Verdes to trade in articles other than salt, these were the least numerous of all. In 1609, excluding ships trading with Brazil, 18 ships traded at Santiago, of which 8 were in the Guiné trade. In 1610 there were 24 ships, including 8 in the Guiné trade. But there were only 2 ships recorded in 1611, only 4 in 1612, and only 3 in 1613. Similarly, in a four-year period during 1642-45, only 30 ships paid customs duties at Santiago, an average of only 7 or 8 per year.[104] These figures include few or none of the ships trading to Brazil.

The trade to Brazil, a small-scale affair involving cottons and salted meats, was a by-product of the passage of the sugar ships through Cape Verdean waters on their outward journey. The sugar ships may also, on occasion, have purchased slaves in the Cape Verdes. The ships trading to the Cape Verdes brought in wines, haberdasheries, olive oil, wheat, nautical supplies, weapons, gunpowder, ammunition, and a wide variety of European manufactures. During most of the seventeenth century, the Cape Verdeans lacked the money, as well as a sufficient quantity and variety of desirable island products, to be able to acquire the full range of commodities they needed.

When all the scraps of information about Cape Verdean shipping are put together, one can arrive at a hypothetical picture of the volume of shipping in the whole archipelago, in good years and bad, during the period 1650-1700. Table 29, it should be stressed, is hypothesis, not fact, but it may help to form a provisional picture of Cape Verdean commerce. These projections indicate, or assume, that ships substantively engaged in the commerce of the Cape Verdes were outnumbered

104. AHU, Cabo Verde, Caixa I, doc. 22; Caixa II, certificate dated Ribeira Grande, Santiago, 28 February 1647. For my use of the word "Guiné" see chapter 9, note 9, below.

TABLE 29

Shipping in the Cape Verdes, 1650–1700
(number of ships)

	Hypothetical Year of High Activity	Hypothetical Year of Low Activity
West Africa trade	12	5
Brazil trade	8	4
Madeira-Azores-Canaries trade	5	1
West Indies slave trade	5	0
Subtotal: trading ships	30	10
Ships loading salt	90	30
Ships revictualing*	150	50
Total	270	90

*Does not include ships in previous categories that may also have revictualed.

by salt ships, and by ships revictualing, by a factor of 8 to 1. The patterns of wind and current made the Cape Verdes the crossroads of the central Atlantic; but this circumstance alone, unaided by other factors, did not transform the archipelago into a great emporium. The words "food and water," symbolizing the most basic of human necessities, summarize and circumscribe the elemental Cape Verdean contribution to Atlantic navigation.

9
The Slave Trade in the Cape Verdes

Racially and socially the Cape Verdes are very much a creation of the slave trade.[1] The slave trade was the instrument that made of the sparse islands of the Cape Verdes a field of collision, and also of co-operation, between African and European. White and black entered into a series of complex interactions that involved oppression and collaboration, cruelty and concubinage, mutual accommodation and intermarriage, and much else. In the sea-isolated laboratory of the archipelago there emerged a hybrid and syncretic society of unusual intellectual and historical interest.

The late Archibald Lyall entitled his book on the Cape Verdes and Portuguese Guinea *Black and White Make Brown* — an allusion to the African and European blood strains whose fusion produced the mixed-blooded brown-skinned mestiços or mulattoes, who predominate numerically in the islands. According to the 1950 census, the tiny white population of 3,000 persons and the black population of 36,000 persons were both far outnumbered by the 101,000 Afro-European "browns."

---

1. In addition to the many sources cited in chapter 8, note 1, the following are also useful, especially for topics involving Portuguese Guinea, slavery, and West African trade: Walter Rodney, *History of the Upper Guinea Coast, 1545–1800* (Oxford, 1970), and his "Portuguese Attempts at Monopoly on the Upper Guinea Coast, 1580–1650," *Journal of African History* 6 (1965), 307–22; António Carreira, *Panaria Cabo-Verdiano-Guineense* (Lisbon, 1968); João Barreto, *História da Guiné* (Lisbon, 1938); Avelino Teixeira da Mota, *Guiné Portuguesa,* 2 vols. (Lisbon, 1954); Edmundo Arménio Correia Lopes, *Escravatura* (Lisbon, 1944); and Georges Scelle, *Histoire politique de la traite négrière aux Indes de Castille,* 2 vols. (Paris, 1906).

Cape Verdean culture itself, particularly as expressed through its major instrument, the Creole or *crioulo* tongue, represents an eloquent compromise between African and European elements. The *lingua crioula*, deeply embedded in the emotional and psychological makeup of the average Cape Verdean, although essentially Portuguese in vocabulary, syntax, and grammar, is also perhaps African in intonation and interior feeling, having grown out of the historical exigencies of the West African situation.[2]

The collision between African and Portuguese cultures — resulting eventually in a kind of coalescence, a coalescence in which African predominance is overwhelming on the ethnic side and Portuguese predominance overwhelming on the intellectual and religious side — creates a difficult question concerning the Cape Verdean identity. Who, after all, is the Cape Verdean? and how does one define Cape Verdean culture? The Cape Verdean writer Manuel Ferreira, after analyzing the question of Cape Verdean identity for some 230 pages, couched his conclusion in a crisp formula: "Afinal: Africa? Europa?: Cabo Verde"[3] ("After all: Africa? Europe?: Cape Verde").

The assertion that "Cape Verde is Cape Verde," of course, fails to satisfy, for the tautology begs the question. One can sympathize with the emphasis the Cape Verdean intellectuals place upon what they call "cabo-verdianidade"; but in their awkward and self-conscious rejection of their African heritage there is much that is hypocritical. For the roots of the problem of Cape Verdean identity lie deep in the past, particularly in the slaveholding and slave-trading past, when the characteristic form of Cape Verdean society first took shape, and a particular pattern of racial relations progressively emerged. The specific task of the Cape Verdean intellectuals is to recognize and acknowledge the realities of past historical experience — a historical experience which, in the archipelago, has been particularly grim, brutal, and cruel.

The statement has been made, repeatedly, that race relations in the Cape Verdes are all but completely harmonious, and that there is no

2. The Creole dialect of the Cape Verdes has been studied in: Baltasar Lopes, *Dialecto crioulo de Cabo Verde* (Lisbon, 1957); Mary Louise Nunes, "The Phonologies of Cape Verdean Dialects of Portuguese," *Boletim de Filologia* 21 (1963); Jorge Morais Barbosa, ed., *Crioulos: Reedição de artigos publicados no Boletim da Sociedade de Geografia de Lisboa* (Lisbon, 1967); and W.A.A. Wilson, *The Crioulo of Guiné* (Johannesburg, 1962).

3. Ferreira, p. 236.

race prejudice in the islands.[4] One would prefer to hear such assertions come, not from the light-skinned Cape Verdean intelligentsia, but from the dark-skinned, lower-class peasant and villager, who might well be the target of whatever prejudice existed; but the lower classes are all but silent on such questions. The lower-class black people of Santiago, indeed, are capable of the most amazing silence; in the great famine of 1940–41, when the death rate soared from the "normal" 13 or 14 per thousand to a high of 107 per thousand,[5] thousands of persons expired virtually in silence, without a gesture of revolt. Over 30,000 Cape Verdeans died during 1940–41, a slaughter that claimed the lives of 17 percent of the population, and tens of thousands of others were left dangerously undernourished; and the weight of these calamities fell largely on the dark-skinned lower classes, while the powers that be, at Praia and at Lisbon, shrugged it all off as just another *crise* (crisis), an ineluctable fact of nature for which no one was responsible. In all this official and unofficial passivity, one senses the worst kind of race prejudice, the prejudice of indifference: what, after all, do the deaths of blacks and mulattoes, in the Cape Verdes or elsewhere, matter?

In the Cape Verdes the common people live out their short existence, caught in the dreadful balance of water and drought, of food and scarcity. In the drought of 1774–75, starvation claimed 22,000 lives; in 1831–33, 12,000 lives; in 1863–65, 30,000 lives; in 1902–4, 15,000 lives; in 1920–22, 17,000 lives; and so forth and so on. In the two-hundred-year period from 1748 to 1947 there were twenty-four years of great famine, an average of one year in eight.[6]

One-half of this overwhelming problem consists of periodic drought and cyclical starvation; the other half consists of traditional fatalism

4. As Ferreira (p. 39) expressed it: "We wish to say – from the social, cultural, and psychological point of view – there are no black Cape Verdeans, no white Cape Verdeans, and no *mestiço* Cape Verdeans. There are, yes, rich Cape Verdeans, poor ones, the well-off, and the wretched; there are Cape Verdeans of humble occupations and of prestigious occupations. That is all." Or again, in the words of Nuno de Miranda: "At present the existing social classes are detached from all notions of race. Thus the expression 'white people' is commonly used not to designate persons who are ethnically white, but for all those who occupy a good social position, whatever their color may be." *Compreensão de Cabo Verde* (Lisbon, 1963), p. 40. The authors seem unconscious of the bias implicit in such assertions.

5. Mendes Corrêa, p. 168.

6. *Colóquios cabo-verdianos*, p. 103; Mendes Corrêa, p. 165; Amaral, pp. 187–89, 228.

and official negligence and indifference, attitudes with a long history going back to the days of the exploitation of one race by another. The common people do not place their trust in bureaucrats; their sarcastic popular saying, "The best governor is rain,"[7] reflects this fact. Only during the drought and famine of 1959–61, with a compassionate governor in office, were measures taken, at last, to prevent wholesale death.[8]

References to starvation in Santiago go at least as far back as 1582–83. During the droughts of 1609–11 food was procured from Gambia, slaves were set "free" by "generous" masters who could not or would not feed them, and many Africans managed to find their way back to the coast of Guiné.[9] Slaves brought to the Cape Verdes, subjected to all the usual horrors of captivity, had additional cruelties to face: the certain prospect of malnutrition, and the recurrent possibility of a long, wasting death through hunger.

Most slaves brought to the Cape Verdes, however, were not intended for service in the islands, but for sale and re-export to the Americas. The merchants of Santiago, advantageously placed off the Guiné coast, hoped to create a great slave entrepôt at Ribeira Grande. Statistics on the slave trade and on ship movements in the Cape Verdes are scarce, but those that exist provide a glimpse of what occurred. In the three-year period 1513–15, 29 ships brought 2,966 slaves into Santiago, with an estimated value of 11:092$815 réis according to the customshouse valuation. Eleven million réis was a great deal of money in 1515, equivalent to perhaps over £9,000 in sterling; and the nearly 3,000 slaves were far too many for the tiny settlements on the island to absorb in so short a period of time. It seems likely that most of these slaves were destined for re-export, and there are records showing the sale of some of them to Spaniards, for shipment to the Canaries and the Spanish West Indies.[10]

The Spanish West Indies was the most common, the most lucrative, and the most important market for Cape Verdean slaves prior to 1640.

7. "O melhor governador é a chuva"; *Colóquios cabo-verdianos,* p. 18.
8. Ferreira, p. 25; Araujo, p. 6.
9. Carreira, pp. 23, 37–38, 44, 56–57. I use the word *Guiné* (which is clearly differentiated in spelling from the English, French, Dutch, and Spanish versions of the word *Guinea*) to indicate only the coast lying between Senegal and Sierra Leone, where Cape Verdeans and Portuguese were very active, a region sometimes called Upper Guinea. Areas to the south and east of Sierra Leone, also known as Guinea, are largely irrelevant to this study.
10. Sena Barcelos, 1: 74–75.

The massive study of the Spanish-American trade by Huguette and Pierre Chaunu, *Séville et l'Atlantique,* lists the slave ships authorized to carry slaves to Spanish America during the years 1551–1640, gives facts or estimates concerning tonnage, and states destinations.[11] Of a total of 1,222 slave ships, 146 (or 12 percent) were listed as going to "Cabo Verde."[12] According to the usual interpretation, Cabo Verde "meant neither the actual cape where Dakar now stands nor the Cape Verde Islands, but rather the 'Guinea of Cape Verde' stretching roughly from the Cape Verde peninsula to the Sierra Leone River"[13] — that is, it referred to the region I call Guiné, and which the seventeenth-century Portuguese called the "Rios de Guiné," or Rivers of Guinea. Many of these slave ships, however, *did* go to the islands, and insofar as the Seville statements of destination have any meaning (for there is no proof that the ships actually went to the destinations stated), the destination "Cabo Verde" must also include the islands.

The Chaunu tables show that the destination "Cabo Verde" became less frequent toward the middle of the seventeenth century. During the years 1596–1610, of 458 slave ships, 255 listed destinations, with 26 ships (or 10 percent of those giving a destination) going to Cape Verde. During the years 1617–30, of 321 slave ships, all but 6 gave their destinations, with 32 of them (or 10 percent) going to Cape Verde. But during the ten-year period 1631–40, out of 158 ships, only 3 (or less than 2 percent) listed a Cape Verde destination.[14]

Doubts arise concerning the accuracy and completeness of the Chaunu tables, and also about certain assumptions — that, for instance, slave ships were usually of about 100, 120, or 140 tons; that the tonnage figure equaled 80 or 90 percent of the authorized number of slave *piezas de India;*[15] that the slavers were more interested in smuggling European merchandise into the Spanish West Indies than in the buying and selling of slaves, which was supposed to be less profitable; and that therefore

11. Chaunu, vols. 3–4.

12. Following the calculation by Philip D. Curtin, *Atlantic Slave Trade* (Madison, Wis., 1969), p. 104.

13. Curtin, p. 103.

14. Chaunu, vols. 3–4.

15. A *peça, boa peça,* or *peça da India (pieza de India* in Spanish) was defined as a male or female slave, aged between 15 and 25 and in good health. Slaves between the ages of 8 and 15, or 25 to 35, in good health, were valued at two-thirds of one *peça.* The old, the very young, the sickly, etc., were valued at less. See Mauro, p. 173; Boxer, *Salvador de Sá* (London, 1952), p. 231.

the slavers carried fewer than the authorized number of slaves.[16] Shipping records from Ribeira Grande in Santiago for the years 1609 and 1610 show the following:[17]

1. The ship *São Diogo* (Roque Álvares of Lisbon, master) left for Cartagena (a Caribbean port in present-day Colombia) on 15 January 1609 with 660 slave *peças da India*.
2. The caravel *Nossa Senhora de Boa Viagem* (Diogo Mendes of Sesimbra, master) left for New Spain (Mexico) on 27 February 1609 with 558 peças.
3. The ship *Nossa Senhora do Rosário* (Vicente Leitão of Lisbon, captain) left for Cartagena on 28 February 1609 with 411 peças.
4. The caravel *Nossa Senhora do Rosário* (Nicolau Lopes of Lisbon, master) left for the Canaries on 12 June 1609 with slaves, hides, and wax, carrying an estimated 164 peças.
5. The caravel *Nossa Senhora de Boa Viagem* (Pedro Gonçalves, master) left for the Canaries on 18 November 1609 with slaves, hides, and wax, carrying an estimated 162 peças.
6. The pinnace *Vera Cruz* (Vincente Pinheiro, master) left for Cartagena on 1 January 1610 with 381 peças.
7. The ship *Santa Ana* (Manuel Fernandes of Lisbon, master) left for Cartagena on 13 February 1610 with 438 peças.
8. The caravel *Nossa Senhora do Rosário* (Baltasar Godinho, master) left for Cartagena on 18 March 1610 with 372 peças.
9. The caravel *São Diogo* (Manuel Rodrigues Menica, master) left for New Spain on 22 March 1610 with 501 peças.
10. The ship *Nossa Senhora da Conceição* (André Preto of Matozinhos, master) left for Cartagena on 16 April 1610 with 602 peças.
11. The ship *Santo António* (Luís Manço, master) left for the Canaries on 26 May 1610 with slaves, hides, and wax, carrying an estimated 51 peças.
12. The caravel *Santo António* (Jerónimo Fernandes, master) left for the Canaries on 26 July 1610 with slaves and hides, carrying an estimated 125 peças.
13. The ship *Santo António* (Manuel Ribeiro, master) left for the Canaries on 4 September 1610 with 14 peças.

The above list shows 8 ships leaving Santiago for the Spanish Americas with 3,923 slave peças, and 5 ships leaving for the Canaries with an estimated 516 peças. Thus, in the two-year period 1609–10, 13 ships carried 4,439 peças out of one port in the Cape Verdes. It is difficult to trans-

16. Chaunu, 1: 310–13; Curtin, p. 105.
17. AHU, Cabo Verde, Caixa, I, doc. 22.

late numbers of peças into numbers of people; one thing is certain – there were more people than peças. If 3 peças equaled an average of 4 persons, then 4,439 peças would come to 5,918 African slaves.

Because Spanish and Portuguese ships used only a small number of names, it is difficult to trace a particular ship from one record to another. In the above list of thirteen ships, only seven names were used (there are two *São Diogos*, two *Nossas Senhoras de Boa Viagem*, three *Nossas Senhoras do Rosário*, and three *Santo Antónios*). When comparing different lists of ships, for certain identification, one must be sure that the names of both ship and master match and that other factors, such as chronology and location, are congruent. It is curious that only one of the above-named ships can be securely located in the lengthy lists supplied by the Chaunus. The Chaunus (4: 260-61, ship no. 185) list the slave ship *N.S. de Buen Viaje* (Diego Mendez, master), leaving Seville in 1608; and this vessel must surely be the *Nossa Senhora de Boa Viagem* (Diogo Mendes of Sesimbra, master), which loaded at Santiago late in February 1609. The Chaunus say this ship was of 140 tons, bound for "Guinea" (which has been interpreted as meaning the coast from Sierra Leone to the Bight of Benin),[18] and then New Spain, and authorized to transport 160 *piezas*. The Ribeira Grande records show that the ship was a caravel, bound for New Spain, but had called at Santiago (not "Guinea"), and actually loaded 558 peças. It is clear that this ship greatly exceeded the authorized number of slaves; and it is also clear that the other America-bound ships at Santiago, with loads of 660, 411, 381, 438, 372, 501, and 602 peças each, greatly exceeded the "average" figures of 120, 140, or 160 peças suggested by the Chaunus. In 1609-10, at least, slave-trading to the Spanish Americas seems to have been lucrative in itself, not just a pretext for Portuguese ships to smuggle European manufactures into the Spanish West Indies, and the slavers exceeded the permissible number of peças, rather than fell short of it.

Shipping records for the years 1609-10 show that Santiago imported slaves and wax from the African mainland as follows:[19]

1. The caravel *Santo António* (Domingos Teixeira, master) arrived from the "River of São Domingos"[20] on 21 January 1609 with wax and an estimated 90 peças of slaves.

18. Curtin, p. 104.
19. AHU, Cabo Verde, Caixa I, doc. 22.
20. The River of São Domingos refers to the Cacheu River, where the Portuguese had two or three trading posts.

2. The ship *São João Baptista* (Bernardo da Lomba of Santiago, master and owner) arrived from São Domingos on 6 February 1609 with an estimated 152 peças.
3. The caravel *Santo António* (Pedro da Costa, master) arrived from São Domingos on 7 February 1609 with wax and an estimated 51 peças.
4. The caravel *Espírito Santo* (Luís Pereira, master) arrived from São Domingos on 7 February 1609 with wax and an estimated 65 peças.
5. The ship *São Diogo* (Baltasar Moreira, master and pilot) arrived from Gambia on 31 May 1609 with wax and an estimated 20 peças.
6. The launch *Nossa Senhora de Jesus* (Diogo Dunhão, master) arrived from São Domingos on 22 June 1609 with 14 peças.
7. The pinnace *São João Baptista* (Paulo Gomes, captain) arrived from Guiné on 12 September 1609 with 12 peças.
8. The ship *São Bartolomeu* (Baltasar Moreira, captain) arrived from São Domingos with wax and an estimated 71 peças.
9. The pinnace *São Miguel* (Dinis André, master) arrived from São Domingos on 21 January 1610 with wax and an estimated 144 peças.
10. The ship *Santa Helena* (Dinis Eanes da Fonseca, captain) arrived from São Domingos in (March?) 1610 with wax and an estimated 41 peças.
11. The ship *São Brás* (Francisco Fernandes, captain) arrived from São Domingos on 26 March 1610 with 96 peças.
12. The ship *São João Baptista* (Bernardo da Lomba, captain) arrived from São Domingos on 25 March 1610 with wax and an estimated 24 peças.
13. The ship *Nossa Senhora da Boa Viagem* (Manuel Ribeiro, master) arrived from São Domingos on 9 April 1610 with 16 peças.
14. The above-named ship (with the same master) arrived from São Domingos on 3 July 1610 with 25 peças.
15. The pinnace *São Miguel* (Dinis André, master) arrived from São Domingos on 23 September 1610 with 42 peças.
16. The ship *São João Baptista* (Bernardo da Lomba, master and captain) arrived from São Domingos on 15 December 1610 with 85 peças.

The above list, which shows 16 ships bringing into Santiago an estimated total of 948 peças (amounting to at least 1,264 persons), has various points of interest. It shows that the number of peças coming in (estimated at 948) was far less than the number exported (4,439) during 1609–10, meaning that a reservoir of slaves must have been built up at Santiago before 1609. It shows that the ships engaged in the back-and-forth Guiné-to-Santiago trade were probably small craft (the average estimated slave cargo was only about 60 peças), few in number, and probably locally owned. It shows, furthermore, that there was a significant entrepôt trade in beeswax, a commodity that was important in West African trade for several centuries.[21]

Slaves paid an import tax of 1$725 réis per peça, and an export tax of 2$000. This meant that a peça transshipped through Santiago paid a total of 3$725 (or about £2 17s.) in tariffs, which was expensive, although the customs books show that many exemptions and exceptions were made, particularly on behalf of permanent residents (*vizinhos*) of Ribeira Grande. The customs books show that, during 1609–10, two ships from Seville paid duties on merchandise brought to Santiago (Portuguese slave ships paid no duties on the cargoes they brought in), and fifteen Spanish ships, going to or coming from the Canaries, paid duties on miscellaneous items, chiefly on the wines, pitch and tar, flour, and manufactures they brought into Santiago, and on the slaves and wax they took out.

Total customs receipts in Santiago during the years 1609–10 came to 10:814$844½ réis (or over £8,300). This amount, by my rough calculations, came from the following sources:

Tariffs on slaves exported	7:970$000
Tariffs on slaves imported	1:577$000
Tariffs on European imports	715$000
Tariffs on wax imports	285$000
Tariffs on wax and hides exported	267$000
Total	10:814$000

In addition, the tariffs which privileged and exempted persons did not pay would have amounted to 1:471$372 réis if they had been paid.[22] No tariffs were paid on goods imported from Portugal, Madeira, and the Azores aboard Portuguese ships, and no tariffs were paid on slaves and merchandise exported on Portuguese ships to Portugal, Brazil, the Azores, and Madeira.

21. Rodney, *Upper Guinea*, p. 158.
22. Portuguese customs officers kept careful records of the exact amounts that importers and exporters would normally have paid if the goods had not been exempted for one reason or another. These amounts were carefully totaled at the end of every year and can be considered to have been an indirect subsidy received by privileged persons from the royal treasury.

The king's treasury collected the following amounts, from all sources in the Cape Verdes, during 1609-10:[23]

Santiago customs revenues	10:814$000
Santiago internal taxes (*dízimas*)	1:220$000
Fogo internal taxes (*dízimas*), est.	510$000
Maio taxes	84$000
S. Antão, S. Nicolau, Boavista taxes, est.	672$000
Total	13:300$000

This total of 13:300$000 was equivalent to slightly more than £10,000 sterling for the two-year period. Customs revenues accounted for 81 percent of the total, and duties levied on slave imports and exports accounted for no less than 72 percent of the entire public revenues of the Cape Verdes. The royal treasury was overwhelmingly dependent on the slave trade.

The customs registers reveal that shipping movements at Santiago during 1609-10 ran as follows: ships in the Canaries trade, 16; in the Spanish slave trade, 10; and in the West African trade, 16. This total of 42 ships did not include Portuguese ships trading in nondutiable commodities; the unlisted ships might be estimated as follows: ships trading to Azores, Madeira, and Portugal, 12, and those trading to Brazil, 20. The addition of these 32 ships, as conservatively estimated, to the 42 ships paying customs duties, makes a total of 74 ships, or an annual average of 37 ships trading at Santiago during the years 1609-10.[24]

The 1609-10 statistics for slaves and ships, unfortunately, were probably not representative. The customs registers for the period from 10 June 1611 to 30 June 1613 show a steep decline in the slave trade, a decline that may have been caused by the raising of the export tax per peça from 2$000 to 6$000 réis. Even though the import tax on slaves seems to have been dropped (there are no records of slave imports in the registers of this period), the total tax paid on the transshipment of a peça had risen from 3$725 to 6$000, an increase of nearly 60 percent.

23. AHU, Cabo Verde, Caixa I, doc. 22. The *dízimas* from Fogo in 1609 came to 280$000; in 1610 they have been estimated at 230$000 (which was the price at which they were farmed in 1615-16, according to doc. 46), making a total of 510$000. The taxes collected in the three Windward Islands (Santo Antão, São Nicolau, and Boavista) during a seven-and-a-half-year period (January 1606 to June 1613) came to 2:523$005, or an average of 336$000 per year, making a two-year total of 672$000.

24. This excludes the salt ships, the revictualers, and any ships that may have traded in Fogo.

Such increases in tariffs either encouraged smuggling (an operation which left no trace in the customshouse records) or drove ships away from the Cape Verdes and toward the African coast, where slave cargoes could be acquired directly.

In any event, the registers for the period June 1611 to June 1613 reveal only the following:[25]

1. The caravel *São Tiago* (Manuel Rodrigues Menica, master) left for New Spain on 4 July 1611 with 168 peças of slaves.
2. The ship *Madre Teresa de Jesus* (Roque Álvares of Lisbon, master) left for Cartagena on 20 July 1611 with 38 peças.
3. The ship *Madalena* (António Pecheco, master) had loaded slaves at Cacheu in Guiné, was driven into Santiago by stress of weather, and there took on another 37 peças, leaving for Cartagena on 16 January 1612.
4. The caravel *Santo António* (André Preto of Matozinhos, master) left for Seville(?) on 19 July 1612 with 120 peças and wax.
5. An unnamed caravel (with an unnamed master from Setúbal) arrived from the Canaries on 16 November 1612 with 85 pipes of wine.
6. The pinnace *São Francisco* (Sebastião Rodrigues, master) arrived from the Canaries on 8 January 1613 with 25 pipes of wine.
7. The caravel *São Pedro* (no master mentioned) arrived from the Canaries on 8 January 1613 with 108 pipes of wine.

This means that the two-year period from June 1611 to June 1613, when compared with the two-year period 1609–10, shows steep declines in shipping, in revenues, and in the numbers of slaves exported. The ships in the Canaries trade fell from 16 to 3, those in the Spain-and-Spanish-Americas trade from 10 to 4, the number of slaves exported dropped from 4,439 peças to 363 (or from an estimated 5,918 persons to an estimated 484 persons), and customs revenues declined from 10:814$844 réis to only 2:649$802. The 1611–13 revenues seem to have come from the following sources: tariffs on slaves exported (plus other charges on slave ships), 2:400$540 (90.6 percent); on wine imports, 234$600 (8.8 percent); on wax exports, 14$662 (0.6 percent); making a total of 2:649$802. The amount not collected in tariffs, be-

25. AHU, Cabo Verde, Caixa I, doc. 22. Note that in this list the first ship mentioned is identical with ship no. 9 in the previous list of slaves exported (*São Tiago* and *São Diogo* are different versions of the same name), and on neither occasion was this ship mentioned by the Chaunus. Also André Preto (of Matozinhos, a town and harbor near Oporto) was named on both lists, nos. 4 and 10, commanding two different slavers.

cause of privileges and exemptions, came to only 47$200. During the 1611–13 period 218 pipes of Canaries wine were imported, and each pipe paid a tax of 1$100. Exports of wax fell off sharply, and the registers record no imports of wax. Nothing concerning the West Africa trade was recorded in the books of 1611–13.

A statement of accounts for the first six months of the year 1615 showed the following income:[26]

Tariffs collected from 6 ships in the Canaries trade	376$506
Tariffs collected from 5 ships in the Guiné trade	501$488
Taxes collected in the Windward Islands	268$137
Santiago internal taxes (*dízimas*)	302$500
Fogo internal taxes (*dízimas*)[27]	115$000
Total	1:563$631

The 1615 statement shows that no slave ships in the Spanish trade called at the Cape Verdes between 1 January and 7 July of that year, although at least 2 ships had purchased slaves for the Spanish Americas during 1614.[28]

The pattern of the Cape Verdean slave trade to the Spanish Americas during the years 1601–40 is one of abrupt fluctuations. In a brisk year the Santiago slavers loaded between 2,000 and 3,000 slaves for the Spanish Indies aboard 5 or 6 ships; in a slack year there were no ships, and no slaves were sold at all. An "average" year (if there had been such a thing) might have brought from 1 to 3 ships loading between 200 and 800 slaves. Philip D. Curtin (p. 107), using the Chaunu tables (6: 402–3), calculated that only 5,230 peças were extracted for the Indies from "Cape Verde," or Guiné, during the forty-year period 1601–40; but since it has been shown that in 1609–10 a total of 4,439 peças for the Indies was loaded at Santiago alone, this would leave only 791 peças to cover thirty-eight years (1601–8 and 1611–40) – an average of only 20 peças per year!

Walter Rodney, on the other hand, following contemporary Portuguese sources, asserted that Guiné shipped at least 3,000 slaves per year before 1640.[29] If this annual average were reduced to 2,000 (which

26. AHU, Cabo Verde, Caixa I, doc. 46.

27. The *dízimas* of Santiago were farmed out for two years at the rate of 605$000 per year (or 302$500 for six months); those of Fogo for two years at the rate of 230$000 per year (or 115$000 for six months).

28. AHU, Cabo Verde, Caixa I, doc. 55.

29. Rodney, "Portuguese Monopoly," p. 312. In his *Upper Guinea,* p. 98, Rodney suggested an annual figure of 5,000 slaves for all the Guiné coast during the period 1562–1640.

seems more reasonable to me), it would make a forty-year total of 80,000 slaves. The Cape Verde Islands, by my own rough estimates, transshipped approximately 20 percent of the slaves extracted from Guiné; that is, the islands transshipped an average of 400 slaves per year, or a total of 16,000 slaves during the years 1601–40. Most of the slaves re-exported from the islands went to the Spanish Indies, for there is little indication in the Santiago records of sizable slave cargoes to Brazil.

The entrepôt trade in slaves at Santiago faced formidable obstacles, including foreign competition, many legal restrictions (such as the prohibition of the sale of guns and ammunition to Africans), heavy taxation, and the direct and difficult rivalry with the Afro-Portuguese trading posts on the "rivers of Guiné." Especially irksome to the Cape Verdeans were the monopolistic practices imposed by Europe: the sale of *asientos*, or slave quotas, in Seville to West Indian suppliers, and Lisbon's imposition of a single monopolist contractor who alone had the right to extract slaves from Guiné (to be explained hereafter). The characteristic Cape Verdean responses to monopolistic restriction involved public protest and official denunciation of the monopolist, accompanied by secret fiscal evasion and mass smuggling.

After Portugal proclaimed her independence from Spain on 1 December 1640, thus inaugurating twenty-eight years of war (1641–68), the prospects for the continuation of the slave trade between Portuguese Africa and the Spanish Indies were very clouded. The Cape Verdes, however — as well as Guiné, Angola, and Benguela — needed the Spanish slave trade more than the Spaniards needed the Portuguese. A scant twenty days after his accession, the new Portuguese king, John IV, decreed that Spanish ships could trade with Guiné and the Cape Verdes if they deposited security in Lisbon;[30] moreover, in petitions which Santiago, Cacheu, and Luanda addressed to Lisbon, the Portuguese traders argued that, war or no war, the slave trade with the Spanish Indies must continue, or else Portugal's African enterprises would fall to ruins.

The question of obtaining Spanish-American silver, in return for slaves, was all-important and aroused the cupidity and interest of Lisbon. The Portuguese authorities decided that Spanish ships could acquire slaves in Portuguese Africa provided the ships sailed directly from the Indies to Africa, purchased slaves only with bullion and precious stones, and paid high tariffs and a *donativo*, or special gift, for the privilege of trading during wartime. In an unconsciously amusing directive to Angola,

30. Rodney, "Portuguese Monopoly," p. 316; AHU, Cabo Verde, Caixa II. This decree was confirmed later by the *alvará* of 1 June 1647, in AHU, Guiné, Caixa I.

the Overseas Council advised that Spanish ships "were to take no merchandise other than gold and silver, pearls and emeralds, and each ship must take 60,000 cruzados of these, or more"![31] The stipulated minimum sum of 60,000 cruzados (the equivalent of £12,000 sterling per ship!) was exorbitant, and this requirement was soon dropped.[32] The *donativo* was very heavy, running from 600$000 réis (£300) for a small ship to 1:600$000 (£800) for a large one, and seems to have been set at the rate of 4$000 per ton, but the Spanish slavers (some of whom were undoubtedly Portuguese sailing under a Spanish flag, but who by Spanish law were subjects of the king of Spain) often refused to pay it. Yet the evidence suggests that the Indies slavers agreed to do business, more or less on Lisbon's terms, and continued to acquire slaves in the Cape Verdes, Guiné, and Angola.[33]

A letter from Jorge de Mesquita de Castelo Branco, governor of the Cape Verdes, dated 9 August 1652, complained that two Spanish ships had refused to pay the *donativo* of 600$000; the previous year, before Castelo Branco took office, another two Spanish slave ships had paid 1:862$200 (£931) in customs duties, but had not paid the *donativo* — and neither had three other Spanish ships before 1651.[34] These remarks clearly confirm that the slave trade between the islands and the Spanish Indies was continuing at a rate only slightly lower than before 1641.

Customs records at Santiago for the first six months of 1652 show the arrivals and departures of eight ships, three of them caravels bringing slaves from Guiné, and two of them Spanish frigates loading slaves for the Indies. The frigate *Nuestra Señora de la Concepción* (Pedro Antonio Afonso, master) arrived from Havana in April 1652, loaded a full complement of slaves, paying 1:897$200 in customs duties, and then left for Havana. A few days later a frigate from Cartagena (Francisco Gomes of Lisbon, master) arrived looking for slaves. There were no slaves immediately available; so the master agreed to wait until some were procured. The Cartagena ship eventually paid 155$200 in duties, which

31. AHU, Angola, Caixa IV, *consulta* 14 January 1654 (confirming previous decisions).

32. Ibid., 16 June 1655.

33. Sena Barcelos, 2: 19. Luanda was in Dutch hands during the years 1641–48. After its recovery from the Dutch a brisk trade was kept up with Spanish slave ships. In 1655 nine Spanish ships (of which one was confiscated) and one Genoese ship paid 11:509$000 (£5,754) into the Angola treasury. During the sixteen months from November 1654 to February 1656, 25 ships (including Brazilian slavers) loaded 13,945 peças at Luanda. AHU, Angola, Caixa IV, governor's letters 17 September 1655, 25 February 1656.

34. AHU, Cabo Verde, Caixa II.

may mean that she purchased only about 25 peças. Both ships paid for their slaves with American silver.[35]

The customs duties levied on the two Spanish ships came to 2:052$400, which was 65 percent of the total six-month tariff revenues of 3:144$557 (£1,572). At least 425 slaves were loaded for the Spanish Indies in 1651, and at least 455 in 1652. Nearly ten years later, in 1661, an angry letter from the citizens of Ribeira Grande, denouncing the corruption of their governor, said that six Spanish slave ships had called at Santiago during the years 1658–60 (an average of two per year), and the citizens claimed, perhaps incorrectly, that the Spaniards paid 9,000 cruzados in *donativos*, which the governor had kept in his own hands.[36] The citizens also complained that another Spanish frigate, which had arrived at Santiago on 20 January 1661, had evaded paying customs duties by bribing the governor. They also charged that the governor (Francisco de Figueiroa), who had several ships of his own, tried to monopolize the Cape Verde trade with Guiné.

In the 1660s the Cape Verdean slave trade continued its usual uneven rhythm. A letter written at Santiago in June 1664 remarked that there had been no Spanish slave ships for three years, but that more ships were expected soon.[37] In 1665, an inquiry from Cayenne in French Guiana concerning the opening of trade with the islands brought the eager reply that the slaves in the Cape Verdes were better than those in Guiné and cost "only" 58$000 réis (£23) per peça, including the 8$000 in customs duties.[38]

After the Luso-Spanish war came to an end, in 1668, the Lisbon authorities refused to allow the Spaniards to resume the slave trade under the old prewar terms — when Spanish ships from Seville had bartered for slaves with European commodities — but insisted the Spanish ships must come directly from the Americas and pay with silver. The authorities at Santiago, nevertheless, in 1677, allowed two Spanish ships to buy slaves, even though they had come directly from Seville. The first ship purchased 260 slaves, and the second, which wanted 600 slaves, could obtain only 290. The municipal chamber at Ribeira Grande, in a letter to Lisbon, insisted that the Spanish had paid with silver *patacas*,[39] and

35. Ibid., docs. 16 and 22 June 1652.
36. Ibid., Caixa III, doc. 433.
37. Ibid., doc. 488.
38. Ibid., Caixa IV, doc. 30 June 1665.
39. *Pataca* was the Portuguese name for the famed 8-*real* silver coin (the Spanish dollar or "piece-of-eight"), once worth $320 réis or slightly less than a Portu-

TABLE 30

*Numbers of Slaves Transshipped in the
Cape Verdes, 1601–1700*

Years	Annual Average	Total
1601–40	400	16,000
1641–70	225	6,750
1671–1700	175	5,250
1601–1700	280	28,000

not with merchandise; they had refused to pay the *donativo*, but, since the war was over, the Portuguese had not pressed the issue. The aldermen felt that this influx of silver was vital to Santiago, since no "money" ships had come in for several years.[40]

In the final thirty years of the seventeenth century, the trade between the islands and the Spanish Indies slackened. The Brazilian market, although less lucrative, probably became more important for Santiago than the Spanish Americas. Santiago's poor relations with the Afro-Portuguese settlers in Guiné, and Lisbon's recourse to monopoly trading companies, made difficult the maintenance of the entrepôt slave markets in the Cape Verdes. The number of slaves involved in transshipments in the Cape Verdes during the whole century can be roughly estimated (see table 30). The total extraction of slaves from the Guiné coast during the century probably came to under 150,000.

The question might well be asked: why should a ship go to Santiago and acquire slaves at an expensive price (60$000 and more per peça) when she could go to one of several points along the Guiné coast and load a slave cargo in exchange for cheap commodities? The answer depends on an awareness of the complicated realities of the coastal commerce, where trading took place very largely on the terms set by African tribal leaders. Trading on the Guiné coast was often unduly delayed, protracted for many weeks or months, because the longer a ship stayed,

---

guese cruzado, and the most important unit in the metallic currency of the Cape Verdes.

40. AHU, Cabo Verde, Caixa IV, docs. 3 October 1674, 6 June 1677; AHU, Codex 489, fol. 6

the more presents and bribes the Africans expected to receive. Barter itself involved complex transactions, for the Africans would not, for instance, exchange slaves for iron bars but wanted the proper "mix" of commodities, involving quantities of a dozen or more articles (such as iron bars, cloth, haberdashery, brandy, guns, gunpowder, knives, metal manufactures, ribbons, beads), and the lack of a single item, such as a sword or a hogshead of wine or a copper cauldron, might nullify the whole transaction.[41] The ship's crew was often too long exposed to the unhealthy climate of the Guiné coast; and the coast itself, with its tricky tidal estuaries, was hazardous to navigation. A small miscalculation could leave a ship high and dry on a mudbank, in which case the nearest African tribe might quickly claim her as their own legal prize, according to the Guiné customs governing castaway vessels.

In these circumstances a ship captain who headed directly from Europe to the Cape Verdes bought the slaves he wanted from the stock maintained at Santiago, stayed only three or four days in the Cape Verdes, long before the onset of the unhealthy rains, and then went on his way to the Spanish Indies — such a captain might have been the one who arrived first in the Americas, obtained the best prices, kept his overhead expenses down to the lowest level, made the most efficient and economical use of his ship, and conserved the lives of his crew and his slaves. In short, such a captain might well have been the one who made the biggest profit.

The slaves at Santiago may have been expensive, but — as the Cape Verdeans claimed — they were "better" than the slaves available at Guiné. "Better" in the sense that the most unfit, the most sickly, and some of the most obdurate had already been culled. At Santiago the slaves had already endured the trauma of their first sea passage; their bonds with the mainland were already loosened; their incentive for escape was weakened, and the opportunity to do so much diminished. The slave trader at Santiago found perhaps a more resigned, a more bewildered, and a more manageable slave cargo than he would have found on the Guiné coast. Much of the very difficult preliminary work, particularly the exasperating bartering, had already been done for him by the Cape Verdeans. Given the excellent geographical position of the Cape Verdes, along the most favorable Europe-to-Indies route, the "expensive" slaves of Santiago may have been the biggest bargain obtainable in the West African slave trade.

41. Rodney, *Upper Guinea*, pp. 186–87.

Even if a slave trader went directly to the Guiné coast, he would probably still find himself involved with Cape Verdean intermediaries, and
perhaps obliged to buy Cape Verdean cloth, for the Cape Verdean presence in the Guiné trade was long-standing, extensive, and fundamental.
Without the Afro-Portuguese middleman, who was often of Cape Verdean or half Cape Verdean origin, and without the elegant Cape Verdean
textiles (the *barafulas, oxós, panos pretos, panos de obra, de agulha, de
bicho,* etc.)[42] that dressed the upper-class people of Guiné, the coastal
slave trade would have had a different complexion, with other personnel and other directions. The middlemen were *tangomaus, lançados,
grumetes,* and *ladinos,* individuals that emerged as the result of Portuguese social, commercial, maritime, and sexual contacts with African
peoples in a tropical environment.

The *tangomaus* were originally black traders, who left their African
societies and picked up Portuguese ways, and who handled much of the
bartering, particularly in the interior. The *lançados* were originally white
Portuguese who left the Cape Verdes and picked up African ways, living
precariously at the sufferance of local chieftains, managing the water-
borne commerce of rivers and coast. The tangomaus and lançados eventually fused, indistinguishably, into a single mulatto Afro-Portuguese
trading class, speaking both creole and African tongues, professing Chris-
tianity and practicing paganism, tolerated by African societies but not
part of them, imbued with certain European racial concepts, and wedded
to the notion that they were "Christian," "Portuguese," and "white."

The *grumetes* were originally African deckhands employed aboard
Portuguese ships. The term eventually applied to most black or mulatto
servants of the lançados, particularly those who handled cargoes and
who worked the boats. *Ladinos* (that is, "Latinos," or "Latins") were
slaves, or other Africans, who could speak Portuguese or creole. Contact
between the lançados and the Cape Verdes was regularly maintained. To
the lançados the Cape Verdean archipelago was their place of origin, a

42. These terms, and many others, are defined in Carreira, pp. 84–97. *Barafulas*
were the standard six-banded cloths, often with alternating strips of white and
blue, used as a unit of account. *Oxós* (from the Mandingo *nhantchó,* meaning
"noble") were fine, well-worked, decorative cloths, to "dress up" the wealthy.
Panos pretos (black cloths) were fine, expensive, deep-blue cloths woven at Fogo,
which were favored by Wolof women, and others. *Panos de obra* (worked cloths),
de agulha (needle cloths), *de bicho* (animal cloths, that is, with designs that suggested the skins of leopards, snakes, etc.; see note 58, below) were all expensive,
ornamental weaves.

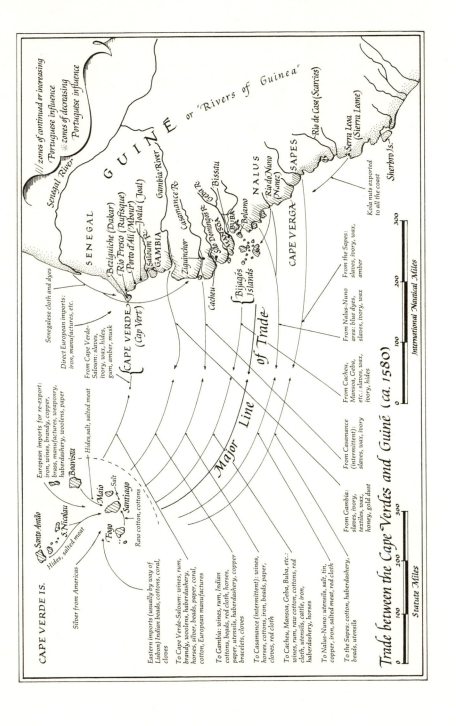

Trade between the Cape Verdes and Guiné (ca. 1580)

CAPE VERDE IS.

Silver from Americas

Eastern imports (usually by way of Lisbon) Indian beads, cottons, coral, cloves

To Cape Verde-Saloum: wines, rum, brandy, woolens, haberdashery, horses, silver, beads, paper, coral, cotton, European manufactures

To Gambia: wines, rum, Indian cottons, beads, red cloth, horses, paper, utensils, haberdashery, copper bracelets, cloves

To Casamance (intermittent): wines, horses, cottons, iron, beads, paper, cloves, red cloth

To Cacheu, Mansoa, Geba, Buba, etc.: wines, rum, raw cotton, cottons, red cloth, utensils, cattle, iron, haberdashery, horses

To Nalus-Nuno: utensils, salt, tin, copper, iron, salted meat, red cloth

To the Sapes: cotton, haberdashery, beads, utensils

European imports for re-export: iron, wines, brandy, copper, brass, manufactures, weaponry, haberdashery, woolens, paper

Senegalese cloth and dyes

Direct European imports: iron, manufactures, etc.

From Cape Verde-Saloum: slaves, ivory, wax, hides, gum, amber, musk

Hides, salt, salted meat

From Gambia: slaves, ivory, textiles, wax, honey, gold dust

From Casamance (intermittent): slaves, wax, ivory

From Cacheu, Mansoa, Geba, etc.: slaves, wax, ivory, hides

From Nalus-Nuno area: blue dyes, slaves, ivory, wax

From the Sapes: slaves, ivory, wax, amber

Kola nuts exported to all the coast

zones of continued or increasing Portuguese influence
zones of decreasing Portuguese influence

Senegal River

G U I N E or "Rivers of Guinea"

SENEGAL

Beziguiche (Dakar)
Rio Fresco (Rufisque)
Porto d'Ali (Mbour)
Saloum R.
GAMBIA Joala (Joal)
Gambia River
Casamance R.
Ziguinchor
Cacheu
São Domingos R.
Geba R.
BUBA
Bissau
CUBA
Bolama
Bijagós Islands
NALUS
Rio do Nuno (Nunez)
CAPE VERGA
SAPES
Rio de Case (Scarcies)
Serra Leoa (Sierra Leone)
Sherbro Is.

CAPE VERDE (Cap Vert)

Santo Antão
S. Nicolau
Fogo
Maio
Santiago
Boavista
Salt
Raw cotton, cottons
Hides, salted meat

Major Line of Trade

Statute Miles
0 100 200 300

International Nautical Miles
100 200 300

cultural and religious reference point, a bastion of support in time of trouble, a busy entrepôt market, and both a commercial partner and a commercial rival, depending on circumstances.

Two sixteenth-century accounts — Francisco de Andrade's report to Philip II (26 January 1582) and André Álvares de Almada's excellent *Tratado breve dos Rios de Guiné do Cabo Verde* (1594)[43] — provide a comprehensive view of Guiné commerce and indicate the extent of Cape Verdean involvement with the coast. In the northern area of Guiné, from Cape Verde proper to the Saloum River — at such places as Beziguiche (Dakar), Rio Fresco (Rufisque), Porto d'Ali (Mbour), Joala (Joal), and Saloum — the Portuguese extracted slaves, ivory, wax, hides, gum, amber, and musk in exchange for cottons, haberdashery, wines, metals, horses, silver coins, beads, paper, and miscellaneous manufactures. The Portuguese were ousted from this trade after 1570 and replaced by the French and English. From the Gambia River, the lançados obtained slaves, ivory, African textiles, wax, honey, and gold dust in return for wines, India cottons, Portuguese red cloth, Indian and Venetian beads, horses, paper, cloves, copper bracelets, and utensils. In spite of foreign competition, the Portuguese position on the Gambia was fairly stable. At the Casamance River, trade was intermittent, being interrupted by local wars, although Portuguese influence there would eventually increase. At Casamance the lançados bartered for slaves, wax, and ivory, and offered wines, iron, cottons, horses, beads, paper, cloves, and Portuguese red cloth.

In the central Guiné area, south of Cacheu — at the estuaries and tidal river courses of Cacheu, Mansoa, Geba, Buba, etc. — Portuguese influence was at its strongest. Here slaves, wax, ivory, and some hides were obtained in return for iron, cottons, wines, horses, cattle, and kola nuts. Offshore, in the Bijagós Islands, the fierce, seagoing, independent Bijagós sometimes permitted the exchange of slaves for iron, Portuguese red cloth, cows, copper cauldrons, and brass basins. Farther south, at the Rio Nuno (Nunez), the lançados obtained slaves, ivory, and wax in return for iron, tin, copper, utensils, salt, Portuguese red cloth, and salted goatmeat. And still farther south, from the Sapes, the Afro-Portuguese traders bartered for slaves, ivory, wax, and amber in exchange for cottons, haberdashery, Indian black cloth, basins, and beads. The same kind of exchanges occurred in the region from Cape Verga to Sierra Leone (originally the "Serra Leoa," or Lioness Range, so named by the Portuguese), although foreigners were encroaching in this area.

43. Brásio, 3: 97–107, 229–378.

The reports make no mention of weapons, guns, and gunpowder, which the Portuguese could not legally supply to the Africans, but undoubtedly the lançados ignored the law and bartered weapons and ammunition, particularly when they were forced to do so by French and English competition.

The lançados were deeply involved in strictly African commerce itself: in carrying rice, millet, salt, palm wine and other foodstuffs, condiments, and beverages from regions of abundance to regions of scarcity; in importing from Senegal fine white cloth (*xereos*) and white-and-blue banded cloth (*galans*) for barter in Guiné; in transporting Mandingo and other cloths from central Guiné to south Guiné; in taking indigo blue dyes from Nunez to Cacheu, and from Senegal to points south; and in supplying all of Guiné with kola nuts from Sierra Leone.[44]

The patterns of commercial exchange in Guiné should not be drawn in lines too bold and simple, for there were a large number of complicated transactions in which local, regional, interior-coastal, intercoastal, and international trading were all jumbled together. The exchange of metals, textiles, alcoholic beverages, and weapons for slaves, ivory, and wax summarizes the essentials of the international Luso-African trade, but many other commodities, and many other trades, were also vital parts of the commercial machinery.

Two points should be noted: (1) the Cape Verdes, in the sixteenth century, served as a center for collection and distribution of products of diverse origins that were destined for Guiné; and (2) textiles, of many types and provenances, were curiously prominent in Guiné commercial transactions. To the Cape Verdes from Europe, for re-export, went metals, manufactures, wines and brandy, haberdashery, Portuguese red cloth, paper, bracelets (of copper, tin, brass, and pewter), Venetian beads, and many "baubles" (mirrors, buttons, combs, bells, bangles, etc.). To the Cape Verdes from Spanish America, via Europe, went silver coins (melted down by the Africans and used for jewelry, not as currency). From the East, mostly by way of Lisbon, came Indian cottons and beads, Eastern coral, and cloves from the Moluccas. The Cape Verdean islands themselves supplied Guiné with raw cotton, cotton cloth, salted goatmeat, horses, and cattle.

The trade in textiles was peculiarly complex. The Guiné coast absorbed Portuguese red cloth, Indian cottons, Cape Verdean cottons, and sometimes also French textiles; while at the same time there was an

---

44. Carreira, pp. 36, 87, 90; Rodney, *Upper Guinea*, pp. 171–82, 206–7, *et passim.*

intensive intercoastal trade in textiles from Senegal, Gambia, and central Guiné (woven by the Mandingos, Fulas, Beafadas, Wolofs, Casangas, etc.), the general movement being from north to south. Central Guiné absorbed whatever raw cotton the Cape Verdes could supply and also used the indigo dyes from south Guiné. With indigo the Africans dyed their cloth light blue, dark blue, or black blue, and then arranged the narrow strips of dyed cloth in contrasting bands with narrow strips of white cloth, or else interwove blue and white threads into intricate patterns, giving Guiné cloth its characteristic and unmistakable look.[45] Yet however proficient the Guiné Africans were at weaving, they did not seem to be interested in tailoring, contenting themselves with sewing the narrow strips together and producing large flat pieces of cloth that were simply wrapped and draped around the body. Thus European tailored articles, particularly hats, coats, shirts, socks, stockings, trousers, etc., always commanded a market, both in Guiné and in the Cape Verdes, regardless of how much of their own cloth these areas produced.

Such was the situation in the sixteenth century. During the seventeenth century, as far as the islands were concerned, there were three notable changes: (1) there was a great increase in the activities of the English, French, and Dutch; (2) the role of the Cape Verdes as the entrepôt market for the transshipment of many diverse commodities ceased to be of much importance; and (3) Cape Verdean cotton textiles, of ever increasing quality, assumed a dominant position in the Guiné trade, ousting European, Indian, and even African rivals.

As for the foreigners, Portuguese efforts to keep them out of Guiné were foredoomed to failure, unless the Portuguese committed strong naval forces, and this the profits and volume of the trade in no way justified. The lançados had few loyalties and no prejudices in the matter: they would trade with anyone; and the Africans themselves insisted on open trade, with all comers, and without Portuguese tariffs or any other artificial barriers. Efforts to build forts, such as at Cacheu and Bissau, in order to monopolize commerce and levy tariffs, were counterproductive and drove trade elsewhere.[46]

Even Lisbon's attempts to keep foreign ships out of the Cape Verdes met with no success, for compelling motives of sheer economic survival drove the Cape Verdeans to trade with foreigners. If Lisbon forbade the

45. See the photographs in Carreira.
46. Rodney, "Portuguese Monopoly," pp. 321–22; and his *Upper Guinea*, pp. 92, 147.

trade, then the merchants became smugglers, avoided royal warehouses, and paid no customs dues; the only effect of such prohibitions was to diminish the royal revenues. The aldermen of Ribeira Grande, the ecclesiastics, the officials of the king's law courts and treasury, and even the king's governor himself, once he had been in the islands long enough to appreciate the economic realities of the archipelago, all connived at promoting the contraband trade with foreigners. For instance, the governors Jorge de Mesquita de Castelo Branco (1651–52), Pedro Ferraz Barreto (1653–58), and Francisco de Figueiroa (1658–63) – during their respective terms in office – traded extensively with foreigners and were themselves the chief smugglers in the archipelago.[47] The bitter denunciations which the aldermen and other officials made against these governors arose not because of disapproval of the illegal activities as such but because the governors tended to eliminate their commercial rivals, monopolizing the commerce with Guiné, raising freight charges on the Santiago-Guiné route (the charges for carrying one slave from Guiné to Santiago increased, during the 1650s, from 1$000 to 2$000 réis),[48] preventing competitors from participating in the trade with foreigners, and engrossing the import and sale of wines. The officials complained only when the governor's personal share was disproportionately large, and when he prevented them from doing more smuggling and illegal trading themselves.

Occasionally the governors, for motives of immediate profit, would suddenly enforce the old laws ordering the confiscation of foreign ships. The infamous Castelo Branco, who was remanded to Lisbon in chains after one year of extraordinary misrule and who was said to have amassed a private fortune of 50,000 cruzados (£10,000) in Santiago, confiscated the Dutch schooner *Halvemaan* and all her cargo (even though many of her ship's company were Portuguese), and seized the 14-gun English ship *Walsingham*. The crew of the *Walsingham*, on a routine call to pick up salt at Maio, were tricked by Castelo Branco and murdered in cold blood.[49]

These actions were exceptions to the general practice, and they took place at a time when other foreign ships were trading peaceably in the islands. Yet the influx of foreign ships to the Guiné coast in the seven-

47. There is ample evidence of this in the papers of the AHU, Cabo Verde, Caixa II.

48. AHU, Cabo Verde, Caixa III, doc. 431.

49. AHU, Codex 15, fols. 25–26; AHU, Cabo Verde, Caixa II, docs. 14 and 24 February, 28 September, 29 October 1652; and 22 August, 5 November 1653.

teenth century created a serious problem for the Cape Verdeans. As early as 1615 a memorandum from Santiago lamented the fact that "what we pay today for one bad Negro would formerly have purchased two good ones."[50] The reason for the price rise lay in the large influx of iron brought by foreign ships; for iron was "the principal sinew and strength in the bartering of slaves."[51] Iron bars, nine inches long, were a standard unit of account in Guiné. Portugal produced very little iron and its export was forbidden; so the iron brought into Guiné by the Portuguese in the sixteenth century came in small quantities, transshipped through Lisbon. Foreigners flooded Guiné with iron bars, thereby lowering their value, while increasing the demand for slaves, thus increasing slave prices. Prior to 1641, Spanish ships supplied the lançados with iron bars; after 1641, English ships supplied both the Cape Verdes and the Guiné coast with iron bars.

There is no doubt that the scarcity of iron bars in the Cape Verdes and in Cacheu-Bissau was the chief weakness in Portugal's commercial position in the Guiné slave trade. Fortunately for the Portuguese the rising demand for Cape Verdean textiles among the upper-class Africans forced the English and French to trade with the Cape Verdeans, exchanging iron bars and manufactures for the coveted cloth. In the 1680s one standard bar of iron was exchanged for two Cape Verdean standard *barafula* cloths.[52] At about that time the Afro-Portuguese traders were selling one slave for 30 iron bars (60 barafulas), one quintal of ivory for 18 bars (36 barafulas), and one quintal of wax for 16 bars (32 barafulas).[53]

How the barafula became the general standard of value in the Cape Verdes and indeed how weaving first started in the islands and how it progressed to a high level of exquisite design, far surpassing the finest creations of Guiné itself, are matters buried in considerable obscurity.[54] The archipelago was at an early date an exporter of raw cotton, sent to the Guiné weavers, but not an exporter of cloth or thread. In Guiné the

50. AHU, Cabo Verde, Caixa I, doc. 57.
51. Ibid.
52. Carreira, pp. 21, 85.
53. Rodney, *Upper Guinea,* p. 207.
54. Carreira's excellent monograph, *Panaria,* published in 1968, opened up this line of investigation for the first time. Carreira himself, born in Fogo but taken to Guiné at the age of eleven, is uniquely qualified to explore the textile question and the relations of the Cape Verdes to the coast, for he speaks and understands not only creole, but also Fula, Mandingo, and Manjaco.

spinners (mostly female) and the weavers (mostly male) seem to have been slaves.[55] By the middle of the sixteenth century, slave spinners and weavers (who also took care of the planting, harvesting, cleaning, carding, and dying of the cotton) were normal members of the retinue of domestic slaves in the larger plantations and households of Santiago. The Wolof women were particularly prized because, in addition to being skilled spinners, they were often very beautiful.[56]

The Cape Verdean textile manufacture was West African in origin, technique, execution, and personnel, although eventually also partly Moorish and partly Portuguese in its patterns and designs. The weavers used a very crude, simple, and fragile loom, probably of Mandingo origin. The loom produced only very narrow bands of cloth, usually 5 or 6 inches wide (and never more than 7 inches wide), and between 5 and 6 feet long. Six of these strips, never more nor less than six, were sewn together, side by side, to make a piece of cloth about one yard wide by no more than two yards long. The fact that six separate bands always went into the making of one *pano* (or cloth) provided the opportunity for many ingenious variations, worked out within the framework imposed by the six-banded arrangement. Alternating bands of indigo-dyed blue cloth with bands of white cloth produced the so-called striped cloth (*pano listrado*) mentioned in many records. The barafulas, it seems, were mostly cloths of this type.

Cape Verdean textiles ran a gamut from the plainest white cloth (*panos simples,* or *cates*) to cloths of the most elaborate weave, with silk woven into the cotton (in imitation of the Guiné *bantans*),[57] or with white, blue, and black threads combined in geometric designs of great intricacy and beauty. To European eyes the symmetrical designs had the look of Arabic mosaics; to the West Africans they looked like leopard markings, or the patterns on snakeskins, and hence the name *panos de bicho.*[58] Decorative motifs of Portuguese inspiration can also be found

55. So says Carreira, p. 53, although Rodney, *Upper Guinea,* pp. 261–62, and others, might disagree.

56. Carreira, p. 40.

57. In Guiné there was a large tree whose seeds contained a silk-like fiber, which was interwoven with cotton to produce a luxury cloth called *bantan* by the Mandingos. In 1686 the bantans were worth slightly more than the barafulas (2 iron bars = 3 bantans = 4 barafulas). In the Cape Verdes a similar cloth, but of higher quality, was made with imported silk. The Cape Verdean weavers also mixed wool and cotton in special weaves. Carreira, pp. 86–87.

58. Carreira, p. 96. *Bicho* is a Portuguese term that, strictly speaking, refers to insects, worms, grubs, and other small forms of life; but popular usage has con-

in the cloths, particularly the square blunt cross, which was copied from that painted on the sails of the caravels and which was the emblem of the Order of Christ.

Cape Verdean slaves cultivated the indigo plant, which had been brought over from Africa, and produced good blue dyes by simple methods. Female slaves would pick the indigo leaves, macerate them with their African wooden pestles, make them into small loaves, and dry them in the sun. The loaves would then be placed in pots, with water and ashes added, and left to ferment. The mixture had to be stirred frequently, for stirring oxidizes the colorless *indican* to produce blue indigo. The shade and strength of the dye was controlled by the amount of water added. The procedure took about two weeks, and usually each group of spinners and weavers made their own dye. In 1704 and 1708 efforts were made to construct large vats and produce the dye in commercial quantities, for export, since there were good markets in Europe for indigo; but indigo exports never seem to have attained a high volume, and the local market consumed most of what was produced.[59]

In the seventeenth century Cape Verdean textiles surpassed the best Guiné cloths in quality of weave and richness of design. Cape Verdean textiles drove out Indian cottons and European cloth. The privileged classes in Guiné preferred Cape Verdean cloth, not just because of its West African appearance, weave, and feel, but because it was superior in quality and design to the European and Indian imports. African chieftains insisted that a certain number of quality Cape Verdean cloths must form a part of the "mix" of commodities in every large bartering transaction. Africans often used the most attractive cloth they could find for funeral shrouds;[60] expensive textiles also figured prominently in marriage-contract exchanges. On ceremonial and other public occasions, the well-dressed African liked nothing better than to appear wrapped in an elegant Cape Verdean *bantan,* or *oxó,* or *pano de bicho.* As far away as the Gold Coast the Cape Verdean *panos* helped to dress the elite. The cloth was also exported to Brazil.[61]

---

verted it into an all-purpose word, designating everything in the animal world from gnats to elephants. Carreira, pp. 135–36, believes the designs used in Cape Verdean cloth were essentially of North African origin or inspiration, transmitted to the islands by the Portuguese and deriving from the Portuguese-occupied towns in Morocco.

59. Chelmicki, 2: 15–16; Sena Barcelos, 2: 169–72, 174–75, 185.
60. Carreira, pp. 79–80.
61. Dampier, 3: 23.

TABLE 31

The Pará-Maranhão Company's Cloth Exports
from the Cape Verdes to Guiné, 1757–82*

Types of Cloth	Quantity	Value
Panos ordinários	62,039 (46.6%)	93:058$500 (14.8%)
Panos de bicho	49,985 (37.5%)	405:245$625 (64.2%)
All other types	21,241 (15.9%)	132:454$700 (21.0%)
Total	133,265 (100.0%)	630:758$825 (100.0%)

*Based on statistics in António Carreira, *Panaria Cabo-Verdiano-Guineense* (Lisbon, 1938), p. 127.

Facts about the volume of the Cape Verdean textile trade in the seventeenth century are all but unobtainable. The first reliable figures come from the eighteenth century and are derived from the records of the General Company of Pará-Maranhão (Companhia Geral do Pará-Maranhão, or Companhia Geral do Grão Pará). The company held a monopoly of the Amazon and Maranhão trade and supplied that region with 28,167 Guiné slaves during the years 1756–78, making a profit of 103:380$784 réis (over £25,000) on the slaves. The company also monopolized the Guiné and Cape Verdean trades and enjoyed exclusive rights of orchil extraction in the Cape Verdes, the Azores, and Madeira. The enormous quantity of 2,284 tons of orchil (85 percent of it from the Cape Verdes) was extracted during 1759–74, realizing a profit of 204:380$784 (over £50,000). Cape Verdean textiles accounted for a substantial part of the company's business. During twenty-six years (1757–82) of activity the company exported 133,265 *panos* from the islands to Guiné, with a value of 630:758$825 (or about £160,000). During its most active years (1758–78), the company's cloth exports ran to an average of 6,243 *panos* per year, although in 1775, the year of highest volume, 12,759 *panos* were sent from the islands to the mainland.[62]

The General Company's cloth exports can be broken down by categories (see table 31). It will be seen that the *panos ordinários* (equivalent to the old barafulas) which had an average unit price of 1$500 apiece, accounted for nearly 47 percent of the volume, but less than 15 percent of the value of total exports; while the luxury *panos de bicho*,

62. Carreira, pp. 115–17, 125–27, 129.

with an average unit price of 8$625, with less than 38 percent of the volume, accounted for over 64 percent of the total value. This movement of cloth was directly related to the company's slave-trading activities: 133,265 cloths went from the archipelago to the coast, while the coast supplied 28,167 slaves for Pará-Maranhão. African slaves in the Cape Verdes manufactured the cloth, which went to Guiné and helped to pay for the purchase of more slaves.

The island of Fogo was the biggest producer of Cape Verdean cloth. The origins of nearly one-half of the company's 133,265 cloths can be traced, as follows: cloths produced by Fogo, 43,696 (67.6%); by Santiago, 19,272 (29.8%); by Brava, 1,713 (2.6%); making a total production of 64,681 cloths.[63] Fogo not only produced more cloth than the other islands, but also produced the best quality cloth.

The Cape Verdean cloth trade as a whole, inextricably bound to Guiné and to slavery, can be regarded as a symbol of the Africanization of the Cape Verdes. The objective commercial realities of the Guiné coast guided and even dictated the kind of economic structures that emerged in the archipelago, while the overwhelming presence of Africans in the islands, whether as slaves or as freedmen, seemed to guarantee that trading would follow the Guiné traditions of barter and that fiscal and currency questions would be looked at from an African perspective. English captains new to the islands, desiring a cargo of salt, or eager to purchase victuals, were often astounded when their gold and silver coins were refused, and the Cape Verdeans demanded instead old clothes, hats, pots and pans, knives, swords, etc. For the ordinary Cape Verdean, trade meant barter, and currency meant the barafulas, which were articles that could be put to ready use. For him a shirt had a self-evident and visible practical utility, and hence an immediate value, but a gold coin did not. As late as 1797, João da Silva Feijó wrote that "in any one of those islands a dress coat, an old waistcoat and breeches, a torn hat, a patched shirt, etc., are the best coin with which everything can be obtained, many times even in preference to money."[64]

For the official and mercantile classes of Ribeira Grande and Praia, however, metallic currency was essential. Many of them wished to make a fortune and then retire to Portugal; a fortune in Spanish silver *patacas* (the principal coin in the islands) could be carried to Portugal, but a fortune in barafulas had little value outside of the West African sphere of activity. Salaried officials and ecclesiastics complained constantly of the

63. Carreira, p. 128.
64. Lereno, p. 73.

poverty of the treasury, the interminable arrearages in pay, and the shortage of coin. But, whether they liked it or not, salaries were paid mostly in barafulas (as they were paid with wine in Madeira and with wheat in the Azores), and fines were levied in barafulas. The merchants and shopkeepers of Santiago grumbled that money, even when it arrived in quantity on a Spanish slave ship, quickly disappeared, used up in the purchase of imports, or else hoarded. Their remedy, which was formally proposed at least a dozen times during the seventeenth century, was to raise the legal value of the coin above its face value, and encourage the influx of gold and silver coins. Lisbon promptly, emphatically, and repeatedly vetoed all such designs, which the Portuguese felt would draw coin out of Portugal and to the islands. It seems clear, nonetheless, that the coins circulated in Santiago above their official values — Lisbon to the contrary notwithstanding — and that each island in the archipelago went its own sweet way, some doing without metallic currency, some accepting it only as bullion, reckoned by weight, and others setting arbitrary values far higher than those obtaining in Santiago. For if Santiago wished to draw coin out of Portugal, it was equally true that Fogo, Santo Antão, and São Nicolau wished to draw coin out of Santiago.

Metallic currency, however, was restricted to the narrow commercial and official white circles in the port towns; everywhere else the barafulas prevailed. Even the white landed rural proprietors, committed to spending their lives in Santiago, tended to accumulate barafulas rather than coin. For instance, when the wealthy Diogo Ximenes Vargas died in 1624, the inventory of his property included much real estate, buildings, animals, 150 slaves, and some gold — but his "cash" reserves consisted of cloth. He left 1,800 barafulas, each worth $400 réis, in 45 large rolls (each containing 40 cloths), adding up to 720$000 in value; he also left 840 plain white cloths, worth $120 each, in 21 rolls (also containing 40 cloths apiece), equivalent to 100$800 in value. The total "cash" value of all the cloths came to 820$800 (about £630).[65]

The Vargas estate, with its 40-piece rolls of cloth, suggests a regular scheme of cloth values, which in the middle 1620s ran as follows:

1 barafula	$400 (£0 6s. 2d.)
1 roll of barafulas	16$000 (£12 6s. 0d.)
1 plain white cloth	$120 (£0 1s. 10d.)
1 roll of plain white cloth	4$800 (£3 13s. 10d.)

---

65. Carreira, p. 85; AHU, Cabo Verde, Caixa I, doc. 125. Vargas bequeathed his entire estate to the Jesuits.

The ratio of barafulas to réis fluctuated considerably, depending on the supply of coin, and was always somewhat artificial, since there was no quick way of exchanging a large number of barafulas for coin. The rolls of barafulas provided a unit of high value especially useful for expensive transactions, for 10 such rolls, in 1624, were roughly equivalent to £122 in sterling. When slave prices were stated (as they often were) in terms of 80 or 120 or 160 barafulas, the implicit unit was the barafula roll of 40 pieces (that is, 2 or 3 or 4 rolls).

On the Guiné coast and among the lançados, metallic currency was seldom seen; there barafulas and iron bars provided the standard measures of value, and little notice was taken of theoretical equivalencies in European coin. Even the Portuguese government had to function within the African system — such as in 1676, when they levied a tax on slave shipments at Cacheu of 3 barafulas per slave;[66] and again in 1690, when they fined the rebellious Bibiana Vaz and her cohorts 9,500 barafulas.[67]

Lisbon, in spite of repeated petitions from Santiago, would not recognize the barafulas as legal tender in the islands, even though the barafulas were the actual medium of exchange until the beginning of the nineteenth century, in most places in the archipelago. With the single exception of the policy on customs duties, Lisbon's intrusions in economic questions damaged the fragile Cape Verdean economy. Since it was nearly impossible to collect customs fees on the Guiné coast, Portuguese ships were required to call at Santiago and pay their duties there, both before and after visiting the coast; needless to say, many or most ships, especially after 1620, ignored the law, went directly to Guiné for their slave cargoes, and paid no duties. Revenues allocated for the support of the bishop and his cathedral staff, and for payment of the governor and his military garrisons, went uncollected, and chronic arrearages became the rule. Lisbon's attempts to force the treasury at Madeira to support the ecclesiastics in Santiago had little result.

Yet on the question of customs duties, the law, if not the practice, continued to favor Santiago, and Lisbon held firm to this principle; but on all other economic matters, Lisbon sacrificed the islanders to the mercantilistic self-interest of the homeland. The slave trade, in particular, was subject to artificial regulation that was intended to extract the

66. Carreira, p. 85.
67. Ibid., p. 21. This fine was supposedly equivalent to 1:900$000 réis, rating the barafulas at a very low $200 apiece. For information on Bibiana Vaz, see Rodney, *Upper Guinea,* pp. 209–11. The documentary evidence is in AHU, Codex 489, fol. 54, and in Cabo Verde, Caixa V.

maximum possible benefit for the king's Lisbon treasury, regardless of adverse consequences for the Cape Verdes and Guiné.

Prior to the breach with Spain, in 1640, contracts for the extraction of slaves from Guiné were sold, for a term of six years, to a single monopolist contractor, who in turn let out subcontracts to other merchants. In 1609 the contractor, João Soeiro, agreed to pay the crown the extraordinary sum of 16:000$000 réis (£12,300) every year for six years.[68] In six years this would have come to 96:000$000 (£73,800) — an immense amount of money at that time. Although there is considerable evidence that João Soeiro juggled his accounts, diverted profits to his brother in Flanders, and evaded Cape Verdean customs duties by trading directly with Guiné, it is unlikely that he cleared enough to meet the full sum of 96:000$000 within the stipulated time period. When he could not or would not make his payments, he was arrested and spent six years (1614–20) in a Lisbon jail.[69]

One year after the expiration of Soeiro's contract, the Treasury Council at its meeting on 23 January 1616 considered letting out a new contract. The merchant Francisco Carlos da Silva had submitted a bid of 12:000$000 per year, plus another 500$000 for monopoly rights in the supply of iron to Guiné, but this sum of 12:500$000 was deemed insufficient. Another merchant, Duarte Pinto de Elvas, offered 13:500$000 per year and argued that this amount was generous because "the Rivers of Guiné are all occupied by the Dutch."[70] Most of the councillors were in favor of accepting the 13:500$000 bid, but the president of the council, Duarte de Castelo Branco, count of Sabugal, dissented, saying that the amount was too little, that Soeiro had really been able to pay 16:000$000 but tried to cheat the treasury, and that the slave trade was still very lucrative.

It was assumed at that time (1616) that an energetic contractor could extract 3,000 slaves per year from Guiné and make an average profit of 10$000 per slave, or 30:000$000 per year;[71] if he paid 16:000$000 to the king, that would leave him with 14:000$000 (minus certain incidentals, such as 12 slaves sent to the king each year for free, 1 percent,

68. AHU, Cabo Verde, Caixa I, doc. 58.
69. Ibid., docs. 23, 54, 80; Correia Lopes, p. 57. The evidence in this case, as in others, is not completely clear. His enemies depicted Soeiro as a cheat who accumulated profits while complaining of losses and who sent his capital abroad while pretending to be bankrupt.
70. AHU, Cabo Verde, Caixa I, doc. 58.
71. Ibid., doc. 57.

or 160$000, devoted to charitable ends, and other small commitments). These calculations were far too sanguine and stipulated a level of profitability, a regularity of supply, a stability of exchange — as well as freedom from failure, conflict, death, shipwreck, and misadventure — that were rarely characteristic of the Guiné trade.

The contractor for 1616–24, António Fernandes de Elvas, who promised 13:500$000 per year, seems to have run into fiscal difficulties by 1620.[72] A successor, for the years 1627–35, José André da Fonseca, who promised 13:400$000 per year (plus 1 percent, or 134$000, for pious works, and 643$000 annually to the convent of the English Brigittine sisters of Lisbon, and 256 pounds of beeswax and 12 slaves to the king), was arrested for arrearages but escaped and fled to France with his profits, which were popularly believed to run to 200,000 cruzados (80:000$000), an improbable figure.[73] The last contract (1637–42) was let out to Gaspar da Costa for only 9:400$000, although the additional stipulations in the contract brought his annual expenses to 10:837$000.[74] Between 1609 and 1637 the reluctance of the merchants to purchase the contract, and the vicissitudes of the Guiné slave trade, had reduced the crown's annual revenues from such contracts by over 40 percent, from 16:000$000 (£12,300) to 9:400$000 (£7,220). After the break with Spain in December 1640, the contract system, which was designed to supply slaves to the Spanish Indies, came to an end.

Relations between the Santiago traders and the contractors were usually poor. The Cape Verdeans were none too scrupulous in observing the monopoly rights of the contractor, and the contractor evaded the customs duties payable at Santiago and undersupplied the archipelago, charging high prices for essential European imports. The Cape Verdeans were allowed to fetch slaves from Guiné, strictly for employment in the islands, outside of the monopoly contract, but they undoubtedly abused this right, bringing slaves not for their own use but for resale and transshipment at Santiago.

After 1642 the monopoly system fell into abeyance, only to be revived again, in 1675, when the Companhia de Cacheu (as it was commonly known), under the leadership of António de Barros Bezerra, was given a six-year monopoly of the Guiné and Cape Verdean trades. The company undertook crushing fiscal, civil, and military obligations; it was

72. Sena Barcelos, 1: 210.
73. Ibid., p. 234; AHU, Cabo Verde, Caixa I, doc. 153.
74. AHU, Cabo Verde, Caixa I, docs. 165, 172. This contract can be found in printed form: *Contrato do Cabo Verde* (Lisbon, 1637).

charged with fortifying Cacheu, maintaining a fifty-man garrison, and meeting all payrolls. In return, company goods were exempt from taxes. Bezerra, graced with the title of captain-major of Cacheu, held supreme civil and military authority in Guiné but was vaguely responsible to the governor at Santiago. He went out to Guiné in 1676 and ran into immediate difficulties with the Africans, the lançados, and the Cape Verdeans. Both Africans and lançados resented Portuguese efforts to collect taxes, restrict trade, and build forts, and Bezerra waged a year-long armed struggle with the Africans at Cacheu. In addition, the company was undercapitalized — its initial shipments to Guiné were valued at a modest 5:600$000 réis (£613) — and was short of ships, men, and goods.[75]

The Cape Verdeans perceived an immediate threat to their commercial, fiscal, and political position. By the terms of the company's monopoly, the islanders could take to Guiné only Cape Verdean products (cloth, cotton, cattle, rum, salt, maize, etc.), for the company alone enjoyed the right to supply Guiné with iron, wines, manufactures, and all products of European origin. The Cape Verdeans, however, for their own use, had the right to purchase one-third of all cargoes brought from Europe in company ships, and the right to freight one-third of the space in the company's slave ships to the Americas. The islanders, understandably, were not impressed by these concessions. The company threatened Santiago's access to Guiné. The establishment of a captaincy, a customs-house, and a fortress at Cacheu, unless done under the direct auspices of Santiago, undercut the political position of Ribeira Grande, deprived the islands of essential revenues, and seemed to imply a shift in the center of gravity of Portuguese operations from the archipelago to the coast.

The governor of the Cape Verdes, who was usually himself a great merchant, could not tolerate this threat to his authority and prosperity. When Bezerra appeared at Santiago on a routine business mission, he was arrested by the governor (Manuel da Costa Pessoa), kept a prisoner for over a year, and then reluctantly remanded to Lisbon, where he was promptly released (on 13 February 1683). Each side accused the other, probably correctly, of trading with foreigners and of defrauding the treasury. Bezerra said that the Cape Verdeans, in violation of the company's privileges, had stockpiled at Santiago over 28:000$000 (£10,933) in "goods of the North" (non-Portuguese European products), designed for re-export to Guiné.

75. AHU, Cabo Verde, Caixa IV, *consultas* 7 December 1680 and 24 October 1681; Sena Barcelos, 2: 56–59, 71, 73, 75; Rodney, *Upper Guinea*, pp. 139–41.

Lisbon's confidence in Bezerra was not shaken. In 1685 King Pedro II reappointed him captain-major of Cacheu, but now he was to be independent of the jurisdiction of Santiago. He served out his three-year term, was replaced in 1689, and died the next year.[76] By this time a new monopoly company had been established, "The Company of the Islands of Cape Verde and Guiné," with a six-year contract covering the years 1690–95. The new company operated on largely the same terms as the old one, with two interesting additions: (1) the company purchased from the Spaniards a contract to supply the Spanish Indies with 4,000 slaves per year;[77] and (2) the company was made responsible for paying the salary of the governor of the Cape Verdes, whose income was doubled, from 600$000 per year to 1:200$000 (worth only the equivalent of £385 after the coinage debasement of 1688), and who, because of the salary increase, was absolutely forbidden to engage in commerce.[78] Lisbon sought to end the rivalry between the governors and the company by the curious means of removing the governors from commercial activities and placing them on the company's payroll.

The hostility of the islanders to the monopoly trading companies continued. The islanders were soon complaining vociferously to Lisbon that the company undersupplied the archipelago, created artificial shortages in order to charge high prices, sent too few ships to Santiago, and raised the freight charges on the Guiné-Santiago route.[79]

The second Guiné company eventually ran into even greater difficulties than the first one. Since the French maintained a factory at Bissau, from which they had shipped 2,800 slaves during the years 1685–89, infringing the Portuguese monopoly, the Portuguese moved to dislodge them. The sum of 50,000 cruzados (£6,567) was set aside for establishing a factory at Bissau. In the teeth of firm African opposition, the Portuguese built a fort at Bissau and intervened in a bitter tribal succession dispute.[80] These measures wasted time, money, and lives and made commerce unprofitable. The coming of the War of the Spanish Succession

76. AHU, Codex 489, fols. 44, 66, 75.

77. Ibid., fol. 107. The appointment of a Spanish vice consul, resident at Santiago, was also authorized. Sena Barcelos, 2: 103.

78. Sena Barcelos, 2: 95, 97. The prohibition against governors engaging in commerce was lifted in 1708 but reimposed in 1720; yet it is doubtful that it was ever really observed.

79. AHU, Codex 489, fols. 101, 132; Sena Barcelos, 2: 143.

80. Rodney, *Upper Guinea*, pp. 142–51; AHU, Codex 489, fols. 103, 117, 131, 139.

(1701–14), which Portugal entered in 1703 against France and Spain, ended the slave trade with the Spanish Indies, provoked the sack of Santiago by the French (in 1712), and temporarily ruined the commerce of Guiné. Even the fortress of Bissau, but newly built, was abandoned and then torn down (1701–8).[81]

Lisbon's official intrusions into the Cape Verdean and Guiné trade, her selling of contracts during 1580–1642, her establishment of monopoly companies during 1675–1700, and her repeated prohibitions of all trade with foreigners, all had damaging effects on the commercial prosperity of the islands. The restrictions on foreign trading, though partially ignored, were particularly irritating. Slaves could be sold only to Portuguese or to Spaniards bearing silver, but not to Frenchmen and certainly never to English and Dutch "heretics." The Cape Verdes had a profitable business in selling livestock to the British West Indies, but it was illegal and had to be carried on surreptitiously. The foreigners wanted to buy Cape Verdean cloth and to assist in the bartering for slaves in Guiné; but Lisbon forbade the sale of Cape Verdean cloth to foreigners, and so again the Cape Verdeans had to sidestep the law. Even the salt, acquired by close to one hundred foreign ships per year, could not legally be sold to foreigners.

During the last two decades of the seventeenth century the authorities in Santiago and Cacheu exerted considerable pressure on Lisbon for the liberalization of foreign trade, a liberalization that would have meant, in part, merely the legalization of existing practice. On 3 November 1694 King Pedro II wrote to the aldermen of Ribeira Grande that, despite their repeated requests, trade with foreigners was not to be permitted.[82] A further Cape Verdean request — that foreign ships be permitted to barter for victuals and beverage (as they had been doing for a century or more) and need not be held to money payments — was, however, granted in 1698; the king warned, nonetheless, that such barter should take place only through the office of the comptroller of the treasury and must not be used as a pretext for illicit trade.[83]

In 1699 António Salgado, the first person to hold the title of governor-general (*governador geral*) of the Cape Verdes, argued forcibly that free

81. Correia Lopes, pp. 65–66, believed that these events brought about a permanent decline in the Guiné slave trade, at least as far as the Portuguese were concerned. This view, it seems to me, should be tested against the evidence available for Guiné slave-trading after 1715.

82. AHU, Cabo Verde, Codex 489, fol. 103.

83. Arq. Dist. Évora, Codex CXVI/2-10, fol. 30.

commerce with foreigners was the only method left for restoring the prosperity of the islands. Finally Lisbon began to give way; in a royal letter to the governor, dated 13 March 1700, free commerce with the ships of friendly foreign nations was allowed, provided the foreigners paid all customs duties. But aliens were still prevented from buying Cape Verdean cattle, horses, or cloth and were not to acquire slaves under any circumstances.[84]

This liberalization, although hedged with restrictions, represented a revolutionary break with traditional policy. Twenty years later, in 1721, Lisbon went all the way, and granted the Cape Verdes, Guiné, and São Tomé all the trading privileges enjoyed by the Azores.[85] For religious reasons, the sale of slaves to foreigners was still forbidden; but otherwise the Cape Verdes enjoyed the same liberties as Madeira and the Azores.

Various other kinds of legal restrictions also applied to the slave trade. A sense of imperative religious obligation weighed heavily with the Portuguese; if Africans came under Portuguese control, then their instruction, baptism, and salvation were urgent and essential tasks. Theologians argued that God permitted African slavery to exist only because it was, or could be, the instrument for the salvation of tens of thousands of souls. Emphatic and repeated legislation, constant royal orders and instructions, and the full weight of ecclesiastical pressure incorporated paramount religious objectives into official policy. The law specified that slaves awaiting embarkation should be instructed, converted, and baptized, and kept in special "houses of catechism," where priests would be in constant attendance. When it was objected that few slaves could understand Portuguese or Creole, the king ordered Santiago and Cacheu to find priests who could speak African languages so that the spiritual needs of African slaves would not be neglected.[86] João Pinto, a Wolof priest engaged in converting slaves at Santiago in 1587, was given a stipend of 60$000 réis per year, which was twice the salary paid to Portuguese parish priests.[87]

Once aboard ship, the slaves would receive guidance from the ship's chaplain, who preferably should be a friar, but if not, at least drawn from the most devout of the secular clergy. The slave ship's chaplain, according to the law, would continue catechism and would baptize, say

84. Sena Barcelos, 2: 151–52; Arq. Dist. Évora, Codex CXVI/2-10, fol. 21.
85. Sena Barcelos, 2: 233–34.
86. Arq. Dist. Évora, Codex CXVI/2-10, fol. 30; AHU, Codex 489, fol. 134.
87. Brásio, 3: 153.

mass, attend the sick, and give the last rites to the dying. As for the slaves who remained in the Cape Verdes, according to a decree of 1697, they had to be instructed and baptized within six months, or their owners would lose all title to them. Owners were also required to give their slaves time off to attend mass on Sundays and holy days and were to feed them on those days, even if they did no work.[88]

In addition to the laws directing religious instruction, there was legislation that sought to maintain the physical welfare of the slaves and to guarantee a minimum standard of humane treatment. The laws of 28 March 1684 were directed to the problem of overcrowding aboard ship.[89] These laws determined that all Portuguese slave ships should be measured by competent officials, and their tonnage, or cubic volume, exactly ascertained; official records of these measurements would be kept. The tonnage would set the limit on the number of slaves a vessel could legally carry: specifically, a ship could carry seven slaves for every two tons, provided the slaves were below decks, or under shelter, but only five slaves for every two tons if the slaves were carried on the open deck, without shelter. Thus a 100-ton ship would be allowed to carry a maximum of 350 slaves under shelter, or a maximum of 250 without shelter, or if she carried equal numbers of sheltered and unsheltered, not more than 300 in all. The legal limits on slave shipments, in relation to tonnage, can be easily calculated (see table 32).

The 1684 laws on overcrowding, though they prevented such clear abuses as the loading of 600 slaves aboard a 100-ton ship, still allowed considerable overcrowding, for the master of a 400-ton ship could still, by the terms of the law, cram between 1,000 and 1,400 slaves aboard her. The laws further specified that small boats were not to come alongside a loaded slaver and that, when a slave ship sailed, a guard was to remain on deck until she was two to four leagues distant from shore. Aboard ship the slaves were to be fed three times per day and given at least one *canada* (about $3\frac{1}{3}$ pints) of water per day per person. Ship captains must store sufficient quantities of victuals and beverage, based on realistic calculations of the probable duration of the voyage; for instance, Lisbon specified that ships from Angola to Pernambuco must carry enough supplies for thirty-five days, from Angola to Bahia enough for forty days, and from Angola to Rio de Janeiro enough for fifty days. Slaves falling ill during the voyage were to be separated from their fel-

88. Arq. Dist. Évora, Codex CXVI/2-10, fols. 10, 27, 31; Sena Barcelos, 2: 163.
89. Arq. Dist. Évora, Codex CXVI/2-10, fols. 9–12.

TABLE 32

*The Maximum Number of Slaves That
Portuguese Ships Could Legally Carry*

Tonnage	Slaves with Shelter	Slaves without Shelter	Slaves Half-Sheltered Half-Unsheltered
25	88	63	75
50	175	125	150
75	263	188	225
100	350	250	300
150	525	375	450
200	700	500	600
250	875	625	750
300	1,050	750	900
400	1,400	1,000	1,200
500	1,750	1,250	1,500

lows, to prevent the spread of infection, and given special care in a separate part of the ship. Penalties for violations were severe, ranging from six years exile in India to lifetime exile, sometimes accompanied by heavy fines and confiscations, depending on the status of the offender. Officials who were responsible for executing the law, such as ship guards, were to be punished with special severity.[90]

The question naturally arises as to the enforcement of these laws; for as always in Portuguese colonial legislation, there was a large gap between theory and practice, between legislative intent and actual compliance. The king's laws were certainly not observed in Guiné, but at Santiago there was a measure of control. The enforcement of the measures commanding the religious instruction of slaves, and their proper care while awaiting embarkation, depended not so much on the royal officials, who may have been largely indifferent, but on the sincerity, zeal, and concern of the local clergy. An energetic prelate like Bishop Vitoriano Portuense (in office 1688-1705), who at midnight invaded the houses of the wealthy and routed the slave-girl concubines from their master's beds, could be a thorn in the side of slave traders. Vitoriano, who had once served as acting governor of the Cape Verdes for

90. Ibid.

twenty-two months (17 April 1688 to 28 February 1690), was pre-vented, on the death of Governor Diogo Ramires Esquivel on 16 Sep-tember 1690, from serving in a similar capacity again. The aldermen and merchants of Ribeira Grande and Praia would not willingly submit once more to his rigid and moralistic rule.[91]

The Jesuits, during the years of their Cape Verdean mission (1604–42), and the Capuchins after 1647, were both active in the catechizing and protection of slaves. Nor was the question of African languages a decisive barrier to communication with slaves, for most of the cathedral clergy at Ribeira Grande were Africans. As Vieira wrote during his visit to Santiago in 1652: "Here there are clerics and canons as black as coal, but so grave, so respectable, so learned, such great musicians, so discrete, and so temperate that they could arouse the envy of those we see there in our own cathedrals."[92] Moreover the *ladinos* (slaves understanding creole) and the Afro-Portuguese lançados provided the priests with a wealth of interpreters.

In Santiago, at least, there were opportunities to give some instruc-tion to slaves in transit and much instruction to slaves in residence. Al-most all slaves, at some time or other, received baptism. Scrupulous clerics, like Bishop Vitoriano, would not baptize African adults until they had received some instruction; but other priests sometimes bap-tized uninstructed slaves en masse, rapidly sprinkling water over a crowd of people who did not know what was happening.

In the Cape Verdes the religious and social acculturation of the Afri-can proceeded slowly and reached only a certain point. Religious syn-cretism, with Catholic saints woven into the African pantheon, and cultural fusion, with an amalgam of European and African elements, were the rule. The Cape Verdean crushes his corn with both African and European implements; he beats out African rhythms on a Portuguese peasant triangle (*ferrinhos*); he cultivates an American plant, maize, by African methods, in fields laid out according to a Portuguese pattern. Again, in his Cape Verdean folk tales, the vicious, scheming wolf of European legend appears in semi-African guise, as a lovable, guitar-play-ing scamp;[93] while in the *crioulo* language, African "soul" finds expres-sion in Portuguese speech. At many levels of sensibility, and of social contact, African elements interpenetrate the imposed European pattern.

91. Sena Barcelos, 2: 92, 95, 103, 173–74.

92. This passage has often been cited. See Ferreira, p. 71; *Cabo Verde: curso de extensão,* p. 511; etc.

93. Amaral, pp. 19, 217–18; Ferreira, p. 157.

If, in the archipelago, the African was Europeanized, so was the European Africanized, content to gauge his wealth by African measures and conduct his trade by African rules. The mulatto was the biological and cultural meeting point of African and European. It was in vain that royal orders such as that of 20 October 1620 were issued, requiring the exile of large numbers of white women convicts to the Cape Verdes, "so that the race of mulattoes may be extinguished as soon as possible."[94] For the white woman never came to the islands in large numbers, and the African woman was the mother of the mixed-blooded Cape Verdean, just as across the sea she was the mother of so many mixed-blooded Brazilians.

The landholding mulattoes of Cape Verde, whatever their color, creed, or tongue, always considered themselves to be "white," Christian, and Portuguese, and sometimes even fidalgos and "nobles." They were outraged when an arrogant Portuguese judge, João António da Silveira e Sampaio, called them *"negros e mulatos."* The judge said "that the 'whites' of the land [*brancos da terra*] were only 'white' by their fathers, who were merely the servants of bishops, governors, and judges, and that by their mothers they descended from the gentiles of Guiné"[95] — most of which was perfectly true but gave deep offense.

Massive promiscuity, involving whites, blacks, and browns, was and remains the rule. Marriage is an infrequent ceremony of little importance that imposes almost no limits on sexual conduct. In Fogo, "twins" is the name given to children born of different mothers on the same day but having the same father.[96] Promiscuity extends even to the clergy. A celebrated black priest who owned much land near Cidade Velha (Ribeira Grande) and who died about 1938, named sixty-eight sons and daughters in his will, but admitted that there were many others he had forgotten.[97]

Men of pure white blood have never been numerous in the Cape Verdes. A document of 1743 reported that there were only about twenty white men in Santiago,[98] although in the sixteenth and seventeenth centuries there were probably more than ten times that number, including a few fidalgos. The "time of waters" (*tempo das aguas*), or rainy season, from July to October, was particularly hard on newly

94. Sena Barcelos, 1: 210.
95. Bivar Guerra, p. 183.
96. Ribeiro, *Fogo,* p. 169.
97. Fontoura da Costa, p. 48, n. 123.
98. Amaral, p. 194.

arrived Europeans. The rain brought life to the plants, but death to humans. The lagoon at Ribeira Grande and the stagnant pools and swamps around Praia, which were not drained until 1877, filled with mosquitoes, and the inhabitants came down with what the old physicians called "remittent" and "intermittent" fevers. Many a European did not survive his first rainy season. Governor João Cardoso Pisarro, who arrived at Santiago on 30 June 1676, died seven weeks later, and his wife, his son, and several servants followed him to the grave.[99] During the seventeenth century five other Cape Verdean governors died before completing their short triennial terms of office.

The mortiferous climate of Santiago had a very bad reputation, and Lisbon had trouble finding people who would fill offices in the archipelago. In Portugal even fairly humble and obscure persons turned down the high but dangerous honor of appointment as bishop or governor of Cape Verde. Of the half-dozen bishops who came to Santiago in the seventeenth century, three died after brief terms of service. Of seven Jesuits who arrived in 1604 and 1606, four died within a few weeks of their arrival, and the order eventually closed its mission because of so many lives thrown away.[100] Humble people suffered the same fate: of six gunners and masons who reached Santiago in June 1678, four were dead by the end of the year.[101]

Whites who survived the first few years and settled in Santiago usually reared mulatto families. The great slave plantations of Santiago, known as *morgadios* and *capelas*, fell eventually into mulatto hands. The senior officials in church and state were always white Portuguese, although the lower ranks were filled with mulattoes and blacks. Persons with special skills, such as master gunners, physicians, architects, and master masons, were almost all white, as were many of the merchants. But the commercial classes of Ribeira Grande and Praia, and the seamen who maintained the connections between the islands and Guiné, included many mulattoes, blacks, and Afro-Portuguese of the lançado type.

Life for the African slave in Santiago was hard, brutish, and, in times of famine, short. There is no doubt that, when the rains failed, the African slave suffered sooner and more severely than any other class. In 1690 the governor informed the king that, after several years of drought, "close to four thousand souls may have died, the larger part of them

99. Sena Barcelos, 2: 62.
100. *Cabo Verde: curso de extensão,* pp. 515-25.
101. AHU, Cabo Verde, Caixa IV, *consultas* 28 March, 5 November 1678, and 5 July 1679.

Negroes."[102] The habit of certain *morgados* of "freeing" their slaves in times of drought, when food was expensive and there was no agricultural work to be done, ironically compounded the difficulty of the slave's position.

For the slave in Santiago there were only a few avenues of escape. Some may have found other islands in the archipelago more congenial. Brava, where many Madeiran whites lived, offered greater agricultural freedom, with many small-property holders and no large estates. Conditions on lonely but productive Santo Antão, with its mostly African population – or on the barren but much frequented and happy-go-lucky salt islands – may have been attractive to certain Santiagoans. It was possible for a fortunate few to go back to Guiné, but as the generations passed, the black African slave turned into a mulatto Cape Verdean freedman, and the ties with Guiné were broken. Nonetheless, in our own day, many Cape Verdeans have emigrated to Guiné and Senegal. In the nineteenth century, American whalers provided another avenue of escape; for instance, half the crew of the famed *Cachalot* were dark-skinned Cape Verdeans.[103] In recent decades many Cape Verdeans have gone to São Tomé as contract laborers, only to work under wretched conditions and return as poor as they left. And finally, from time to time, emigration to the United States, Argentina, and Brazil has been possible.

For the mass of the slave population, trapped in the interior mountain recesses, escape to the outside became all but unthinkable. The land-bound Cape Verdean peasant was not maritime-minded but lived within restricted horizons. The island of Santiago became a kind of mainland, known only as "Cabo Verde"; the other islands were only "as ilhas," whereas Santiago was Cape Verde, the center of a narrow world. The dark-skinned Santiagoan was seldom a boatsman, a fisherman, a boat builder, or a sailor. The sea did not attract him; his mountains were world enough for him. Many reached old age without having even once left the interior highlands to descend to the water's edge.[104]

The land-bound Cape Verdean found escape from the misery of life, if ever, not in other lands (which few could reach), but in music, poetry, and the dance. For the Cape Verdean, as for some of the American and Brazilian slaves, emotional release came in bodily movement, in rhythm,

102. AHU, Cabo Verde, Caixa V, letter 25 June 1690; Codex 489, fol. 75; Lereno, pp. 26–27.
103. Frank T. Bullen, *Cruise of the "Cachalot"* (London, 1898), pp. 24, 31.
104. Mendes Corrêa, pp. 236–37.

and in the tender lyrics of the melancholy *morna*; for what the *samba* is to the Brazilian, and spirituals and "blues" to the American Negro, the *morna* is to the Cape Verdean, and more. In the archipelago amusements are few, the range of pursuits narrow, and vocations and avocations limited; so in the *morna* a full compass of emotion and experience finds expression, with surprising intensity.[105]

The most popular of *morna* composers was the Bravan poet Eugénio de Paula Tavares, whose verses in the Bravan Creole dialect touched the hearts of the people. After his death, on 1 June 1930, a girl from the hamlet of Fonte Vinagre in Brava is reported to have said: "Quando nhô Eugene morrê 'm pensa Braba djâ cabâ" ("When master Eugénio died, I thought Brava was done for").[106] It was Eugénio Tavares who, in his famed *Morna de despedida* ("The Farewell *Morna*"), gave poignant expression to the mood of the Bravan at the moment of emigration, when he left a wife or lover for a separation that could last ten or twenty years:

Hora di Bai	Hour of going
Hora di dor	Hour of pain
Ja'n q'ré	I wish
Pa el ca manchê!	That it would not dawn!
De cada bez	Each time
Que 'n ta lembrâ,	That I remember thee,
Ma'n q'ré	I would choose
Ficâ 'n morrê! [107]	To stay and die!

Lack of opportunity compelled emigration, but the *dinheiro do mar* (sea money), as the people called money earned abroad, came at a high personal and emotional price; or, in the words of another *morna*: "Dinhêro di mar, dja bu caro" ("Money from the sea, how costly you are").[108]

The foreigner, the outsider, looks upon the Cape Verdeans – with their problems, their *mornas*, and their literature – with some impatience. In his critical view the islands need fewer guitar players, poets, *mornistas*, and littérateurs, and more agronomists, engineers, physicians, and hydrogeologists. But Cape Verdean problems, with their artistic and

105. See the discussion in Ferreira, pp. 127–48, who calls the *morna* "the maximum exponent of the sensibility of a people."

106. Often quoted, but perhaps apocryphal; Ferreira, p. 138; Araujo, p. 63.

107. Tavares, *Mornas: cantigas crioulas* (Lisbon, 1932), p. 38; Ferreira, p. 140.

108. João Baptista Amancio Gracias, *Monografia sobre a Província de Cabo Verde* (Praia, 1922), p. 72.

psychological reflections, arise from the social and economic situation, which is itself the end product of a society once composed of masters and slaves.

In the seventeenth century, slaveholding and slave-trading were the archipelago's *raison d'être*, were the very basis of its existence as a social and economic complex. The archipelago serviced the ships of all nations and produced large quantities of salt for the international trade; but its population, in itself composed largely of slaves or the descendants of slaves, lived mainly off slavery and its proceeds. The slaves of Santiago and Fogo wove the fine cloth that was used to purchase more slaves in Guiné. The relationship of Santiago and Guiné was ambiguous, with Santiago dependent on but also in competition with Guiné. The slaves procured in Guiné were largely destined for re-export to the Spanish Indies; Santiago relied on Spanish America as a slave market and as a source of silver currency. Those slaves who stayed in the archipelago underwent a process of partial acculturation and progressive hybridization in a society dominated by white urban officials and traders and mulatto rural patriarchs.

Lisbon gave the archipelago its overall political direction, and its dominant cultural and religious institutions. Lisbon was also the source of a stream of unenforceable mercantilistic legislation, of useless instructions and ill-informed memorandums. Monopoly systems of trade, favored by Lisbon, met much opposition in the islands. From Lisbon came an occasional zealous cleric and a considerable number of self-seeking, quarrelsome, and greedy officials.

Portugal, Guiné, and the Americas provided the economic and social connections that, across the centuries, have intersected in the archipelago. All contributed in a complex pattern of relationships to create the social and cultural enigma which is Cape Verde.

10
Conclusion: The Insular Nexus of Maritime Movement

Today the Portuguese islands lie hidden under veils of obscurity and neglect. Aside from questions relating to the discoveries, during the past half-century the Western world (the Portuguese alone excepted) has not produced more than a dozen books dealing with the Portuguese mid-Atlantic archipelagoes. It may be hard for us today to realize how recent this slide into obscurity has been, for our forefathers, in the normal course of travel, were more likely to make lengthy visits to the islands and were generally more familiar with them than we are. From 1830 to 1910 a considerable literature appeared describing the islands to a wide audience that was both instructed and entertained.

The Cape Verdes received much attention in the works of Horatio Bridge (1845), Charles Sainte-Claire Deville (1848), Charles W. Thomas (1860), Alfred B. Ellis (1885), and Immanuel Friedländer (1913). In addition Charles Darwin, stimulated by observing the differences between life forms on the oceanic islands and on the mainland, began his journal of the voyage of the *Beagle* with brief notes concerning the flora, fauna, and geology of the Cape Verdes.

The Azores were described in books and essays by John Fowler (1830), Edward Boid (1835), Joseph and Henry Bullar (1841), Thomas W. Higginson (1860), and C. Alice Baker (1882), and mentioned in many diaries and memoirs of whaling voyages. Madeira attracted a host of writers: John A. Dix (1851), Edward Vernon Harcourt (1851), Rudolph Schultze (1864), W.J. Quintus (1866), Richard Greeff (1872), William Longman (1875), Alfred B. Ellis (1885), L. Manchon (1888), Eugene Jones (1895), A.J. Drexel Biddle (1896), W.H. Koebel (1909), and many others. Between 1889 and 1910, Samler Brown's detailed tourist guidebook to the islands of Madeira, the Canaries, and the Azores ran through ten editions.[1]

The nineteenth-century importance of the archipelagoes can also be deduced from the large number of consuls, vice consuls, and consular agents stationed at the islands. During the 1850s, for instance, over twenty nations maintained representatives in Madeira; and Britain, the United States, Spain, Greece, and Uruguay each kept both a consul and a vice consul there. In the Cape Verdes eleven countries retained twenty-seven representatives scattered among seven islands. Britain had a consul and a vice consul at Praia, a consul at Mindelo, and vice consuls at Sal and Boavista; the United States had consuls at Praia and Mindelo, and vice consuls at Sal, Maio, Fogo, and Brava; and Brazil had a consul at Praia and vice consuls at Mindelo, Sal, Boavista, and Maio.[2] Today it would be inconceivable for any nation to keep representatives in such forsaken places as Sal, Maio, Fogo, Boavista, and Brava.

In the Azores the maritime powers stationed consuls and agents at the three international ports of Ponta Delgada, Angra, and Horta. The Dabney family of Boston and Fayal, owners of the ship-supply firm of Dabney and Sons, itself the largest business enterprise in Fayal, held the United States consulship of Horta from 1815 to 1892, passing on the office from father to son and to grandson.[3] Today there are only two

1. The works by most of the authors named can be found in the bibliography. The list is intended to be representative, not comprehensive, for another two dozen names could be easily added to it. Recently, since about the middle 1960s, there has been an upsurge of interest in the publication of books about Madeira and the Azores written by non-Portuguese authors. The following may be noted: R.H. Bryans, *Azores* (London, 1963); K.E. Gygax, *Beiträge zur Geographie von Ponta Delgada, Angra do Heroismo und Horta (Azoren)* (Zurich, 1966); Albert t' Serstevens, *Le périple des îles Atlantides: Madère, Açores, Canaries* (Paris, 1966); L.C. Andrade, *The Open Door* (New Bedford, 1968); Egerton Sykes, *The Azores and the Early Exploration of the Atlantic,* 2d ed. (London, 1968); Bernard Venables, *Baleia! Baleia! Whale Hunters of the Azores* (New York, 1969); and Aake Berg, *Madeira* (Stockholm, 1970). But Araujo's book (1966) seems to be the only recent substantial foreign work on the Cape Verdes.

2. Travassos Valdez, *Six Years,* 1: 18, 46, 91, 128, *et passim.* But it should be noted that, in the lesser Cape Verdes, the same man, usually a prominent local merchant, would serve as vice consul for two or three countries.

3. John Bass Dabney (d. 1826) was U.S. consul at Horta, 1815–26; his son, Charles William (1794–1871), was consul 1826–71; and his grandson, Samuel Wyllys (1826–93), was deputy consul, 1858–71, and consul, 1871–92. The third consul, Samuel Wyllys Dabney, was particularly distinguished, and earned an international reputation for his acts of hospitality, philanthropy, and courage. Other

or three vice consuls at Horta and Angra; in all of the Portuguese island communities, only Funchal and Ponta Delgada retain some pretensions to diplomatic importance.[4]

Today the islands have largely lost their consuls, their international trade, and much of their prominence in the bunkering of ships. Their strategic position alone, Madeira excepted, commands attention. All calculations of naval and air strategy in the North Atlantic must, at some point or other, involve the Azores. Ponta Delgada served as an Allied naval base during World War I; Britain's Royal Navy used the facilities at Horta during 1943-45; and both British and Americans, despite the formal neutrality of Portugal, built air bases in Santa Maria and Terceira during 1943-45. The Terceiran air base is still manned by American forces, who were also, during the late 1960s, constructing harbor facilities at Praia. The strategic prominence of the Azorean geographical position has always been apparent, almost from the days of the discoveries. Philip II recognized this fact when he built his gigantic fortress at Angra; and the Portuguese made use of the islands as a base from which to extend armed protection to the harassed returning East Indiamen.

The strategic position of the Cape Verdes, in principle and in potential, is equally crucial, although its significance is partly concealed by the fact that the Cape Verdean region has never been the scene of major military campaigns by the great powers. A naval "confrontation" in the vicinity of 15° north latitude, or extensive military conflict in the Senegal-Gambia mainland, could bring the strategic location of the archipelago into prominence. Certainly, across the centuries, the Portuguese have found the Cape Verdes to be very useful as a staging ground for political and economic ventures on the African mainland. The island of

---

members of the Dabney family include: William Henry Dabney (1817-88), U.S. vice consul at Terceira, 1845-48, and consul-general at Tenerife, 1862-82; Robert Lewis Dabney (1820-98), theologian; Lewis Stackpole Dabney (1840-1908), a Boston lawyer; Charles William Dabney (1855-1945), president of the universities of Tennessee and Cincinnati, and assistant secretary of agriculture (1893-97); and Julia Parker Dabney (b. 1850), a painter and novelist. See *Lamb's Biographical Dictionary of the United States* 2 (Boston, 1900): 309-11; *Herrinshaw's Encyclopedia of American Biography of the Nineteenth Century* (Chicago, 1906), p. 275; *National Cyclopaedia of American Biography* 4 (New York, 1897): 474.

4. Eleven countries (Belgium, Brazil, Britain, France, Greece, Holland, Italy, Monaco, Spain, Switzerland, and the United States) had some kind of consular representation at Funchal during the 1960s, and nine countries (Belgium, Brazil, Britain, France, Italy, Norway, Spain, Sweden, and the United States) at Ponta Delgada.

São Tomé in the Gulf of Guinea, although far less strategically located than the Cape Verdes, has played a similar role and was recently used as a base for foreign intervention in the Biafran war of 1966-70.

The strategic uses of the islands, clearly apparent in the 1970s, project into the future, with no foreseeable point of cessation. On the other hand the commercial functions of the islands, which show signs of stagnation, decay, and crisis in the 1970s, seem to have little future at all. Tourism may rescue Madeira and could assist the Azores, helping to bring commercial accounts into balance, but a revival of trade seems unlikely, and it is improbable that either tourism or trade will flourish in the Cape Verdes. In the seventeenth century the commercial position of the islands was far stronger, and insular commerce contributed substantially to Atlantic trading operations.

Insular trading in the seventeenth century can be summarized under various headings. First, in each archipelago, there was a purely local trade carried on by caravels and other small vessels, or even by launches and boats. Madeira traded with the Canaries and the African coast; the nine Azorean islands traded with each other, exchanging wines and cereals, and transshipping foreign imports; and the Cape Vèrdes carried on a voluminous business with the coast of Guiné, transshipping European imports, offering Cape Verdean cloth, rum, and maize, and acquiring slaves, ivory, and wax.

Second, there were the trades within the Portuguese Empire. Portugal sent olives and olive oil to all the archipelagoes, salt to Madeira and the Azores, and wines and cloth to the Cape Verdes. In theory, though not always in practice, all Eastern spices reached the islands by way of Lisbon, and all foreign commodities to the Cape Verdes had to be transshipped at Lisbon. The Azores supplied Madeira, Lisbon, and the Portuguese garrison towns in North Africa with wheat and the Cape Verdes and Brazil with wines. Madeira sent wine to the Cape Verdes, Angola, Brazil, and North Africa, and occasionally a few pipes to Lisbon. The Cape Verdes sent salted meat to Madeira and Brazil, and African-styled cloths to the black population of Brazil; the archipelago also sold slaves to Brazil.

In the seventeenth century Portuguese imperial commerce constituted an appreciable portion of the total Atlantic commercial effort, and the islands contributed much to the flexibility, variety, and frequency of various trades. A document showing customshouse incomes at various Portuguese ports in 1681 illustrates the significance of Madeira and the Azores within the Portuguese system (see table 33). By percentages, the

TABLE 33

Customshouse Income at Portuguese Ports in 1681*
(in réis)

1.	Lisbon	269:856$000	(£ 86,590)
2.	Oporto	60:763$000	(19,495)
3.	*Madeira*	25:412$000	(8,153)
4.	*Terceira*	14:822$000	(4,755)
5.	*Pico-Fayal*	7:912$000	(2,538)
6.	*São Miguel*	4:500$000	(1,444)
7.	Faro	3:058$000	(981)
8.	Portimão	1:999$000	(641)
9.	Buarcos-Figueira	1:654$000	(531)
10.	Viana	1:203$000	(386)
11.	*São Jorge*	1:144$000	(367)
12.	*Graciosa*	1:024$000	(329)
13.	Setúbal	908$000	(295)
14.	Tavira	766$000	(246)
15.	Conde	609$000	(195)
16.	Aveiro	226$000	(72)
17.	Lagos	144$000	(46)
18.	Castro Marim (Vila Real)	100$000	(32)
19.	Peniche	62$000	(20)
20.	Caminha	53$000	(17)
21.	Milfontes	40$000	(13)
22.	Albufeira	26$000	(8)
	Total	396:281$000	(£127,154)

*Arq. Dist. Évora, Codex CXIII/2–28, fols. 5–6.

contributions to customs duties of the various Portuguese ports can be construed as follows: Lisbon, 68.34; Oporto, 15.33; fourteen other continental ports, 2.53; and island ports the remaining 13.80 percent. Lisbon, as one of the great harbors of western Europe, dominated the other ports overwhelmingly; but this predominance, at least as expressed in the figures for 1681, is slightly misleading, since official policy encouraged payments at Lisbon rather than at other ports. Thus Portuguese ships with cargoes for the islands paid all their duties at Lisbon and none at the island ports, so that an undetermined percentage of the Lisbon total actually reflected commercial movement generated by the islands. Moreover the mercantilistic laws of the empire forced the Brazilian sugar trade, and all Eastern spices, to be centered exclusively at Lisbon and required all foreign manufactures destined for the colonies to be transshipped at Lisbon, thereby artificially stimulating the commerce of the capital.

If Lisbon is left out of the reckoning, the percentage of customs duties contributed by the islands can be seen in dramatic terms: Oporto, 48.05; fourteen other continental ports, 8.60; Madeira, 20.10; all Azorean ports 23.25. Thus, with Lisbon excluded, the islands contributed over 43 percent of all duties collected. The six Azorean and Madeiran port complexes rank among the top twelve Portuguese ports, and four of them among the top six. Particularly notable was the port of Funchal, which contributed two and a half times more revenue than fourteen continental ports combined.

The Cape Verdean contribution to Portuguese commerce cannot be delineated so precisely. João de Andrade Corvo, minister for Portuguese colonies during 1872–77, calculated annual Portuguese imperial incomes, toward the close of the sixteenth century, as follows:[5]

India and the East	697:810$000 (£476,817)
Brazil	63:000$000 (43,050)
Cape Verdes	27:400$000 (18,793)
Mina	24:000$000 (16,400)
Angola	22:000$000 (15,033)
São Tomé	9:500$000 (6,492)
Total	843:710$000 (£576,585)

These figures, which are hardly more than rough guesses, help to illustrate the comparative contributions of different parts of the empire to crown revenues. As is to be expected, the rich Eastern trade, which after 1600 was to undergo a long decline, accounted for nearly 83 percent of the total revenue. If the Eastern ventures are excluded, the comparative position of the various Atlantic possessions, expressed in percentages of contribution to the total revenue, ran as follows: Brazil, 43.18; Cape Verdes, 18.78; Mina, 16.45; Angola, 15.08; and São Tomé, 6.51. In these terms the Cape Verdean contribution, considering the great disparity between the islands and the mainland in size, population, and resources, was quite remarkable.

The same minister and author, Andrade Corvo, made another calculation of imperial revenues as they existed in 1835, on the eve of the ex-

5. Andrade Corvo, 1: 9–10.

tinction of the Portuguese slave trade. This second set of figures, much diminished in comparison with the sixteenth-century figures (the given sterling equivalencies indicate this more clearly than the sums in réis), again shows the Cape Verdes occupying a strong position:[6]

Goa, Macau, and the East	288:000$000 (£	64,000)
Angola	132:879$000 (	29,529)
Cape Verdes	92:522$000 (	20,560)
Mozambique	56:154$000 (	12,479)
São Tomé	8:490$000 (	1,887)
Total	578:045$000 (£138,455)	

Eastern incomes account for about one-half of the total; apart from the East, the percentage contributions of the various colonies ran as follows: Angola, 45.81; Cape Verdes, 31.90; Mozambique, 19.36; and São Tomé, 2.93. Again the Cape Verdes, before the end of the slave trade, show considerable strength.

In the seventeenth century, however, the Cape Verdes contributed very little to general revenues. Lisbon's unrealistic interventions in the Cape Verdean and Guiné trade, the prohibitions on foreign commerce, and Lisbon's incomprehension of the monetary and trading systems in the islands, all forced Cape Verdean trade into illicit and contraband channels. Much of Cape Verdean commerce went untaxed, and the Santiago ecclesiastics were forced to ask the treasury at Funchal to pay their salaries.

In summary, it can be said that the three archipelagoes of Madeira, the Azores, and the Cape Verdes occupied positions of prominence in the maritime economy of Portugal. But, in addition to this, from an international perspective, the islands made signal contributions to the Atlantic commercial world in general. If there had been no islands, seventeenth-century maritime commerce would have been distinctly different, and navigation itself appreciably more difficult and more hazardous. Madeiran wines, Pico wine, and Cape Verdean salt — all three — were staples of Atlantic commerce by the close of the seventeenth century. Other island products — such as Azorean pastel, wheat, brandy, and linen, Madeiran sugar and confectionery, and Cape Verdean raw cotton, cotton cloth, orchil, and livestock — at certain times and seasons, figured in international trade and were carried in foreign bottoms.

6. Ibid., p. 19.

The three archipelagoes, moreover, although their total populations in 1700 came to well under 170,000 persons, were nonetheless consumers of international products. To the islands went fair quantities of English textiles and manufactures, Newfoundland salted codfish, New England pipestaves, timber, fish oil, and cereals, Carolinas rice, Brazilian tobacco, French perfumes and textiles, and Baltic pitch, tar, and cordage.

In addition, the trade in slaves, a major activity in the Cape Verdes, deeply affected the social and economic structures of the Atlantic world. The Cape Verdes both "consumed" and supplied slaves; in return for silver, wines, clothing, and manufactures, the islands sent slaves primarily to the Spanish Americas and secondarily to Brazil, while within the archipelago the institution of slavery shaped, or misshaped, social and economic development.

The products of the various islands, with the notable addition of São Miguel oranges, which were shipped mostly to England, flourished and prospered in the Atlantic trade all through the eighteenth century and well into the nineteenth. And then disaster struck. The heaviest blows came in the area of greatest activity and profit — the wine trade. In the United States a slow alteration in manners and taste threatened the traditional markets for Portuguese and island wines. The notion that wine was essential for good health began to be challenged. American-made whiskey won more consumers year by year, while, paradoxically, movements for total abstinence were on the increase. The citizens of Fayal were puzzled by the behavior of teetotaling American sailors from so-called "temperance" ships, who refused to buy any wine whatever. Worst of all were the plagues of oidium and phylloxera, which destroyed almost every single vine in Madeira and the Azores. Pico wine never recovered. The vintners of Madeira managed very slowly to regain volume and quality, but in the interim they lost their vital North American market.

A similar fate overtook other branches of insular commerce. Virus disease and insects devastated the orange groves of São Miguel (damagingly in 1844 and fatally in 1895). The mass marketing of unprecedented quantities of wheat by Canada and Argentina undermined the demand for the inefficiently raised Azorean wheat surplus. In the Cape Verdes the end of the slave trade also brought an end to the cloth trade with Guiné, and the old skill in weaving ornate cloth slowly died out. Even the salt trade, toward the end of the nineteenth century, lost much of its former volume.

Yet, when all is said and done, trade, whether it flourished or whether it decayed, did not limit or express the essential importance of the islands to the Atlantic world. Throughout the seventeenth century, insular commerce generally grew in volume and value, but that commerce by itself did not explain the complete significance of the islands to Atlantic shipping. The vital service of the archipelagoes lay in ship supply; in watering, victualing, repairing, rescuing, manning, and protecting ships of all kinds, from many ports of origin and bound for many destinations, and belonging to all the maritime nations of the West — including East Indiamen, West Indiamen, Brazilmen, codfishers, slavers, men-of-war, sugar ships, wine ships, salt ships, and vessels with mixed and miscellaneous cargoes.

From the perspectives of general Atlantic commerce and navigation, the availability of good fresh water in the islands was of more consequence than the availability of the finest malmseys, just as in the central and south Atlantic, hard dry salted Cape Verdean goatmeat was a commodity of more consideration than beefsteak, and hardtack, in all the reaches of the maritime world, more vital than pure white bread.

Testimony of the prominence of the mid-Atlantic archipelagoes in their function of ship support is implicit and explicit in a wealth of sources, but it is not the kind of evidence that lends itself to quantification. At the present state of knowledge, over-all shipping statistics for the Portuguese islands can be arrived at only by hypothetical projections, based on crude multiplication of the small samples of data that do exist. Such projections suggest that the three archipelagoes, during the period 1670–1700, serviced from 500 to 1,200 ships per year, depending on conditions. Almost all these ships were watered and victualed, but less than half of them, and sometimes only a third of them, transacted any trade (see table 34).

Trading and victualing suffered certain differences in emphasis from one archipelago to another, and from island to island. Madeira, because of its closeness to Europe, was much less important in victualing than the Azores; and within the Azores, victualing was all-important at Horta, but of little significance at Ponta Delgada. In the Cape Verdes, Santiago did most of the victualing and watering; ships went less frequently to São Nicolau, Fogo, Brava, and Boavista, and almost never to Santo Antão.

The chronological dimension is also of fundamental importance for understanding the general development of the islands. After 1580, when Portugal came under the crown of Spain, the islands were drawn into Spain's long wars with the French Huguenots, the Dutch, and the English. The archipelagoes had their shipping and trade interrupted and were victimized by some damaging raids. Fortunately, after 1603, the

TABLE 34

Number of Ships* in the Portuguese Islands, 1670–1700

Islands	Traders		Victualed		Total	
	High Vol.	Low Vol.	High Vol.	Low Vol.	High Vol.	Low Vol.
Madeira	120	80	60	40	180	120
S. Miguel–Sta. Maria	70	30	20	10	90	40
Terceira-Graciosa	60	40	30	20	90	60
Pico-Fayal-Flores-S. Jorge	110	50	460	150	570	200
Cape Verdes	45	12	240[†]	80[†]	285	92
Total	405	212	810	300	1,215	512

*Estimated annual averages of numbers of ships in hypothetical years of high-volume and low-volume activity.

[†] Including salt ships, which are not counted as traders because they generated very little commercial activity in the Cape Verdes.

Anglo-Spanish war came to an end, and English merchants began to build up the trade between England, on the one side, and Madeira, the Azores, and the Canaries, on the other. English merchants took up permanent residence in Funchal, Ponta Delgada, and Angra — joining older groups of Flemish and Italian merchants — and opened up English markets for Azorean pastel. The nascent British communities in North America pointed the way to future commercial growth; the increasing European interest in North America and the West Indies meant an inevitable acceleration of trade that would benefit all participants in the commerce of the Atlantic.

Wars, nonetheless, kept interfering with normal development. Spain's long struggle with the Netherlands (1570–1609, 1621–48), the most formidable of the maritime powers, deeply disrupted all branches of Portuguese seaborne commerce. At the end of 1640 Portugal rebelled against Spain and managed to make a shaky truce with the Dutch. These events plunged Portugal into a twenty-eight-year struggle (1641–68) with Spain, during which Spanish fleets no longer called at the Azores, the Cape Verdean slave trade went into crisis, and the trading relations of all three Portuguese archipelagoes with the Canaries were completely broken off. These years of crisis were years marked by new commercial departures and new economic trends. São Miguel's pastel trade withered away, but Pico-Fayal began to export wine to North America for the first time. English merchants arrived in the islands in greater numbers, including the first New Englanders, followed by Frenchmen. Salt extraction from the Cape Verdes increased as the English expanded their West Indian ventures, and as the Newfoundland salted codfish trade flourished. In the meantime, Dutch failures in Angola, Brazil, and São Tomé (1648-54) and England's vigorous and victorious assault on Dutch shipping (1652-54) diminished the Dutch threat in the Atlantic while enhancing the value of England to Portugal as a maritime and commercial partner.

After the Luso-Spanish peace of 1668, Portugal remained at peace for thirty-five years (1669-1703), and the islands entered a phase of rapid and general development. The coming of age of the English plantations in the Americas, the development of English Jamaica, the emergence of Yankee and Virginia traders, and the striking diversification and evolution of the trades in wine, fish, slaves, sugar, rum, tobacco, maize, wheat, textiles, manufactures, metals, oils, and salt brought swarms of ships to the mid-Atlantic archipelagoes. After the end of the War of the Spanish Succession (1701-14) the shipping and commerce of the islands continued to grow until the days of the American Revolution.

The ties between the islands and Anglo-America were particularly interesting. In the seventeenth and eighteenth centuries, shipping and trade provided the points of contact. In the nineteenth century the effort to man whaling ships brought Azoreans and Cape Verdeans together with Americans in the same vessels. At the end of the nineteenth century and into the first two decades of the twentieth, long after the decline of New England whaling, the last phase saw the immigration of substantial numbers of Azoreans, Cape Verdeans, and Madeirans to the United States, where they supplied cheap labor for factories and farms and were particularly useful in the once flourishing textile mills of Massachusetts, Connecticut, and Rhode Island.

When the islanders had made a little money, or reached retirement age, they often went back to the islands, where they would buy land and build homes and be known as the rich "Americanos." There is both wonder and envy in the happy refrain from a Bravan *morna*:

> Amaricano tem dólar,
> Tem dólar comà burro! [7]

7. Ribeiro, *Fogo*, p. 176; rough translation: "The 'Americano' has dollars,/He has dollars to burn!"

The "Americanos" brought strange clothes, strange manners, and strange words into the islands. In the Cape Verdes, particularly in Brava and São Vicente, the following modified English words are or were common: *ariope* (hurry up), *blaquefela* (black fellow), *seiló! seiló!* (sail ho! sail ho!), *sore* (sorry), *troba* (trouble), *reite* (right), *djobe* (job), *fulope* (full up), *grogue* (grog), *ovataime* (overtime), *alrai* (all right), *gotchôr* (go ashore), and, inevitably, words of profanity and cursing, *sanababitche* and worse.[8]

English America affected the islands very greatly, but the islands exerted very little influence over English America — except in small things, such as in inducing the Americans to drink madeira wine. The position that madeira once held in the thirteen colonies, and later in the United States, was very remarkable. Madeira was once the wine of choice in North America, and testimony to that fact lies ready to hand. In 1762 Benjamin Franklin, on his way from Europe to America, visited what he called "the delightful island of Madeira," where the ship replenished her stores and "took in many refreshments"; later he collected and published information on how to grow madeira grapes in the Americas, for he wished that his country, in this desirable commodity, could become independent of foreign suppliers.[9]

George Washington sent his own cargoes to Madeira to be traded for choice wines and requested cuttings from Madeira vines. With his own hand he wrote such requests as: "Order from the best house in Madeira a pipe of the best Old Wine, and let it be secur'd from pilferers" (1759).[10] He preferred madeira to all other wines and was very knowledgeable about madeira vintages; the impossibility of obtaining his favorite madeira was not the least of the hardships of Valley Forge.[11] John

---

8. Some of these words were popularized by immigrants; others arose during the whaling days at Brava; and still others emerged during São Vicente's bunkering activities. The name of the Cape Verdes' most distinctive dish, *cachupa* (boiled cornmeal with beans, fish, meat, etc., added), is said to derive from *ketchup*, itself originally a Chinese or Malaysian word; but the derivation of *morna* from English *mourn* has been convincingly challenged. See Lyall, p. 103; Araujo, p. 11; Ferreira, pp. 129, 131.

9. Franklin, *Papers*, ed. Leonard W. Labaree, 10 (New Haven, Conn., 1966): 167; 12 (1968): 6–7.

10. Washington, *Writings*, ed. John C. Fitzpatrick, 2 (Washington, 1931): 321.

11. "Washington was a one-bottle man. This means that at dinner he customarily drank a pint of Madeira, besides rum punch and beer. He preferred Madeira to all other beverages, but he was catholic in his drinking habits, and often drank cider, champagne and brandy." W.E. Woodward, *George Washington* (New York, 1946), p. 153.

Adams, Washington's successor as president of the United States, entered the following in his diary (22 September 1774): "I drank madeira at a great rate and found no inconvenience in it";[12] ten years later Adams assured the Portuguese ambassador at the Hague that, in America, "madeira was esteemed above all other wine," and that "it was found equally wholesome and agreeable, in the heats of summer and the colds of winter."[13]

Conclusive witness to the place of madeira in American life comes from Thomas Jefferson, the most notable gourmet and oenologist ever to occupy the White House. He purchased and served madeira by the pipeful, drank it as his beverage of choice, and fought hard against increasing tariffs on Portuguese wine. Once, in 1786, when he was in Paris — surrounded by the incomparable vinous variety of France, of whose excellence he was fully cognizant — he nonetheless felt deprived, for there was no madeira, so he ordered a pipe of madeira from America ("I would prefer that which is of the nut quality, and of the very best").[14]

Washington, Adams, and Jefferson provide testimony of no ordinary kind, from no ordinary men. They were all good eaters and discriminating drinkers, of catholic and sophisticated taste, in addition to being great statesmen, presidents of the United States, and founders of the Republic. Madeira needs no finer friends than these.

Wine was but one article in the Atlantic trade, one of many bonds between east and west in the Atlantic community; fortunately for themselves, Madeira and the Azores supplied the Americas with copious quantities of wine, thereby maintaining their economic independence, but even if the islands had had no wine — or salt or sugar or wheat or cloth — they would still have played the role that geography had assigned to them in the great Atlantic world.

The seventeenth-century Atlantic, with its coasts and islands and ports, with European enclaves in Africa and European colonies in the Americas — which were largely confined to the litoral, or placed inland on the banks of navigable rivers, where ships penetrated from the sea — constituted a great maritime community with a certain mutuality of interest and of experience. This great community extended both north and south, was frigid and equatorial, African and European, black and white, and it wedded the Old World to the New World.

12. Adams, *Diary*, ed. L.H. Butterfield, 2 (Cambridge, Mass., 1961): 136.
13. Adams, *Works* 8 (Boston, 1853): 127.
14. Jefferson, *Papers*, ed. Julian P. Boyd, 9 (Princeton, 1954): 274.

Conclusion

The indispensable instrument of the Atlantic community was the sailing ship, the carrier of commodities, and the vehicle responsible for the two greatest human migrations known to history — that of the European to the Americas, and that of the African, unwillingly, to those same Americas. The Portuguese mid-Atlantic islands provided essential assistance to ever increasing fleets of ships. The islands were pivots around which the wheels of international commerce turned. They were the still points of succor and reference in a moving world of wind, water, and sail. As such, the now neglected islands were the purest symbols of the Atlantic world.

Appendix I

Geographical Facts

Location

Archipelago	Northern Extremity (Lat.)	Southern Extremity (Lat.)	Eastern Extremity (Long.)	Western Extremity (Long.)
Madeiras	33°08′N	32°24′N	16°16′W	17°16′W
Azores	39°43′N	36°55′N	24°47′W	31°15′W
Cape Verdes	17°13′N	14°48′N	22°40′W	25°22′W

Areas, Dimensions, and Elevations

Island	Area (in sq. miles)	Maximum Length (miles)	Maximum Width (miles)	Maximum Elevation (feet)
The Madeiras				
Madeira	286.0	35.4	13.6	6,105
Porto Santo	16.2	9.3	3.1	1,663
Deserta Grande	3.2	7.2	1.1	1,601
Bugio	0.8	4.7	0.4	1,348
Baixo	0.4	1.7	0.6	584
Chão	0.2	1.0	0.3	322
The Azores				
São Miguel	288.2	41.0	9.9	3,543
Pico	167.2	29.8	9.3	7,716

Island	Area (in sq. miles)	Maximum Length (miles)	Maximum Width (miles)	Maximum Elevation (feet)
Terceira	153.1	19.2	11.1	3,500
São Jorge	91.7	34.1	3.7	3,497
Fayal	66.3	13.6	9.3	3,421
Flores	55.1	11.1	8.6	3,090
Santa Maria	37.4	10.8	4.9	1,935
Graciosa	23.4	8.6	4.9	1,299
Corvo	6.7	4.3	2.7	2,549
The Cape Verdes				
Santiago	382.5	34.1	17.8	4,566
Santo Antão	300.7	26.5	14.8	6,492
Boavista	239.3	19.1	17.9	1,269
Fogo	183.7	16.3	14.8	9,281
São Nicolau	132.4	27.6	13.6	4,278
Maio	103.8	14.9	10.1	1,430
São Vicente	87.6	15.0	10.0	2,378
Sal	83.3	18.4	7.3	1,332
Brava	24.7	6.5	5.7	3,202
Santa Luzia	13.5	7.6	3.3	1,285
Raso	2.7	2.2	1.7	538
Branco	1.1	2.4	0.7	1,072
Grande	0.7	1.4	1.1	311
Cima	0.4	1.4	0.4	252
The Archipelagoes				
The Madeiras	306.8	–	–	6,105
The Azores	889.1	–	–	7,716
The Cape Verdes	1,556.4	–	–	9,281
Total area	2,752.3			

Appendix II

Historical Demography

The Population of the Islands at Different Periods

Island	1580*	1650*	1720*	1800*	1900[†]	1960[†]
The Madeiras						
Madeira	25,000	32,000	45,000	67,000	148,300	264,600
Porto Santo	500	500	450	800	2,300	3,500
The Azores						
São Miguel	25,000	30,000	40,000	60,000	121,300	168,600
Terceira	16,500	18,000	21,000	30,000	48,800	72,500
Pico	3,500	6,000	11,000	19,000	24,000	21,600
Fayal	5,000	8,000	10,000	16,000	22,300	20,300
São Jorge	3,000	4,500	8,000	9,000	16,200	15,700
Graciosa	3,500	4,200	5,700	6,900	8,400	8,600
Santa Maria	2,000	2,400	3,600	4,500	6,400	13,200
Flores	2,000	2,500	3,400	5,800	8,100	6,600
Corvo	450	500	550	600	800	670
The Cape Verdes						
Santiago	8,000	9,500	12,000	26,000	64,900	88,900
Fogo	1,200	2,500	5,000	8,000	17,600	25,500
Santo Antão	400	1,000	3,000	12,000	29,900	34,600
São Nicolau	140	300	650	4,000	12,000	13,900
Brava	100	400	1,200	3,000	9,200	8,600
Boavista	50	150	1,000	2,200	2,600	3,300
Maio	50	120	250	700	1,900	2,700

Island	1580*	1650*	1720*	1800*	1900†	1960†
Sal	0	10	30	50	500	2,600
São Vicente	0	0	0	100	8,800	21,400
The Archipelagoes						
The Madeiras	25,500	32,500	45,450	67,800	150,600	268,100
The Azores	60,950	76,100	103,250	151,800	256,300	327,770
The Cape Verdes	9,940	13,980	23,130	56,050	147,400	201,500
Total	96,390	122,580	171,830	275,650	554,300	797,370

Estimated Population Densities:
Numbers of Persons per Square Mile

Island	1580*	1720*	1800*	1900†	1960†
Madeira	87	157	234	519	925
São Miguel, AZ	87	139	208	421	585
Terceira, AZ	108	137	196	319	474
Graciosa, AZ	150	244	295	359	366
Santa Maria, AZ	53	96	120	171	353
Brava, CV	4	48	121	372	348
Fayal, AZ	75	151	241	336	306
São Vicente, CV	0	0	1	100	244
Santiago, CV	21	31	68	169	232
Porto Santo, MAD	31	28	50	142	216
São Jorge, AZ	33	87	98	176	171
Fogo, CV	7	27	43	96	139
Pico, AZ	21	66	114	143	129
Flores, AZ	36	62	105	167	120
Santo Antão, CV	1	10	40	99	115
São Nicolau, CV	1	5	30	91	105
Corvo, AZ	67	82	90	119	100
Sal, CV	0	0.4	0.6	6	31
Maio, CV	0.5	2	7	18	26
Boavista, CV	0.2	4	9	11	14

*Based on estimates derived from a wide variety of sources, both published and unpublished; the most important are the following (see Bibliography for full references): Maldonado, Diogo das Chagas, Monte Alverne, Frutuoso, Henriques de Noronha, Cordeiro, Chaves e Melo,

Principal Towns and Settlements in the Islands in 1720
(with estimates of their populations)

1. Angra, Terceira, AZ (cidade)	13,500
2. Funchal, MAD (cidade)	12,000
3. Ponta Delgada, São Miguel, AZ (cidade)	9,500
4. Ribeira Grande, São Miguel, AZ (vila)	5,800
5. Praia, Terceira, AZ (vila)	3,150
6. Horta, Fayal, AZ (vila)	3,000
7. Vila Franca do Campo, São Miguel, AZ (vila)	2,800
8. Santa Cruz, Graciosa, AZ (vila)	2,400
9. Lagoa, São Miguel, AZ (vila)	2,300
10. Ribeira Grande, Santiago, CV (cidade)	2,200
11. Ponta do Sol, MAD (vila)	2,200
12. Machico, MAD (vila)	2,000
13. Câmara de Lobos, MAD (vila?)	1,800
14. Calheta, MAD (vila)	1,800
15. Rabo de Peixe, São Miguel, AZ	1,800
16. São Vicente, MAD	1,800
17. Fenais do Rabo de Peixe, São Miguel, AZ	1,800
18. Vila de Porto, Santa Maria, AZ (vila)	1,700
19. Arco de Calheta, MAD	1,700
20. Estreito de Calheta, MAD	1,600
21. Santa Cruz, MAD (vila)	1,500
22. Nordeste, São Miguel, AZ (vila)	1,300
23. Ribeira Brava, MAD	1,300
24. Rosto do Cão, São Miguel, AZ	1,300
25. Agua de Pau, São Miguel, AZ (vila)	1,200
26. Caniço, MAD	1,200
27. Canhas, MAD	1,200
28. Velas, São Jorge, AZ (vila)	1,100
29. São Sebastião, Terceira, AZ (vila)	1,100
30. Porto Moniz, MAD	1,100

Brásio, Sena Barcelos, Chelmicki, Dampier, Boid, and Ashe. In accuracy these estimates range all the way from the scrupulously careful count by certain priests of all the "souls" in their particular parish, to the wild guesses of travelers. Local officials trying to justify their salaries, and local "boosters" (such as the historians of certain islands), naturally tended to exaggerate the numbers of persons living in their own region, as well as its wealth and importance. My method, generally, has been to choose the lowest and most conservative estimates. Where there has been no information for a particular year or period, I have made projections on the basis of information for other years or periods.

†Based on the census reports for the years 1900 and 1960, published by the Portuguese National Institute of Statistics.

31.	Ponta Delgada, MAD	1,100
32.	Povoação, São Miguel, AZ	1,100
33.	Praia, Santiago, CV (vila)	1,000
34.	Lajes, Pico, AZ (vila)	1,000
35.	Santana, MAD	1,000
36.	Estreito da Câmara de Lobos, MAD	1,000

Note: Since in some of the islands, such as Madeira, there is little level terrain, the towns and villages are not as compact and well defined as those of continental Portugal, but the houses are scattered about the countryside, with perhaps only a church, a market place, and a few other structures at the urban nucleus. For many of these places, therefore, the population figure cited refers to the population of the parish as a whole, but it is an old tradition of Portuguese administrative practice to regard a village as co-extensive with its parish. The status of "vila," with its attendant political privileges, by 1720 had more to do with antiquity of settlement and geographical location than with intrinsic importance; thus there were Azorean vilas with less than 400 inhabitants, while places five times as large were denied that status. Câmara de Lobos in Madeira claimed to be a vila, but was not officially recognized as such; Praia in Santiago was officially recognized as a vila, although there are no documents to prove when this status was granted.

Appendix III

Portuguese Weights and Measures

Weights

In international commerce, for many commodities, the following weights were standard:

QUINTAL (hundredweight) = 4 arrobas = 128 arratéis = 129.5 lbs. av. = 58.744 kilograms.

ARROBA (rove or quartern) = 32 arratéis = 32.37 lbs. av. = 14.686 kilograms.

ARRATEL (pound) = 16 onças = 1.01 lbs. av. = 458.938 grams.

ONÇA (ounce) = 1.01 oz. av. = 28.683 grams.

There was also a lighter, but less commonly used, version of the above weights:

QUINTAL = 4 arrobas = 112 arratéis = 113.32 lbs. av. = 51.401 kilograms.

ARROBA = 28 arratéis = 28.33 lbs. av. = 12.850 kilograms.

In addition, in various localities in Portugal and the islands, depending upon custom and the commodity involved, an arroba could contain from 25 to 32 arratéis, and an arratel from 12 to 16 onças. English merchants called the 128-arratel quintal the "quintal of Lisbon," or the "greater quintal of Lisbon"; the 112-arratel quintal was called the "lesser quintal of Lisbon." The Portuguese arratel was only 5.348 grams, or less than one-fifth of an ounce, heavier than the English pound avoirdupois (so that for calculations in this book, I have regarded the two as identical).

Wine Measures

For Portuguese wines in the international trade, the following measures, derived from Lisbon, represented the most common standard:

TONEL (tun) = 2 pipas = 6 terços = 8 barrís = 50 almudes = 600 canadas = 252 English wine gallons = 953.89 liters.
PIPA (pipe) = 3 terços = 4 barrís = 25 almudes = 300 canadas = 126 English wine gallons = 476.94 liters.
MEIA PIPA (hogshead) = 1.5 terços = 2 barrís = 12.5 almudes = 150 canadas = 63 English wine gallons = 238.47 liters.
TERÇO (tierce) = 1.33 barrís = 8.33 almudes = 100 canadas = 42 English wine gallons = 158.98 liters.
BARRIL or QUARTOLA (barrel or cask) = 6¼ almudes = 75 canadas = 31.5 English wine gallons = 119.23 liters.
ALMUDE = 12 canadas = 48 quartilhos = 5.04 English wine gallons = 19.07 liters.
CANADA = 4 quartilhos = 3.36 English pints = 1.589 liters.
QUARTILHO = 3.36 English gills = 0.397 liters.

The old English "wine gallon" corresponds to the present-day United States gallon of 231 cubic inches (not to the larger imperial gallon of Britain). The *pipa* or pipe was by far the most commonly used measure in the Portuguese wine trade; the *tonel* or tun was seldom used (probably because it was too bulky and heavy); while *almudes, canadas,* and *quartilhos* were for retail and tavern measures.

Within Portugal there were many local variations. In Oporto the local *almude* was 50 percent larger than the Lisbon *almude*, and the pipes much larger than elsewhere. In the islands pipes ranged in size from the "small" Angra pipe of 18.75 *almudes* to the extra large Funchal pipe of 27 *almudes* for measuring must. But since the Angra *almude*, at 2.2 liters per canada, seems to have contained 26.4 liters (Sousa Lima, p. 171), the Angra pipe of 495 liters actually came out larger than the Lisbon pipe of 477 liters.

Wine measures, indeed, were always rather imprecise, because of the continuous loss of volume through evaporation. It is quite probable that merchants buying wine for storage or shipment demanded and received very generous measures, with eight, or ten, or fifteen extra canadas to the pipe, for they knew that evaporation and seepage would "shrink" the wine. At the end of a voyage, or after a period of storage, a "pipe" seldom contained a full pipe of wine.

Measures of Dry Capacity

In the Portuguese trade the following were used, especially for grains and salt:
MOIO = 10 sacos = 15 fanegas = 60 alqueires = 23.1 English bushels = 814 liters.
SACO = 1½ fanegas = 6 alqueires = 2.31 English bushels = 81.4 liters.
FANEGA = 4 alqueires = 1.54 English bushels = 54.266 liters.
ALQUEIRE = 0.385 English bushels, or 1.54 pecks = 13.566 liters.

These were the Lisbon standards, which by law were measured flat. In the Azores, however (but not in Madeira), heaped-up measures were legally required for wheat, and these were supposed to conform to the following standard:

MOIO = 68 Lisbon alqueires = 26.18 English bushels = 922.522 liters.

In the Cape Verdes, by the nineteenth century, two very large moio measures had become customary and won legal recognition:

MOIO (general Cape Verdean) = 180 alqueires = 69.3 English bushels = 2,442 liters.

SALT MOIO (island of Maio) = 135 alqueires = 51.975 English bushels = 1,831 liters.

The salt moio of Maio was raised to the general Cape Verdean standard in 1846. The Cape Verdean moio was exactly three times as large as the Lisbon moio. The Cape Verdean moio, nonetheless, does not appear to have been used in the seventeenth-century salt trade. In Oporto there was a large alqueire measure, of which only 45 were required to make up one Lisbon moio; this would mean that 3 Oporto alqueires = 4 Lisbon alqueires.

Portuguese Cloth Measures

Cloth was sold by *varas* and *côvados*, the precise lengths of which seem to have been as follows:

VARA = 5 palmos = 43.11 English inches = 109.5 centimeters.
COVADOS = 3 palmos = 25.86 English inches = 65.7 centimeters.
PALMO = 8.62 English inches = 21.9 centimeters.

The *vara* of 43.11 inches was analogous to, and nearly identical with, the English *ell* of 45 inches.

General Note

Trade in Madeira and the Azores in the seventeenth century seems to have been conducted largely on the basis of the weights and measures of Lisbon. Three circumstances contributed to this result: (1) official discouragement of the proliferation of local measures in the islands; (2) the decree of 13 September 1561 (see Drummond, 1: 589–94) reducing most island measures to the standard of Lisbon; and (3) the pressure of the foreign merchants, who preferred the well-known and understood Lisbon standards to any local system of measures.

Accurate information about old Portuguese weights and measures is not easy to find, and the researcher must pick and choose among conflicting and confusing sources. Portuguese authors frequently explain the internal arrangement of Portuguese measures but seldom suggest accurate metric equivalents or compare the measures with those of other countries. In compiling the above tables, I have found the following authors helpful: Wyndham Beawes, *Lex mercatoria* (Dublin, 1754), pp. 724-25, 729, 733, 742-43, and his *History of Spain*, 1: 262-355; F. Altés, *Traité comparatif* (Marseilles, 1832), p. 329; Samuel Ricard, *Traité general du commerce* (Amsterdam, 1705), pp. 39, 72, 80, 97; John Penkethman, *Accompts of Merchandise Ready Computed* (London, 1648), not paginated; Silva Sampaio, p. 364; Soares de Azevedo, "Açores e o Norte," p. 39; Samler Brown, p. 16; *Universal Dictionary of Trade*, 2 vols. (London, 1757), 2: 508-9; Sousa Monteiro, pp. 362-63; and Mauro, pp. lxvi-lxviii.

Appendix IV

Portuguese Money

Currency systems ran on a silver standard in the seventeenth century; gold coins were adjusted to the silver standard, occasionally, as the bi-metallic ratio changed. During the entire Philippine period, from 1580 to 1640, Lisbon issued coins at the fixed ratio of 2$800 réis to one mark of silver. During the wars of 1641–68, and after, Portuguese currency was seriously strained by military expenses and by the shortage of silver. In an effort to increase the supply of money, in the face of shrinking bullion reserves, and as a means of affording temporary relief to the treasury, the Portuguese government devalued the currency by altering the silver standard four times. Thus, the value of one mark of silver was changed as follows:

Before 1641	2$800
1 July 1641	3$400
8 June 1643	4$000
22 March 1663	5$000
4 August 1688	6$000

After 1688 the silver ratio remained stable for forty-six years; not until 10 February 1734 was the currency again devalued, to the ratio of 7$000 per mark of silver.

The four seventeenth-century devaluations of Portuguese coin make it desirable to establish a correspondence in value between Portuguese coins of various periods and some stable foreign money unit. The English pound sterling is ideal as a stable unit against which to measure Portuguese currency, particularly since so much of Portugal's international trade was with England. In England the mint value of one troy mark of sterling silver between the years 1601 and 1694 fell in the narrow range between £1 19s. 8d. and £2 1s. 4d.; the market value was slightly higher, coming between £2 1s. 4d. and £2 2s. 8d. In 1694 and 1695 there was a severe credit inflation which drove the price of silver to as high as £2 11s. 4d. per mark, but in the general recoinage of 1696–98, all the coins were recalled and the price of a mark of silver was driven down to the mint standard of £2 1s. 4d. The treasury thus returned to the standard of £2 1s. 4d., which can therefore be regarded as the normative standard of English coinage for the seventeenth century as a whole.

The basic unit of Portuguese money was the *real* (plural *réis*), or $001, a unit so small as to be worth only 0.081 of an English penny in 1700. The smallest copper coin in circulation was worth only 1.5 réis; and the smallest silver coin was worth $010. The silver *vintem* ($020) was a useful small unit, and prices were often quoted in terms of 2, 3, and 4 vintens ($040, $060, and $080). The silver *tostão* ($100) was equally useful; the expression *dez tostões* (ten *tostões,* or 1$000) can still be heard in Portugal, and was common in Brazil until the 1940s. The *cruzado* of $400, which before 1641 was roughly equivalent to the English crown, or to ten Spanish *reales*, was the most important silver coin, and prices and salaries were often quoted in terms of cruzados rather than réis, especially for large sums.

Gold coins with values ranging from $400 to 12$000 were minted in the seventeenth century, but the lesser denominations were gradually dropped. The most important gold coins were the *moeda, meia moeda,* and *quarto de moeda*, which made their appearance after 1640, and were eventually worth 4$000, 2$000, and 1$000 respectively. Portuguese gold coinage came into its own in the eighteenth century, after Brazil became the world's greatest gold producer. Portuguese *moedas de ouro* (the famed "moidores") and the gigantic *dobrão* ("doubloon") of 24$000 displaced Spanish silver coins as the most important currency in international maritime trade. Partly as a result of the influx of Brazilian gold, the silver standard was overthrown, and England adopted a permanent gold standard based on a mint price of £3 17s. 10½d. per ounce of fine gold.

If the rate of £2 1s. 4d. per mark of silver is accepted as a general standard for seventeenth-century English currency, then it is possible to work out exact sterling equivalencies for Portuguese currency of different periods, depending on whether it was coined at the ratio of 2$800, 3$400, 4$000, 5$000, or 6$000 per mark. Two other factors, however, have to be taken into account in making the mathematical calculation. First, the English troy mark, equivalent to 248.828 grams, was nearly 8.5 percent heavier than the Portuguese mark of 229.469 grams; and, second, the English sterling silver standard represented a higher standard of fineness than the Portuguese silver standard. English silver coins contained 11.1 parts pure silver out of 12 parts, leaving only 0.9 parts for the alloy; but Portuguese coins contained 11 parts pure silver to 1 part alloy. Thus the sterling standard was 0.92499 in fineness, and the Portuguese standard only 0.91666 – a difference of about 0.9 percent. When these variables are included in the calculation, the Portuguese *milréis* (1$000) was worth the following in sterling at different periods:

1601–41	13s. 5.8d.
1641–43	11s. 1.3d.
1643–63	9s. 5.3d.
1663–88	7s. 6.6d.
1688–1734	6s. 3.5d.

Or, conversely, the pound sterling (£1) was worth the following amounts in Portuguese réis at different periods:

1601–41	1$482
1641–43	1$800
1643–63	2$117
1663–88	2$647
1688–1734	3$176

These figures express ideal exchange ratios based on the silver content of coins in mint condition; they do not express the actual exchange ratios that prevailed historically at any particular place. The actual historical exchange ratios were affected, often dramatically, by the condition of the coin (which was usually underweight, and sometimes seriously underweight), by the desirability of the coin, and by geographical location. Spanish coin was the most desirable of all; in London, Spanish coin with ten marks of silver was worth more than Portuguese coin with an identical ten marks of silver, because Spanish coins were familiar and were acceptable everywhere, while Portuguese coin was not well known. In Lisbon, Spanish money was legal tender, while English money was almost unknown. My own exchange calculations, as they occur throughout this book, are based on rates more favorable to Portuguese currency than those expressed above; for it is obvious that, in the islands, Portuguese coin was worth more, and had more purchasing power, than its strict bullion equivalent in English coin.

Exchange rates, therefore, varied greatly from locality to locality. In Madeira and the Azores, Spanish money was fairly common, and foreign merchants were usually paid in that coin. In the Cape Verdes coin was very scarce, but what coin there was was usually Spanish. The islands continued to use the coins of many different countries until nearly the end of the nineteenth century. In the eighteenth century Portuguese gold coinage became abundant, until the Brazilian mines began to fail, after 1760. In the nineteenth century the English gold sovereign was legal tender in Portugal. Foreign coinage was only driven out of the islands after the collapse of the gold coinage system and the introduction of paper currency.

For information on Portuguese money, see Beawes, *History of Spain* 1: 274, 277; Peres, *História de Portugal* 6: 375–88; Mauro, pp. 395–432; and Magalhães Godinho, vol. 1. On English money, see Albert Feaveryear, *The Pound Sterling: A History of English Money*, 2d ed. (Oxford, 1963), pp. 48–154; and John Craig, *The Mint: A History of the London Mint from A.D. 287 to 1948* (Cambridge, 1953), pp. 140–99.

Bibliography

Sources in Manuscript

The following six institutions, with fundamental collections for the history of the islands, are listed alphabetically, by geographical location.

Azores, Angra. Biblioteca Pública e Arquivo Distrital de Angra do Heroísmo. This important Terceiran archive, which collects materials from the central Azorean administrative district, was founded in 1948, and permanently housed in fine and ample quarters in 1957. It contains municipal and regional government documents, ecclesiastical records, and two or three important codices. I worked with the following:
Câmara de Angra. Registo Geral. Livros I (1557-1592), II (1593-1623), III (1652-1707).
Livros da Capitania Geral, da Provedoria da Fazenda e Alfândega Real, Registos de alvarás, etc. Livros nos. 1 (1694-1702), 118 (1650-1700), 184 (1693-1727), 238 (1666-1693), 252 (1609-1619), e 291 (1685-1723).
Maldonado, Manuel Luís (1645?-1711). "Primum vivens da Phoenix Angrense: no alento do ser e substancia dos primeiros povoadores da Ilha Terceira." Terceira, ca. 1705. An unpublished codex of high historical value, known usually as the "Fénix Angrense."

Azores, Ponta Delgada. Biblioteca Pública e Arquivo Distrital de Ponta Delgada. The library dates from 1841 and has a large collection of Portuguese rare books; the archive is more recent and has collections of government, ecclesiastical, and private papers. The customshouse and treasury records are fundamental for the commercial history of São Miguel and form the basis of chapter 5, above. I worked with the following materials:
Livros da Alfândega e Fazenda Real de São Miguel. Anos 1620, 1621,

1624, 1639, 1640, 1646, 1648, 1663, 1669, 1670, 1671, 1676, 1677, 1678, 1679, 1680, 1686, 1688, 1689, e 1694.

Diogo das Chagas. "Espelho cristalino em jardim de varias flores." São Miguel, ca. 1646. Fundamental for the history of São Miguel, but unpublished and little known.

Frutuoso, Gaspar (1522-91). "Das saudades da terra." In 6 books. São Miguel, finished in 1589. The complete original manuscript, a large codex (14 x 9 in.) with 583 leaves.

Henriques de Noronha, Henrique. "Memorias seculares e eclesiasticas para a composição da historia da dióçesi do Funchal na Ilha da Madeira, destribuidas na forma do systema da Academia Real da Historia Portugueza. Anno 1722." Full of information about Madeira, little used, and unpublished.

Machado, Carlos. "Livro de genealogias." (With additions by Ernesto do Canto.) São Miguel, ca. 1890-1900.

Maldonado, Manuel Luís. "Primum vivens da Phoenix Angrense." An 1875 copy of portions of the codex in the Arq. Dist. Angra.

Manuel da Purificação. "Principios, creação e progresso da congregação heremitica dos padres e irmãos do Valle das Furnas da Ilha de Sam Miguel." Copied and edited by António da Assunção, at Água de Pau, São Miguel, in 1665.

Pereira de Agrela, João Agostinho. "Genealogias da Ilha da Madeira." In 6 vols. Ca. 1820.

Évora, Portugal. Biblioteca Pública e Arquivo Distrital de Évora. A well-organized, well-run, and much used archive; some interesting materials on the Cape Verdes were found here. The following were the most useful codices: CV/1-19, CIX/1-13, CXII/1-36, CXIII/2-28, CXV/1-21, CXV/2-13, CXVI/1-14, CXVI/1-39, CXVI/2-10, and CXVI/2-15.

Lisbon. Arquivo Histórico Ultramarino. The main depository for official colonial or "overseas" papers; reasonably well arranged and heavily used. Its materials, by physical condition, fall into two main categories — loose leaves (*papéis avulsos*) and codices — as follows:

Papéis avulsos. These materials were divided into geographical areas, by captaincies, then placed in boxes (*caixas*), arranged in rough chronological order. Subsequently the papers were cataloged, or are being cataloged, placed in numbered folders, arranged in strict chronological order. (In my notes I have referred to cataloged manuscripts as, for example, Caixa I, doc. 1, and to uncataloged manuscripts by caixa number and date [e.g., Caixa I, doc. 1 January 1600]. The process of cataloging involves, of course, some shuffling of papers from one caixa to another, so that notes referring to old caixa numbers may not be strictly accurate.) Some materials on the islands can be found scattered about in such collections as those of Angola, Bahia, India, Mozambique, Pernambuco, and Rio de Janeiro (all of which I have used for other purposes), but the main materials for the islands run as follows:

Açores. Caixa I (1600-1700).

Cabo Verde, Ilhas do. Caixas I-V (1600-1700).

Guiné. Caixa I (1614-1700).

Madeira e Porto Santo. Caixa I (1599-1760).

São Tomé e Príncipe. Caixas I-II (1594-1700).

Codices. I have used the following codices for this study: nos. 13, 14, 15, 45, 46, 81, 82, 83, 92, 114, 169, 275, 278, and 489.

Lisbon. Arquivo Nacional da Tôrre do Tombo. The Portuguese national archives, which have undergone several improvements in recent years, have an exceedingly rich collection of Madeira materials, which took all my attention while I was there. These materials are the account books kept by the customshouse and treasury of Funchal. While I was using them, they were in process of being recataloged and rearranged. I cite them by their old numbers, which may have been or will be changed:

Arquivo da Provedoria da Alfândega e Fazenda Real da Madeira (also referred to as the "Arquivo da Repartição da Alfândega [etc.] . . . do Distrito do Funchal," which, for the seventeenth-century volumes, at least, is anachronistic). Codices nos. 35 (1689-1706), 40 (1640), 145 (1642), 1126 (1649-52), 1136-39 (1611-74), 1142 (1569-90), 1144 (1632-37), 1145 (1600-1653), 1146 (1645-67), 1147 (1667-71), 1148 (1675-80), 1149 (1680-1700), 1232 (1646-60), 1233 (1650), 1234 (1699), 1235 (1722), 1503 (1620), 1505 (1675-89), 1506 (1682), 1507 (1687), 1509 (1696-99).

Madeira, Funchal. Arquivo Distrital do Funchal. This is a small archive in cramped quarters, with rich seventeenth-century materials, of which I had time to use only the minute books of the municipal chamber, as follows:

Câmara da Cidade do Funchal. Livros de Vereações. Anos 1603, 1605, 1606, 1607, 1610, 1611, 1613, 1616, 1617, 1618, 1619, 1620, 1623, 1624, 1625, 1626, 1627, 1629, 1631, 1632, 1634, 1635, 1637, 1638, 1639, 1640, 1641, 1642, 1644, 1645, 1647, 1648, 1649, 1650, 1651, 1653, 1654, 1655, 1656, 1657, 1658, 1660, 1661, 1662, 1663, 1664, 1665, 1666, 1667, 1668, 1669, 1670, 1671, 1674, 1675, 1676, 1677, 1678, 1679, 1680, 1681, 1682, 1683, 1684 (and there are other yearbooks in this ample collection, beyond 1684, which I did not get to).

Bibliography

Materials in Print

A full bibliography of works dealing with the islands would run to over 1,800 items. Most of them are poor in quality, unequal in emphasis, and often extremely hard to find (books issued in small runs and printed on obscure presses in such places as Ponta Delgada, Horta, Praia [Santiago], and Mindelo, which have sometimes escaped the European and North American book trade completely). Four islands alone (Madeira, Terceira, São Miguel, and Santiago) are the subjects of over 95 percent of this literature, while the other twenty inhabited islands have been neglected by most authors. Certain favorite topics dominate the bibliography: volcanism, tourism, travel literature, the discoveries, and the Cape Verdean language and literature; but a great number of other topics are neglected. The general history of the islands for the period 1580 to 1820 is largely unwritten, and commercial and economic history, in particular, all but untouched. The following bibliography, which is limited to about 150 items, is mostly confined to works cited in the notes (although not all authors cited in the notes, particularly if they were not specially concerned with the islands, are named again here) and to works that otherwise contributed to this study. For fuller bibliography, the reader is referred to: Campos de Castro de Azevedo Soares, 1: 20–28, and 3: 17–24; Soeiro de Brito, pp. 199–207; Hartnack, pp. 154–77; Amaral, pp. 377–412; Ferreira, pp. 239–67; and Mauro, pp. xxxiii–xxxv *et passim.*

The following list is divided into four sections: (1) General works; (2) Works on Madeira; (3) Works on the Azores; and (4) Works on the Cape Verdes.

General Works

Abstracts of English Shipping Records Relating to Massachusetts Ports; from original records in the Public Record Office, London, compiled for the Essex Institute, Salem, Massachusetts. Part I: Entrance and Clearance, 1686–1717. London, 1931. Typescript. (Photostatic copy in University of Chicago Library.)

Allen, Herbert Warner. *A History of Wine: Great Vintage Wines from the Homeric Age to the Present Day.* London: Faber and Faber, 1961.

Andrade Corvo, João de. *Estudos sobre as provincias ultramarinas.* 2 vols. Lisbon, 1883.

Bannerman, David Armitage, and W. Mary Bannerman. *Birds of the Atlantic Islands.* 4 vols. Edinburgh: Oliver & Boyd, 1963–68.

Beawes, Wyndham. *A Civil, Commercial, Political, and Literary History of Spain and Portugal.* 2 vols. London: R. Faulder, 1793.

Boxer, Charles Ralph. *The Dutch in Brazil, 1624–1654.* Oxford: Clarendon Press, 1957.

_____. *The Portuguese Seaborne Empire, 1415-1825.* London: Hutchinson, 1969.

_____. *Portuguese Society in the Tropics: The Municipal Councils of Goa, Macao, Bahia, and Luanda, 1510-1800.* Madison, Wis.: University of Wisconsin Press, 1965.

Brito Freire, Francisco de. *Relação da viagem que fez ao Estado do Brazil a Armada da Cõpanhia, anno 1655.* Lisbon, 1657.

Carvalho e Vasconcelos, Ernesto Júlio de. *As colonias portuguezas: geographia physica, politica e economica.* 2d ed. Lisbon, 1903.

Chaunu, Huguette, and Chaunu, Pierre. *Séville et l'Atlantique (1504-1650).* 8 vols. Paris: Ecole Pratique des Hautes Etudes, 1955-60.

Cordeiro, António. *Historia insulana das ilhas a Portugal sugeitas no oceano ocidental.* 2 vols. Lisbon, 1866.

Cortesão, Armando, and Teixeira da Mota, Avelino. *Portugaliae Monumenta Cartographica.* 6 vols. Lisbon, 1960.

Diffie, Bailey Wallys. *Prelude to Empire: Portugal Overseas before Henry the Navigator.* Lincoln, Neb.: University of Nebraska Press, 1960.

Embid, Florentino Perez. *Los descubrimientos en el Atlántico y la rivalidad castellano-portuguesa hasta el Tratado de Tordesillas.* Seville, 1948.

Great Britain. Foreign Office. *Portuguese Possessions.* Peace Handbooks, vol. 19, nos. 115-21. London, 1920.

Great Britain. Naval Intelligence Division. *Spain & Portugal.* Vol. 4: *The Atlantic Islands.* Oxford, 1945.

Innes, Harold A. *The Cod Fisheries: The History of an International Economy.* New Haven, Conn.: Yale University Press, 1940.

Leite, Duarte. *História dos descobrimentos: colectânea de esparsos.* Edited by Vitorino Magalhães Godinho. 2 vols. Lisbon, 1958-60.

Magalhães Godinho, Vitorino. *Os descobrimentos e a economia mundial.* 3 parts. Lisbon, 1963-67?

Magnino, Leo. "António de Noli e a colaboração entre portugueses e genoveses nos descobrimentos marítimos." *Studia* (Lisbon), no. 10 (1962), pp. 99-115.

Mauro, Frédéric. *Le Portugal et l'Atlantique au XVIIᵉ siècle, 1570-1670. Etude économique.* Paris: Ecole Pratique des Hautes Etudes, 1960.

Morison, Samuel Eliot. *Admiral of the Ocean Sea.* 2 vols. Boston: Little, Brown and Company, 1942.

_____. *The European Discovery of America: The Northern Voyages.* New York: Oxford University Press, 1971.

_____. *Portuguese Voyages to America in the Fifteenth Century.* Cambridge, Mass.: Harvard University Press, 1940.

Peragallo, Prospero. "Cenni intorno alla colonia italiana in Portogallo nei Secoli XIV, XV, e XVI." *Miscellanea di Storia Italiana,* Year 40, ser. 3, 9 (Turin, 1904): 379-462.

Peres, Damião, ed. *História de Portugal.* 9 vols. Barcelos, 1928-54.
Peres, Damião. *História dos descobrimentos portugueses.* 2d ed. Coimbra, 1960.
Portugal. Instituto Nacional de Estatística. *Anuario demográfico.* Lisbon, 1929-.
Prestage, Edgar. *The Portuguese Pioneers.* London: A. & C. Black, 1933.
Rogers, Francis Millet. "Insular Portuguese Pronunciation." *Hispanic Review* 14 (1946): 235-53; 16 (1948): 1-32; and 17 (1949): 47-70.
_____. *The Travels of the Infante Dom Pedro of Portugal.* Cambridge, Mass.: Harvard University Press, 1961.
_____. *Precision Astrolabe: Portuguese Navigators and Transoceanic Aviation.* Lisbon: Academia Internacional da Cultura Portuguesa, 1971.
Serstevens, Albert t'. *Le périple des îles Atlantides: Madère, Açores, Canaries.* Paris: Arthaud, 1966.
Silveira, Luís. *Ensaio de iconografia das cidades portuguesas do Ultramar.* 4 parts. Lisbon, 1955.
Simon, André Louis. *The History of the Wine Trade in England.* 3 vols. London: Wyman & Sons, 1906-9.
Sousa Monteiro, José Maria de. *Diccionario geographico das provincias e possessões portuguezas no Ultramar.* Lisbon, 1850.
Southey, Robert. *Lives of the British Admirals.* Vols. 3-4. London: Longman, Brown, Green & Longmans, 1837.
Steckley, George Franklin. "English Merchants in the Canaries, 1648-1661." Unpublished M.A. thesis, with the edited text of Public Record Office MS. Lynch, C. 105/12. University of Chicago, 1967.
Stephens, W.B. *Seventeenth-Century Exeter: A Study of Industrial and Commercial Development, 1625-1688.* Exeter: University of Exeter, 1958.
Taft, Donald R. *Two Portuguese Communities in New England.* New York: Columbia University, 1923.
Tenreiro, Francisco. *A Ilha de São Tomé.* Lisbon, 1961.
U.S. Naval Oceanographic Office. Charts of the Madeira Islands: H.O. 1275, 1277, 1312. Charts of the Azores: H.O. 1224, 1736, 1739, 5278. Charts of the Cape Verde Islands: H.O. 5720, 5721, 5722.
U.S. Naval Oceanographic Office. H.O. 51. *Sailing Directions for the West Coasts of Spain, Portugal, and Northwest Africa and Off-Lying Islands.* 6th ed. Washington, 1952.

Works on Madeira

Aguiar, Fernando de. *Cousas da Madeira.* 2d ed. Lisbon, 1951.
Arquivo Histórico da Madeira. Funchal, 1931-.
Augusto da Silva, Fernando. *Dicionário corográfico do Arquipélago da Madeira.* Funchal, 1934.

_____. *Elucidário madeirense.* 3 vols. Funchal, 1940–46.

Berg, Aake. *Madeira.* Stockholm, 1970.

Biddle, Anthony Joseph Drexel. *The Madeira Islands.* Philadelphia: Drexel, Biddle & Bradley Publishing Company, 1896.

Bolton, William. *The Bolton Letters: The Letters of an English Merchant in Madeira, 1695–1714.* Edited by André L. Simon. London: T. Werner Laurie, 1928.

Bowdich, Thomas Edward. *Excursions in Madeira and Porto Santo during the Autumn of 1823.* London: G.B. Whittaker, 1825.

Brown, A. Samler. *Madeira and the Canary Islands with the Azores: A Practical and Complete Guide for the Use of Invalids and Tourists.* 6th ed. London: Sampson Low, Marston & Co., 1901. (13 eds. were published between 1889 and 1927.)

Bryans, Robert Harbinson. *Madeira, Pearl of the Atlantic.* London: R. Hale, 1959.

Dix, John Adams. *A Winter in Madeira and a Summer in Spain and Florence.* 4th ed. New York: William Holdredge, 1851.

Esteves dos Santos de Freitas Ferraz, Maria de Lourdes. "A Ilha da Madeira na época quatrocentista: elementos para o seu estudo." *Studia,* no. 9 (1962), pp. 143–98.

Harcourt, Edward Vernon. *A Sketch of Madeira; Containing Information for the Traveller, or Invalid Visitor.* London: J. Murray, 1851.

Harcourt, Susan Vernon. *Sketches in Madeira.* London, 1851.

Hartnack, Wilhelm. *Madeira: Landeskunde einer Insel.* Hamburg: Friederichsen, de Gruyter & Co., 1930.

Koebel, William Henry. *Madeira Old and New.* London: Francis Griffiths, 1909.

Nascimento, João Cabral do. *Apontamentos de história insular.* Funchal, 1927.

Pita Ferreira, Manuel Juvenal. *O arquipélago da Madeira, terra do Senhor Infante, de 1420 a 1460.* Funchal, 1959.

Porto da Cruz, Alfredo António de Castro Teles de Meneses de Freitas Branco, visconde do. *Folclore madeirense.* Funchal, 1955.

Quintus, W.J. *Het Eiland Madera.* Groningen, 1866.

Ribeiro. Orlando. *L'Île de Madère: étude géographique.* Lisbon, 1949.

Schultze, Rudolf. *Die Insel Madeira.* Stuttgart: Cotta, 1864.

Works on the Azores

Açoreana: revista de estudos açorianos. Angra, 1934–.

Afonso, João. "O trigo e outros géneros para pagamento de ordenados, ao fim do século XVII." *Boletim da Comissão Reguladora dos Cereais do Arquipélago dos Açores* (Ponta Delgada), vol. 15 (1952).

Andrade, Laurinda C. *The Open Door.* New Bedford, Mass., 1968.

Bibliography

Araújo, Miguel Cristóvam de. "A Restauração na Ilha Terceira 1641–1642." *Boletim do Instituto Histórico da Ilha Terceira* 6 (Angra, 1948): 38–116.

Archivo dos Açores. 13 vols. Ponta Delgada, 1878–1904.

Ashe, Thomas. *A History of the Azores or Western Isles; containing an account of their government, laws, and religion, the manners, ceremonies, and character of the inhabitants: and demonstrating the importance of these valuable islands to the British Empire.* London: Sherwood, Neely, and Jones, 1813.

Ataíde Machado de Faria e Maia, Francisco de. *Subsídios para a história de São Miguel.* 3 vols. Ponta Delgada, 1944–49.

Baker, Charlotte Alice. *Summer in the Azores, with a Glimpse of Madeira.* Boston: Lee and Shepard, 1882.

Baptista de Lima, Manuel Coelho. *A Biblioteca Pública e Arquivo Distrital de Angra do Heroísmo.* Angra, 1957.

Belo, A. Raimundo. "Brasileiros na Ilha Terceira e outras notas genealógicas terceirenses." *Boletim do Arquivo Distrital de Angra* (Angra) 2 (1952–53): 3–27.

Boid, Edward. *A Description of the Azores, or Western Islands; from personal observation, comprising remarks on their peculiarities, topographical, geological, statistical, etc., and on their hitherto neglected condition.* London: Edward Churton, 1835.

Bryans, Robert Harbinson. *The Azores.* London: Faber and Faber, 1963.

Bullar, Joseph, and Bullar, Henry. *A Winter in the Azores; and a summer at the baths of the Furnas.* 2 vols. London: John van Voorst, 1841.

Campos de Castro de Azevedo Soares, Eduardo de. *Nobiliário da Ilha Terceira.* 3 vols. Oporto, 1944–45.

Carreiro da Costa, Francisco. *Açores.* Lisbon, 1967.

————. "A cultura do pastel nos Açores." *Boletim da Comissão Reguladora dos Cereais do Arquipélago dos Açores* (Ponta Delgada), no. 4 (1946).

Chaves e Melo, Francisco de. *Descripção da Ilha de São Miguel.* Lisbon, 1723. (Summarized in *Archivo dos Açores* 1: 200–224.)

Comissão Reguladora dos Cereais do Arquipélago dos Açores. *Boletim.* Ponta Delgada, 1945–.

Drummond, Francisco Ferreira. *Annaes da Ilha Terceira.* 4 vols. Angra, 1850–64.

Félix, Emanuel. *Angra no último quartel do século XVI.* Angra, 1970.

Figueiredo, Jaime de. *Ilha de Gonçalo Velho: Da descoberta até ao aeroporto!* Lisbon, 1954.

Figueiredo Côrte-Real, Miguel de. *A construção naval na Ilha de São Miguel nomeadamente na Ribeira da Povoação nos séculos XVI e XVII.* Ponta Delgada, 1970.

Fowler, John. *Journal of a Tour in the State of New York in the Year*

1830; with remarks on agriculture in those parts most eligible for settlers: and return to England by the Western Isles, in consequence of shipwreck in the "Robert Fulton." London: Whittaker, Treacher and Arnot, 1831.

Frazão Pacheco, Cristiano. *As cinco desgraças do Arquipélago dos Açores: em defesa do Arquipélago e dos seus habitantes.* Ponta Delgada, 1961.

Freire, Anselmo Braacamp. *O Conde de Villa Franca e a Inquisição.* Lisbon, 1899.

Frutuoso, Gaspar. *Saudades da Terra.* In 6 books. The original MS is in the Arq. Dist. Ponta Delgada; it has been published only in fragments, intermittently, in different places. Bk. I publ. Ponta Delgada, 1939; and portions from it, in Spanish trans., at Tenerife, 1964. Bk. II publ. Funchal, 1873; Oporto, 1925; and Ponta Delgada, 1968. Bk. III publ. Santa Maria, 1922. Bk. IV publ. in 3 vols., Ponta Delgada, 1924-26. Bk. V publ. Ponta Delgada, 1964. Bk. VI publ. Ponta Delgada, 1963.

Gygax, Katharina Elisabeth. *Beiträge zur Geographie von Ponta Delgada, Angra do Heroismo und Horta (Azoren).* Zurich: Juris-Verlag, 1966.

Higginson, Thomas Wentworth. "Fayal and the Portuguese." *Atlantic Essays,* pp. 227-68. Boston: Lee and Shepard, 1882.

Instituto Histórico da Ilha Terceira. *Boletim.* Angra, 1943-.

Jardim Cunha da Silveira, Martim Afonso. "Do contributo flamengo nos Açores." *Boletim do Instituto Histórico da Ilha Terceira* (Angra) 21-22 (1969): 1-142.

Kellenbenz, Hermann. "Historiker und historische Institutionem der Azoren." *Aufsätze zur Portugiesischen Kulturgeschichte* 5 (Münster, 1966): 248-65.

Lima, Marcelino. *Famílias faialenses: subsídios para a história da Ilha do Faial.* Horta, 1922.

Machado, Frederico. *Actividades vulcânicas da Ilha do Faial, 1957-1958.* Lisbon, 1959.

Machado Gonçalves, Alfredo. *Notícias de algumas espécies de maior valor bibliográfico da Biblioteca Pública de Ponta Delgada.* Ponta Delgada, 1965.

Monte Alverne, Agostinho de. *Crónicas da província de S. João Evangelista das Ilhas dos Açores.* 2 vols. Ponta Delgada, 1960-61.

Rebelo, Ernesto. "As uvas: Ilha do Pico." *Archivo dos Açores* 7 (1885): 65-75.

"Relações comerciais da Ilha Terceira com o Brasil no século XVII." Documents in *Boletim do Instituto Histórico da Ilha Terceira* 4 (1946): 39-64.

Rogers, Francis Millet. "Os Açores: Plataforma no Atlântico." *Boletim da Academia Internacional da Cultura Portuguesa,* no. 2 (1966), pp. 193-209.

_____. "Brazil and the Azores." *Modern Language Notes* 62 (1947): 361–70.

Sá, Aires de. *Frei Gonçalo Velho.* 2 vols. Lisbon, 1899–1919.

Sarmento Rodrigues, Manuel Maria. *Ancoradouros das Ilhas dos Açores.* 3d ed. Lisbon, 1967.

Schaw, Janet. *Journal of a Lady of Quality.* 2d ed. New Haven, Conn.: Yale University Press, 1934.

Silva Ribeiro, Luiz da, ed. *Livro das avaliações dos ofícios das Ilhas dos Açores, 1691.* Angra, 1955. Separata do *Boletim do Instituto Histórico da Ilha Terceira,* vol. 13.

Silva Sampaio, Alfredo da. *Memória sobre a Ilha Terceira.* Angra, 1904.

Silveira Macedo, António Lourenço da. *História das quatro ilhas que formam o districto da Horta desde a época do seu descobrimento até a presente.* 3 vols. Horta, 1871.

Soares de Azevedo, João. "Os Açores e o comércio do Norte no final do século XVII." *Boletim do Arquivo Distrital de Angra* 2 (1952–53): 29–41.

_____. "Nota e documentos sobre o comércio de La Rochelle com a Terceira no século XVII." *Boletim do Instituto Histórico da Ilha Terceira* 6 (1948): 1–23.

_____. "Relações comerciais da Ilha Terceira com o Brasil no século XVII." *Boletim do Instituto Histórico da Ilha Terceira* 4 (1946): 39–64.

Soeiro de Brito, Raquel. *A Ilha de São Miguel: estudo geográfico.* Lisbon, 1955.

Sousa Lima, Helder de. "Os Açores na economia Atlântica: contribuição para o seu estudo nos séculos XV, XVI e XVII." Unpublished licentiate thesis, University of Lisbon, 1960.

Sykes, Egerton. *The Azores and the Early Exploration of the Atlantic.* 2d ed. London: Markham House, 1968.

Vasconcelos Arruda, Luís de. *Terra Nostra: excerptos da Ilha de São Miguel.* Lisbon, 1943.

Velho Arruda, Manuel Monteiro. *Coleção de documentos relativos ao descobrimento e povoamento dos Açores.* Ponta Delgada, 1932.

Venables, Bernard. *Baleia! Baleia! Whale Hunters of the Azores.* New York: Knopf, 1969.

Webster, John White. *A Description of the Island of St. Michael, Comprising an Account of its Geological Structure; with remarks on the other Azores or Western Islands.* Boston: R.P. & C. Williams, 1821.

Works on the Cape Verdes

Amáncio Gracias, João Baptista. *Monografia sobre a Provincia de Cabo Verde.* Praia, 1922.

Amaral, Ilídio do. *Santiago do Cabo Verde: A terra e os homens.* Lisbon, 1964.

Araujo, Norman. *A Study of Cape Verdean Literature.* [Chestnut Hill, Mass.] Boston College, 1966.

Barreto, João. *História da Guiné, 1418-1918.* Lisbon, 1938.

Bivar Guerra, Luiz de. "A sindicância do desembargador Custódio Correia de Matos as Ilhas de Cabo Verde em 1753 e o regimento que deixou a Ilha de São Nicolau." *Studia* (Lisbon), no. 2 (1958), pp. 165-293.

Blake, John William. *Europeans in West Africa, 1450-1560.* 2 vols. Hakluyt Society Publications, Ser. 2, vols. 86-87. London, 1942.

Boletim Trimestral de Estatística: Província de Cabo Verde. Praia, 1949-.

Botelho da Costa, Joaquim Vieira. "A Ilha do Fogo e o seu vulcão." *Boletim da Sociedade de Geographia de Lisboa,* ser. 5, no. 6 (1885), pp. 376-98.

Brásio, António. "Descobrimento, povoamento, evangelização do Arquipelago de Cabo-Verde." *Studia,* no. 10 (1962), pp. 49-97. Also printed in *Cabo Verde: Boletim de Propaganda e Informação* (Praia), Year 14 (1962-63).

_____, ed. *Monumenta Missionaria Africana: África Ocidental.* Ser. 2. Vols. 1-3 (1342-1600). Lisbon, 1958-64.

Bridge, Horatio. *Journal of an African cruiser: comprising sketches of the Canaries, the Cape De Verds, Liberia, Madeira, Sierra Leone, and other places of interest on the West Coast of Africa.* London, Wiley and Putnam, 1845. Reprinted London: Dawsons, 1968.

Cabo Verde: Boletim de Propaganda e Informação. Praia, 1949-.

Carreira, António. *Panaria Cabo-Verdiano-Guineense: Aspectos históricos e sócio-económicos.* Lisbon, 1968.

Chelmicki, José Conrado Carlos de. *Corografia cabo-verdiana, ou descripção geographico-historica da provincia das Ilhas de Cabo-Verde e Guiné.* 2 vols. Lisbon, 1841.

Colóquios Cabo-Verdianos. Lisbon, 1959. Articles by Manuel Lopes, Luís Terry, Almerindo Lessa, J. Bacelar Bebiano, were the most useful for my purposes.

Correia Lopes, Edmundo Arménio. *A escravatura: subsídios para a sua história.* Lisbon, 1944.

Corry, Joseph. *Observations upon the Windward Coast of Africa.* London: G. & W. Nicol, 1807. Reprinted London: Cass, 1968.

Curtin, Philip D. *The Atlantic Slave Trade: A Census.* Madison, Wis.: University of Wisconsin Press, 1969.

Dampier, William. *A Collection of Voyages.* 4 vols. London: Printed for J. and J. Knapton, 1729.

Drake, Francis. *The World Encompassed by Sir Francis Drake.* Edited by W.S.W. Vaux. Hakluyt Society Publications, Ser. i, vol. 16. London, 1854.

Ellis, Alfred Burdon. *West African Islands.* London: Chapman and Hall, 1885.

Ferreira, Manuel. *A aventura crioula ou Cabo Verde: uma síntese étnica e cultural.* Lisbon, 1967.

Fontoura da Costa, Abel. *Cartas das Ilhas de Cabo Verde de Valentim Fernandes, 1506-1508.* Lisbon, 1939.

Freire, Gilberto. *Aventura e rotina.* Rio de Janeiro, 1953.

Friedländer, Immanuel. *Beiträge zur Kenntnis der Kapverdischen Inseln.* Berlin: D. Reimer (E. Vohsen), 1913.

Kellenbenz, Hermann. "Jácome Fixer: Deutsche Handelsbeziehungen zu Portugal um 1600." *Aufsätze zur Portugiesischen Kulturgeschichte* 8 (Münster, 1970): 251-74.

Lacerda, João Cesário de. *Relatório do Governo Geral da Província de Cabo Verde.* Lisbon, 1901.

Lereno, Álvaro. *Dicionário corográfico do Arquipélago de Cabo Verde.* Lisbon, 1952.

———. *Subsídios para a história da moeda em Cabo Verde, 1460-1940.* Lisbon, 1942.

Lindbergh, Anne Morrow. *Listen! the Wind.* New York: Harcourt, Brace & Co., 1938.

Lisbon. Universidade Técnica de Lisboa. Instituto Superior de Ciências Sociais e Política Ultramarina. *Cabo Verde, Guiné, São Tomé e Príncipe: Curso de extensão universitária – ano lectivo de 1965-1966.* Lisbon, 1965? Articles by Raquel Soeiro de Brito, António da Silva Rego, João Ameal, António de Almeida, José Júlio Gonçalves, Joaquim Angélico de Jesus Guerra, Óscar Barata, are the most useful for my purposes.

Lopes, Baltasar. *Cabo Verde visto por Gilberto Freyre.* Praia, 1956.

———. *O dialecto crioulo de Cabo Verde.* Lisbon, 1957. Lopes de Lima,

Lopes de Lima, José Joaquim. *Ensaio sobre a statistica das Ilhas de Cabo-Verde no Mar Atlantico e suas dependencias na Guiné Portugueza ao norte do equador.* 2 vols. Lisbon, 1844.

Lyall, Archibald. *Black and White Make Brown: An Account of a Journey to the Cape Verde Islands and Portuguese Guinea.* London: William Heinemann, 1938.

Mendes Corrêa, António. *Ultramar português.* Vol. 2: *Ilhas de Cabo Verde.* Lisbon, 1954.

Miranda, Nuno de. *Compreensão de Cabo Verde.* Lisbon, 1963.

Osório de Oliveira, José. *As ilhas portuguesas de Cabo Verde.* Oporto, 1955.

Bibliography

Parsons, Elsie Clews. *Folk-Lore from the Cape Verde Islands.* 2 vols. New York: American Folk-Lore Society, 1923. Also publ. in Portuguese: *Folclore do Arquipélago de Cabo Verde.* Lisbon, 1968.

Ribeiro, Orlando. *Aspectos e problemas da expansão portuguesa.* Lisbon, 1962. Contains: "Primórdios da ocupação das Ilhas de Cabo Verde," pp. 129-59.

_____. *A Ilha do Fogo e as suas erupções.* Lisbon, 1954. 2d ed. 1960.

Rodney, Walter. *A History of the Upper Guinea Coast, 1545-1800.* Oxford: Clarendon, 1970.

_____. "Portuguese Attempts at Monopoly on the Upper Guinea Coast, 1580-1650." *Journal of African History* (Cambridge) 6 (1965): 307-22.

Scelle, Georges. *Histoire politique de la traite négrière aux Indes de Castille.* 2 vols. Paris: L. Larose & L. Tenin, 1906.

Sena Barcelos, Cristiano José de. *Subsídios para a história de Cabo Verde e Guiné.* 7 vols. Lisbon and Coimbra, 1899-1913.

Silveira, Onésimo. *Consciencialização na literature Cabo-Verdiana.* Lisbon, 1963.

Teixeira da Mota, Avelino. *Cinco séculos de cartografia das Ilhas de Cabo Verde.* Lisbon, 1961. Also publ. in *Garcia de Orta* 9 (Lisbon, 1961): 11-16.

_____. *Guiné Portuguesa.* 2 vols. Lisbon, 1954.

Thomas, Charles W. *Adventures and Observations on the West Coast of Africa and Its Islands: Historical and Descriptive Sketches of Madeira, Canary, Biafra, and Cape Verd Islands.* New York: Derby & Jackson, 1860.

Travassos Valdez, Francisco. *África Occidental: Notícias e considerações.* Lisbon, 1864.

_____. *Six Years of a Traveller's Life in Western Africa.* 2 vols. London: Hurst and Blackett, 1861.

Index